ROLE OF MEDIA IN KASHMIR CRISIS

ROLE OF MEDIA IN KASHMIR CRISIS

Deepa Viswam

KALPAZ

Role of Media in Kashmir Crisis

Rs. 880

ISBN: 978-81-7835-862-8

Published in 2010 in India by
Kalpaz Publications
C-30, Satyawati Nagar,
Delhi-110052
E-mail: kalpaz@hotmail.com
Phone : 9212729499

Lasser Type Setting by: Rudra Computer Graphics, Delhi
Printed at : Chawla Offset Printers, Delhi

Contents

four reports in The Hindu and Thirty - five in the New Indian Express. (h) Coverage of waller barrage / tribal project and other related stories. During the period of study there twenty two reports in The Hindu and eleven reports in the New Indian Express (i) Coverage of siachen issue. There were twelve reports in The New Indian Express and twelve reports in The Hindu. (j) Coverage of report on sir creek. There were 5 reports on Sir Creek in The New Indian Express and only two in The Hindu. (k) Coverage of reports on third party mediation. The New Indian Express had ten reports on third party mediation wherelse the Hindu, only seven. (l) Coverage between separatist and pak government m. Coverage of army. During the period of study there were eleven started in the Hindu and 6 reports in the New Indian Express. (n) Coverage of militancy related stories in the state. During the period of study. There were forty three stories in The Hindu and sixty three stories in the New Indian Express. (o) Development in the state during the course of composite dialogue. During the course of study there were five stories in The Hindu and two in the New Indian Express. (p) Coverage of report justifying and glorifying the past. There are five reports in TNIE where else there were no reports in The Hindu. (q) Coverage of other stories. During the period of study there were forty two stories in The New Indian Express and seventy three stories in The Hindu.

6. Editorials 192

(a) Editorials covering eco and cultural co-operation. (b) Editorial covering cbms. (c) Editorials on the art of diplomacy. (d) Editorials suggesting terrorism. (e) Editorial with precautionary note on the evolving peace. (f) Editorials covering cross-border terrorism. (g) Editorials coverage of n - cbms. (h) Editorial on sir creek. (i) Editorial on the composite dialogue. (j) Editorial on third-party mediation. (k) Editorial on factors affecting delay conflict resolution. (l) Editorials suggesting the views of the political parties opposing peace process. (m) Editorials on hurriyat. (n) Editorial of the previous govt. Vs. Upa govt. (o) Editorials covering separatists peace process. (p) Editorial for progress of peace process. (q) Coverage of the role of the army. (r) Editorial on pok (s) Editorials of human rights violation. (t)

NEWSPAPERS ATTITUDE ON CONFLICT RESOLUTION. There were three features in The Hindu and two features in The New Indian Express which dealt more on conflict resolution. (k) NEWSPAPERS ATTITUDE TOWARDS BILATERAL PEACE. There were four features towards Newspapers attitude toward bilaterial peace compared to the Hindu which carried only one. (l) FEATURE COVERAGE OF SIACHEN ISSUE. During the period of study there 3 features in The Hindu and two such features in the New Indian Express. (m) FEATURES COVERING ENDING OF VIOLENCE AND PROMOTION OF PEACE. There were seven features in The New Indian Express wherelse The Hindu carried only two features. (n) FEATURES ON THIRD - PARTY MEDIATION. There were two features related to third party mediation in The Hindu wherelse four features in The New Indian Express during the period of study. (o) FEATURES OF PoK. During the period of study there was one feature in The Hindu and one feature in the New Indian Express. (p) FEATURES RELATED TO HUMAN RIGHTS VIOLATION. During the period of study there was one feature. (q) FEATURES RELATED TO BAGLIHAR NEWSPAPERS ATTITUDE TOWARDS CONFLICT MANAGEMENT & PEACE. Conflict management in the backdrop of the disaster had five features in the New Indian Express and two features in The Hindu. (r) FEATURES ABHORRING UN RESOLUTIONS AND OTHER PROPOSALS MOOTED. During the period of study there two features in the Hindu abhorring in resolutions and other proposals mooted but the New Indian Express has no such features. (s) FEATURES ON POLITICAL DEVELOPMENT. During the period of study there are six features in the New Indian Express and two in The Hindu.

8. Letters to The Editor **303**

9. Interviews, Cartoons and Photographs **321**

10. Conclusion **352**

Index **359**

Preface

The issue of what role media plays in conflict resolution is very ambiguous and produces endless discussion. However most of the expert agrees that the issue is not fully researched and the answer for it cannot be easily found. When the news media are playing a constructive role in the process as the talks are being held in a mostly supportive press coverage is less likely to have negative influence negotiations. If other hand the news is more likely playing a negative role in the overall process they are more likely to have a negative influence on talks. The relationship between government and the media is an ongoing who tells the story.

In February 2004, India and Pakistan resumed the process to normalize their relations after half a decade of confrontation over Kashmir, which could have had catastrophic consequences. The renewed normalization process, described officially as 'composite dialogue,' includes Kashmir as one of the most important issues to be resolved incrementally by top officials of the countries. A similar process in 1997-1998 had resulted in the February 1999 signing of Lahore Declaration, which had mentioned Kashmiri settlement as a key to South Asian peace. However, the ensuing conflict over Kargil in the disputed region brought India and Pakistan back to the confrontational path. The book will attempt to assess the viability ofthe renewed 'composite dialogue' vis-a.-vis Kashmir, with reference to on goings in the print media, a sort of comparative study of the two national newspapers from the second round of composite dialogue to the third round of composite dialogue until the break of Mumbai blast of 2006. The book examines the role news media in any political process is start by looking at the political context attempt to understand the role of news media political leaders and journalists interact within a given situation and then examine resulting news stories influence the process itself.

Deepa Viswam

1

Introduction

One of the most common premises of all peace negotiations is to keep the news media out. The greater the level of media involvement, it is claimed, the more likely the talks will fail. When the news media are playing a generally constructive role in the process as the talks are being held in a mostly supportive environment, press coverage is less likely to have a negative influence on negotiations. If on the other hand the new are more likely a playing a negative role in the overall process they are more likely to have a negative influence on talks. The relationship between government and the media is an ongoing struggle over who tells the story. It is helpful to think of that role in terms of a continnum of independence. One side of that continnum would be those situations in which the news media become government tools that simply pass on whatever they are told. The opposite extreme would be devoted to those cases in which the news media were unwelcome intruders in the process. Here the media become major obstacle as government leaders find themselves constantly reacting to stories either uncovered by the press or planted by other actors. In the middle of the continnum one finds those cases in which the press plays the role of informative intermediary which many consider an ideal situation the media provides independent reports and analysis about what is going on.

The Political Environment and Media Independence

Government leaders and the opposition are in a constant battle to take control over the political environment. the struggle over the news media should be seen as simply one element within this more general competition for political control. The press is more likely to react to political developments than to initiative them. A useful way to understand the role of news media in any political process to start by looking at the political context and an attempt to understand the role of the news media political leaders and journalists interact within given situation and then examine how resulting news stories influence the process itself. This idea can be labeled as the politics-media cycle.

Changes in the political environment lead to changes in the role of news media then lead to further changes in political environment. There are two major indicators of governments level of control over the political environment surrounding a peace process. (1) their ability to mobilize consensus among elite in support of the process. (2) Their ability to take control over events and the flow of information associated with the process. The first factor shapes the general political context in which journalists are operating, while the second determines the nature of inputs journalist will use to control news stories. The greater the leader's success in each of these stories in each of these stories the more likely the news media will do bidding. If they fail in these task, the news media have the potential of becoming serious obstacles. As always it is best to think of success and failure in terms of a continnum rather than as a dichotomy.

By far the most important challenge is to mobilize as many successes as possible in support of peace process. This sets the stage for everything that follows. Journalists depend on their sources to give them a sense about which policies are controversial and which are not. They only reflect those beliefs that advance them. They often become advocates for the cause and help define the borders of legitimacy by treating them dissenters as deviants.

The role of the united nations news media in two different wars demonstrate this principle. Hallins work on the Vietnam war shows how in the early years of that conflict, the American news media was extremely supportive of government efforts to stop communism. Anti-war protestors were framed as either crazy or dangerous. Only when elites began to raise questions about war, the role of the media began to change, which increased the rate of political change. There was a reverse trend in the Gulf War, albeit in much shorter intensive and the news media reflected that level of dissent and division. Once the hostilities began, however, most elites decided to come together in support of war effort and the resulting coverage would be described as celebratory. These are both good examples of the politics-media cycle.

There is a good reason to believe that the level of consensus has a similar influence on the role of the news media in a peace process. When there are deep divisions over the process the news media will justifiably focus on these divisions and thus play a more critical and independent role. In those in which the opposition to a peace process is relatively small, on the other hand the new media will feel obligated to run with the tide and become part of consensus, As noted this may involve marginalizing those who disagree.

The high level of consensus should also have an influence on the role news media play in negotiations. First journalists may be less aggressive looking for stories that serious questions about the process. Once the storyline has been established journal sits search for information that fits and either ignore or underplay information that runs in a different directions/. Second even when journalists do publish negative stories about negotiation they are likely to be less damaging. Without serious challenger able to exploit such information for political advantage, such stories are unlikely to resonate with the general public. Finally leaders enjoying a high level of support are in much better position to take some flak and move on. What negative coverage can completely undermine a weak government, its effects on a powerful government will be considerably less significant. This goal for leaders is to take control over events it and the flow of information. When governments are in opposition to initiate events it provides them with important advantage in their relation with the news media. It allows to them carefully orchestrate what happen in the field and to prepare the accompanying spin.

On the other hand, when governments either lose control lover events over events, or are forces to react to the actions of others they find it more difficult to control media coverage. Journal sits become less dependent on official sources when they find stories elsewhere. The control over events and the flow of information can be especially important with regard to the negotiations government must keep the negotiations moving also must keep a tight lid on information coming out of talks. The greater the friction between the two sides the more each will turn to news media in an attempt to mobilize outside support for their position .The news media are seen as weapon that can be used against the other side.

There is an important lesson here. The path of influence between the level of media involvement and the success of the negotiation runs in both the directions. Not only does increased media involvement decrease the likelihood of success but the lower level of success the more the media are likely to become involved .When this does take place the resulting coverage has potential of making matters even worse. This is another example of the politics –media cycle that was mentioned earlier, difficulties in the negations lead to damaging press leaks that make it even more difficult to move forward in the negations.

When people think about the role of the new media in negations they usually focus exclusively on the flow of information. The fact that this topic comes up relatively late in this discussion places on many fronts, not only in negations. News about the peace process is also based on what journalists gather from opposition leaders, from alternative local and foreign sources, from movement leaders, and from public leader opinion polls. Whoever provides the best news stories is in the best position to complete for the public agenda.

The greater the level of elite support for a peaceful process, the less likely thee will be massive protests that cast a negative light on the situation and place the government on the defensive. Even more importantly when things do go wrong the media will emphasize the need to get the process back on track. A crisis will probably be framed very differently, however when a peace process is considered controversial. There will be an intensive debate over the meaning of the crisis and the more critical and pessimistic storyline.

Every government that is involved in peacetalks, however must inevitably cope with the trade-off between the need for secrecy and the need for transparency. If all negotiations are kept completely secret it violates the public right to know. It also limits the ability of the government to prepare for the types of concessions that will have to be made in order to move the process forward. If on the other hand there is no secrecy, the talks have very little chance of succeeding.

Why is secrecy such an essential element in such negotiations? The most important reason has to do with leaders needs for public posturing. The public wants to achieve peace by paying the smallest price possible. Political leaders interested in moving forward must continually try to convince the public that they are winning. When speaking to their constituencies, leaders stress the need to remain firm and often place their messages within a colorful wrap of patriotic myths and symbols above all, they will avoid any appearance of weakness that would play into the opposition hands. Premature leaks of concessions will severely undermine strategy.

When both sides begin playing to their constituencies it sours the atmosphere surrounding the talks. Valuable time can be wasted in dealing with public declaration that are offensive to the other side. Negotiators will also find themselves severely limited in their ability to compromise when leaders have promised to remain firm. The type of communication required within the negotiating room is in many ways the exact opposite of what is needed when speaking to the public. Genuine negotiations demand flexibility and at least a minimal; empathy. Message tailored for the public usually steadfastness and ethnic loyalty.

The struggle for control over events and the flow of information concerning a peace process is in many ways a microcosm of the overall conflict between officials and journalists. The most important commodity, the government has to offers to the press is newsworthy information. When leaders are able to maintain a monopoly on that information. When leaders are able to maintain a monopoly on that information .., it provides them with tremendous power over the media. When on the other hand journalists are in a position to cultivate alternative sources of information it increases their ability to play an independent role. The government loses its power to dictate story lines his is for the most part a healthy development for it provided citizens with a more balanced picture of what is happening. Nevertheless when governments lose all control over the flow of information media coverage can become a serious obstacle to moving forward.

From the Middle East to Northern Ireland

One of the most important differences among the three cases was the governments level of control over the political environment. The oslo peace process represents a case in which the Israeli government had the least control. The same government, on the other hand, had a tremendous amount of control over the environment surrounding the peace process with Jordan. The level of control in the Northern peace process appears to fall between the other two, but not in the middle.

Israel and the Palestine

The Oslo talks where Rabin kept the media out led to major breakthrough in august 1993. But at the same time talks were going on United States at the same time. The news media were covering these meaningless talks kept the on going negotiations in complete secrecy. Which led to the success of the talks.

The government had complete monopoly against these talks and the short period was termed as "peace festival" where the government could initiate a number of peace programme. But the government did not mobilize the necessary consensus in support of the process, but had a very little control of events and information about the process. The Israel public and the Knesset were completely split over whether the country would territorial concessions to Gaza and west bank. Rabin never recognized the PLO as the representative of Palestine Arafat as a terrorist leader. The governments inability to control the terrorist attack on Israelis and the Israeli were competing with one another to cover more gruesome incidents. The terrorist attacks provided tremendous advantage to Oslo's opponents.

The information garnered from two set of negotiations varies and it is necessary that we compare them. The first ended with the signing of the Cairo agreement and the media was involved in majority of the discussions which they provided continual briefings to the press but they found that the media may be avoided in which the Oslo B agreement was signed.

The Peace Process with Jordan

The peace agreement with Jordan received an overwhelming support of 91-3 in the Knesset as there was a high level of consensus surrounding the agreement. It is hard to imagine a more problem –free peace process between two enemies. The press was informed the place where it would take place but no the substance. Neither Israel nor Jordan leaked stories to the press so the success of talks. This case provides a good example of how political success leads to media success.

Northern Ireland

The multi-party talks chaired by former US senate majority leader George Mitchell got the consensus of the the Ultsar Party, the Unionist Party, Social Democrats and Labour Party. It was also endorsed by the paramilitary groups, Sinn Fein, the Progressive Unionist Party and the Ulster Democratic Party. The only groups that opposed this accord were Democratic Unionist Party and the United Kingdom Party. The talks were kept in complete secrecy when Mitchell announced that a tight lid on the discussion. The Northern Ireland news media was vocal supporter of Good Friday Agreement. The Belfast newsletter of the Unionist paper and the nationalist Irish news published common editorials in favour of the peace process. The culmination of this co-operation was the fact that both newspapers asked the readers to vote yes in the referendum.

The terrorist attack at Omaghin August 1998 led to the Northern Ireland press avoiding the intent of the terrorists which was aimed at derailing the peaces process, but after examining the news coverage and listening to the interviews the bomb had done reverse effect. This was very different from what had happened in Israel. The journalist worked in a conducive manner in Northern Ireland when news media moved a closer to the government tools to end the continuum, they were most likely to either ignore or discredit opponents.

Territorial Options

The redrawing of boundaries (as securing of independence) is seldom easy. Boundaries when redrawn, frequently leave bitter legacies, as in Ireland and India\Pakistan\Bangladesh. When redrawing of boundaries cannot be achieved sovereignty over the disputed territory can be shared. In history condominiums represent this sharing, as over the Sudan (between the British and the Egyptians) or the new Hebrides (between the British and the French). Temporary periods sovereignty may be expressed by the UN over South Africa and East Timor.

Self-determination

The autonomy is the manifestation of self-determination, the greater involvement of UN or consortia of states in the settlement of conflicts has also helped to develop the concept of self-determination as implying autonomy in appropriate circumstances.

Resistance to Autonomy

There are fears that autonomy is spring board to secession. Autonomy may affect the operation of the economy especially when there are regional taxes and restrictions on the mobility of labor. The civil war in America (when Arab ham Lincoln justified the stance of northern states by saying that This country cannot endure permanently half slave and half free.

The Future of Autonomies: A Frame Work

Is is always found that majority community is usually opposed to autonomy of minorities.

In India too there are limits to the use of violence although in the Punjab and Kashmir the scale of violence has been high. The more democratic and pluralistic a state is, the better the chances that autonomy may be successfully negotiated and operated.

Global Media

The shrinkage of once influential players, Breakups, rapid growth of new players, do not receive front page treatment, but the merger of Time inc with warner communications and then with America online dominate headlines.

Some media companies own properties internationally or provide some content across borders (for example, vivendhi canl+ distributers movies internationally, but no large conglomerate owns newspapers, book publishers, radio stations, cable companies, or television licenses in all major world markets.

News Media corp comes closest to being a global media enterprise in both content and distribution, but ona global scale it is still a minor presence-that is minor percentage of global media revenue, global audience, and the in the number of markets it covers. The pervasiveness of a handful of media companies looks even less relevant when one looks at media ownership across countries. The united nations "human development report 2002" examined ownership of the five largest newspaper and broadcast enterprises in 97 countries. It found that 29% of the worlds largest newpapers are state owned and another 57% are family owned. Only 8% are owned by employees or public for radio stations, 72 percent and 24% family owned. For television stations, 60 percent are state owned, 34 percent are family owned. These data suggest there is little foreign direct investment in the media sectors of most countries.

Corporate Ownership is Killing Hard-Hitting Journalism

Conclusion

Government who are to mobilize a good deal of political in support of their efforts and to exert control and information have little to fear from the news media. The good news is that the media can play extreme constructive role in peace process in the jordian and Northern Ireland the news media were important agents for creating conducive environment. An agreement that enjoys a good deal of political support should receive much more positive coverage than one that is marred by controversy. The news media make it more difficult to create peace process. So there are more international conflicts than peace process. They are more likely to deal with threats than opportunities especially in coverage of the enemy. The new media are more likely to reinforce national stereotype than change them.

The new media are best thought of as fair –weather friends .In times of trouble when they could do the most good they only make things more difficult. The mews media can make a positive contribution to a peace process. However they do so when most of the difficult work has already been done.

Global Media, Neoliberalism and Imperialism

The notion of globalization which is usually described as telos of capitalism is misleading. Economic and culture globalization arguably would be impossible without a global commercial media system to promote global markets ant to encourage consumer values. Instead the neoliberal politics that have come to forefront today. This refers to the set of national and international policies that call for business domination of all social affairs with minimal countervailing force. Any activity that undermines the business and wealthy has to be avoided for neoliberalism relies on the ability of markets to use technologies to solve social problems for better than any other alternative course. To achieve this target the commercial media and communication media are to be deregulated. They are re-regulated to serve corporate interests.

The Global Media System

In the past few years a global commercial media has emerged, where else previously media systems were primarily national. The global oligopoly has two distinct but related facts. First it means the dominant firms –nearly all us based are moving across the planet at breakneck periods. The point is to capitalize on the potential for growth abroad- and get outflanked by competitors since the us market is well developed and only permits incremental expansion. As Viacom CEO sunner redstone has put it "companies are focusing on those markets promising the best return which means overseas" Frnak Biondhi, former chairman of vivendhi universal studio asserts that 99 percent of the success of these companies long term is going to be successful execution offshore.

Huge global media conglomerates are becoming more and more concentrated and dominant players in each media increasingly are subsidiaries. The level of mergers and acquisitions is breath taking.

In the first half of 2000, the volume of merger deals in global media, internet, and telecommunications totaled $300 billion, triple the figure for the first six monthsof 1999 and exponentially higher than the figure from ten years earlier.

The global media market has come to be dominated by seven multinational corporations:Disney, AOL-Time warner, sony, news corporation, Viacom, Vivendhi and berltmann.

Of the seven only three are truly usfirms studios,all but one of the us televieon network the few companies that control 80-85 % of the global music market the preponderance of satellite broadcasting world wide a significant publishing all or part of most of the commercial magazine publishing all or part of most of the commercial able TV channels in the US and world wide a sinifanct portion of European terrestrial televiwepn and on and on and on.

Rupert Murdoch new's corporation may be the most aggressive global trailblazer, although cases could be made for sony, Bertelsmann or AOL,Time warner.Murdoch has satellite TV services that run from Asia to Europe to Latin America. His star TV doiminates in Asia with thirty cahnnelsin seven languages, News corporation TV service for china, pphonenixTV, in which it has a 45% stake, now reaches forty –five million homesthere and has had an 80% increase in advertising revenues in the past year. And barely begins to describe News corporation entire portfolio of assets:Twentieth century fox films, fox TV network, haper collinspublishers, TV stations, CableTV channels, magazines, over 130 nespapers, and professional sport teams.

Why has this taken place? The conventional explanation is technology i.e. radical improvements in communication make global media empires feasible and lucrative manner unthinkable in the past. This is similar to the technological explanation for globalization writ large. This is only partial explanation at best. The real motor force has been the incessant pursuit for profit that marks capitalism, which has applied pressure for a shift to neo liberalsim deregulation. In media this means the relaxation or elimination of barrier to commercial exploitation of media and concentrated media ownership. There is nothing inherent in the technology that required neoliberalism, new digital communication could have been used, for example to simply enhance public service had society elected to so. With liberal values however, television, which has been a non-commercial preserve in many nations, suddenly became subject to transnational commercial development. It has been at the centre of the emerging global media system.

Once the national deregulation of media began in major nations like the United States and Britain, it was followed by global measures like the North American Free Trade Agreement and the formation of the world trade organization all designed to clear the ground for investment and sales by Multinationals Corporation in regional and global markets. This has laid the foundation rations in regional and global markets. This has laid the foundation for the creation of global media system, dominated by the aforementioned conglomerates. Now in place; the system has its own logic. Firms must become larger and diversified to reduce risk and enhance profit making opportunities and they must straddle the globe so as to never be outflanked by competitors this is market that some anticipate having trillions of dollars in annuals revenues with in decade.

The development of the global media system is challenged by the media conglomerates for even though they crave for their domination of markets through the world strong tradition of protection of domestic media and cultural industries persist. Many countries like Norway, Denmark and Spain to Mexico keep their small domestic film production industries alive. With government subsidies Manu countries like México Sweden, Italy and Ivory Coast met in Ottawa to prepare ground rules to protect the culture from Holly wood juggernaut.

Neoliberalists argue that subsidies generally inhibit the ability of nations to develop their own competition media firms and also affect the trade barriers and regulation harm consumers. Commercial media lobbies within nations perceive that they have more to gain by opening up their borders than by maintaining trade barrier.

The executive arm of the EU European commission is in the middle of the controversy exits concerning media policy and it has considering more power than ITU. The EC is committed to building powerful pan-European media giants that can toe with European giants. The EC is committed to building powerful pan European media giants' that can go toe-to toe with the U.S based giants.

Global commercial media system is linked to the neoliberal global capitalize economy is to consider the risk of advertising. The commercial media system is necessary transmission by for business to market than wares across the world a whopping three quarter of global spending on advertising ends up in the pockets of mere 20 media companies.

Ad spending has grown up leaps and bounds in the past decade as tV has been opened to commercial exploitation and it is growing at more than twice the rate of GDP growth.

There has been a shake out in national and regional markets with small firms getting eaten by medium firms and medium firms by large firms. A much smaller number of larger of larger firms now dominated the media at national and regional level. Fourth estate one of the few remaining independent book publishers was sold to Murdoch Hopper Collins in 2000.The chairman of can west global communication stated in 2000 uttered that second tier corporation like those of in the first tier need to reach beyond national borders. The borders are gone we have to grow. The ceo of bonnier Sweden largest media conglomerate says that to survive we want to be leading media company in northern Europe, Australian moguls following the path blazed by Murdoch have the mantra "expand or die".

Second tier meida firms are hardly oppositional to global system. México's televise, Brazil's globo, argentina's clarinnand venezula's Cisneros group for example are among the worlds sixty or seventy largest media corporations.These firms tend to dominate their own national and regional markets which have been experiencing rapid consolidation as well.

Global Media and Neoliberal Democracy

The problems of having wealthy private owners dominate the journalism and media in society have been well understood all alone journalism, in particular which is the oxygen necessary for self government to be viable will be controlled by those who benefit by existing inequality and the preservation of statuesque.

Even a wealthy capitalist launch a commercially viable company that can go toe- to-toe with media giants. The market is effectively closed off to outsiders. The competitive marketplace and the traditional means the commercial media system that the trained profession was to be nonpartisan. the neoliberal transformation of media and communication has taken part the attack on professional autonomy of journalism.

All public service broadcasters and institutions that interfere with profit maximization have received a severe set back and this felt even in the case of media as this is very much evident from the fall of grace of public service broadcasting in much of the world.

Neoliberalism is more than an economic theory however. It is also apolitical theory. It posits that business domination of society proceeds most effectively when there is a representative democracy but only when it is weak and ineffectual poli ty typified by high degrees of depolitician especially among poor and working class. It is here that one can see why the existing commercial media system is so important to the neoliberal project, for it is singularly brilliant as generating the precise sort of bogus political culture that permits business domination to proceed without using a police state or facing effective popular resistance.

The global corporate media system is politically conservative, once capitalist relations have become pre-eminent because the media giants are significant beneficiaries of the current social structure. Corporatee lords like Rupert Murdoch impose their neo-liberal political; positions on the underlings and the bias is subtle and purely to commercials concerns. The best journalism is pitched to the business class and suited to its needs and prejudice.

In India, for, example influenced by the global media system, the revamped new media now focus more on fashion designers and beauty queens than on the dark realities of a poor and violent country. This slant is font quite subtle, indeed the genius of the commercial –media system is generally lack of overt censorship as George Orwell noted in his unpublished introduction to animal farm censorship in free societies is infinitely more sophisticated and through than in dictatorship because unpopular ideas can be silenced and inconvenient facts kept dark, without any need for an official ban.

The Global Media and Imperialism

In the 1970's Third world developed plans for new world Information and communication order (NWICO) to address their concerns that western domination over journalism and culture made it virtually for newly independent nations to escape colonial status. The NWICO campaign was part of a broader struggle at that time by Third world nations to address formally the globally economic inequality that was seen as a legacy of imperialism. The us cultural domination remain central concern in many countries for obvious reasons. Even though the leftists intellectual's decrying American films, a cultural nationalist like France had nine of its top ten grossing films in 1999 produced by the Hollywood giants. the crux of the story for many European filmmakers is that you have to work in English and employ Hollywood moviemaking convention to succeed.

As the media conglomerate spread their tentacle there is reason to believe they will encourage popular tastes to become more uniform in at least some forms of media. Bollywood film industry is also developing close ties to the global market. The music industry the least capital intensive industry is open to experimentation and new ideas.

The entire global regime is the result of neoliberal political policies urged on by the US government.

2

Media and Conflict

While a considerable amount of analysis has focused on the media's potential to support democracy efforts and build sustainable peace, no similar effort has been given to analyze the role media can play in a conflict prevention. Nor has the media's capacity to incite conflict been sufficiently analyzed and the lessons learned.

B.R. Nand in Indian Foreign Policy—The Nehru Years notes that in early 1950s Pakistan could have embraced India if during discussions both direct and under United Nations auspices it had agreed to vacate its aggression or if had not insisted on Admiral Nimitz as the plebiscite administrator. But apparently it did not feel secure enough to accept a leading figure from a neutral country like Burma, Indonesia or Ceylon as the plebiscite administrator. Its intransigence negated the commitment that India had made to hold a plebiscite within the terms of the United Nations resolution of 13th August 1948. Meanwhile the situation within Jammu and Kashmir in the Indian subcontinent evolved in a manner that made the original Indian offer of a plebiscite wholly out of date.

Singh, LP in his book India's Foreign Policy: *Shastri* Period refers to second Kashmir War in 1965. He described that in 1964, Gulzarilal Nanda, the then home minister took several measures to end Kashmir's special status within the Indian union. In launching military offensive during the second Kashmir war Pakistan not only crossed the cease fire line but also violated a part of the international boundary between two countries. It became quite obvious to India that the Pakistan objective was not a limited one intended merely to balance the Indian control of three military posts in Azad Kashmir.

The news of Pakistani military success in southern Kashmir electrified Indian public opinion. By its bold diversionary move India frustrated Pakistan's well nursed plans to force India to accept Pakistan terms for settlement in Kashmir.

Sailen Chaudhari focuses is in his work Beijing-Washington-Islamabad entente points out that on the insistence of Lord Mountbatten the first Governor General of free India, the dispute was taken to the United Nations. But naturally India did not get justice there since the Anglo-American block dominating the world body at the time took a definite pro-Pakistani stand and acted in a way so that the Kashmir issue was kept alive to keep the two countries at loggerheads for perpetuity. Moreover with a view to make its presence in this strategic area more tangible, the US managed to include seventeen American nationals in the 36 member team supervising the truce in Kashmir. Thus began active involvement of the USA in Pakistan's affairs. The US support for Pakistan on Kashmir issue was prompted by a desire to acquire military bases in Pak-held Kashmir adjoining the Soviet Union.

S. Rama Malkote pointed out that the line of control was recognized as the international boundary between India and Pakistan. An important feature of the Simla Pact is that for the first time the two countries settled their dispute without a third party interference.

According to *Haksar* the ideological basis of Pakistan was the so-called two nation theory. President Bhutto insisted on the validity of this theory and in proof says that because Bangladesh after its liberation did not join India the theory remains inviolable. But, he forgets that if Bangladesh did not join India it certainly establishes a three-nation theory rather than two nation state. And insofar as Pakistan is driven to dissolve even the one unit in west Pakistan into its components of Sindh, Baluchisthan, Frontier and Punjab it recognized that the unity of what remains of Pakistan cannot be maintained by monolithic theory of Muslims being one nation but on the recognition of the fact that despite the common faith the Punjabis, the Sindhis, the Baluchis and the Pathans must have a federal structure through which the diverse aspirations of the people of Pakistan can be satisfied.

Madhu Limaye opines that question of Indo-Pak relations is not a simple question and it is quite complicated. According to him, it is intimately connected with the larger problem of Hindu-Muslim relations. The long story of these relations have been characterized by both conflict and co-operation, often cooperation has been overtaken by conflict. He recommends the resolution of this age-old conflict and calls for the highest statesmanship, generosity, mutual tolerance and to put it candidly downgrading of religion in public life.

S.S Brinda in her study of the Kutch episode points out that both the countries succeeded in resolving the dispute with the help of peaceful means. The international tribunal set up to solve the problem gave its 100 page judgment on 19 February 1968 and awarded to Pakistan nearly 320 sq.m of Indian territory or roughly about 1/10 of the territory of the Rann of Kutch she claimed from India. The award was a healthy example of arbitration and mediation and it was hoped that both the countries would rely on these methods to solve their outstanding issues.

E.S. Reddy and A.K. Damodaran (1992) highlight Krishna Menon's legendary role on Kashmir. They pouch out that we have many reasons for terminating because it is not always administered according to us with the degreee of impartiality that is required of those concerned. What is more Pakistan even after making of the ceasefire line has taken territory which we could retake by force, but that would lead to an aggravation of the situation, so, striking the balance we let them keep it. There have been as many as 140 violations of the cease fire line in the year of 1962 alone. There are an average ninety or ninety five incidents inside Kashmir organized by Pakistan in the way of violence and sabotage in which Pakistan, British and American ammunition has been found.

Panagriya (1994) opines that the US during the Kargil War brought pressure on Pakistan to withdraw intruders, continuous exchanges of views between president Clinton and PM Vajpayee brought the two democracies together. On Aug 17, 1999, India made public the Draft Nuclear Doctrine (DWD) spelling out the minimum nuclear deterrent, command, control system and broad thrust on nuclear forces, even while reiterating its strict adherence to the objectives of no-first use and non-use against non-nuclear weapon states.

Bhattacharya (1994) points out that there was a difference as time wents on in contrast to 1947 and 1965 as all the Mujahideen did not come from outside.

They were mostly young Kashmiri's who sneaked across the line of control to acquire training in the use of advanced weapons and in guerialla tactics. They then returned to eliminate selected official targets, take hostages, provoke police and paramilitary reaction against local people and generally try to paralyse the administration. They knew their way around the valley and could count on sympathizers. Pakistan hoped by setting up training camps and contributing sophisticated arms and also money. Thus Pakistan avoided provoking a military confrontation with India.

Khilani (1995) opines that it was Nehru who in his mistaken magnanimity had said that when conditions in Kashmir settled down then India would conduct a plebiscite to confirm the option of Kashmiris. But the condition in Kashmir did not settle down due to continued aggression of Pakistanis, Sir Owen Dixon had also stated clearly that Pakistan must withdraw from the so-called "Azad Kashmir" before India can hold the plebiscite. By 1954, the conditions deteriorated as Pakistan acquired then ultra sophisticated weapons from the Eisenhower administration, this increased political and military strength of the aggressor state and so changed the delicate balance in Indo-Pakistani affairs that Krishna Menon the Indian representative told the Security Council in 1955 that vacation of Pakistani aggression from Kashmir was the man issue.

Chitkara (1996) states that the accession of Kashmir became a legal fact when Maharaja Hari Singh of Kashmir signed the instrument of accession and the same was accepted by the then Governor General of India Lord Mountbatten. Instead of taking the obvious cause of clearing the whole territory of the state of Kashmir of tribal invaders who were guided, assisted and supported by Pakistan armies India was persuaded to stop her armies short, leaving of state's territory in the hands of Pakistan. He opines that had the soil of Kashmir been freed from the aggressor there perhaps would have been no Kashmir problem.

Bose (1997) in his analysis of the struggle for self-determination in Kashmir in notes that mass opinion in the valley (and among the Kashmir Muslim majority in Doda is only not confused but by and large unambiguous and unequivocal in the belief that only independent statehood would constitute genuine emancipation. He quotes Benazir Bhutto on the subject who said India might win (a hypothethetical referendum) since the Muslim vote will get badly divided while the Jammu, Hindus, Kashmir Pandits and Ladhaki Buddhists vote enmasse for India. Such statements seem to represent an unique yet unmistakable acknowledgement that a very significant pro-independent constituency exists in Jammu and Kashmir and serves as a reminder that many pro-Pakistan elements like prejudiced and misinformed Indians tend to the Kashmir insight in terms of extremely reductive amid superficial categories.

Bose (1997) points out that there is no alternative to democratic debate and discussion between representative of various groups and political tendencies in the different regions of Jammu and Kashmir, if progress is to be made towards a durable political settlement. This is especially because kashmiris leaders almost always decline to countenance truncation as the price of self-determination. He cites that the Jammu and Kashmir Liberation Front (JKLF) chairman Yasin Malik asserts that (JKLF) may accept partition, with much regret, only after major majorities in Jammu and Ladakh vote against unity with Kashmir in a free and fair referendum on self-determination in which all parties including those advocating unity are able to campaign and canvas among the electorate in all three regions. Rejecting proposals of trifurcation as unacceptable and a part of BJP communal politics Malik has stated that even if we have to give our blood for it, we want to live as the people of Jammu, Kashmir and Ladakh.

Dixit (1998) is of the strong view that Pakistan has remained and will remain antagonistic and intrusive vis-a-vis India, despite the interlude of the Gujaral doctrine and the restoration of the cosmetic dialogue between two countries. What is more important is the fact that the Pakistani power structure expected the Gowda and Gujaral governments in India to be vulnerable and indecisive. Such an expectation augmented adventurism trends in Pakistan's India policies. According to him this was illustrated in Pakistan trying to sabotage the assembly elections in Jammu and Kashmir in 1996. Pakistan sponsored intrusive violence and terrorism in the state continues to generate instability and disaffection there as well as in other parts of India, taking advantage of the frustration and alienation in different sections of our citizenry.

Jetly (1999) in a study of India's policy and Dialogue on Kashmir has varied suggestions from differing domestic and foreign quarters for a political solution, greater autonomy for Kashmir with the LOC being converted into a permanent border, the creation of a separate entity of Jammu and Kashmir under UN supervision, the bifurcation of Kashmir between Ladakh valley and Jammu valley, and having autonomous status providing equal access and political connections to Pakistan and India.

Rajdam (1999) points that an average Indian tax payer is not aware of the reasons that trigger explosions in the ranks of Indian leadership when anyone asks seeks to implement the United Nations resolution to settle the Kashmir issue once for all. The will of the people of Kashmir has been held supreme in these solutions. According to him if this will is with the state of India, as the Indian media would want Indians to believe then why do we fritter our energy in fighting nine-year old bloody proxy war in the state. Sadly the media of the gigantic democratic country has been playing galleries when it comes to facing truth particularly in the valley. Had the Indian media done its job faithfully without compromising professional ethics, the people of Kashmir would have been in gratitude and may have accepted the conversion to Indian secularism along time ago.

Quereshi (1999) observed that Pakistan is concerned only with the Kashmir region and is willing to let Jammu and Ladakh remain with India. According this provides adequate proof of its intentions? Pakistan's role in Gilgit Baltistan and the repeated rejection of the independence option for Kashmir strengthens his observation. However, the solution for Kashmir is not an armed conflict but the two countries must adopt a peaceful dialogue.

Patil and Jha (1999) discussing peace and co-operative security aspects in South Asia. He opine that the next step in confidence-building is glasnost or transparency. In this area the Pakistan has to do lot of home work. Pakistan does not publish detailed defense, space and atomic energy reports as India does not annual reports on these activities. While in India itself the information availability is less than what many of us would like to see, in Pakistan it is abysmally less than in India. This of course was an inheritance of the milital/ regimes. Before there can be meaningful discussion of any should start publishing detailed budgets on defense, space, and atomic energy.

Ashtosh Kumar Sharma and Chodhury (1999) focus on the politics of autonomy in Jammu and Kashmir and opine that negotiation settlement demands equally sensitive appreciation of feelings and demands of Jammu and Ladakh regions, it calls for autonomous sub-region status for Jammu to be a part of the process of restoration of more autonomy for the state of J&K. He points out that restoration of pre-1953 position is not possible and it was not done even in the 1975 accord with Sheikh Abdullah. The federal question is not settled by the opinion of anyone generation, because it is question of growth. Every successive stage of our political and economic development gives it a new aspect, makes it a new question.

Banerji (2000) in his discussion of conflict resolution in the post cold war era stresses that the spatial strategy of the status quo accepting the line of actual control is also no longer possible to adopt because public opinion both in India and in Pakistan disfavours it. Pakistan has no reason to jump at the proposal as it is already enjoying what the proposal offers it. Even in India LOC finds few buyers. In February 1997 the then Chief Minister of J&K, Dr. Farooq Abdullah, suggested handing over the (PoK) Pakistan occupied Kashmir to Pakistan and retaining what it controls at present in the border state and drew vituperation from the BJP. But in April 1997 Prime Minister I.K. Gujaral also ruled out the possibility of converting the Line of Control in Jammu and Kashmir into a permanent border.

Dixit (2001) discussing India's foreign policy opines that the possible interaction of the Hurriyat is the focus of political and media attention. According to him the question to be asked to whether it would be right to deal with the Hurriyat as the sole or major group representing the people of Jammu and Kashmir. The objective answer to this question would be in the negative. The Hurriyat does not have any representatives from Ladakh or Jammu. It does not even have representation from some militant groups which not part of it. The Hizbul and Pakistan based groups insist on retaining their separate identity. Equally importantly India cannot ignore or marginalize Chief Minister Farooq Abdullah and National Conference which have fought elections and have affirmed their commitment to India's territorial integrity. He opines that the Hizbul or other violent groups arrogating to themselves the role being the sole representatives of the citizens of Jammu and Kashmir is not actually correct and should not be politically accepted.

Krishna Ashok, Chari P.R. (2001) trace the genesis of the Kargil and say it lies in Pakistan's repeated failure to annex Jammu and Kashmir. Conventional wars, fifteen years of fighting in Siachen and 12 years of militancy has led to exasperation. From the period of 1995, militancy in the Kashmir valley was on the decline and this was the cause of concern to the Pakistani political and military establishment. Its strategic and diplomatic aim was to bring back the J&K issue into focus because global attention was flagging and draw, India into a negotiating position wherein it would be forced to accept the international community as mediators and observers in Jammu and Kashmir dispute.

Chitkara (2002) agrees that converting the LOC into international border that will be tantamount to rewarding aggression, and where was the guarantee that Pakistan will respect an international border anymore then the LOC. The original boundary of Kashmir was an international border when it was invaded in 1947 by Pakistan. In fact India never consented for autonomy nor conversion of LOC but an impression went to the people.

Sharma (2002) alleges that autonomy has led to baneful results. He is critical of the leadership has removed the secular and socialist character of the state officially by an amendment act. According to him has a separate flag, a separate constitution a special status and it needs only independence in foreign relations with countries bordering the state to emerge as a Sultanate, the key note to the Anglo-American conspiracy umpiring the Kashmir-situation at all stages since partition against India and in favour of Pakistan.

Genicot and Skarperdas (2002) state that Peace does not come without negotiations, without the development of a measure of trust, and ultimately without the presence of institutions that will maintain it to the future. All these require effort and expense that must be undertaken by all interested parties. Making peace is an endeavor that entails much uncertainty, and the chance of success should depend on the degree of effort and the size of the investments in conflict management. Jodi Nach Tway and Tensler Mark, (2002). In sum, the theoretical linkage between economic considerations and attitudes toward foreign policy may be direct or indirect. In the former case, citizens judge foreign policy alternatives by weighing costs and benefits and then give or withhold supular policy. Moreover, this calculation may be made with strategic considerations in mind, so that costs and benefits are also considered in relation to the implications for other actors, particularly adversaries. In the latter case, support or opposition to a particular foreign policy may be determined to a greater degree by confidence in the government. The substantive qualities of an individual policy mean little if the government is viewed as being too inept or dishonest to implement it effectively and with the public interest at heart. Policy alternatives thus may not be evaluated independently, with respect to their merits but rather in terms of confidence in the policy's architects.

Although distinct, these theoretical approaches are not mutually exclusive. Citizens may use or combine both types of reasoning when formulating opinions about foreign policy, including issues of war and peace.

Redd B. Steven (2002) describes, The poliheuristic theory of foreign policy in which decision making incorporates the conditions surrounding foreign policy decisions, as well as the cognitive processes associated with these surroundings (Mintz and Geva 1997). In other words, it concentrates on the "why" and "how" of decision making, which makes the theory relevant to both the contents and the processes of decision making. The term *poliheuristic* can be subdivided into the roots *poly* (many) and *heuristic* (shortcuts), which refers to the cognitive mechanisms decision makers use in attempts to simplify complex decision tasks (Geva, Redd, and Mintz 2000; Mintz and Geva 1997; Mintz et al. 1997). Abelson and Levi (1985, 255) citing Braunstein (1976), define heuristics as "problem-solving methods which tend to produce efficient solutions to difficult problems by restricting the search through the space of possible solutions". The poliheuristic theory of decision making proposes that decision makers employ a two-stage decision process in which decision makers, in the first stage, initially screen available alternatives using cognitive-based heuristic strategies. In the second stage, when the decision matrix has been reduced to a more manageable number of alternatives and dimensions, decision makers resort to analytic, expected utility, or lexicographic rules of choice in an effort to minimize risks and maximize rewards (Mintz and Geva 1997; Mintx et al. 1997).

Simons A. Beth (2002) considers arbitration and adjudication as examples of cases that raise issues of second-order compliance. Although there are important differences between the two legal procedures, these differences are not severe enough to exclude one at the expense of reducing the sample. Not surprisingly, arbitration is used more frequently than adjudication because the former allows the disputants to choose the arbitrators and the exact issues to be decided. Adjudication, on the other hand, invokes an existing legal framework and institution. The result in both cases, however, is a legally binding ruling, carrying similar obligations with respect to compliance.

Maoz, Ifat, Ward, Andrew, Kotz Micheal (2002) opine that these psychological barriers (see Mnookin and Ross 1995; Ross and Ward 1995, 1996) might being with cognitive dissonance (Festinger 1957), which can lead disputants to reject present settlement offers to rationalize past struggles. The list would also include optimistic overconfidence (Kahneman and Tversky 1979, 1984), whereby negotiators reject proposed trades of concessions because they attach greater weight to prospective losses than gains. An additional barrier arises from the fact that disputants are likely to demand a settlement that not only advances their individual positions over the status quo but does so in a fair and equitable manner that is, in a manner that gives appropriate weight to the relative strength and legitimacy of rival claims (Adams 1965; Rawls 1971). Given that most disputes have their roots in a history of events and rival claims that the parties see through the prism of their conflicting interest and ideologies, the search for an agreement that satisfies both sides' equity needs is apt to be a frustrating one.

Bose (2003) in a study of Kashmir, roots conflict, paths to peace has delineated that there is some resemblance between the ways in which the conflicts over Palestine and Kashmir have got transformed over tbe decades. Initially both conflicts had manifested themselves in the form of interstate wars—1948, 1956, 1967 and 1973 in the former case and 1947-48, 1965 and 1971 in the latter case. As Intifada changed the Palestine struggle into an internal one in 1987, militant actions converted the Kashmir conflict in 1989 from an interstate one to an internally located one no doubt with extensive external Support. According to the study, the conflict holds one major lesson for Pakistan that secession is not a practical proposition in today's world. In 1994 and in 200], the LTTE had fought Colombo to a military stalemate a feat that the Pakistani sponsored fighters in Kashmir have never ever begun to approach. Similarly the LTTE has controlled substantial areas of Srilanka territory since 1990, areas from where state authority has been excluded. Nothing like it has ever happened in Kashmir. Therefore if Pakistan believes that any part of the areas currently with India can be separated it is a delusion that can only serve to prolong the conflict without a strategic purpose.

Bose (2003) has compared the positions of the Irish Free State in 1921 and that of Pakistan in 1947 which had a good deal in common especially with respect to the perception of having received a raw deal. The IRA attempts to spark violence in the 1930s and 1950s had failed utterly for want of popular support. But when the IRA entered the fray in 1968 it met witb success because of the changed popular mood. This has a close parallel to the failure of Pakistan's efforts in 1965 and 1970-71 to influence the valley and the success they met in 1989. Bose also notes that despite the huge problems IRA violence had created for them stringent policing by the government and reprisals by the paras, large sections of Catholics continued to support the IRA-passively and surreptiously just as much the same has happened in Jammu and Kashmir.

Bose (2003) points to the difference between Jammu and Kashmir and Northern Ireland that British-Irish intergovernmental co-operation on Northern Ireland was greatly facilated by two countries common membership in a dynamic regional organization of integration and co-operation the European Community (EC) known since 1992 as the European Union which both nations joined since 1972. According to Bose (2003) it is substantially easier for countries embroiled in a contentious bilateral dispute to cooperate on settling the problem under an overarching regional framework of cooperation and integration which links the countries through supra state institutions and reduces the salience of rigid sovereignty discourses and state borders.

When there is no time pressure, the differences just hypothesized are expected to hold; namely, peacekeepers are expected to be more assertive in the severe versus the nonsevere disputes. By contrast, whenever there is time pressure, the predicated differences decrease or do not cccur. The logic here is that peacekeepers who manage severe disputes under a time constraint may wish to use more techniques, but the time constraint limits their freedom to do so. This approach will not differ significantly from that used by the peacekeepers who manage nonsevere disputes under time pressure. In this latter case, the number of techniques used will be low because the peacekeepers conclude that the dispute does not deserve an extensive effort on their part. Thus, time pressure serves to mask the difference in approaches to meditation between severe and nonsevere disputes. *Wall Jr. and Druckman (2003)*

Chiozza and Goeman (2003) show that leaders who participate in international disputes improve their chances to remain in office. They argue that leaders want to stay in power and will only become involved in disputes if such actions are likely to increase their tenure. From this perspective the results suggest that leaders are choosing their fights well (Bueno de Mesquita et al., 2001: 196-97). This pattern holds regardless of domestic regime type: democratic and nondemocratic leaders, that is, benefit to almost the same degree from international conflict participation. Victory as compared to both defeats and draws also increase tenure, and effort that is particularly pronounced for democratic leaders. Distinguishing low-density conflict from war, they find that conflict participation short of war is beneficial to the office tenure of both democratic and nondemocratic leaders This is not the case for war, however. Fighting a war generates one of the largest degrees in the risk of office removal for democratic leaders, whereas it produces a sizable but statistically insignificant increase in the hazard of losing power for nondemocratic leaders.

Ghiozza and Choi (2003) suggest that leaders with a history of conflict involvement, use of major force, and military successes and leaders with a previous career in the military should be less likely to take steps that might lead to the resolution of a dispute. This is because such a decision would undermine the reputation that defines their identity as political actors. As soon as an accommodative move is made, reputation for toughness evaporates and is not to be recovered again. Although any bargaining process might potentially entail reciprocal concessions from the contending parties, territorial matters are less likely to be amenable to such forms of give and take; their peculiar features and the underlying indivisibility that makes them so intractar'e militate against this possibility.

Butler *(2003)* analyes U.S. decision making in historical cases of intervention. He suggests that greater insight is needed regarding the decision to rule out or commit to the use of a military option. A broader interpretation of the term is used, encompassing not only these standard elements of military action but also what Brecher and Wilkernfeld (2000) refer to as "indirect" military action. Such action can and does include crisis behavior such as the deployment of conventional forces to countries neighboring the conflict, major transfers in arms and military hardware to one or more parties involved in the conflict, dispatch of military advisors to one or more parties involved in the conflict, introduction of extensive convert operations in one or more countries involved in the conflict, and so forth. The United States need not be directly involved in the fighting but must, at a minimum, be directly involved in altering the context of that fighting through the application of military influence. "Military intervention" henceforth should be understood to construe any deliberate introduction or application of military weaponry, personnel, or intelligence intended to alter the dynamics of a conflict.

Mediation is described a assistance to interacting parties by a third party who may or may not have authority to impose an outcome (Wall, Stark, and Standifer 2001). A through review of the decision-making (Beach 1997), motivation (Locke 1991), and mediation (Carnevale 1986) literatures revealed that decision makers (e.g., mediators), when given different options (e.g., techniques), eliminate some and select from the remainder as they pursue their own goals. As they do so, various factors affect the decision makers' or mediators' decisions. Some of these factors are internal 10 the dispute, whereas others are external constraints. As these orders are applied to the peacekeepers' potential techniques, it appeared that the third order, which instructs the peacekeeper to be and appear to be neutral, eliminated the following techniques from the peacekeepers' feasible set (i.e., the set of techniques available, given the constraints of the role): stating one side's point of view to the other, calls to apologize, calls for empathy, having a drink with one side, and praising one side to the other. The fourth order, no personal assistance, eliminates the "peacekeeper assists" technique and prescribes the inclusion of the "third-party assist" technique (e.g., calling on nongovernment organizations for assistance). The final order, not to the problem solve personally, seems to eliminate the techniques of arguing for concessions, citing dependency, educating/advising, analyzing the disputants, and the peacekeepers' provision of data. It is hypothesized that peacekeepers will use more mediation techniques (i.e., a more complex and costly approach) in severe disputes than in nonsevere ones (hypothesis (1) Specifically, it is hypothesized that peacekeepers, on average, will use more of these techniques in severe (compared to nonsevere) dispute (hypothesis (2) This reasoning leads to hypothesis 3: peacekeepers will more frequently use the set security techniques in severe (vs. nonsevere) disputes. *Wall A. Jr. and Druckman (2003)*

Mathew and Moove H. Hill, (2003) studied the sources of heterogeneity that might exist in foreign policy series. We identify two such sources below: different actors and different issues. The most likcly source of short-memoried and long-memoried heterogeneity is aggregation across different actors. One manner in which researchers might study the behavior of multiple actors is to aggregate across multiple countries. Most studies of foreign policy examine directed dyads that are pairs of countries, but in a few cases researchers have aggregated the behavior of several countries to create a single, series (Davis and Ward 1990; Goldstein and Pevehous 1997). For example, Goldstein and Pevehouse (1997) study the behaviour of the United Na:ions (UN) and NATO countries toward Serbia during the Bosnian conflict of the 1990s. They thus created an international actors series that was the sum of the behavior of each actor (i.e., the UN and the NATO countries). Because there is little reason to believe that the UN and each of the NATO countries used the past in the same way when responding to the Serbs, this international actors series is an aggregation across heterogeneous actions.

Dixi (2004) in a discussion of India and regional development described that the ceasefire line was drawn between Indian and Pakistani forces in Jammu and Kashmir at the end of Indo-Pakistan War on July 17, 1949. The Prime Ministers of India and Pakistan Indira Gandhi and Zulifiqur Ali Bhutto decided to re-delineate it as "Line of Control". This was agreed upon in accordance with paragraph 4(II) of Simla Agreement. This new line of control signifies an important political transition from the ceasefire line being a military line separating two armies, to line demarcating a political divide which was to evolve into an international boundary in Jammu and Kashmir between India and Pakistan.

Prakash and Shrama (2004) calls for Enforcing effective media control measures and dissemination of maximum information to the masses. According to him there should be not any communication gap between the government and the people. Reorganing opera-military forces to effectively undertake law and order and combat the growing militancy and special forces to be integrated into them. Improving their leadership training fire power, mobility and flexibility; restoring faith by good clean administration by introduction of social services to better the lot of the people and mobilizing Indian Muslims in the cause of saving Kashmir are some measures suggested by the author.

Mintz (1993, 1995) introduced noncompensatory (decision making as part of poliheuristic theory. One immediately eliminates alternatives that imply major losses on key value dimensions, typically the political dimension. For example, during the Cuban missile crisis, the Kennedy administration had two goals: (1) get the missiles out and (2) avoid war with the USSR. The constraint version involved getting the missiles out under the constraint of avoiding war. Options that scored low on either goal were never very seriously pursued. Diplomatic protest was unlikely to get the missiles out; military invasion was likely to cause war. According to accounts of the decision-making process, neither of these options was followed up in a serious way. *Geortz (2004)*

Rajan and Sethi (2005) stressed that it may not be proper to speak in terms of quick settlement as the United Nations assisted efforts tend to. It is a process that requires years of discussion and learning educating the public, broadening the agenda re-perceiving the enemy, and workshops the so-called Gujral doctrine appeared to be a small beginning. So for only a law and order approach has been predominant in the Indian government's attitude and approach towards the issue. India has to accept the militants as political actors and engage in constructive talks with them. It is necessary that the conflicts of this kind be transformed so as to create a more hospitable environment for negotiation. *Rajan and Sethi (2005)* noted that the moment the Palestine took to a civilian based movement intifada, a constituency more responsive to their demands could be created within Israel and outside, This paved the way for the peace agreement. The authors opine that as long as the Indian and Pakistani government engage in dialogue only to score a point, the Kashmir problem will exist.

Verghese and Kothari (2005) opine that since 1989 four major developments have had a role in the India-Pakistan conflict, the nuclearisation of the sub-continent, the post 9/11 world, the widening of the India-Pakistan power gap and the increased alienation of the Kashmiris. On the Indian side preferences with regard to autonomy and the allegiances that underpin them range widely. Large numbers in Jammu and Ladakh and the Pandits of Kashmir do not want a structure that would permit valley Muslims to dominate. But many in Jammu do not also want to be in the ascendancy of the majority group over there. The vast mountainous tract of Doda district and adjacent parts of Udampur district have Sunni Muslim majorities and substantial Kashmir links. Poonch and Rajouri district of Jammu with 90% and 65% Sunni Muslims respectively have no great ties with Kashmir but there is a great disquiet about Jammu Hindus. Within Ladakh where half the people are Muslim there are different elements on political structuring.

Iyer (2005) in his study of the Indus treaty and India-Pakistan water dispute points out that disputes can crop up over the difference between run-of-river projects and storages. The run of the river means absence of storage. When a project is described as the run of the river it means denying the existence of any storage. He states that the treaty prohibits storages by India on the western rivers except to a limited extent, but permits run of the river scheme subject to several conditions.

Gazdar (2005) studying the Baligar project opines that it was already in the public domain since 2000, well before the peace process started during that period confronting the project was not seen as an important priority as it did not challenge the military governments definition of the core national interests. The Pakistan government's stand is seen as more to do with its disillusionment with the broader bilateral negotiation. The Baglihar dispute might be the pretext rather than the cause of a cooling off in the peace process.

Sorlie, Mirjam, Gleditch, Pelter, Nics, Strandi (2005) stress that ensuring diversified economic development remains the key to preventing future conflicts. Improved management of resources, natural as well as human, and the development of more transparent and legitimate, if not democratic, regimes proved the most efficient means toward preventing new conflicts in the Middle East as in other developing regions.

Regan and Aydin (2006) suggest that mediation facilitates the transfer of information quite efficiently. An outside mediator serves as the conduit for information, ideas, and possible concessions that civil war parties would not possibly convey without a third-party intermediary. Outside interventions can provide a more objective view of conditions and possible outcomes of the conflict, which help adversaries to update their beliefs about the likely outcomes. Absent an outside intervention, the information held by the warring parties is at best asymmetrical, and neither side has a unilateral incentive to honestly convey its military capabilities, expectations of victory or defeat, or the value of a settlement that it would accept for the fear of exploitation by its adversary. Third parties can therefore influence the value of a settlement by transmitting information on the preferences of adversaries and offering inducements that make a negotiated outcome more attractive than other solutions. In this respect, diplomatic initiatives can help parties find a cooperative solution that both sides can agree to and allows the parties to make the credible commitment required of negotiated ends to civil wars (Walter 2002). The key to successful interventions, therefore, is to reduce the asymmetry of information about capabilities and incentives and, in doing so, help civil war parties find a peaceful solution that can benefit both sides.

Events data-based approaches, analyzing the presence of conflict in short time intervals as measured by articles published in newspapers or issued over news services, offer yet another quantitative way of observing early warning signals on a weekly or even daily basis. *Poe C. Steven, Rost, Nicholas, Carey C. Jabine (2006).* Early projects, such as the Conflict and Peace Data Bank (COPDAB), the World Event Interaction Survey (WEIS), or the Global Events-Data System (GEDS), have largely relied on human coded data and have generated some useful predictions (Davies and Gurr, 1998).

Events data approaches use machine-coded data and are therefore in a position to analyze much more information (Gerner et al. 1994; Bond et al. 1997; Bond et al. 2003). Such approaches have been applied to examine the political situation in the Middle East (Schrodt and Gerner 1997, 1998, 2000; Gerner and Schrodt 1998) and in Kosovo (Pevehouse and Goldstein 1999). The FAST early warning system of the Swiss Peace Institute combines qualitative and quantitative events data approaches and monitors a number of countries in Africa, Asia, Europe, and the Middle East. *(Steven, Rost and Carey)*

3

Methodology

The research aims to study and compare the coverage of the second round composite dialogue between India and Pakistan as treated by both the newspapers (The Hindu and The New Indian Express) with wide circulation in the south India. The operational definition of a major newspaper in this study is taken as a daily newspaper in the English newspaper with multiple editions in India.

Objectives of the Study

1. To study the role of print media in covering the conflict
2. To study the role of print media in highlighting ways of resolving conflict.
3. To analyse the coverage of the Kashmir conflict in the National Press.
4. To make comparative content analysis, of the Kashmir conflict in two newspapers.
5. To study the various issues involved in the Kashmir conflict and process of conflict resolution.

Content analysis has been used to analysis the course of conflict reports, editorials, features, photos, letter to the editor. Content analysis is used to study the manifest and latent content in the media and it is used here as a quantitative and qualitative method to supplement each other to draw inferences. The sample consisted of two national English dailies The New Indian Express (Madurai Edition) and The Hindu (Madurai Edition). The news report, editorials, features, interviews, photos and letter to the editor, were gathered from April 3, 2005 to November 29, 2006.

Sample Frame and Size

The sample was spread for over a year as the confidence building measure gained great momentum between two countries with more frequency of reports until there was a sudden halt with the Mumbai blasts where the economy of the country received a setback and impasse that emerged between both the governments and the illusory note of Confidence Building Measures (CBMS) with violence exerted by the neighbouring country (Pakistan). A total of 250 samples of each newspaper totaling to 500 samples welt analysed during the period of study.

A news story is defined as information about the event or persons associated with the event. Apart from news stories on the front page and in other pages, editorials, features, including news analysis and opinion pieces, interviews, and letter to the editor were content analysed to study and compare the coverage in terms of the issucs reported, the nature and the extent of coverage and the difference in news treatment.

HYPOTHESIS

H0: There relationship between is no composite dialogue and the conflict report in media.

H1: There is relationship between composite dialogue and the conflict report in the media.

Data Collection and Analysis

Content analysis was applied to the entire sampie for categorsing and analysing the data in both the newspapers for study. The news report, features, interviews, editorials, photos and letter to the editor were coded under various categories and subcategories. The coded data were subjected to quantitative analysis or both after an inter-reliability test to check for the subjectivity of the coder and mutual exclusivity of categories. Content analysis has been used to analyse the latent content -deeper layers of meaning embedded in the reports. The data were analysed both quantitatively and qualitatively. Comparative content analysis was also carried out to study the differential coverage of events in the two newspapers.

Quantitative Analysis

Quantitative analysis has been undertaken to study exactly how far print media through its report coverage of the Kashmiri conflict presents various issues of composite dialogue. The composite dialogue initiated during the tenure of the Vajpayee government has gained momentum in the Manmohan Singh government. The issues discussed are:

1. Peace and securely including (CBMs) Confidence Building Measures
2. Jammu and Kashmir
3. The Siachen Glacier
4. Wullar barrage / Tulbul navigation project.
5. Economic and commercial co-operation
6. Sir Creek mission.
7. Terrorism and drug trafficking
8. Promotion of friendly exchanges.

The Hindu		*The Ney / Indian Express*	
Direct News	767	Direct Stories	591
Editorial	46	Editorial	64
Features	90	Features	69
Letter to the Editor	428	Letter to the Editor	36
Cartoon	17	Cartoon	4
Photos	217	Photos	134
Interview	7	Interviews	0
Total	1572		898

There were 767 direct news reports in The Hindu as against 591 news reports in The New Indian Express. 46 editorials figured ia The Hindu as against 64 editorials in The New Indian Express. There were 90 features in The Hindu as against 69 features in The New Indian Express. The Elndu had given much importance to wide range of public opinion with 428 letter to the editor as against 36 letters to the editor in The New Indian Express. 17 cartoons appeared in The Hindu as against 4 in The New Indian Express. There was 217 photographs in The Hindu as against 134 photographs in The New Indian Express. There was absolutely no interview in The New Indian Express whereas The Hindu carried only 7 interviews.

Discriminant analysis tests in predictor (independent) variables as discriminators of the differences between k groups of a single discrete (categorical) dependent variable. The dependent variable is interval scaled.

Discriminant analysis

Two-group discriminant analysis

In discriminant analysis we predict classification into a given category as a function of the predictor variables. Here we assume a linear function. In case of Two-group Discriminant Analysis, only two categories are involved.

The Objectives of a Two-Group/Analysis:

(1) Finding Linear combinations of the predictc variables that enable the analyst to separate the groups by maxirrizing between-variable variation relative to within-groups variations identity.

(2) Establishihg procedures for assigning new individuals into the groups. For these individuals, a profile on the predictor variables are known, but not for group identity.

(3) Testing whether significant differences exist between the means of the two groups on the predictor variable profiles.

(4) Determining which variables account for most of the differences in mean profiles of the groups.

The analysis is designed to achieve two goals. To indicate the overall power of all to differentiate between the two groups variables of composite dialogue in (a) The New Indian Express and (b) The Hindu. To find out the relative importance of each of those variables in describing the two groups of composite dialogue, six measurement components of the variables were introduced into discriminant function. The discriminant coefficient were computed for all the measurements, the centriod value for each of the two groups was arrived at an significance was tested by Wilkslambda.

Qualitative Analysis

The issue of what role the media would play in conflict resolution is very ambiguous and has received scant treatment. However, most of the experts agree that answers cannot be easily found and the media's role in conflicts can be both positive and negative depending on the circumstances. But it is interesting that many diplomats agree that in the midst of a conflict media silence is often better than media coverage. 'Media diplomacy' is quite a new term, not yet broadly used, but considering the growing public concern about conflict resolution, it may become a powerful tool of diplomacy in the future. Due to time constraints journalists often do not have enough time to gather, digest" nd filter information. Coupled with the instinctive assumptions made by policy makers, diplomats, and the military the information gets skewed many times before reaching the audience.

The function of diplomacy is conducting negotiations between representatives of groups or nations with political affairs between countries that can result in government -sponsored programmes to inform or influence public opinion in other countries. In brief, it's called public diplomacy negotiations around conflict prevention and peace building which are normally conducted in a discrete way without involving too much of media attention. The media cannot be directly involved it) conflict resolution, but its watcher - teacher function can be very useful for the prevention of any negative processes in society.

Media diplomacy can be defined as a tool of communication through the media, which should help diplomats to perform their key function of leading the processes of conflict resolution and prevention. At the same time, it is worth considering a suggestion made recently by Joann Byrd, wliting as ombudsman for the Washington post in covering conflict stories, Byrd (2000) states journalists should add 'S' for solution and "C" for common ground to the traditional five W's formula (Who, What, When, Where, Why)

Two newspapers may editorially take very different stands on the same event or issue. The volume of news in different categories does not give one an idea about the contents and issues that are projected nor how and event can be reported and interpreted. It is to explain the question of how an event is reported that qualitative analysis has been carried out at four levels.

1. The first level of analysis looks at how the second round of composite dialogue and its developments has been reported according to the constructed news stories and sub themes in both the newspapers.
2. The second level compares the two newspapers where the various mediators and disputants (Parties to the conflict) view the composite dialogue.
3. The third level of analysis includes how both the newspapers have taken enough initiative to identify the common ground "C" and all possible solutions "s" to resolve the conflict.
4. The fourth level of analysis incorporates how both the governments rely on the initiated composite dialogue to avoid conflicts and avert a nuclear disaster.

These events are included in features and editorials which substantiate how the government to government via media resolution or Track III unlike the Track II, a non-government initiative, may help futher the peace process with the neighbouring country which views with much distrust the eight issues that fall under the gambit of the composite dialogue:

1. Kashmir peace and security Siachen Issue
2. Sir Creek mission
3. Wullar Barrage / Tulbul navigation project
4. Terrorism and Drug trafficking
5. Economic and commercial co-operation
6. Friendly exchanges.

4

Composite Dialogue

The incentives - disincentives structure has caused South Asia to oscilate between cooperation/stability and confrontation / instability. With Pakistan's return to democracy in 1988, relations temporarily improved. By the summer of 1990, however, the two were nearly at war over Kashmir. After the crises, relations once again improved, and a flurry of confidence - building measures were agreed upon. In 1992, the two resumed discussions on bilateral negotiations and presented each other with a series of "nonpapers". The following year, India and Pakistan were reputed to be on the verge of signing a series of agreements on the Siachen, Sir Creek, and Wullar conflicts. However, in 1994 - 95, relations deteriorated. India was in the midst of a full-blown insurgency in Kashmir and held Pakistan responsible. Pakistan charged India with maltreating Kashmiris and campaigned for international mediation in the dispute. Nonetheless, in 1996, the two countries began the so-called six-plus-two talks that covered Kashmir, security, trade, and other bilateral issues. By 1997, India's problems in Kashmir had perceptibly eased. India's security forces seemed to have gained the upper hand against the militants. Elections had returned a civilian government to Kashmir, and this further reduced tensions.

The nuclear tests of May 1998 caused India and Pakistan to once again trade charges. The two governments then surprised the world by agreeing to a historic summit in the Pakistani city of Lahore in February 1999. The summit produced a number of accords on nuclear weapons, confidence building, trade and economic relations, and, most importantly, resuming a dialogue on Kashmir. Within months, however, the two countries were at war. Pakistani troops and Kashmir militants crossed the line of control in Kashmir along the heights in Kargil and a short, sharp war ensued. In the aftermath of the war, both sides took strong stands. India insisted that Pakistan stop aiding the Kashmiri militants and Pakistan repudiated the Lahore agreements. The military coup in Pakistan in October 1999 and the hijacking of an Indian civilian aircraft from Kathmandu to Kandahar by Kashmiri militants led to further tensions. In the summer of 2000, relations once again improved. A series of cease-fires in Kashmir (led off by a Kashmiri militant group in July and extended by the Indian government in November 2000), military retrenchment by Pakistan along the line of control, and Track II contacts between India and Pakistan led to a perceptible warming of relations. In July 2001, Indian and Pakistani leaders finally resumed negotiations. The summit in Agra did not, however, produce an accord, and once again relations deteriorated.

The most important of these disputes is the India-Pakistan quarrel over Kashmir. The two countries are still at odds over other territorial issues: Siachen and Sir Creek. Between 1989 and 1993, the two countries made progress on the smaller quarrels. From 1996 onward, India and Pakistan once again began discussions on Kashmir and the lesser territorial issues, in the so-called six-plus-two dialogues. The talks foundered on substance and also on differing that deals with all bilateral issues simultaneously without giving priority to any one issue, especially Kashmir.

The two States of India and Pakistan were born in August 1947. When India was partitioned at the end of British colonisation it was hoped that the relation between India and Pakistan would be normal and cordial because the partition was affected with the consent of the leaders of two nations. The people of two areas had shared a common history for centuries and the economies of the two countries were complimentary to each other. But unfortunately that did not happen.

Two major reasons for constant conflict between the two States were 1. Partition was affected in haste without formulating suitable and detailed rules of the game. The result was mass exodus of population from each country, large-scale killing, abduction of women, forced conversions, problems of recovery of evacuee property, and many such other problems. This caused bad blood between the two countries bad things could not be forgotten for long.

Secondly the basis for partition was not laid down in unambiguous terms. Pakistan's leaders advocated and accepted partition on the basis of two-nation theory. In contrast while the Indian leaders accepted partition, they never approved of two-nation theory. They accepted partition on the basis of some type of territorial self-determination and more on account of compulsions created by the prevailing situation of widespread riots and the unhealthy intentions of the British rulers.

As regards, undoing partition of India had the country shown some courage things would have been much easier immediately after partition, particularly when Pakistan provided an excuse to us by sending forces in Kashmir. Instead of availing of that golden opportunity, India under the stewardship of then Prime Minister Pandit Nehru went to the United Nations and accepted ceasefire. The Pakistan army at the time was weak and the job could have been done at a minimum cost. The second opportunity came in 1965 when Pakistan again attacked Kashmir; India fought and won the war here but returned all occupied areas to Pakistan under the Tashkent agreement.

Kashmir Problem

Under the terms of the Independence of India Act of 1947, the sovereignty of his Majesty over Indian State's lapsed. The states were free to accede to India or to Pakistan, or if they such as, to remain independent. In October 1947 faced with the invasion of the State by armed raiders backed by the regular army in plain clothes, the ruler of the State, Maharaja Hari Singh backed by the leader of the popular political party Sheikh Abdullah requested India to accept the accession of Kashmir to India and to intervene with her armed forces. India accepted the accession and thus Kashmir became part of Indian Territory. The letter dated 27th October 1947 of Lord Mountbatten the then Governor General of India, accepting Kashmir's accession to India laid down that as soon as law and order have been restored in Kashmir and her soil cleared of the invaders, the question of the State's accession should be settled by reference to the people.

Accession to India

The accession of the State of Jammu and Kashmir to India, signed by the Maharaja on the 28th October 1947 was completely voted in terms of the Government of India Act (1935). The Indian independence act (1947) and the international law was total and irrevocable. The largest political party in the State, the National Conference, supported the accession. Lord Mountbatten's acceptance of the Instrument of accession was unconditional. He said, "I do hereby accept this instrument of accession. This instrument of accession was complete with the offer and acceptance".

Reference to United Nations

India made a reference to United Nations on 1st January 1948 under Article 35 of the Charter, which permits any member state to bring any situation, whose continuance is likely to endanger international security, to the attention of the security council. The intention behind this reference was prevent war between two nearly independent countries.

Pakistan consistently misled the world regarding the involvement in Kashmir. It claimed initially in 1947 that it was not in any way assisting tribal invaders and was only not actively opposing their passage out of fear that they may turn against the local Pakistani population. Pakistan later claimed that its own forces were not involved directly in operations in Kashmir. But the United Nations commission that visited India in July 1948 found Pakistani forces operating in Pakistan Occupied Kashmir (POK).

Non-implementation of UN Resolution by Pakistan

Despite India's completely legal and valid position on Jammu and Kashmir, in order to find a solution to the situation created by Pakistan's aggression, India had accepted the option of holding a plebiscite in Jammu & Kashmir. It had, however been made clear by the Indian leaders that holding of such plebiscite would be conditional upon Pakistan fulfilling part I & II of the UNCIP resolution of 13th August 1948 which inter alias, required that all forces regular and irregular under the control of both sides shall ceasefire. In 1946 Mohammed Ali Jinnah conferred the leaders of Jammu & Kashmir for merger with the proposed new State of Pakistan, but did not get a favourable response.

On October 22,1947 Pakistan not to the standstill agreement with the Maharaja Jammu & Kashmir launched an invitation of Jammu & Kashmir by tribals led by Pakistani army officers promoting the Maharaja Hari Singh to sign Instrument of accession. October 26,1946 in which he mentioned that he acceded to the Dominion of India to fight Pakistani aggression of Kashmir the first batch of Indian troops were flown to Srinagar on 26th October 1947, it was becoming increasingly clear that Pakistan was giving all support to the invaders in the shape of transport, arms, ammunition and military leadership and even Pakistani soldiers without uniform were actively fighting.

For peaceful settlements, India offered various proposals. On 30th December 1947 while the operations were still in progress the Indian political leadership appealed to the United Nations to intervene and ask Pakistan to withdraw its troops.

Thus on Jan 1,1948 India submitted a formal complaint to the Security Council under chapter VI of the charter, as India was anxious to avoid direct conflict with Pakistan.

On 17th April 1948, the Security Council declared that the situation in Jammu and Kashmir was likely to endanger international peace and security and therefore recommended through a draft resolution the setting up of Commission of five members to proceed once to the Indian subcontinent and place their good officers and mediation at the disposal of the government's of India and Pakistan.

India however rejected the draft resolution but the Security Council adopted it on 21st April and 7th May the membership of United Nations commission on India and Pakistan. The fighting on Kashmir had become more expensive and more serious. Therefore the Commission addressed itself to bringing about a ceasefire and adopted a resolution on 13th Aug. 1948. After negotiations it was accepted by the government of India on 23rd December and Pakistan on 25th December 1948. A ceasefire was ordered from 1st January 1949.

United Nations Commission on India and Pakistan: Basic Resolution of 13th August 1948

Part I

Require a ceasefire, non-augmentation of military potential on either side and the maintenances of peaceful atmosphere.

Part II

Pakistan had to withdraw all her forces, regular and irregular while India was required to keep sufficient troops for the security of the state including the observance of law and order.

Part III

The Government of India and the Government of Pakistan reaffirm their wish that the future status of Jammu and Kashmir shall be determined in accordance with the will of the people and to that end up on acceptance of the truce agreement both the governments agree to enter into consultation with the Commission to determine fair and equitable conditions whereby such free expression of will be assured.

Obviously Part III of the resolution could come into force only after Part Part II and I had been fully implemented.

Plebiscite proposals shall not be binding upon India if Pakistan does not implement Part I and II of the resolution of 13 August 1948.

Thus legality of the State's accession to India was rever questioned by the Security Council or the Commission.

However right from the time of cease fire the efforts of the commission and its various representations and mediators were to induct into office the plebiscite administrator appointed in pursuance of the United Nations resolution of 13 August 1948.

The proposals from Mr. Mcnaughter of Canada, followed by those of Sir Owen Dixon. Dr. Graham laboured from 1950 to 1953 to find a solution to the holding of a plebiscite.

But since Pakistan was not willing to withdraw the troops from the territory occupied by it, the missions failed.

As Pakistan was guilty of the invasion of Jammu & Kashmir it did not abide by the UN resolution and neither withdrew its troops and infiltrators. Instead it built airfields in the occupied territory and imposed a full civilian and military control while claiming the territory as Azad Kashmir.

For the violations the UN could not impose sanctions on Pakistan, as the resolution was not under chapter VII of the charter.

To win Chinese support, it gifted 4853 sq. km of the Kashmir territory in the Shakakogm valley China in I 963, thus disrupting the territorial of the state of Jammu & Kashmir.

Pakistan has made a great deal of play with the idea of self-determination. What is the self that has the right to determine its destiny, to determine whether it would be a part of one country or part of another country or would be independence? It is clear that the self-contemplated in the enunciation of this democratic principle is not and cannot be, a constituent part of the country.

It can be operative only when one is dealing with a nation as a whole and the context in which it can be applicable is the context of conquest or of foreign domination or of colonial exploitation.

The government of Pakistan wrecked any possibility of plebiscite being conducted by not implementing Part II of the resolution, perhaps because it was fully aware of what the result of such an excuse would be. As V. Krishna Menon stated in the Security Council (763 meeting, 23 Jan 1957) if an offer is made and it is not accepted at the time it is made, it cannot be held for generations over the heads of those who made it. In fact the representative of India M.C. Chagla had stated in the Security Council as far back as in 1964, that he made it clear on behalf of the government of India that under no circumstances can India agree to a holding of a plebiscite in Kashmir.

Solutions Proposed by Resolutions: Time and Context

Since 1957 there have been no UN resolutions on the substantive aspects of the Jammu & Kashmir issue. Over fifty years after partition the ground situation in the State to which the resolution referred to has considerably changed. Pakistan unilaterally ceded a part of the State to China in 1963. There has been demographic change on the Pakistan's side with the generations of non-Kashmiris allowed to take residence on the parts of Jammu & Kashmir occupied by Pakistan. The above position is increasingly being acknowledged by the world today. UN Secretary General highlighted the fact that UNCIP did not come Under chapter VII and were therefore not self enforcing. He stated at a press conference in Islamabad in March 2001 that the two parties should discuss these issues and find a peaceful way out.

India-Pakistan Discussion on Jammu & Kashmir

In fact, in the decades of the 80s and 60s several rounds of bilateral discussions took place between India and Pakistan over 1950-51, 1953-54, 1956- 57, 1962-63, to resolve the differences over Kashmir. Jammu & Kashmir is one of the subjects identified for dialogue under the composite dialogue set up at India initiative in 1988.

1965 War: Its Implications

By imposing war, Pakistan negated the very reason for which reference had been made to the UN in 1948. All the arrangements that were arrived at with Pakistanis through instrumentality of the Security Council were based on the integrity and inviolability of the ceasefire line established after the 1947-48 skirmishes. By violating this line in 1965, Pakistan rendered the dead resolutions of 1948 and 1949 in the context of which ceasefire line had been established through the Karachi Agreement of 1949.

Simla Agreement - **Its Implications**

Pakistan imposed yet another war on India on 1971. After the conflict, bilateral talks were held in June-July 1972 and the Simla Agreement was signed between 2nd July 1972. In terms of this agreement, which was duly ratified by the two governments in 1972, the two countries undertook to resolve all differences bilaterally and peacefully.

The Lahore visit of the Prime Minister of India

The Prime Minister A.B. Vajpayee took a historic initiative and visited Lahore from Feb. 2001, 2002. The visit was aimed at conveying India's deep desire to establish peaceful, co-operative and friendly ties with Pakistan. The Lahore Declaration which committed the two countries to build trust and confidence and develop mutually beneficial co-operation to resolve the outstanding issues including J&K through bilateral negotiations, provided a blue print for India-Pakistan relations into the 21st century.

Kargil

However the ink had barely dried on the Lahore Declaration that the Pakistan army manifested its compulsive hostility towards India by launching a military operative in May 1999 across LOC in an attempt to occupy the dominating heights along a 140 km stretch of Srinagar - Leh highway. India's policy of maintaining the sanctity of the LoC and the tremendous restraint shown by India it its firm action against the intruders without crossing the LOC found wide international support and endorsement.

Agra Summit

Notwithstanding the continued sponsorship of cross-border terrorism by Pakistan, on May 23, 2001, India again took the initiative to establish a high level political dialogue with Pakistan by inviting General Musharaff to visit India. Then the Pakistan President General Musharaff visited India from July 14 to July 16, 2001 and had talks with PM Vajpayee in Agra.

Constituent Imbalance

Sheikh Abdullah, the then Prime Minister of the state tried to manage special status for the state. The Chairman of the Indian Constituent Assembly, Dr. B.R. Ambedkhar categorically told Sheikh Abdullah "You want that the responsibility of defense etc. of Kashmir should remain the headache of India, but the Indian Parliament should have no control over the state. "I am the Minister of Law of India and I have to protect the interests of India. So I cannot accept such a proposal." But Pandit Nehru, then through the good offices of Gopalamany Ayyangar, managed special status under Art. 370 for Kashmir for a temporary period and that too was vehemently opposed by the Members of the Constituent Assembly. This temporary provision was later modified as temporary and transactional by the 13th Amendment Act, 1962. But even temporary provisions remain as good as permanent. (Virender, 1995).

The study of the provisions of the special status for Jammu and Kashmir under Article 370 of the Constitution of India throws up, at the outset, four mutually incompatible propositions simultaneously operative in the state.

(a) Special status of Kashmir vis-a-vis other states.

(b) To be governed by its own constitution.

(c) To be an integral part of India.

(d) Citizenship, First class, Second class, Third class and the people without the right to citizenship.

Under this article any citizen of Jammu and Kashmir can contest decision to any state Assembly or the Lok Sabha or the Rajya Sabha, seek service, do business, trade or set up industry and purchase property anywhere in the country. But none from any other part of the country enjoys those rights in Jammu and Kashmir.

In relation to Kashmir itself, Article 370 provides sovereignty within sovereignty, a special status of state (Kashmir) within a state (India). Article 370 by providing special status to the state generates false notions in the minds of the youth of the valley. There are often disparities within the state. The whole set up in Jammu and Kashmir was manipulated to keep out the Hindus and also to keep the power knob in the hands of the Muslim majority in the Kashmir valley. This was manipulated under cover of article 370. It is for this reason that Jammu, a Hindu Majority Zone, was to send one member to the State Assembly for every 90,000 people while the valley sent for every 73,000. Likewise Ladakh and Leh were apportioned a lesser share than lawfully due to them just to keep the valley always in power. Shri Jagmohan, a former Governor of the state, wrote that for the Lok Sabha, Jammu returns one member for every 1.4 million people, while Kashmir sends one representative for every million. Jammu's total area is seventy percent larger than Kashmir's and has 45% of the state's population. Jammu has 32 seats out of the 76 in the State Assembly, and Kashmir has 42. Why such a step motherly treatment to Jammu? The reason is so obvious. One cannot avoid feeling that Jammu is a Hindu majority region of the state, and combined with Ladakh and Leh the Buddhist areas, may not sometimes come to power in the state.

As the prominent Kashmir independent leader Shabhir Shah frankly admitted to me in the Autumn of 1996, the reality is that the question of re-opening the issue of the state's accession to India is not acceptable to the majority of inhabitants in the Jammu and Ladakh region. One conceivable solution to this compendium would be to limit the question of self determination to Kashmir proper. The entire political spectrum in Kashmir is united it is opposition to any suggestion of dividing J & K how much popular support the trifurcations concept enjoys even in the Jammu region).

India's implacable opposition to any notion of plebiscite and Pakistan's lack of manifest interest in the idea except for propaganda purposes makes it likelihood of any such exercise extraordinary remote. Illustrations drawn from experiences in Quebec and Bowie show that a plebiscite is hardly an appropriate instrument for resolution of highly sensitive and complex questions of self-determination. The other salient issue that any autonomy process will have to confront and resolve concerns of the major social and political variables between three distinct regions. Any process intended to grant J&K autonomy must ensure equitable sharing of political power, natural resources, and budgetary allocations between regions particularly between Kashmir and Jammu, the two major regions.

Siachen Issues

The Karachi agreement signed on July 27,1949, by Lt. General S.M. Shainagash on behalf of India and Major General J. Cartheran for Pakistan specifies the Cease Fire Line to follow the general line along Charbet La (point 16,700) chalander (on the shioyk river) thence north to the glaciers. The line up to point NJ 9842 was naturally accepted, and the lines run in the North-South direction for quite some distance before reaching NJ 9842 (from where the line was to extend further north as per the agreement). This on itself negates Pakistan's China and basis for its cartographic aggression of CFL joins NJ 9842 with Karakoram pass, which lies well to North East.

This includes not only the Siachen glaciers system, but also the upper reaches of the Nehru valley into which the Siachen glacier descends.

General Arif agreed that the Karachi agreement continues to remain in force except where deviation has taken place by mutual consent meaning under Simla agreement. The violation had been authorized by the Pakistani leadership which laid claim to the area of the line running north from point NJ9842 to Karakoram pass rather than glaciers as specified in the Karachi agreement.

The confirmed Pakistan military patrols in the Siachen glaciers in August 1983 while foreign mountaineering expectations are mentioned, no reference is make to the Pakistan was setting from patrolling to trying to locate military posts in the area in 1984 where India pre-empted the make.

Pakistan claim to 10,000 sq.km K2 Karakoram pass NJ 9842 triangle has been sought to be justified by quoting India protects regarding the Indo-Pak boundary agreement of March 2, 1963.

The Indian protest detail May 10, 1962, categorically defined this area to be under the unlawful occupation of Pakistan which had been achieved by military force. The UN resolution itself required Pakistan to vacate the territory occupied by forces in the State of J & K. Pakistan's case for the Siachen area is claimed to be based on five historical realities. First the foreign mountaineering expedition invariably sought permission from the Pakistan government because of the fact that her right ran in the area. The is inherent on three counts.

1. As per understanding arrived at before accepting the August 1948 resolution of the UN Commission for India, Pakistan, these areas remained under the control of J&K state.

   The UN resolution and Karachi agreement defined the nature of Pakistan control of century in J&K as temporary

2. Pakistan's writ in 1962 ran in Skarch-Kapadu areas but not on the Saltro ridge and the Siachen Nabra region. Even if the Pakistani claims was true, permission given to Mountaineering expeditions does not bestow sovereign rights. So, Expedition between 1957-61 is initial to support this argument. The print media of the world has generally supported Pakistan case. No map shows that the official Atlas of Pakistan shows the Loc joining point NJ 9842 with Karakoran pass.

3. Pakistan's own maps are highly inconsistent. Some maps in the Atlas of Pakistan appear to show the northern areas (of Pak) extending Gilgit Agency as falling entirely within the disputed territory of J&K state. While others show the northern areas and J&K state as a part of Pakistan on page listing the jurisdictional divisions of Pakistan however Gilgit agency and J&K is listed as disputed. The fallacy in such depictions is obvious; no boundary in such high mountains ranges can possibly conform to a straight line cutting across valleys and ranges nearly at right angles over a distance of 140 km. The US government issued instructions on March12, 1987; the future deprivation of the CFL\Loc would be extended to the Karakoram pass as has been the previous practice. Third, Pakistan claims that communications infrastructure in the entire region limit it with the northern areas of Pakistan. This is factually incorrect.

   The population in the inhabited region North West and north point NJ 9842 is administratively dependent on Pakistan. In trying to find a peaceful solution, India has not tried to claim areas west of the Saltro Range, although it has legal, political and moral right to do so. The census report of 1941 lists the Frontier districts of the State of Jammu and Kashmir do not really include the Siachen Area. The critical element of General Arifs statement of launching attacks on Indian Positions on the Saltro range.

4. Mountaineering expeditions had gone on in the area and in to the higher peaks to North from early days. But in the 1970s, Pakistan slowly

started charging license fee from international mountaineering expeditions. By 1978 Pakistan had started to send liaison officers with such expeditions and soon military officers were used for such liaison duties. This was followed in 1983 by military patrols and the mountaineering activities came to the attention of the Indian government.

Since the early 1960s Pakistan pursued a quiet approach to regularize the imaginary line which marked a straight line joining point NJ 9842 with Karakoram pass to the East. Many more atlases started to show the line joining point NJ 9842 with Karakoram pass as the Loc this was not agreed upon. Pakistan used this cartographic aggression to support its claim. India appeared to have taken note of Pakistan's activities in the marked area. Mountaineering expeditions from Pak to Siachen has been discontinued by 1983. The Pakistan government protested and on August 21, 1983 for the first time staked its claim over the area north of the line joining NJ 9842 with Karakoram pass. This was reiterated in another note on August 29, 1983. Pakistan decided to establish permanent posts in September/October 1983 to occupy key posts on the Saltro ridge.

The dispute started in April 1984, when the Indian troops had launched operations Megadoot, which brought most of the area under the control of India. Though both sides came close to solving the issue in 1989, they are yet to arrive at a solution to date. The 1972 agreement specified the northern most part of the LoC as the one defined by the ceasefire line of 1949 Karachi Agreement-NJ 9842. India intreprets the extensions of CFL from this point to North up to another point Indira col whereas Pakistan interprets the line to run North East from NJ 9842 to the Karakoram pass.

What are the notions behind each other's proposal? India's emphasis on the Saltro Range action from the ground reality that Siachen Glacier is totally under India's control. Thus it appeared that India is delinking the Siachen Glacier from the scope of talks, since India considered Siachen a misnomer. The issue is at stake in Pakistan's attempt to dislodge Indian troops from the Saltro Range bordering Pak. Pakistan agreeing to this would mean accepting India's hold over Siachen. Pakistan would not agree to such proposals.

For India, Pakistan's proposals are not acceptable because of the following resources. Firstly, India rejects Pakistan's positions that there was an agreement in Siachen between both the countries in 1989. In Saltro range beyond NJ 9842. One significant aspect of the current proposals from the Indian side is India's emphasis on the term Saltro range instead of Siachen. All the four proposals from the Indian side only mentioned Saltro. Pakistan rejected all these proposals.

Pakistan's proposals included (A) implementation of 1989 agreement between India and Pakistan (according to which India and Pakistan are to redeploy positions held when the ceasefire was declared in 1971 and (B) a ceasefire only if it involved the monitoring of such a ceasefire by a third party like the United Nations military group in India. One significant aspect of Pakistan stand during the current round of Siachen talks was the linking of the Siachen issue with the core problem of Kashmir. India rejected both stands of Pakistan.

During round of talks on Siachen in 1992, India denied that there was any final agreement and stated that both sides had only agreed to carry forward the process of discussions, which had remained suspended since 1989, secondly India would never agree to have a third party mediation on any bilateral issue between India and Pakistan dispute. These are various perspectives surrounding the Siachin dispute.

- From an Indian perspective, the Siachen glacier is the wedge of territory that separates Pakistan occupied Kashmir (PoK) from Aksai Chin, the part of Kashmir claimed and occupied by China. In Indian perceptions, Siachen's geostrategic importance lies in the fact that its control would support Indian defence of Ladakh, Jammu and Kashmir against Pakistani or Chinese threats. It would prevent of the outflanking of India forces in Leh and Kargil sectors and connecting the Aksai Chin highway with Karakoram pass. Control over Siachen would enable to India to keep watch over the Karakoram highway and the Khunajarab pass, while fortifying India's position in border negotiations with China.
- In order to block Pakistan's access to the Siachen glacier India has no option but to maintain its hazardous posts on the Saltro Ridge.
- India's declared policy on the Siachen dispute is to interpret thence Northwards to the glaciers to mean that the LoC proceeds from NJ 9842 along the watershed line of the Saltro Range. However, India's declared policy is not a sufficient indicator.
- Any Indian withdrawal will leave Pakistan with an open door to the commanding heights. Pakistan would gain in a negotiations what it has been unable to obtain on the battlefield. What ever the cost India is compelled to therefore stand firm and maintain its current deployments.
- After the India-Pakistan wars of 1965-1971, neither side attempted to delineate a ceasefire line or line of control in the Siachen region because of the nature of the terrain and the absence of any physical military

presence. Pakistan interprets the vague language contained in 1972 Simla agreements to mean that the LoC should extend in a straight line in a North easterly direction from NJ 9842 toward the Karakoram Pass. At the same time Pakistan recognizes the disputed nature of the Siachen region. In the 1963 Sino-Pakistan agreement, for example, in which the Karakoram Pass was defined as the terminal point for the delineation of the Sino-I'tkistan boundary. The areas south of the border with described as the contiguous areas the defence of which is under the actual control of Pakistan and not as Pakistani territory. Pakistan also claims that the Siachen glacier and its approaches full within.

- The Pakistani controlled and administered territory of Jammu and Kashmir, more specifically in the Baltistan district in the Northern areas. The claims that Siachen is a part of Pakistan's Northern Areas is significant because Pakistan has, since independence, gradually incorporated the northern areas, within the state. Pakistan officials have also taken the stand that the northern areas were never under the direct jurisdiction of the state of Jammu and Kashmir in undivided India while no steps have been taken so far, to integrate the northern areas formally within Pakistan, such a move is possible in the future. The anomalous status of the Northern areas provides Pakistan the Justifications, when the need arises, to separate the Siachen Conflict from the larger dispute over Kashmir. Siachen is thus portrayed as a regional issue by Pakistani officials as opposed to Kashmir, which, it stressed, is an international issue.
- The dispute over the Siachen region is recognized as a byproduct of partition, because all Pakistani governments have claimed permanent government control over this subdistrict of Baltistan.
- Pakistan was willing to accept the territory and no man's land until India deployed forces in the Siachen area in 1984.

Agreements

As early as 1984 and 1985, flag meetings were held, with little success between Indian and Pakistani sector commanders. Since January 1986, several high-level talks have been held between Indian and Pakistani defence and foreign secretaries as well as senior military personnel, reflecting their desire to reach a peaceful and negotiated settlement. At the fifth round of talks between defence secretaries in June 1989, an understanding was initially reached to resolve the dispute. According to the joint statement issued at the conclusion of talks, there was agreement by both sides to work towards a comprehensive settlement, based on the redeployment of forces to reduce the chances of a conflict, avoidance of the use force and the determination of future positions on the ground as to confirm the Simla agreement and to ensure durable peace in the Siachin areas. In 1989, and once again in 1992, the two countries came close to a resolution of the dispute.

The joint statements stated that the army authorities of both sides will determine the position. At the fifth round of the defense secretary talks in November 1989, with the assistance of military experts, an India-Pakistan agreement was reportedly reached that envisaged (1) the military withdrawal of forces from key passes to new positions and (2) the creation of a "zone" of a result of troop disengagement and redeployments. The delineation of this area of "peace and tranquility" would be without prejudice to the known position of either side.

The formation of a joint commission that would be responsible for delineation of the line of control beyond NJ 9842 until the area was formally delineated; monitoring mechanism would be devised to prevent the occurrences of violations. The difficulty in reaching or implementing any mutually agreeable proposal was due to a number of factors, ranging from domestic political constraints to differences over the determinations of redeployment positions, the demarcation of the proposed demilitarized zone, and ensuring the inviolability of such a zone.

1. Once Pakistan's map stretching the LoC to the Karakoram pass gained currency and it began granting permits to mountaineering expeditions, Indians fears were rightly aroused (Salvi, 1985). It decided to move into the area before Pakistan could shortly before his assassination in May 1991; Rajiv Gandhi told the foreign correspondents Associations in New Delhi we almost signed a treaty on Siachen with Zia. The only reason it wasn't signed was that he died in August 1988.

Rajiv Gandhi tacitly acknowledged breach of the Simla Agreement when he said on November 16,1989 in Kolkata that India had recovered about 5,000 square kilometers from the occupied area of Siachen and that India would not forgo are square kilometer of that. It was this mind set that wrecked the June 1989 understanding. There have been seven round of talks between representatives of the two countries from January 1986 to November 1998. The last three round of talks the fifth (June1989), sixth (November 1992) and seventh (November 1998) between the defence secretaries reflect poorly on Indian leaders.

Pakistan sought to revive the 1989 agreement by formally making a proposal which was a major concession to India, namely the existing positions would be recorded, albeit in annexure and that on understanding that it would constitute a basis for a claim to the area legally, morally or politically, the annexure would mention the point at which the troops will redeploy demarcations of the LoC will follow thereafter. India did not respond to the proposal, and the talks ended.

The source of the encroachment is said to be maps that were initially produced by the US Defense Mappings Agency, which depicted LoC running from the vicinity of NJ 9842 north east to Karakoram Pass, in the 1970s and the 1980s. The best explanation for this error by America's map makers appears to lay in the possible 'translation' Air Defense Information Zone (ADFI) markings which provide zoning boundaries for air controllers in card and military error action, into an extension of the LoC from NJ 9842 to the Karakoram pass. These have becomes an article of faith for Pakistan. But the publication of such map by many of the world leading atlases, further encouraged the Pakistani army to contest security of the LoC. And so, General Zia-ul-Haq decided to occupy Siachen Glacier, in the 1980s, as a means to alter the status quo of the LoC. After the Sino-Indian conflict, the Indian army took preempting action in April 1984 and occupied the Saltro ridge which marks the western wall of Siachen glacier. As Lieutenant General Mc.Chobber, former Northern Army Commander who initiated the Indian pressure on the glacier admitted, the strategic importance of the area was not a major consideration, nor was to own purpose to capture any territory. It was simply to ensure that India was not presented with a fait accompli like the Aski-china in the early fifties. Their defeat in Kargil has only strengthened Pakistan's resolve to look resolution of Siachen to the Kashmir issue.

A military solution to Siachen dispute could be found with both sides arguing to a formal demarcation of these positions as it exists today-called the AGPC. With joint patrolling by both sides, this could include first a disengagement and not withdrawal for a period of two years. And eventually to either convert the region into a peace park or to establish a Siachen Science Centre to be operated by scientists from India and Pakistan so that the world's most instances, cruel, strategically observed and highest attitude war can be put to an end.

Taskent Agreement

After the ceasefire of 1965 war, both the countries agreed to hand back captured areas of each other in Tashkent agreement NJ 9842 remained undisputed.

Simla Agreement

After the war of 1971, Simla Agreement was signed according to which the captured areas were given back. More over the ceasefire line was turned into the line of control.

Sir Creek Mission

Shastri had encouraged Jaya Prakash Narayan to explore the possibilities of rapproachment with Pakistan, Shastri himself believed that he had the ability to persuade Ayub on terms of the settlements that would be acceptable to India. Ayub on the other hand was convinced of his ability to persuade Shastri to agree to a settlement on terms favorable to Pakistan. When Shastri met Ayub in Karachi in 1964 both leaders appeared to give each other such an impression. Pakistan began its probe in the marsh land known as the Rann of Kutch, the weakest link in India's defence links. The Rann is an area of 7,000 sq.m which is covered by water for half of the year and is desert for the other half of the year, very little vegetarians to be found there except certain grounds where some grass grows, gazers from nearby places use this area for cattle grazing.

Ever since 1947 Pakistan had insisted that the boundary between Kutch and Pakistan's province of Sindh was in dispute. India, on the other hand decided that the border was in dispute the only thing that was unsettled was the demarcation of the boundary. Legally speaking, all of the Rannbelonged to the princely states of Kutch during the British period. There is some evidence, which suggests that the British period exercised some administrative jurisdiction in the northern part of the Rann. Boundary pillars have been erected between Kutch and Sindh as far as back as 1924. The collector of Tharparkar districts disregarded these pillars and issued grazing permits to cattle owners who went beyond these boundaries. In 1947 cattle owners from Sindh were asked by the agents of the Kutch Durbar to pay fees for the grazing facilities, those who argued that they had a license from Pakistan were harassed by these agents. Those incidents promoted Pakistan to raise the question of border with India. New Delhi took the position that the border was settled; all that there was there to be done was a demarcation of certain parts of the border. The difference over the interpretation of their respective jurisdiction led to skirmishes in 1956. Pakistan intruded six miles inside Indian Territory and took over chad bet. India, however, pushed the intruders out immediately. Similar incidents in following years induced the two countries to discuss the matter. The Ministerial talks in 1959 provided no agreements. Both countries agreed to collect more information and come back to the negotiation table in due course. They further agreed that if negotiations remained unproductive, they would refer the question to impirtial arbitrations.

During the 1960s and 1964 the Director General of the Survey on India wrote to his counterpart in Pakistan several times so as to begin work on the demarcation of the border. There was no response from the Pakistani side. There the matter rested until January 1965, when Pakistan decided to use force to settle the issue. Pakistan argued that the dispute existed regarding the border between Kutch and Sindh since 1874. She claimed nearly half of the area of north of the 24th parallel-an area of roughly 3,000 square miles. Pakistan argued that the Rann was a dead sea or land sea and as such, should be equally divided between India and Pakistan. India argued that the Rann was not an inland sea but a salt marsh and therefore there was no territorial or boundary dispute, all that was left to be done was the demarcation of the border in certain sectors.

The outlines of a final settlement emerged in June 1965 after a meeting between Wilson, Shastri and Ayub in London on the occasion of the Commonwealth Prime Minister Conference. In their private consultations with British Prime Minister, Shastri and Ayub gave concessions to each other-gestures that facilitated the eventual settlement of the Rann dispute Shastri agreed to withdraw Indian troops from the border posts inside Azad Kashmir. Ayub agreed to the restorations of the status quo ante and gave up his demand for linking the rann dispute with the Kashmir dispute. On June 30th 1965 the officials of India and Pakistan finally signed an agreement. According to this agreement, a cease-fire was to become effective on July 1st 1957. Pakistan agreed to restore the status quo ante and withdraw behind the line regarded by India as the international border between Kutch and India. Besides vacating biar bet and Point 84, Pakistan was to dismantle its post at Kanjurkot. India was to continue its post at chadbet, but she agreed to pull out from sardar part and vigo court. Both sides were given two months for the withdrawal of the troops. The agreement provided that India and Pakistan would continue to patrol their respective tracks that they had been patrolling before January 1st 1965. After the restoration of the status quo ante officials of the two countries would begin negotiations for the settlement of the Rann dispute. In the absence of any agreement, the two sides would refer the matter to a judicial tribunal as envisaged in the Indo-Pák agreements of 1960. Pakistan managed to secure a sort of consolation prize. The preamble of the agreement expressed the hope that the settlement over the Rann would pave the way for an eventual settlement of the other outstanding disputes between two countries.

On January 25th Pakistan intruded about one and a half miles inside the Indian Territory and set up a post near the Kanjarkat Fort. A few weeks later, the Gujarat state police spotted Pakistani soldiers patrolling inside the Indian territory on February 12. India protested and demanded the withdrawal of Pakistani forces. She proposed that the status quo ante be restored and the officials from the two sides should meet to discuss the demarcation of the border. Pakistan, in reply, invested that the Kanjakat Fort was inside these area of the Rann actually controlled by fear since 1974. While the two sides were complaining against each others' intrusions, two Pakistani army battalions advanced into Indian territory near sardar post on April 9th 1965 and forced the Indian police to withdraw to Urgo court, a miles south east. The Indian troops, however, reoccupied the sardar post the following day. The Pakistani tactics were similar to those employed by China against India's border in 1962, it would occupy Indian territory and then call for a cease fire and peaceful settlement of the dispute.

Pakistan now proposed that all Indian troops and civilian personnel be withdrawn from the area north of the 24th parallel. It was obvious that Pakistan had asked for India's withdrawal from the entire area she was claiming. While these notes were exchanged Pakistan launched a massive attack on several Indian points in the period April 24th to April 29th. Pakistan forces struck against Indian posts-points 84, Sardar, Vigo court and chad bet about 8 miles inside Indian Territory. In one of these attacks, Pakistani forces of a brigade strength were by tends and air planes. They were also able to use their armour. It was an undeclared war between the two countries.

The Pakistani attack came at the time and place where India was soft and marshy that tanks could not be used. Pakistan's line communication and transpirations were better and shorter than that of India. Faced with overwhelming odds India could not possibly hope to recover the lost ground right away. A realization of this difficult situation aroused the vocal demand in India for hitting Pakistan elsewhere—a proposition that was brought with the risk of an all out war along the entire border between the two countries.

Basically, it has been another case of India belatedly discovering her own frontiers. To a lay lawyer, India's claim to the whole of Rann of Kutch looks considerably better than Pakistan's theory that the northern half of it is disputed. When it all began, India found Pakistan in occupation of territory in the Rann which she considered her own, as were the Chinese in Ladakh. As in Ladakh India pushed her forces further and further forward behind those of intruders until the Pakistanis, like the Chinese before them, became concerned about the safety of their rear, and gave Indians a shock and a bloody reminder (Hari, 1969).

When the public and press in Pakistan were jubilant, the mood in India was one of indignation and anger. There were demands to teach Pakistan a lesson at a time and place of India's choosing. Responding to the nation's mood Prime Minister Shastri announced in the Lok Sabha that if Pakistan persists in its aggressive activities, the army would defend the country. It soon became clear that Shastri was under serious pressure from various quarters in his own party and senior ministers, some of whom would be quite pleased to see Shastri replaced if he did not handle the situation to their satisfaction. There Chevervister demands coming from since Singh and Para socialist party. It was in such a context the British Prime Minister Harold Wilson offered to mediate. Wilson suggested immediate ceasefire to be followed by a withdrawal of troops by both sides and the restoration of status quo anti as of January 1 1965. Pakistan wanted to open all the outstanding disputes between the two countries.

The dispute over the Rann was merely a pretext to forceful action by Pakistan over Kashmir. Nearly all segments of public opinion called upon Shastri to remain firm and reject and suggestion of linking the Rann dispute with the Kashmir question. Responding to internal pressure, Shastri advanced three demands that the status quo ante of first be restored, secondly that the Rann dispute should not be used as a lever to open discussions on other border disputes and thirdly that the procedures agreed to in 1959 for settling the Rann of dispute may be adopted for settling issues arising out of the present conflict. It is clear that while Shastri was equally firm in not being provided into a drastic and hasty action against Pakistan. He was supported in such policy by the army leadership which did not think of the Rann as being as vital to India's security as to risk a wider war with Pakistan.

General T.N. Chaudhry dismissed the Kutch conflict, pin pricks which while irritating politically were of no major military significance. It is a mistake in the strategic thinking that every inch of the border has to be guarded equally well. This was the line of thinking among the military high command which explains why the border in this corner had been so neglected that Pakistan exercised administrative jurisdiction in certain areas of the northern part of the Rann. As a matter of fact, this area was under the jurisdiction of the Minister of Home Affairs only when the fighting erupted was the area brought under the jurisdiction of the Defence Minister.

Indo-Pak official talks failed to produce any agreement on the dispute. Both sides proceeded to refer the matter to the proposed judicial tribunal

Pakistan nominated ales Bebler of Yugoslavia. As India and Pakistan could not agrees on the name of the Chairman for the tribunal, they requested, as provided for in the agreement, the view secretary general think to nominate the chairmen of the tribunal. Uthant appointed General Gunnar lega gan of Sweden the Chairman for the tribunal. The tribunal begin its work in Feb 1966 and handed down its award two years later. The tribunal, by majority vote formed that: 90% was awarded to Pakistan on the begins that the authorities of the Pakistanis province of Sindh had inscribed superior administrative jurisdiction over the area for a long time. In his dissenting opinion justice ales Babler, the Yugoslavia judge nominated by India, upheld the Indian view that the Kutch-Sindh border lay along the northern edge of great rann. He rejected the authority view on Pakistan display of authority over 10% of the rann on the ground that sporadic grazing of Sindh cattle in the area, being private activity, would not constitute a display of that authority. Justice general Legormen, chairman of the tribunal, himself had observed that the paramount considerations of promoting peace and stability in the region also weighed in favour of giving a margined area south of rahim ki bazar to Pakistan as it was whole surrounding by Pakistan such remarks, together with dissent of justice babler, gave rise to some outcry in India against the onwards. The socialists and jan Sangh demanded rejection of the Bombay award. M.C. Chagla, a former chief justice of the Bombay High Court tent support to this view: we agreed to implement judical, not a political award, we can reject it. Government however accepted the Kutch Award.

The Sir Creek is a surely mile long estuary in the marshes of the Rann of Kutch, sparing inaugural from the Pakistan dispute over Sir Creek can be treated to the 1965 war. Pakistan after these clashes demanded that half of Rann of Kutch along 24th parallel belonged to it. India in its part claimed that boundary ran roughly along the northern edge of the Rann and the matter was referred to arbitration. As represented on a 1914 map, the entire Sir Creek with its eastern bank defined by a green line belong to Pakistan it claimed. India disputed this and claimed that the green line in 1914 map is an indication line which in technical terms can be called a ribbon line. The boundary is defined by the map. Boundary pillars have been erected in the middle of the Creek, indicating the frontier line. According to Lt. General Alkiya, the disputed lines on the demarcation of the boundary from the mouth of Sir Creek and from the top of the Sir Creek eastwards to a point inland is designated as the Western terminus. The boundary was thus fixed.

The ruling in 1913 of the Government of Bombay which resolved the dispute on Sir Creek between the their Maha Rao of Kutch and the ruler of

Sindh was the basis of making several sequencing maps. Rear Admiral K.R. Srinivasan, the chief hydrograph, the mid-channel principle on Sir Creek was endorsed by Para name and Para 10 of the 1914 resolution this was represented in the final map of 1925, the proper boundary symbols. The talks were held after a gap of six years with a view to delineating the maritime frontiers in the Rann of Kutch area. After the talks Pakistan wanted the dispute to be taken to the international tribunal. But rejected it unilaterally stating after the Simla Accord have to be resolved bilaterally. The making of the boundary with Pakistan will have an important bearing on the exploitation of promising sea-based resources in the area. The border once defined can be the basis of determining maritime boundaries which are usually drawn as extension on sea from reference points on land and the Exclusive Economic Zone (EEZ) which extends to commercial exploitation. The Pakistan EEZ would be enlarged by around 250 sq.m in case India accepted the green line showing the Sir Creek eastern bank as the land boundary for drawing maritime boundary. Islamabad rejected the mid-channel principle as this principle applied only to navigable channels and Sir Creek to it is not a navigable channel. India proposed that the two sides should delimit the maritime boundary from several sides. The two sides can proceed towards the land from the extremity of the EEZ limit to a mutually acceptable limit. This limit can be governed by the internationally recognized technical aspects of law of sea, Pakistan however rejected this approach, instead the determination of the land boundary in Sir Creek area and fixing its maritime borders are inseparable for it. Pakistan sources say that foreign companies will not move into the area unless the dispute over maritime boundaries with India was fully resolved.

As a confidence building measure India has shown a readiness to define a common base line along the estuary's current dimensions. The centre of this line can extend into the sea to a distance of 200 nautical miles, forming a maritime boundary with Pakistan. Pakistan got the elevated ground that is not submerged during the raining season containing high hills and lofty sand dunes, commanding the low-lying salt desert, containing the extension terms of grasslands, having fresh water hills and the only permanent habited parts of the Great Rann. Comparing 317 square miles, 9.43% of the lands claimed by Pakistan have been awarded to it. This area is about 32 miles long and 8 miles broad, and a few add regions act both ends. Pachhen Prime Minister is the highest hold in the Rann, 1,450 feet above the level of sea. The other, chorad and Khader, do not exceed 617 feet. The extension grass covered Trent in the Rann on itself; the Banni is a part of Kutch. Thus the strategic and fertile parts go to Pakistan. Lagergan was left with India, the uninhabitable marshy land lying below sea level which will remain largely undefended against Pakistan incursions. According to the award Sardar post, Vigokot, Biar Bet, Point 84, Karins Shahi, Bila Bet and Naran Bet are left with India. The marginal areas to the south of Rahim ki Bagar including Kanjarkat on the west and on both sides of Nagar Parkar in the east together with solved uplands of Dahara Banni and Chad Bet, measuring about 32 miles by 8 miles in the middle sector including pivotal and Valokun are given to Pakistan. The government of India gave her approval to the award. Pakistan's contention rejected by the tribunal (1) that Sindh had continues jurisdiction over the areas, (2) the median line, and (3) the principle of nearness to the shore. The tribunal had accepted the basic argument of India that the Rannon was Kutch territory.

Neither of the other parts India water treaty nor had the Nehru Noon part nor the Taskent declaration brought about the desired friendship.

Tulbul Navigation / Wullar barrage

The partition of British India meant that the Indus basin was now to be shared between two sovereign entities. Besides these two countries there was the state of J & K whose status was not decided in Aug 1947, but which too formed part of the Indus basin. Riparian issues were first anticipated with reference to the future management of Punjab's irrigation system. Failure to arrive at a settlement before independence led to a standstill agreement that maintained existing flows till March 31, 1948.

The water dispute between the two countries arose after the partition of India. Sir Radcliff's Award is considered basically responsible for it. The Indus river system has Sin Rivers, the Indus, the Jhelum, and the Sutlej. Five of the Sin Rivers have their upper reaches in India. Radcliffs alone cuts across the Sutlej and Ravi while the boundary between Pakistan and Kashmir crosses the remaining three. Indus is reached by the remaining five in Punjab In West Pakistan. These rivers are so interlinked with each other by the series of canals that in case there is shortage of water in one, a main look canal can draw water from another. Before the partition, the irrigation system was treated as a whole. In 1947, when the line dividing the former province of Punjab was drawn it cut right across this system and India was given control over the head works of the canal. The Cerozpur were on the Sutlej River from which the Dipal Pur canal takes its start on the border in Indian territory.

The sale mark man in the Montgomery district has its important eastern training works in Ferozepur. The works of the upper Babi Poab cereal which irrigated both Indian and Pakistan soil are with India at Madhopar on the river rawn. The dispute over the distribution of water grew worse when after the partition, India described that Government of Pakistan should replace the supplies she was receiving from the eastern rivers by building link canals from western rivers. Pakistan did not like the suggestion of India and was not prepared to agree to any diminution of supplies of these eastern rivers by building link canals from the western rivers as she not only needed them, but also considered them to be her right as the cover riparian under international law. An agreement was reached between India and Pakistan in May 1948 under which in due course Pakistan was to tap alternative source for the water of the eastern rivers.

The standstill agreements lapsed without progress on a final settlement and Indian Punjab promptly stopped downstream flows on the Sutlej and upper Bari Doab canal systems, triggering a crisis in Pakistani Punjab. Urgent negotiations followed and new agreements were reached on April, 1948 between two provincial governments for the restoring of flows to Pakistani Punjab. The wording of the new agreement implied that W. Punjab governments had accepted E. Punjab's right of pre-emotion over supplies from the head works located in the latter's territory. While west Punjab subsequently did not ratify these agreements it was widely perceived that Pakistan had compromied an otherwise strong riparian claim in return for an expedience of restored supplies for the west crop.

While discussing the impact of the dispute on the Indo-Pak relations, Eugene R Black former president of the World Bank wrote that the relations between the two countries were thus thrown into crisis which was to continue along the border intermittently throughout the decade that followed. Five long years after the partition India and Pakistani troops were still facing each other behind sand bags and barbed wire at irrigation headworks along the frontiers. This was likely to lead to war. At the insistence of Eugene Black, a group of experts studied the problem after a tour of the Indus basin and submitted a plan to him in 1954. After nine years of the hard work, he succeeded in convincing the two countries to accept the draft treaty. It was formally signed on 19 Sept 1960 at Rawalpindi by the Prime Minister of India and the President of Pakistan. The crux of the agreement is that India should for irrigation purposes issue the three easterly streams in besides Sutlej, Beas and Ravi and Pakistan the three westerly-Chenab, Jhelum, Indus.

The World Bank brokered Indus water treaty between Pakistan and India in 1960 was the culmination of these treaties. The IWT, awarded all flows of the three eastern rivers of the Indus basin (Ravi, Beas, Sutlej) exclusively to India right of three western rivers (Indus, Jhelum and Chenab).

A myth has grown that IWT is a model of good neighborliness is an otherwise conflict ridden bilaterally relationship. The IWT is perceived as perhaps the most successful confidence building measure between two countries having remained intact all these years, surviving two wars and several phases of conflict. The test of the treaty holding through decades of conflict would be that there were no serious violation on either side. The admirers of the treaty appear to be unaware that the term of the treaty actually requires virtually no co-operation between two parties.

The Jhelum and Chenab where the riparian upper states can feasibly interfere with entitlement of the lower riparian-both have unresolved ongoing disputes between the two parties. While discussing the Baglihar issue it needs to be recalled that Pakistan has already taken the Wullar Banage/Tulbul Navigation project dispute on the Jhelum to Indus Water Commission in 1986.

The objective of another project called Wullar Barrage by the J & K government in 1980 was to raise the level of water in Wullar lake. This project would have augmented water transport on river Jhelum, which would have in turn reduced the road traffic on Baramullah-Islamabad (Anantnag) route. In winter, the water falls to a considerably low level in river Jhelum, resulting in the lowering of power generating capacity from 105 MW to mere 35 MW. The construction of Wullar Barrage would have provided required flow of water to lower Jhelum and ensured the maintaining of the power generating capacity during winter also. However Pakistan had serious reservations on the construction of the barrage.

However in the year 1991, Wuller Barrage construction did not figure in the secretary level of talks between India and Pakistan. Pressures on Indus Water Treaty has grown appreeiably over the past few years with increasing demand of waters. The J&K Legislative Assembly of India has even called for scrapping the treaty to harness the enormous hydroelectric power potential of the Chenab.

Economic and Commercial Co-operation

Economic relationship between and Pakistan has been largely confined to trade interaction. Trade between two nations continued till 1964-65 after which the trade relations were severely restricted because of the 1965 war. Pakistan established a surplus in its trade with India right from the beginning, because of exports of raw jute in which India was severely in deficit. Between 1948 and 1967-68, Pakistan had a persistent surplus in its trade with India, except during 1958 and 1959. However, Pakistan's surplus fulgure at from year to year, depending upon exports of raw jute and fish to India. In 1951, Pakistan experts to India were Rs. 51 crore and imports aggregated to only Rs.15.3 crore. Between 1957 and 1967-68 the peak in Pakistan surplus with India was in 1962-63 when its exports to India totalled Rs. 16.7 crore as against imports of Rs. 9.5 crore. Pakistan thus had a surplus of Rs. 7.2 crore. After its war with India in 1965, there was a complete stoppage of trade between India and the western part of Pakistan.

The Simla agreement of 1972, which constituted an enduring basis for the normalization of relations between the two countries, provided that trade and co-operations in economic and other fields will be resumed as far as possible end that to this end delegations from the two countries will meet from time to time to work out the necessary details. The Indo-Pak trade links which were snapped abruptly in 1965 were re-established in 1974, following the Simla agreement signed in January 1975 for three years. The agreements envisaged trade on a government-to-government basis through state trading agencies. Subsequently in 1976, trade was opened to provide sectors by both sides. However, in July 1978, the Government of Pakistan unnaturally stopped its private sector from importing from India. Thereafter trade between the two countries was being handled by the Trading Corporation of Pakistan, a public sector agency, while in India both public sector agencies as well as private sector conducted trade with Pakistan. This particular measure was adopted by Pakistan apparently to prevent over, involving from the Indian side and under-in-voicing from the Pakistan side. However the Pakistani authorities did not give specific reasons for preventing their private sector directly importing from India. This action also enabled Pakistan to effectively supervise its trade with India with care and caution.

In October 1982, the government of Pakistan approved 40 specified items for imports by its private sectors from India. But of the same time imports of these items have been channelised through the Trading Corporation of Pakistan. It was entrusted with the responsibility of processing all documents and opening of letters of credit in favor of Indian exporters. The list of these 40 limits B given in Annexure I.

The two way trade between the two countries also showed a marked see-saw trend which does not fall in any specific pattern. After the resumption of trade between the two countries from 1975-76 to 1982-83 India did experience a surplus in the balance thrice and Pakistan five times. When India constantly showed surplus in bilateral trade for three successive year Pakistan government unilaterally stopped its private sector from importing from India. This particular action swung the trade balance continuously in favor of Pakistan.

The present exchange of commodities is limited to a few items. India's exports to Pakistan largely consist of Beedi leaves, Medicinal herbs, Iron and steel products, Engineering items, Tyres and tubes, Iron ore, Metal manufactories, Stone and gravel, Cotton fabrics and Glassware.

During 1983, since of the additional items that were exported include betal leaves, seamless take, value bladder, aluminium phosphite tables, fresh ginger, onus and tea.

India's imports from Pakistan comprise largely of Waphate, Furnance oil, Rode salt, Pig Nion, Fruits and vegetables, Crude fertilization and crude minerals and Crude vegetables materials.

An effort has been made by the Indian private sector as well as the government to normalize trade relations with Pakistan.

The Fall Out of Terrorism and Drug Trafficking

The increase in drugs and arms resulted in increase in covert operations and advocacy of Islamic jihad came in as a handy cover-up. The BCCI Bank scandal, donations to Pakistan army and elections of **ISI** MP's with deep connections brought out the link of the drugs barons, ISI and later army sponsoring terrorism in Punjab and Jammu and Kashmir and their links with the fundamental organization. The drug barons in NWFP, Lahore and Karachi pushed drugs into India Dera Baba Nawak, Rann of Kutch and Bombay. With its ISI playing a leading role, Pakistan exploited India's vulnerability supporting terrorist and separatist groups. Terrorists are inevitably forced to act in collusion with the smugglers. Religious fundamental organizations conjunction with the underworld network is evident from March 1993 serial blasts in Mumbai and the role played by the Dawood Ibrahim crime syndicate. Narco terrorism is gradually becoming a part of the disturbed environment of these areas.

Indian mafia has also got involved in drugs and arms smuggling and a network of narrow terrorism is emerging in the border states of J&K, Punjab, Rajasthan, Gujarat, Mhastri and North-eastern states.

Integrating opium growing areas of Pakistan and Afghanistan, a transnational network emerged and trafficking gradually started playing a role in the political economy of the area. When opium production declined in Golden triangle (Thailand, Myanmar and Cocos) in late seventies the focus of international drug mafia shifted to the Golden crescent particularly to the poppy growing areas of Afghanistan and Pakistan. These areas have been linked to international trafficking network and introduction of channels and technology for processing opium into heroin.

The Indian drug cartels are mostly dependent on Pakistani patronage and sponsorship of organized crime and terrorism in India. Pakistan support to such ventures has empowered drug syndicates to consolidate and expand their linkages in the region. Nearly over 75% of drug seizure has their origin in Pakistan and Afghanistan. Both Punjab and Kashmir militants are being incorporated into the drug and subversive network.

Conclusion

The composite dialogue which gained moment UIT. in the aftermath of 2004 during the Manmohan Singh government reached his crescendo during the second and third round of composite dialogue. The third round of composite dialogue was a set back with the Mumbai blasts and the fourth round of composite dialogue received a severe jolt with the ongoing election scenario in Pakistan. External Affairs Minister Mr. Pranab Mukerjee will hold talks giving place to the fifth round of composite dialogue after the general elections. Though the sub-continent has been oscillating between terrorism and elections both sides hope the dialogue process will move ahead.

To deal only with the most recent history, bilateral talks at the highest level collapsed in mutual recriminations in 1999 and again in the summer of 2001. Powerful elements in India's and Pakistan's political and business elites have concluded that the policy of brinkmanship, which in 1999 and even more menacingly in 2001-02 brought India and Pakistan to the verge of all-out war and a possible nuclear exchange, has produced ever-diminishing geo-political returns.

5

General Reports

The New Indian Express of Chennai reports the presence of Pakistan men languishing in Indian jails though the Indian government had taken their initiative to repatriate, the Pakistan consulate delayed the process. The anguish of prisoners due to governmental negligence found wide spread coverage of story and the stake of prisoners accompanied by their mental and physical trauma. Such reports did not figure much in The Hindu. There were beginning reports in The Hindu and TNIE of the need to have any discussion with Pakistan, on Kashmir must be focused first and foremost on the need to end to end cross border terrorism including dismantling infrastructure of terrorism across the LOC. The external affairs minister K. Natwar Singh said President that it will not be to set any time frame for the resolution Kashmir issue on numerous occasions General Musharaff has underpinned the need for setting the time frame for resolving the Kashmir issue. Coming of Musharaff after events of September 11, 2001, weeks after the Agra Summit, forced a fundamental shift in Pakisthanis internal orientation Islamabad attempt to insulate its Kashmir policy from the global war on terror, however was tested by New Delhi's decision to confront Pakisthan with all its military might, after the attack on Parliament of Dec 13 2001, the near war situation in the summer of 2002 brought the whole world down on the sub-continent.

Both the news papers did report on the rejection of application filed by Pakistan Information Minister to travel to Srinagar by bus on June 30.

The application processed and was declined to accord permission as he had helped in training 3500 militants in 1988 - 89 at his farm house at Rawal Pandi in the wake of relevation by JKLF leader Yasin Malik in Paksithan. This opportunity would give him to pray at the graves of his of grand parents besides meeting his relatives.

The Pakistan president to the visiting Pakistan journalists said that the onus is on the Hurriyat at leaders to represented the matter but the Indian government stoutly refused such encounters without seeking permission from the Dr. Manmohan Singh. Discussion on the Kashmir issue has to be had within a rigid time frame and indefinite discussion on the broached subject has to be avoided at any cost. On Siachen the maps on both sides have to be corrected and proposing Indus water treaty II, both sides did not have the kind of confidence. Free exchange of newspapers and magazines between India and Pakistan he added that there was lot of material that served propaganda purposes.

The TNIE further reported on the viable solution and phased manner through which a amicably the issue can be resolved. The issue can be resolved. The proposed ruled out a military option on Kashmir, advocated out of box solution without any rigid time frame. Indian and Pakistan need to discuss Kashmir by analysing in deeper context the issues of self government, independence, actonomy, joint control, and joint management, He proposed a three phased approach conristing of broadly ascertaining the will of Kashmiris to set a broad direction evolving a conseasus through debate and discussion. Both the home NPs did not have the same say on the LOC being irrelevant. (April 20, 2006)

The Media had change in the attributes to reporting the Indo-Pak relations, especially after the service of Musaffarabad Srinagar axis of the bus, the spordic increase in the people to people contactt has made the government for speedy redressal of the issues. The demilitarisation emphasised by Pak President Pervez was welcomed by Dr. Manmohan Singh, but the concept of self governance was not acceptable as the state had a separate constitution and federal provision did not alter the status quo, instead maintained the self administration to be logically carried out. TNIE reported the travel of UPA Chair Person Sonia Gandhi to Pakistan and the dates will be worked out through diplomatic channels.

TNIE reported that President Abdul Kalam of endorsed the view that (CBMS) are to put in a incubation so that no one kicks it off and then watch the eggs in goods will gesture.

TNIE a broad frame work was broached up wherein he did not want to deviate from the stand taken earlier and ruled out accepting the LOC as permanent border to settle the Kashmir imbroglio. Mushruff also appreciated the flexibility shown by India over the initiation of the bus service and it was no substitute for the resolution of the Kashmir issue.

The former NDA government along with Mr. Vajpayee did take steps to meet the upcoming visit of President Musharaff to give new thrust to the decisions taken during the tenure of the NDA government with regard to relations between the two countries found reported in the TNIE.

General Musharaff advocated a three phased approach for the resolution of the Kashmir issue. The first stage is to broadly asertain the will of Kashmirs, that can never be ignored. Phase two, he said, is to develop a consensus through debate and discussions, while phase three is take decision.

The Hindu reported the chief of Pakistan based Jihad Council Syed Saludiin expressed his willingness to hold talks with Indian leaders provided these are result oriented, sincere and meaningful.

Troop withdrawal in Kashmir was emphasised by the Hindu and the joint statement of April 18 a land mark statement that such a move by New Delhi would have a very positive impact on the peace process.

Both TNIE and the Hindu the concern over F -165 for Pakisthan by the United States by The Hindu. The newspaper also further stated that it would not acknowledge such failures or diplomatic failure on the part of India. This has become more explicit, as the composite dialogue is on the anvil.

There were critical remarks or more puzzling statements regarding the opening of the issue on soft border would help India and Pakistan move towards a final settlement of the Kashmir dispute - rather representing a final settlement by itself - Dr. Singh would appear to have opened the door to alternative, which satisfy both Pakistan position and Indian position, that the line cannot be redrawn.

The TNIE quoted Farooq Abdullahha had called on Pakistan President Pervez Musharrah to stop terrorism in J & K as well as cautioned the government for monitoring Islamabad's buying of US arms.

The New Indian Express in expressed the talks that will be scheduled between the Indian government and Pak government wherein dates were being scheduled for the ensuring talks earlier between both the governments on Siachen, Sir Creek Wallar barrage, terrorism and drug trackfying promotion of culture and friendly relations, economics and trade relation.

The Hindu quoted especially the Asia - African summit at Jakarta the Kashmir issue has moved to final solution especially it beamed out from the very president of Pakistan General Musharraf.

During his talks in New Delhi President General Mushraff has stated their will not be a U-turn in the policy towards Kashmir, as he has promised that he will not will under pressure from the Indian government. India and Pakistan must co -operate in tackling terrorism the UN secretary General Kofi Annan during a 30 minute meeting with the PM, Manmohan Singh reports The Hindu. The developing countries which constitute the vast majority of the membership should be able to decisively influence the global agenda in all its aspects. TNIE, If India is seeking nuclear reactors from France, Russia and america, can Pakistan be far behind. This is the first time that France and Pakisthan are discussing on nuclear co-operation in paris. France's offer on nuclear energy co-operation appeared conditioned upon Islamabad clearing its name on non-proliferation.

Last years revelation on the nuclear black market run by Pakisthani scientist as Khan and its linkages with weapon programme of North Korea, Libya and Iran, have left a number of questions unanswered. While Indian will closely monitor Pakistan's parallel nuclear energy diplomacy, it will also have to keep an eye on the chinese role in NSG. If and when France, Russia and US go to Nuclear suppliers group seeking a change of nuclear rules favour of India, the big question is whether china would want the new dispensation to be extended to Pakistan on the same terms.

TNIE and The Hindu quotes Pakistan President General Mushraff that given India's Sensitivites of its secular credentials, a solution to the Kashmir issue cannot be on the basis of religious basis. Instead it could be on a people basis, a regional basis. The people basis suggests that he still harps on self - determination, knowing very well that plebiscite has become invalid when the pre - conditions set were not observed by the then Pakisthan government.

Another formulation was maximum (self - governance and it is highly complicated as the solution need to be drawn in favour of different parameters like the solution has to be found within India's stand of no re-drawing of borders, Pakistan's stand of LOC cannot be permanent border and boundaries becoming irrelevant.

The CBM and the conflict resolution need to go in tandem. TNIE quoted the general Mushraff prefers international guarantees for implementation of any pact reached with issue. He also recognised the (Hurriyat conference) HC as the sole representative of the Kashmirs wanted them to share the trilateral talks.

TNIE quoted that Pakisthan was upset when the NDA regime fell last year, as Islamabad had built rapport with ministers like Jaswant Singh and Yashwant singh as well as National Secretary Adviser Brijesh Mishra. (May 28,2005)

Responding to the queried of Journalists especially on General Mushraff statements on maximum autonomy, self - governance and international supervision, he asked Pakisthan to honour its commitment to dismantle terrorists camps in the Pakisthani soil. The foregin office spokes person also made it clear that General Mushraff had not committed anything on autonomy. TNIE Dr. Singh was willing to consider autonomy, if Pakistan ensured dismantling terrorists from the soil. Wherelse The Hindu the BJP president visit to Pakisthan after a gap of 26 years would help keep on tracks the peace efforts started by NDA government. TNIE reported that he was received at the Labour airport by director general protocol colonel Hamdami and deputy Chief of protocol at the Ministry of Foreign Affairs Aman Rashed.

The week long visit of Mr. Advani to pakisthan and the focus of their interaction was going on peace process to resolve outstanding issues, including Kashmir. though the general made a reference to Pakisthan looking forward to the visit of Hurry at leaders beginning on June 2, (June 1,2005 The Hindu) Mr. Advani did not raise the issue of invitation to them to cross into Pakisthan from Pakisthan - occupied Kashmir.

There was only change of intention of in the head lines the Hindu indicating a solution acceptables to all while TNIE that a solution to Kashmir is certain. (June 1, 2005)

The Hindu and TNIE high lighted the vehemence expressed by the leaders of the strong blanket ban extended to travel of Hurriyat leaders beyond LOC for it was outside the bilateral understanding. (June 2, 2005)

The visit to Pakisthan by Mr. Advani has given a need fiilip to India - Pakisthan process and the MMA conglomerate of six parties has supported the peace process but with reservations. Mr. Advani regretted very much on the demolition of the Babri Masjid declared that it was "Saddest day in my life". (June 2, 2005)

The Hindu reported that while speaking at the CNN world report conference that General Mushraff urged the united states and western powers to help resolve political disputes affecting the Muslim world, particularly Pakistan and Kashmir for durable peace in the world, as conflict management is no more option. (June 2, 2005)

The leader of opposition proclaimed that the entire India supported the peace process and demanded the setting up of an association of parliamentations of India and Pakisthan. (June 2, 2005 TNIE)

TNIE & The Hindu during the week long to Pakishthan Mr. Advani extolled the founding father of Pakisthan Moammed Ali Jinnah that he left and inerasable stamp on history, and Quad-e-Millath Ali Jinnah was one of them. (June 5, 2005) He did take back his words on Akand Bharat and mooted that

India and Pakisthan as unalterable reality of history. TNIE Advani praising Jinnah caused a flutter within the Sangh Pariwar that the controversy was played down releasing copies of the Qaid-e-Azam speech in which he favoured the creation of a secular state. Jinnah had said in his address to the constituent assembly on August 11, 1947, according to an excerpt from the book towards Jinnah's Pakistan that you are free, you are free to go to your temples, you are free to go to your mosques or any other places of workship in this state of Pakistan. You may belong to any religion, caste or creed that has nothing to do with the business of the state

TNIE reported that Pakistan president claiming that he had cleared, the Pakisthan was not supporting cross - border terrorism, interference in Afghanistan and selling nuclear technology gaining weightage in global politics. (June 7, 2005) The incidents of violence were not acts of terrorism but sectarian violence.

Sheikh Rashid applied for a special permit to travel by the srinagar - Musaffarabad bus on June 15 as a common citizen and common Kashmir. (June 9, 2005)

TNIE quoted the General assuring that two weeks are enough if India and Pakistan can show their political will can be solved through a Pakistan time frame.

Rashid denied media reports that he had altered his plans to travel to Jammu and Kashmir by the Muzaffarabad - Srinagar bus service.

The Pakistan government rejected opposition demand for a cut in defence budget. The increase was made considering the growing dispartity between India and Pakistan armed forces. Pakistan's navy and air force were technically behind the Indian navy and air force. (June 15, 2005)

TNIE and The Hindu reported that, the JKLF leader Yasin Malik statement that Pakistan Information Minister Sheikh Rashid Ahmed had helped him set up a large militant camp for infiltration into India in the 1990, the government stand on trans LoC terrorist infrastructure has been muted since the beginning of the current round of discussions, through Malik's revelation has given an opportunity to stress on the issue in the context of peace process. (June 15, 2005)

The Hindu and TNIE coverage of the response to Mr. Vajpayee letter, by Dr. Singh especially the June 15 letter of Mishandling of Pakistan's issue Dr. Singh sounded more emphatic. He drew instances from the hosting of Pakisthan's leaders and digastrics from the previous government. (June 22, 2005)

The recent visit of Hurriyat leaders has backing from the past to create a more cordial atmosphere. It is a reminder to the discordant note expressed by Mr. Vajpayee. Mr. Singh also made it clear that the visit of Hurriy at to Islamabad Pakistan has "Violated" on the agreement reached by two government if the Pakistan government claim that Hurriyat the sole representative of J & K has no ground, as J & K has an elected government after a free and fair election sabtoges the claims of the NDA government in stirring a controversy over the visit of the Hurriyat.

There were other leader of the NDA government Jaswant Singh who criticized the UPA government handling of the peace process on several counts. (June 22, 2005)

The Hindu coverage of the Dr. Singh letter Mr.Vajpayee released on June 15, 2005 and it commitment to Jan 6, 2004, found permanent note in the Hindu.

The Hindu and TNIE core coverage of the travel of Rasheed to Srinagar, Musafferad on june 30 was not approved by Indian government in spite of repeated pleas by Pakistan government Rashid in a fitting tribute reciprocated the whole claim as baseless for India too conducted Mukthi Bakimi camps in east Pakistan which subsequently became Bangladesh though India considered the processing of the application, the visit by Sheik Rashed resorted to Kashmir at this stage appeared likely.

Speaking of the energy deficit the defence Minister was apprehensive of Pakisthan's low intensity conflict and trade and transit with and through Pakistan remains highly circumscribed (June 29, 2005 The Hindu) India located in the are fundamental activism, tourism and political instability between North and East Africa and South east Asia has to face full spectrum of threats to security the new India Express unfailingly reported the force addressed by Defense Secretary, the carnegic.

The nuclear CBM was held to discuss on the existing hot lines between the Director General of militancy operations (DGMOS) and establishment of dedicated and secure hotline between foreign secretaries of two countries. (July 17, 2005)

The Pak government conveyed to the US on the negative implications of the acquisition of sophisticated weapon systems by India. (July 5,2005 TNIE) They were worried whether India will perpetuate an arms race. The pak government opposed the movement of Indian religious tourists to visit Pakistan as it affected the two nation theory and it undermined the very rationale of creating Pakistan. (July 10, 2005 TNIE)

Pakistan government leveled spurious charges on the Indian troops that they had violated the LoC in poonch district of J & K after ceasefire came into vogue in November 2003. The Director General of Pakistan Inter service. Public relations claimed that the troops had crossed the LoC and abducted one civilian. Counter charges in India, that the Pakistani troops opened unprovoked firing on the other side of the Poonch sector. But, the New Indian Express failed to report the allegations hurled by the Pakistani government, but instead indicated the ceasefire which came into effect on November 26, 2003 is holding on without any violations from either sides during past 20 months and would continued in future too. (July 19, 2005)

The Pakistan government has convened an inter ministerial meeting to include MFN status to India by Pakistan, transit facilities for Indian goods, for export to Afghanistan and central Asian republic, permitting private Indian airlines to operate in Pakistan, opening of Indian banks and amendment to the shipping political of 1974 to permit third country vessels. (July 31, 2005)

TNIE even during an interaction with 2004 batch India Foreign service probationers PM Dr. Singh stressed the need for a new relationship with Pakistan.The leaders have not failed to inoculate the minds of young probationers on regional co-operation which is a paramount importance to promote a regime, so that unauthorized proliferation of nuclear weapons was stopped.

PM Aziz postponed his visit to US as he wanted to avoid the high profile welcome accorded to visiting Indian PM Dr. Singh.

The talks on nuclear and conventional CBMS were bogged down over Pakistan's proposal (IRR) for a strategic restrain regime (SRR) which proposes parity of weapon systems. But the pre-notification of missile tests as well as establishing hotline contacts between foreign secretaries besides upgrading the hotline telephone links between (DGMOS) were carried out. (July 7, 2005)

The government of India has often reiterated its stand that Pakistan should respect the commitment of the joint statement of January 2004. Reminding the UPA of Pakistan President Pervez Musharaff commitment. L.K. Advani said that (LeT) was reactivating its centre in Muridke area of Pakistan with training camps and the Pakistani soil not to be used for terrorist activities.

The political development in Leh under strain ahead of election, formed a wide coverage in the Hindu. The multi party system here ceased to exist after all the political parties in the Buddhist majority district decided to dissolve their separate identities and contest the 2002 assembly polls.

Under the banner of LUTF. The aim of the front was to fight for unions territory status for Leh. Leaders village heads who would political clout asked the people of their village to vote for the front candidates. This led to the uncontested victory of LUTF candidates in two assembly seats in Leh district.

After the fractured verdict of the 2002 assembly elections the LUTF decided to join the PDP – Congress coalition government. The coalition government gave more power to the Leh autonomous hill development council this move ended the harmony of the Deputy commissioner, the state governments representative in the district and made democratically elected council supreme in the policy matters relating to the district. Difference suffered within the front and election due September the differences appear sharper.

India and Pakistan tonight reached an understanding on the proposed agreement on pre-notification of flight testing of ballistic missiles. After two days of intensive discussions on nuclear CBMS, the two countries also decided to establish by next month the hot line between the two countries. The agreed text of the proposed agreement on pre-notification of test will be referred to the foreign secretaries of the two countries for formalization. Jammu and Kashmir the union parliamentary affairs minister emerged as the hot favourite of the congress high command for the CMs post in the state. Azad was instrumental in reviving the political fortunes of the party in Jammu and Kashmir soon after taking over Pradesh congress committee president (PCC). Mr. Khan during the just – concluded talks on nuclear CBMS as positive, referred to India as creating a bogey of infiltration to deploy more troops in J & K.

The successful test launch of Ground launched cruise missile Half VII will Babur that can carry nuclear and conventional warheads to a range of 500 km, the TNIE did indicate that Pakistan failed to inform in the launch. But similar accusation did not appear in the Hindu. The report also stated that all missiles have the capacity of strike many Indian cities.

In an interview to the Daily Telegraph Gen. Musharaff admitted that previously his hands were tied, either because of 10 mm long confrontation with India in 2002 or the last general elections or political insecurities at home. Expedite the Kashmir peace process is the main agenda.

The test firing of the cruise missile Half and Babur is a major boost to country's deterrence and quantum jump in Pakistan's defense capability. Such a move by Pakistan was Prompted by apprehensions that India would acquire certain weapons system, including Israeli made acro system and US made Pat – 2, Pat – 3 patriot defense missile. More defence related news stories and features and editorials were covered in the TNIE. The Hindu paid less attention to these areas of marked importance.

Pakistan PM Shakat Aziz expressed it in unequivocal terms that his country would not allow transit facility for India for exports to a third country. India has been asking Pakistan to open up the Wagh route for transit trade land locked Afghanistan has also requested Islamabad to consider the Indian proposal. On joint Indo-Russia military exercises along the Rajasthan border armed at pre-empting terrorists activities from a third country Pakistan was capable of defending its frontiers and it would not compromise on tits sovereignty.

Advani accepted that his recent statements on Mohammed Ali Jinnah was completely in line with the policies of NDA.

In the first public sign of co-operation between the investigative agencies, experts from the CBI and Pakistan federal investigation agency will meet in the near future to discuss the issue of mutual interest.

The centre and state followed dual policy on Kashmir accused National Conference (NC) president Omar Abdullah. Union Home Minister Shivraj Patil promised setting up of high powered committee to discuss on autonomy of the state. Giving a chance to thousands of educated unemployed youth who have crossed the age bar, the J & K government today relaxed the upper age limit from 35 to 37 years. As per a MOU between the centre and the state, there was a freeze on fresh recruitment in government services but the ban was removed by PM Manmohan Singh as a part of he reconstruction plan.

The outgoing General Role of army officer commanding of Udampur – based northern command Lt. Gen. Hari Prasad has said that situation in J & K in improving and the army should not be replaced by the BSP, J & K police, or the Jammu and Kashmir police.

The UPSC chairman centre & state S.R. Hushim while inaugurating the 8th National conference of state public service commission stated that a uniform model code of conduct would be scheduled in their work programme. A draft was prepared in this regard by the chairman of Orissa and J & K PSCs. The challenge is to steer the overall growth with fairness, equity and sustainability mainstream.

The opposition national conference president, Omar Adbullah has stressed on the importance of involving elected representatives of the state in the talks, and reiletrated that his party's demand for greater autonomy. Omar Adbullah spelt but the fundamental difference between Hurriyat and NC is that they got thousands of people killed by giving guns in the hands of youth and we pursued a political struggle.

The New Indian Express coverage of PM will host a dinner for Pakistan President Pervez Musharaff and elaborate on the possibilities of greater co-operation.

The reviewable of the dialogue process in The Hindu indicated two views. One is to change the format of the composite dialogue and revive the India – Pakistan joint ministerial commission with four sub-groups. The other is to continue the composite dialogue format and in addition reactivate the ministerial commission. The dominant perception is that whole the composite dialogue format would continue with eight specific items, the revival ministerial commission could provide greater beway in dealing with subjects not listed in the existing format.

The last meeting of the joint commission was held in 1989. Though it was decided to reactivate the joint commission, originally conceived in 1988, there was ambiguity on its jurisdiction. While the Indian side referred to as joint commission on the lines of 1988 body, Riza Mohammed Khan chose to describe it as a joint economic commission.

The New York meet between Dr. Singh and Pervez Musharaff in the UN general assembly had Delphic utterances though the joint statement of January 6, 2004 statement the Vajpayee Musharaff meet, signed at Islamabad) and the April 18, 2005 (the Manmohan Singh - Musharaff document at New Delhi) to reiterate their pledge and that they world not allow terrorism to impede the peace process.

Musharaff address to the united nations were interspersed with imagery and Metaphon which made the sitting journalists raise eyebrows. (Sep 16, 2005) Further this digression over to Kashmir and upholding the UN security council to resolve the Kashmir issue gives the impression that there is no ioto of change ever after the CBMS on full swing.

Equating Israel with Kashmir further entails imputes the Indian government for inaptness in handling imbroligo. Such insinnations added pep to the whole talk of US insisting reducing infiltrations in the towns of Baramulla and Kupwara. The invitees of themeet figured in TNIE, Forcign minister Natwar Singh, National security advisor M.K. Narayan, Foreign Minister Khursheed Mehmouod Kasuir, NSA advisor Tariq Aziz on Pakistan side.

Foreign Secretary Shyam Saran as reported in the Hindu stated that it was unrealistic to arose expectations of spectacular outcomes" every time the president of Pakistan and the Prime Minister of India met. (Sep 16, 2005) But TNIE headlines read as "talks marked by frankness" did quote that it is unrealistic to expect dramatic results whenever the two leaders met. Both the newspapers stand on purity while reporting the Musharaff, Dr. Singh meet in New York. The text of joint statement was exclusively reported in the Hindu with the dates mentioned but TNIE failed to produce such as reports.

The New York meet of Pervez Musharaff and Dr. Singh saw the emergence of three new positions and it would require human ingenuity to reconcile. (Sep. 17, 2005 The Hindu)

The Indian positions that the border will be redrawn.

The Pakistani position that status quo was unacceptable. His own formulation while the border would not be redrawn.

TNIE failed to demarcate the emergence of such proposals. On the position of Iran Dr. Singh clarified that India did not hold 'brief' or offered an 'alibi' for Tehran's nuclear programme and India continued to believe that Iran was under an obligation to fulfil all international commitments. (Sep. 17, 2005) A vivid picture of the UN general assembly speech by General Musharaff and his theatrics, in the venue did genrate – but of interest, to patiently waiting journalists who spared not even his angry demeanour and anxiety Tidden face to be reported. The Pakistani leader's immediate objective was to make PM Manmohan Singh agree to tangible reduction of the Indian security forces in the Kashmir valley.

General Musharaff equating Palestine with Kashmir and harked back to security council resolutions received a lethal blow from external affairs minister who stood his ground by scrutinizing the Pakistani leaders speech at the united nations general assembly. (Sep. 19, 2005) He also politically pointed to General Musharaff, to point out where in 2004 speech was there any comparable reference to the security council resolution or the equating of Kashmir with Palestine. There was no such references during the Bandung and New Delhi meet. Taken aback by the polite but aggressive talk back by Indian side, the general tried to suggest that the speech was drafted at the junior level in the Pakistan foreign office. (Sep. 19, 2005)

In the New York meet, India received assurances from Pakistan on the Iran – India gas pipeline, the general reportedly told America's senior most policy leaders that he would gladly abandon the pipeline in exchange for four nuclear reactors. The best explanation for the non- productive New York Manmohan – Musharaff meeting came from Tariq Aziz, the Pakistan president national security adviser, that last time I had tied up all knot together, but this time the foreign office fellows messed up. (Sep. 19, 2005 The Hindu)

TNIE, (Sep. 20, 2005)after the inauguration of a national fish seed farm at Manabad in Baramullah district Mufti denied any incitation to visit Pakistan. But a Pakistani official announced in New York that Musharaff, had involved Mufti to Pakistan. Mehbooba Mufti, PDP president, Omar Abdullah, President of NC, would visit Pakistani ahead of the CM.

Pakistan was a leading country of muslim "Ummah" and its moral duty and responsibility to carry forward the Palestine cause. (Sep. 20, 2005) Mr. Omar Adbullah urged the centre to set aside the Parlimentary resolution of 1995 that declared PoK as an integral part of Inda and respond positively to Gen. Musharaff, India could consider demilitarization and withdrawal of troops from Urban areas as the government (in the state as well as at centre) had claimed an improvement in the situation. (Sep. 25, 2005)

The former self styled president of PoK expressed serious doubts over the emergence of an independent Jammu and Kashmir after the experience in central Asia and the world will not support any fresh muslim soverign state there was no support for an independent in the occupied Kashmir and it was only a myth created by some vested interests. (Sep. 27, 2005, TNIE)

Agreement on for pre-notification of missile tests, establishing of communication link between Indian coast guard and Pakistan's maritime security agency, press for liberlisation of Visa regime, allowing trade through land route and transit facility for goods, signing of an extradition treaty and mutual legal assistance were a slow of (CBMS) during four – day visit of external affairs minister K. Natwar Singh to Islamabad.

The basic objective of Mr. Singh visit is to review the status of the composite dialogue with Pakistan and to mark the revival of the India – Pakistan joint commission after a gap of 16 years. (Oct. 3, 2005, The Hindu) There is conscious effort on both sides to remove the perception created by a section of the media that the recent contact between Pakistan president pervez musharaff and PM Manmohan Singh in New York on the sidelines of the United Nation general assembly brought about a slump in the bilateral ties. (Oct 3,2005, The Hindu) India and Pakistan signed an agreement making it obligatory for them to notify the other at least 72 hours before testing ballistic missile within a 40 km radius of the inter national boundary and the LoC. (Oct 4, 2005, The Hindu) The communication link would help facilitate the early exchange of information on fishermen who inadvertently stays into each other's territories and also information on smuggling, Pollution and search and rescue operation.

The former PM, Atal Behari Vajpayee and the BJP president L.K. Advani have written separate letter to Pakistan president General. Muharaff express their grief at the tragedy that has struck Pakistani on the wake of earthquake.

Pakistan denied reports that Indian soldiers crossed the LoC to help repair one of its army bunker after the earthquake Direction General of inter services public relation Shakat Sultan refuted media reports expressing concern over the safety of Pakistan's nuclear installation. (Oct 14,2005, The Hindu)

They were robust and shock proof. An earthquake or even direct bomb attack cannot cause harm to the Nuclear installation. A first consignment of relief material for the victims of October 8, earth quake was sent by special air craft.

A total of 82 tonnes of relief material which includes 5,000 blankets, 310 tents, five tones of plastic sheets and 12 tonnes of medicines, has so far been earmarked for Pakistan. (Oct 15, 2005, TNIE) The train carrying the assistance will leave Delhi for Attari – Wagh. Pakistan High commission has opened an account with ABN Amro Bank's Hansalaya Buiiding branch in the capital for Indians wanting to donate money for the earth quake affected victims.

In a dramatic announcement Pakistan president Pervez Musharaff purposed opening up the line of control to assist in the reconstruction of the ravaged areas in (PoK). (Oct 19, 2005, The Hindu) Islamabad would open up routes other than Srinagar – Musaffarabad. A decision has been taken up to allow the mobile companies to operate from both sides. Pakistan was ready to accept the helicopter but not pilots or military personnel. (Oct 15, 2005, The Hindu)

The Pakistani government condemned the killing of minister of state for education Ghulam Nabi Lone, insrinagar, by unknown by persons. (Oct. 19, 2005, The Hindu) After the peacewith India moved into top gear last year, Pakistan had made it a practice to condemn the killing of innocent and high profile targets in J & K. However, Islamabad is careful not to attribute the killing to anyone.

TNIE, History was scripted in J and K after telephone calls were made to (PoK) for the first time in 15 years. The facility was provided on the orders of PM Manmohan Singh. BSNL installed toll –free ISD telephones at the disaster management control rooms in Jammu, Srinagar, tanghar and Uri to facilitate divided families to enquire about the welfare of relatives across the border.

The proposal on easing movement across LoC has been welcomed by several sections in Pakistan and PoK including militant groups operating in Kashmir. General Musharaff in an informal talk with correspondents during the tour of the worst hit area in (NWFP) stated that his government was determined to allow free movement of Kashmiris on either side of the border. It (movement) across the LoC can't be free for all". The ruling and the opposition of PoK, the PoK Muslim conference leader Sardar Ali, the former vice – president of PoK, PDP challenging Lalbul Akbar the JKLF chairman Yasin Malik has advised to evolve an accepted formula to provide relief to the victims.

Chief of relief commission Farooq Ahmed Khan chose to be categorical in his statement about the reported Indian response to softening the LoC when Gen. Musharaff had gone record that he was floating the proposal through the media, and if India agreed, the modalties were to be worked out.

India permitted Pakistani helicopters to fly in the no-fly zone – one KM along the LoC on a case to case basis. Accessing some of the quake – hit areas might require the helicopters to fly close to the LoC and hence permission had been sought no request from Pakistan soldiers to cross LoC for relief work.

PM Dr. Singh issued an appeal to all central government employees and those working in central public sector under takings and automonous bodies to contribute to PM National relief fund to help the victims of the earthquake in J & K.

J & K Mufti Mohammed urged the PM Dr. Singh to ensure that the telephone link from the state to Musaffarabad in PoK was restored soon. The former CM Farooq Abdullah, PDP president Mehbooba Muft, Hurriyat conference chairman Mirwaiz Umar Farooq, JKLF chairman Yasin Malik, National front chief Naeem Khan and DEP Chief Hashim Quereshi have spoken with one another in restoring the phone link.

New Delhi has informed Islamabad of its proposal to open three relief centres on camps near the Kamnpost close to Human Sethu (Uri Sector), tithwal (tangha) and Chakandabegh (Poonch). The Indian decision to open three points along the LoC was in line with the April 18 agreement with Pakistan to allow the divided families to cross the line at the designated place to meet relatives. Soon after the October 8 earthquake PM Manmohan Singh conveyed to Pakistani that New Delhi would undertake relief operations in areas on Pakistani side of the LoC, which had better access from the Indian side.

India expressed concerns over the situation in Gilgit (on Pakistani side of Control) where the curfew was in force after clashes between Pakistani paramilitary forces and Shia students. This is one of the few occasions when India has spoken out on what it believes is an issue of human rights on Pakistani Loc.

The three relief camps proposed by India had not be come operational because India was still waiting concurrence from the Pakistani side. Though India had promised to make these camps operational on October 25, this could not be done since the green signal from Pakistan had not come.

In the after math of the sectarian violence, Pakistan has taken strong exception" to the remarks made by the external affairs ministry, the foreign office is not any single incident incident and Baltistan but the systematic and large scale violation of the Kashmir people by the Indian occupation forces.

India and Pakistan have agreed after four round of official talks to open five points across LoC from nov. 7 to enable people on both sides to participate in the earth quake relief and reconstruction work A joint statement listed Nanseri – Tithwal, chakote – Uri, Rawalkot – Poonch and Tattapani – Mendhar as the agreed routes from where people would be allowed to cross.

The sudden departure of Natwar Singh from the external affair ministry could slow down the peace process with India expecially on the Kashmir issue. Natwar had resigned as the external affairs minister following allegation that he bribed the Saddam led Iraqi authorities to buy oil in the UN sponsored oil – for – food programme (Sep 10, 2005, TNIE) The most important thing is the engagement of Natwar Singh with the Pakistani leadership on Kashmir issue. Pakistan wanted continuity of these behind – the – scene consultation and it had been conveyed to India. The expansion of the SAARC had detailed report in the Hindu, but the TNIE deciphered that there was terror deficit between the two countries. Singh also acknowledged that he saw truth in what Pakistan PM had to say because Pakistan has not fully lived up to the assurance it gave in January 2004 that it will not let its territory be used for terror directed against India. (Nov 14, 2005) It's learnt that Pakistan PM Shakat Aziz attempted to probe the PM on possible movement towards demilitarization of Kashmir by way of some withdrawal of troops during their last meeting was turned down. Singh had underlined to Aziz the need for Pakistan to act on curbing cross border terrorism which is crucial to the turning the deficit into a surplus and is an obligation Pakistan undertook in the January 2004 joint statement. The issues of demilitarization can be discussed only when Islamabd delivered on these assurances.

In his keynote address the international donars conference organized by Pakistan to raise resources for earthquake victims, Gen. Musharaff concluded his speech with detailed references to the opportunity provided to India and Pakistan by the earth quake to move into a new era of bilateral ties several items in the reports have been bracketed to tell public at large General Musharaff's concern in the quake hit people and his attitudinal change which has confronted both the nations that has brought about irreparable damages. (Nov 20, 2005, The Hindu) India, besides sending over 1,300 tents, of relief material such as tents, blankets, and food for quake victims had pledged $ 25 million in kind for the reconstruction.

Minister of state for external affairs E Ahmed stated that India had seen the report on preliminary damage and need assessment, prepared by ADB and

WB and was ready to take up specific projects in sectors such as education and health where India had wide experience and considerable experience.

India permitted Pakistani helicopters to fly in the no-fly zone along LoC to enable them to access their villages close to the LoC. India installed special telephone call centres to enable families to talk to their relatives and friends across LoC free of charge. (Nov 20,2005, The Hindu) But TNIE headline itself was more emphatic and suggestive as 'donate' solution to Kashmir'. (Nov 20, 2005) But the Hindu title of the same story 'a life time opportunity for India and Pakistan, says Musharaff' Both are contradictory. As donation can happen in J & K and in PoK. Similarly life time opportunity to save million in J & K and not in PoK TNIE title is ironical and an extension of a compulsion from the neighbouring country.

General Musharaff was answering a question posed by Chinese journalist on the Post – quake relations between India and Pakistan and prospects for an ultimate resolution of the Kashmir issue. (Nov 17, 2005, The Hindu)

"This opportunity should be utilized to reach a fair settlement of the dispute we cannot clap with one hand, I hope India realizes that the solution has become more possible now in the wake of tragedy in which Kashmir was affected.

Also in yet another indirect reference to India he asked the media to fined for itself how countries affected by the Tsunami did not cut their defense expenditure even though they did not have any threat. (Nov. 17, 2005, The Hindu)

TNIE reported that the foreign secretaries of India and Pakistani have success fully completed two round of composite dialogue process and the third round of composite dialogue process would be on Jan. 17,18.

TNIE, India's comments on Balochitan was intriguing especially at the council of Pakistan Newspapers editors in Lahore as New Delhi noted with concern over the spiralling violence in Balochistan asked Pakistan to exercise restraint (Dec 31, 2005, TNIE) According to Pakistani media reports the Pakistani

TNIE, army has used helicopters gunships in the operations crackdown on tribesmen in Balochistan killing citizens of people the four party Baloch alliance has claimed that 50 people were killed and more than 100 injured in the operation. (Dec 29, 2005, TNIE)

There were information that the Pakistani army is building bunkers, observation towers and new posts in close proximity to the IB. (Dec 22, 2005, TNIE) The minister for Home defended that there was close monitering along the new posts and remedial measured are being adopted to deny advantage to the adversary.

The statistics of infiltrators into India till October 2005 was 220, who were killed and 7,625 were apprehended by the army were found reported in TNIE.

The categorical statement – that the PM had no plans to view any of the three test matches or the five one – day international – put at rest speculation that Dr. Singh would travel to Pakistan in the immediate future. No formal invitation' the the PM had been received so far. The 'television invitation' had been noted by New Delhi, there was no basis to a report filed by a western new agency that Dr. Singh had already accepted an invitation to travel to Pakistan. (January, 2006, The Hindu)

TNIE, also reported that much awaited changes that Pakistani held for years gave way to demilitarization and self – governance in the aftermath of the October 8 earth quake but declined to elaborate and put forward them as proposals. (January 5, 2006)

With Pakistan finding it different to finalise accommodation for its consulate General in Mumbai, the ministry of external affairs has taken up the matter with the Maharastra government to facilitate the process. India's consulate in Karachi is ready after renovation but it is unable to open the mission for want of clearance from Pakistani government. (January 5, 2006)

After the third round of composite dialogue with the Pakistan.

TNIE, suggested that after the third round of composite dialogue yielded two new concepts (1) self – governance (2) demilitarization which is paradigm shift from the deep rooted parameters. (January 17, 2006)

Like the UN solutions or ascertaining the wishes of the people to yet another supra structure that verily needs introspection from Indian the governments. Kashmir to be discussed along with CBMS, peace and security where else the other issues like the sicachen, the sir creek co-operation in trade and economy, friendly co-operation in trade and economy, friendly exchanges and terrorism and drug trafficking in the foreign secretary level talks.

The Hindu reported more on the federal nature especially after the third round of composite dialogues.

The former president of the PoK Sardar Abdul Qayoom flayed the Pakistan establishment not to make use of the help readily made by he Indian government. 'self rule' is a nice new word in the emerging trend but care has to be taken to consider the multi-ethnic, multi – cultural, multi religious state of J & K. (January 29, 2006, The Hindu)

The federal nature of the state can be implemented where every section of society feels empowered and becomes a participant in the dialogue process. The independence of J & K is opposed by him for the present historical factors and the international environment are not conducive for such appraisal. TNIE, terming "force" India assertain of continuing cross border terrorism Pakistan president pervez musharaff has alleged that new Delhi used this as a pretext for not moving forwarded in improving bilaterial ties.

TNIE, also reported that president APJ Abdul Kalam visualized a federation of India and Pakistan like the European union Federation can become a possibility in the next 50 years like the US and Russia , and the unification of Germany. (Feb 3, 2006)

TNIE, Pakistan, president Gen. Musharaff reiterated the need of demilitarization and self governance as a way forward towards the resolution of Kashmir issue. India could pull out its forces out of Srinagar, Baramulla and Kupwara without having the need to amend its constitution. (Feb 6, 2006)

Since 1990, February 5 is being observed all over Pakistan and PoK as Kashmir solidarity day to express solidarity with the separatists and reiterate governments moral, diplomatic and political support to Kashmirs. After the composite dialogue there were initiatives from the Pakistani side to resolve all outstanding issues and out of the box thinking to resolve the Kashmir issues. (Feb. 5, 2006)

TNIE gave an elaborate account and scheduled dates for the commencement of the discussion the eight issues.

The round table conference brought some 60 representatives including CM Ghulam Nabi Azad, NC chief Omar Abdullah, PDP chief Mehbobba Mufti and other attended the round table except the Hurriyat. (Feb 26, 2006, TNIE)

The third round of the composite dialogue (CD) between two countries and the scheduled dated found mention in the TNIE reports. Foreign Minister meet on July 21, 22 economic and commercial co-operation in Islamabd March 28-29. Tulbul navigation project – April 18-19, Siachen in New Delhi – May 23-24 Sir Creek in New Delhi – May 25 – 26 Terirorism and Drug trafficking in Islamabd – May 30 – 31. (Feb 7, 2006 TNIE)

Promotion of friendly exchanges in New Delhi, June – 1-2. The two round started in January in New Delhi discussed new Delhi on peace and security and on Jammu and Kashmir.

Pakistan reacted immediately and welcomed Dr. Singh observation on resolution of Kashmir which he spelt out at the inaugural ceremony of the Amritsar – Nankana Sahib bus service. (March 28, 2006,The Hindu) Pakistan Foreign office spokesperson has been Tsneen Aslam acknowledged that the ideas of a non- aggressive pact or friendship treaty have been suggested by both sides of the past. On Dr. Singh observation that was a 'mistake' on the part of Pakistan to link the normalization of bilateral relations with the resolutions of the Jammu and Kashmir Ms. Aslam argued that Kashmir was at the heart of India – Pakistan relations and it would be unrealistic to expect the improvement in economic ties without resolving the issue.

The peace process with Pakistan must ultimately culminate in a treaty of peace, security and friendship, before flagging off the first Amritsar – Nanasahib bus since 1947. (March 25, 2006,The Hindu)

Borders would not be redrawn should be seen as 'just lines' on the map so that the people on both sides of the LoC were able to move freely and trade with each other. With the on-going composite dialogue there is split in relations like the resolution of Kashmir and bilateral relations. They have to been in different perspective to give impetus to other developments which would other wise get hampered. The title of the New Indian Express was bit ludicurous. Punjab bus returns from Pak. The title indicates as if the two separated Punjab province have come together instead of two governments coming close on heels to further bilateral relations. (March 26, 2006,TNIE) There was absolutely no mention of the treaty of friendship offered by PM Dr. Singh during the flagging off ceremony at Amritsar Namakhana Sahi bus service at Amritsar. The news report of bereft of the initative of the Indian government.

A string of attacks on prominent leaders of Pakistan based Islamist terror groups like the former head of the HM kidnapped and beaten, a Jammat – Ud – dawa leader shot dead, has sparked speculation that Pakistan's ISI may be cracking down on organizations hostile to president Pervez Musharaff's pro – united states policies. Pakistan has also begun to take action against HM, whose leadership recently staged a protest against Gen. Musharaff in Mushaffarabad police in the troubled south waziristion province arrested four HMcadre, charging them with having links to the Taliban and Osama Bin laden's Al-quaida. It was the first Pakistani admission that these links exist. (March 31,2006,The Hindu)

However the Indian intelligence sources noted that there was no sign Pakistan was moving against Jihadi infrastructure, such as offices, training camps, and financial assets.

Pakistan president Musharaff has praised PM Manmohan Singh's efforts to involve all groups in J & K towards finding a solution to the conflict in the state. President Musharaff said in the composite dialogue process with India 'we are going forward on CBMS and conflict resolution'. In conflict resolution, 'kashmir is the key issue and we have to move forward.

TNIE also reported that India's concerns cannot be appeased as long as the Jihadi leaders are roaming free in Pakistan and issuing statements and openly making claims for different acts, Foreign secretary Shyam Saran remarks came as Pakistan said the two countries should go beyond CBM to address contentious issues, including Kashmir problem. (June 8, 2006)

Pakistan president Pervez Musharaff says that 'demilitarisation is his final resolution of the dispute'. Demilitarise Kashmir, give self – governance to people of Kashmir, and joint management at the top. He would discuss Kashmir and other issues with Singh when PM visits Pakistan on a bilateral talk. This is for the first time, a news report stated that Musharaff would discuss issues bilaterally though many a occasions demanded international attention. (June 25, 2006,The Hindu)

TNIE In the Mumbai train blasts, which left at least 190 people dead and 600 injured, India has taken strong exception to Pakistan foreign Minister Khurshid Mehmood kasuri statement which sought to link the blatant and inhuman bomb blasts in Mumbai to so called issue of linking Kashmir with the terrorist attack. (July13, 2006)

The report also stated that that Pakistan will co-operate with India against the scourge of terrorism only if the so-called disputes are resolved.

Though the union home secretary Duggal condemned the softest of the soft targets like the innocent tourist were mostly reprehensible, he added that there was no rethink on the going peace process. (July 12, 2006 TNIE)

Dr. Singh on the nature of CBMS with Pakistan after the Mumbai blasts stated that 'Pakistan in 2004, had solemnly given assurance that Pakistani territory would not be used to promote exchange and about terrorist elements directly against India that assurances has to be fulfilled before the peace process or other processes can make progress. (July 15, 2006 TNIE)

TNIE reported that PM Dr. Singh at the G – 8 summit in St. Petersburg in expected to seek support of the world's top industrialized nations for India's effort to put down the growing threat of foreign backed Jihadi terror on its soil. The Mumbai serial blasts have lent an urgency to the task of bringing international pressure on Islamabad to dismantle terrorist infrastructure.

Pakistan foreign minister Khurshid Mehmood Kasuri, even before the securing agencies could reach any conclusion with regard to those behind the serial bomb blasts in Mumbai, gave interviews to various international media organizations to insist that his country had nothing to do with the terror strikes in India's financial capital "India is a vast country, there are attacks in other parts of India, there should not be knee – jerk reaction that everything happening inIndia starts from Pakistan. (July 14, 2006, The Hindu)

With the Pakistan continuing to allow its territory to be used by terrorists, the question of reducing the number of Indian troops along the Kashmir border did not arise until this ceased, defence minister pranab Mukerjee at a convention organized by the west Bengal Pradesh congress committee in the wake of Mumbai blasts. (July 17, 2006, The Hindu)

From the stated reports even at the end of third round of composite dialogue, the logistics of withdrawing troops proved to be miserable failure among to the threat posed by mayhem by the hawkish militants.

The report stated for the first time Pakistan spokesman mentioning the active co-operation of Pervez Musharaff in tracking the terrorists investigations into the Mumbai blasts if new Delhi, provides evidence. New Delhi promptly wanted the submission of HM Chief Syed Salauddin who is freely roaming in Pakistan, PoK, and sharing the same stage with many minister of the federal government of Pakistan, ban on Jammt – Ud – Dawa at political outfit of let, underworld dawood Ibrahim. (June 22, 2006, TNIE)

The report for the first time told on the co-operation of war on terror, at least after the wake of Mumbai blasts.

The Indian side is also aware that a policy of 'non-contact' with Pakistan cannot last long given the complicated nature of the relationship. The National Democratic Alliance (NDA) which adopted a 'boycott Musharaff attitude after the October 1999 coup was forced to make contact with Islamabad after the December 1999 Kandahar hijacking.

In 2004 and 2005, Gen. Musharaff and Dr. Singh met on the sidelines of the United nations General assembly, with the Pakistan President also paying a visit to New Delhi in April 2005. (July 31,2006, The Hindu)

TNIE, the US congress last month of a possible sale of 36 F – 16C/D Block 50 – 52 aircraft, has notified its intention to supply 60 mid-life update modification kits an falcon star structured life enhancement kits with associated equipment and services F 16 a / P in Pakistan is inventory. (July 27, 2006)

Coverage of The Pok Government and India

There were five stories in The Hindu and absolutely no stories in the TNIE on the future of PoK.

The President of PoK sardar Mohammed Anwar, has fully acknowledged the self rule proposal propounded by Pakistan President Pervez Musharaff as the starting point for any dialogue. The self rule proposal seeks to do this by giving the people a say in their destiny.

The Hindu reports much attention to the on going changes in PoK.

The Hurriyat conference is certainly not the representative of the entire state and a particular region or locality cannot decide the future of the entire state on both sides of the LOC became a wide reputed quote from PM of PoK

Sikandar Hayat. The independence of the state is also ruled out as both sides of the state have budget deficit and economically both are dependent on two countries.

Eighteen Jihadi top commanders staged a hunger strike in Musaffarabad against the betrayal of the jihad in J & K by president Pervez Musharaff. Organised by the United Jihad Council (UJC) a Pakistan based plat form for all major groups operating in India, the hunger strike marked the first instance where Jihadi leadership has staged a protest against Pakistan their protest was being conducted in an ISI run safe houses in Musaffarabad. (March 13,2006 The Hindu)

A suspected HM commander arrested has allegedly disclosed that the terrorist outfit operates from Abotabad in Manseara area of POK. During the interrogation he allegedly disclosed that be rejoined the outfit in September 2000 after which he was sent to PoK along with five other men for training. The former Chief Justice of PoK High court justice Malik future which, has urged India and Pakistan to respect the sentiments of the people of J & K people. (April 18, 2006 The Hindu)

The coming of the former PMs Benazir Bhutto and PMs Shakayar Khan to India which is also praise worthy nature of the Indian democracy and the CBMS in people contact.

The TNIE has gone to the extend of highlighting the warm reception given to Shajaat Hussain the Hindu has explored that the mind set even of the for democratically elected former Ministers shajaat Hussain who still relented on the granting of MEN status to India deferring it to a later period, ventures on the premise of maintaining the status quo ante vis-a-vis India.

Bhutto favour restoration democracy.

Coverage of The Mainstream Parties and Their Urges

There was only one story in The Hindu first and no stories in the TNIE.

On the eve of the first anniversary of the service, the PDP celebrated its launch as Yomi Kasarvan Awam named Karavam-e-Aman and a was launched on April 7 and last year and is as the biggest kashmir centric CBM service between two countries. She regretted that the process of verification for acquitting the trade permit was cumbersome. She advocated the option of self- rule, restoration of political powers enjoyed in 1947, Kashmir youth inducted in the police departments, internal security to the handed over to the J & K police, laws such as disturbed areas act and the armed forces special powers act to be with drawn. (April 8, 2006 The Hindu)

Coverage of CBM Related

There were 79 stories in The Hindu and 91 stories in The New Indian Express.

A The New Indian Express widely reported that Ladakis has been the centre of south Asian track which was cut off from the rest of the country by the state for more than six months due to inclement weather conditions Ladakis have welcomed the PM more of opening up the Kargil to Skardu in the Northern areas of Pakistan and China route to Tibet through Aksai Chin.

The foreign secretaries of both nations had taken the trip of truck across the LoC as first step towards promotion of trade across the border which were severed in 1947 – 48 participants in the intra – Kashmir dialogue process has started on CBM to be obtained further

There was extensive coverage on the Jammu and Kashmir government and this comes in the wake of demands of the Lackhi people that historic and ancient links with China be opened for economic and trade co-operation.

The demand of the Ladakhis to open the trade routes with China is based on practical considerations. Laddkh is cut off from the rest of the country for more than six months, during which all economic activity comes to a complete stand still. Due to the pancity of economic opportunities, many youths turn to suggesting of goods on the both sides of the LoC. The political elite points that the matter needs urgent attention from the central leadership in view of the immense of economic opportunities it presents.

The Indian Express reported coverage of India ready to lift NTBs on September 14, 2005 to lift immediately every single non-tariff barrier to increase bilaterial trade with Pakistan. It is also widely reported that India is ready to import from Pakistan textile, cotton, molasses, etc., The opening of the wagh border has helped the smoothening of relations between nations.

The report in The New Indian Express (April 7, 2005) stated the Jammu – Udampur line is the first phase of the proposed Rs. 3,500 crore, 344 KM line up to Baramulla, the first line linking the rest of the country with the interior areas of the state. There were extreme coverage covering more than half page reports in the Hindu with breath taking stories or the smooth travel of the bus inspite of threats claimed by militants to thwart the host of activities initiated by terrorists. The opening of the Kamman bridge which helped both the passengers

The re-opening of the Srinagar – Muzaffarabad road show case the new mood of reconciliation. (The Hindu, April 8, 2005) Apart from the Prime Minister, the congress president and UPA chairperson sonia Gandhi, the external affairs minister Natwar Singh, the petroleum minister Mani Shankar Aiyar, the Parliamentary affairs minister, Gulam Nabi Azad, besides Jammu and Kashmir Governor Lt. Gen. S.K. Sinha, the Chief Minister Mufti Mohammed Sayeed, and deputy CM Mergat Ram Sharma. The union Home Minister, Shivraj Patil, who had planned to travel to srinagar stayed back in New Delhi to monitor the situation.

The frequency of bus service between Srinagar and Musaffarabad, trucks to ply, open additional routes between Poonch and Rawalket, start rail link between Kokhrapur in Rajasthan and Munabo in Pakistan's Sindh province, interaction and co-operation along the LoC including agreed meeting points for divided families trade, pilgrimage and cultural interactions.

There were no prominent reports in The New Indian Express but The Hindu reiterated on the safety of the passengers and Pakistan also emphasised the threats to Srinagar – Musaffarabad bus service threatened by the militants and the dry run of the bus was postponed due to exchange of threats from militants.

The Hindu reports that Jammu and Kashmir CM Mufti Mohammed Sayeed offering full security to its passengers and the threats from the militants will be kept under check.

The Hindu news reported on April 3, 2005 which covered a whole range of news related to fool proof security to passengers who are to travel to Musaffarabad. For it would be seen by the public as maneuvered to dispel fear linking in th minds of the Indian public who ever shun taking a holiday trip to Kashmir after a spat of militancy in the state.

Advanced arrangements like review meeting by the union Home ministry on the safety of the 29 passengers who boarded the bus and the security agencies were beefed up along the road routes to foil any attempt by the militants to ensure the safety of the passengers. Both Bonhomic were expressed by the people on the other side of the LoC which had number of hoardings and bill – boards to receive the guests. Such reports which would instill confidence in the minds of the public did not figure in The New Indian Express. The Hindu has amicably supported the views of the politician, the senior members and the army to retrieve the spirit of the occasion.

Denial of permission by the Pakistan government to politicians to go to srinagar. Musaffarabad in the Srinagar - Musaffarabad bus was an expected move. The speculation was rife because Pakistan does not recognise any party in the state as the representatives of the people of Kashmir. It has missed no opportunity to describe the state government and mainstream politicians as puppets in the hands of central government. (The Hindu April 2,

2005) The CPI (M) general secretary M.Y. Tarigami, the chief whip of the national conference Mubarak Gen, a number of legislators in the poonch district have been denied permissions.

The only leader who visited PoK Mr. Sheikh Abdullah, in 1964, acted with nod from Pandit Nehru and the ascent given by Ayub Khan to discuss on the Kashmiri tangle. Both newspapers demanded a enthusiastic move by the CM to have discussions with the PM on the issue of permit and travel. (The Hindu, April 3, 2005)

The New Indian Express, the plying of buses between Amritsar and Lahore found prominent coverage in the issue. (May 6, 2005) The Hindu reports with the historic opening of 70 kms. Srinagar – Musaffarabad bus there is enthusiasm that the trade links will get much needed thrust.

Both The New Indian Express & The Hindu (April 14, 2005) reported that the trains to Udampur brings the Kashmir valley closer, which has taken over two decades to complete the Rs.515 crore raiway line that will pass through the treacherous likely terrain of the Pirpangal ranges. The entire 342 kms rail line from Jammu to Baramullah via Udhampur, Ktria, Kaizabad and Srinagar would be completed by 2007.

The New Indian Express and The Hindu there was reported violence ahead of the second bus service killing two civilians and injuring 17 the second bus leaves for Srinagar – Musaffarabad amid heavy security and threat from four militant organisation.

The Hindu coverage of the serious absence of the discussion on Iran pipeline with rice and the NPT discussion that are quiteserious about civilian nuclear power in India. (April 22, 2005)

The predominant move of the Hurriyat a cross the border came to be closely observed in The Hindu. The Hurriyat travel to PoK and the fanfare exhibited by the public at both the places shows remarkable change in the movement of people across, the border. There were no festivities on this side of the LoC (The New Indian Express, June 3, 2005)

Compared to the facilities expressed on the other side of the LoC. Doves were released as the Hurriyat leaders crossed the Aman Sethu.

The CM Mufti Mohammed Sayeed in an exclusive talk with The Hindu demanded the opening of the Srinagar – Musaffarabad bus service weekly and expanded so that real interaction between the people on both sides talks place.

The opening of the Kargil – Skarden road in the Pakistan controlled northern areas is crucial for as the new story states that the passengers wait five decades to make a six – hour journey to meet the near and dear ones. To reach the main towns of northern areas one has to reach Islamabad, the capital of Pakistan .and then take the Karakurans highway. A person making the journey from Kargil has to travel at least 1,500 km to reach the northern areas across the LoC. Skarder is the main town of Baltistan and is home to some of the highest peaks in the world. But locals believe that opening of Kargil – Skarder road would not be an easy proposition for Pakistan. Such lengthy reports failed to get coverage in The New Indian Express. The Hindu has given impetus to other areas of J & K, which is ignored by The New Indian Express which beckons national importance. (The Hindu August 7, 2005)

Only two points of call were identified in each country Delhi – Mumbai in India and Lahore and Karachi in Pakistan. (The New Indian Express, September 9, 2005) Delhi is keen to get the 1976 Air services agreement modified so that multiple carrier can operate between the two countries. This would allow private air lines like jet and sahara to fly to Pakistan. But Islamabad has turned down as request.

The New Indian Express (September 29, 2005) had graphically represented the route of Amritsar, Lahore bus service. The Hindu had other areas to state like the draft agreement protocol and technical modalities for the Nankana Sahib – Amritsar bus service including issues such as designated routes, bus terminals, and facilities for the bus craws. The two countries decided that each Indian passenger would have to pay a fare of Rs.750/- while a Pakistani will have to shell out Rs.900/-. (The Hindu, September 29, 2005)

Though talks on enhanced co-operation in civil aviation between India and Pakistan ended inconclusively, in the latest parleys both sides agreed to let private airlines operate in each other's country. (The Hindu, September 29, 2005) They also agreed on increasing the existing number of 12 flights a week from each country. While Pakistan wanted the number of flights to be increased to 48, India suggested 20 to 22 as a beginning. Perse Pakistani's proposals are sound from the economic angle but their has to be some degree of reciprocity.

The New Amritsar – Lahore bus link, scheduled to begin regular operation from December 23, marks yet another position step for the people of India and Pakistan who have suffered due to the cross border tension. The bus service facilitated restoration of the familial bonds which Kashmirs had lost decades ago. Stories narrated in newspapers and beamed by electronic media about families separated for years reuniting touched upon the human aspect and re-established emotional and familial links between the Kashmiris.

The third round of composite dialogue saw the launch of first Amritsar – Lahore bus service. Amid land slogans in favour of India – Pakistan friendship, Dy CM of Punjab Rajinidhar Kaur Bhatel flagged off the flower – bedecked golden coloured 45 seater Volvo. (The Hindu, January 25, 2006)

Exactly a year after the launch of the Srinagar – Musaffarabad bus service amidst fanfare to bridge the hearts of divided Kashmir, the enthusiasm of travellers on the Indian side of the LoC seems to be waning owing to curbs on travel and long time clearance. The general refrain among the Kashmiri people is that by restricting the travel only among the divided families to travel on board a bus has not served the real purpose of enhancing people-to-people contact. How many divided families would be there on either side of the cease fire line The bus service should have been open of all citizens so that they would interact with each other and under stand each other.

The prisoners who inadvertently entered the Pakistani areas were being suspected to be spices were lodged with Lahore jails. There are reports that states there are many who languish in the Pakistani jails waiting to be released.

The Indian Express widely reported on the measures of Mr Natwar Singh visit to Pakistan. With agreement on pre notification of missile test and establishing of communication link between India coast guard and Pakistan's maritime security agency, Another major development was the immediate notification of detention of nationals, providing consular access and verification during detention period.

Najan Sethi, editor of the daily times and Friday times of Pakistan who conducted the discussion said the media in India was relatively free and Pakistan media had also, by and large been made free now Such conspicuous absence of such reports in the Hindu.

The report The New Indian Express stated the secretary of state Condeeze Rice recently conveyed to Pak foreign minister Khurshid Mehmood Kasuri that the project would violate "Iran and Libya' sanctions Act" passed by US.

The New India Express reported June 23, 2005, on liberalizing visa regime for senior editors and executives of Indian and Pakistani newspapers to facilitate easy travel of Journalists and free movement of publication across the border The INS members took the occasion as an opportunity to dispel the impression among Pakistan journalists and Indian media 'totoe' the government line of vital national issues

Mammon Mathew of Malayala Manorma said that Pakistani and Indian media should exchange reporters and editorial staff for short periods to promote a better understanding of each others country. (The New Indian Express, June 23, 2005)

A day ahead of Pakistan President Pervez Musharaff arrival in the The New Indian Express reported in three decked headline "Hands on the trigger on one of Gen's visit" where vital installation including the place of stay and the General will visit his during his three day stay in the country. The General is a sort of CBM made a trip to India on April 17 Indo – Pakistan one day – cricket match to be watched by Minsraff and prime minister Dr. Manmohan Singh. (April 16, 2005)

The bus service between Srinagar – Musaffarabad has opened more of such routes through the border. The Pakistan Foreign Minister Mr. Kasuri said the opening of more entry points along the LoC was possible as another confidence building measure. The Pakistan President on his recent visit to India said that the peace process was irreversible and his coming India shows hope on the Kashmir issue as Indian government has proposed on many confidence building measures to build mutual trust.

The report in the Hindu with the peace process is now irreversible and The New Indian Express "India, Pak smoke peace pipe" endorsed the view of President Musharaff during the occasion to reactivate the joint economic commission, expedite the issues of sir creek and siachen glacier with existing institutional mechanism.

Both the reports stated the bonhomie that was left behind the arrival, failed Agra summit 2001. The achievements were far more than expected formed the sub headline in the front page of the Hindu. On the LoC settlement both leaders had different views Pakistan President stating the status quo cannot be accepted Indian on the other hand reinforcing no redrawing of the borders, and both on common platform proclaiming that border stands irrelevant. Karachi, Mumbai consulates to be opened by the year end.

BJP president L.K. Advani trip to Pakistan found wide coverage in The New Indian Express but the Hindu failed to report the travel of L.K Advani on the very first day

The coming of President Pervez Musharaff, and cricket enthusiast at Ferozesha Kotla stadium and having a quiet chat with PM Dr Singh for the find ODI India – Pak cricket has bought more furor and change in the rigid atmosphere.

The The New Indian Express expressed the hope that "Kashmir comes before cricket" formed the main link in the first part of the paper. The visit was finalized hectic back door diplomancy was between officials of both the countries to prepare the ground work for talks between Mr Musharaff and Mr Singh. (The New Indian Express, April 10, 2005)

The coming of General Musharaff to India especially after the abortive Agra summit the final one day cricket match between the two sides at Perozha

Kotla brings with him a message of peace and a visit to dargah at Ajmeer. Musharaff coming to India was high lighted elaborately in both the newspapers and the general's intention of moving about in and around India along with the delegates. (The Hindu, April 17, 2005)

The visit of Najam Aziz Sethi, Editor the Friday times and Daily times to India, when peace process achieved new heights with the arrival of Pakistan president General Musharaff leaves a New trail of path for other mess from the Pakistani establishment to venture into India to give more focus on the discussions on the composite dialogue and reinforce the views expressed by their counter part to create more political will and political space for speedy redressal to the decade old conflict. (The New Indian Express, May 4, 2005)

The press spokesperson made amply clear that to a large extent the media on both sides of the border has been provocative in native, perpetuating the conflict at times, with strong editorials against each other, and on the other occasion acting as doves of peace accer lating the peace process. Seth recalled that in 1988 when Benasir Bhutto had clinched a settlement on Siachen with India, the Pakistani press called her naive and misplaced, thereby forcing the Pakistani government abandoned the peace initiative till 1994 It was the same press that hailed the secretary level talks outcome between two countries in 1997. It was here the Indian press stepped up the hostility and soon the Indian government backed up the proposals. The derailment of the 1999 Lahore Summit and the breakdown of the Agra talks had the involvement of the press, the vernacular press was abused by the Pakistani Editor for they had been instrumental by projecting the nations as enemies and not worthy of trust. The BJP led – government had brought in a Hinduvate element in the media through continous war mongering especially after the Pakistan nuclear blast. Mr. Sethi's remarks in the Hindu "in a way, changing the attitude of influential English press is going to be more difficult than in Pakistan. The opinion of the English press is its own and therefore deeply ingrained as conviction, the indoctrinations under democracy is deeper because it gives the illusions of being 'shared' and not 'imposed'.

The ongoing interaction between India and Pakistan was Track III. Diplomacy and not Track II, a non-governmental initiative, it was more of people-to-people dialogue through media, remarkable statements were made by Javed Jabber, co-convenor of South Asian Editors Forum (SAEF). (The Hindu, May 27, 2005)

At joint commission India is likely to present to Pakistan three proposals including liberalization of the visa regime and improvement of consular access.

The proposals include an increase in the number of nationals visiting the other country for pilgrimage and also the number of shrines.

The proposals will be forwarded in the form of amendment to update the 1974 visa agreement, the 1982 protocol on consular access and the 1974 bilateral protocol on visits to religious shrines.

The objective at the end of the fourth round of expert level dialogue on (CBMS) India and Pakistan proposed part to reduce the risk from accident relating to nuclear weapons through radiological leakage. It flows from the framework of (MOU) between the two countries arrived at Lahore in February 1999. The two sides further undertake to notify to each other immediately in the event of any accidental, unauthorized or unexplained incident. That could create the risk of a fallout with adverse circumstances for both sides or an outbreak of a nuclear was between the two countries. This was the first report in the Hindu related to nuclear pact.

The New Indian Express, the top officials of the BSF and Pakistan rangers would be meeting quarterly in Munabai to discuss issues like border activities on the mid – western borders and security matters. The BSF has raised the issue of Pakistan building a platform on zeroline. The meeting will also discuss ways to strengthen joint patrolling and steps to curb inadvertent border crossings.

The Indian government took the initiative of insuring the Pakistan team of Rs. 2 crore for their fourth one day international cricket match against India. The Gujarat Cricket association Amm told reporters that 15,000 men will be employed to protect the stadium and another 50 each advertising insurance cover with as many as 300 tickets have been kept for Pakistani fans.

The Hindu and The New Indian Express reports the Amritsar – Lahore and Amritsar – Nankana Sahib bus service and the establishment of a hotline between coast guards. The communication link between the coast guards could go a long way in alleviating the sufferings of fishermen who inadvertently stray into each other's water. The report appeared for two days in the The New Indian Express. (The Hindu, May 11, 2005)

Wadeace Rehman paid visit to a private hospital in Sringar and offered Salwar Suits, blankets to 30 children of Rahat Vihar, a Shelter for or plans and widows proves how public from different spectrum of life do co-operate in enhancing the peace process.

The New Indian Express, Pakistan has announced new guidelines for Indians wanting to visit the country by procuring the request forms and delivered to relevant authorities at least eight weeks in advance and must be accompanied by photo copies of a valid passport.

Medical Visas were issued by the Indian High Commission to Pakistani patients highlights the enthusiasm derived in the on-going CBMS.

The Hindu coverage of the tourists streaming from different parts of the world, the cultural and ancient sites here are crying for funds. Many of them are decaying and crumbling despite local efforts. The city's cynosure are a crumbled nine storey place of the 16th century. The Zonevar Singh first, Henis Gompa ministry, the Shanti stupa have formed the major tourist attractions.

The New Indian Express, to promote people-to-people contact, Pakistan has given clearance to ferry service linking Mumbai, Karachi and Dubai.

The structural changes for Jinnah House in Mumbai has raised the concern of Pakistani government where the Indian government has planned to convert into SAARC cultural centre. The Indian leadership in the last two years have failed to hand over the house to Pakistan, inspite of Pakistan's preference to acquire Jinnah House for its consulate has repeatedly been raised. Both India and Pakistan plan to open their consulates in Karachi and Mumbai by the year end.

CM Mufti Mohammed Sayeed has advocated the restoration of telephone links with various cities of Pakistan saying it would boost the relations between the two sides o Kashmir. The telephone link between Jammu and Kashmir and Pakistan had been snapped after militancy erupted in the region. But incoming calls from Pakistan are not barred. (The Hindu, September 27,2005)

India offered material to help Pakistan rebuild its earthquake – affected areas but dismissed the probability of its engineers going over to the other side as romanticism. The proposals for setting up relief camps at the three designated points on the LoC was deferred. India would begin construction activity immediately but it was the military engineering services which would have to operate in PoK.

The aversion to indulge came in with their avoidance of military pilots, then how do you expect MSS people to go and construction. Further modalities to help Pakistan could be firmed up after the Geneva conference.

India has offered Rs.112.45 crores in assistance to Pakistan for relief and rehabilitation of the October 8 earthquake. The offer was made by minister for state for statistics oscar Fernando at a conference organized by the united nations office of the co-ordination for Humanitarian affairs in Geneva. This is the largest – ever military assistance announced by Indian for Pakistan since independence. In dollar terms, the assistance pledged is $25 million or Rs.149.44 crores in Pakistani rupees. (October 28, 2005)

Indian technology for prefabricated quake resistant shelters would be made available to Islamabad. A number of news which played a major role in providing relief to thousands of people hit by October 8 earthquake in Uri and Langhhar, the Chennai – based world vision has so far distributed tarpaulin sheets, blankets, food and hygienic kits to over 1,300 families in the affected areas. It has launched a pilot project of constructing small classrooms at schools damaged in the earthquake volunteers of mala Amritanandamayi math have arrived from Delhi and Chennai Ashram branches to help the relief and rehabilitation workers.

The LoC of control was opened on November 7, this is the first time in the history of J & K the LoC has been opened for the movement of goods as per the recent agreement signed between India and Pakistan.

Boundaries disappeared for the moment as officials and scribes crossed over in each other's territory. Twenty seven trucks with 300 tents, 3000 trauplins, medicines, rice and wheat was sent by the government. Pakistan has sent one truck for the quake victims on the Indian side.

The Indian and Pakistani authorities opened the second point along the LoC for exchange of relief material for the earth quake hit people. The third crossing point across the LoC at Tithwal Tangdhar would open on November 12 as a foot bridge across the Kishanganga is constructed by Pakistani army. The other two crossing points – Balnoi (Mendher) and Sikkat (Uri) to be opened on November 14 x 16 Two close relatives on either side of the LoC made unsuccessful attempts to hug each other at a distance of IoM. It was yet another grim remainder of how thousands of families on either side were desperate to meet each other. (The Hindu, November 10, 2005)

24 Indian citizens crossed the LoC the newly constructed bridge near the Krishan Ganga river in Teetwal . They were warmly received by the Pakistani army. Kishan ganga also serves as the dividing line between the two parts of Kashmir. The bridge was laid by the Pakistan army in a record time.

The fifth and the last relief point for the exchange of relief material along the LoC was opened at 12.30 p.m. by colonel Gyan Mishra of the Indian army and it col. Basit Irfan of the Pakistan army. (The Hindu, November 17, 2005)

To work on the finalization of "Border ground rules for implementation along theinternational border" as part of the conventional (CBMS) between the two countries airmed at avoiding conflict was arrived here at the third round of he Pakistan – India expert level dialogue in continuation of the composite dialogue. (The Hindu, April 28, 2006)

The two sides agreed on the modalities for holding quarterly flag meetings on need basics at sector level commanders in agreed sectors. It was agreed that consistent with the intent of the part reached on development of no new posts and defence work along LoC, the existing posts and defence works would not be fortified. Both sides agreed to periodically discuss further CBMS and review, monitor the implementation of existing conventional (CBMS as called for in the Lahore move of 1999 and as mandated by Foreign secretaries on both sides).

There were several reports of tripartite framework agreement for Iran – Pakistan – India project by December. Gail and IOC identified as project partners in the expected one third Indian participation in the tripartite project.

There was a contradictory report of one column story in the The New Indian Express on India willing to permit trade via Wagah border. The export of four items through the Wagh border like Cattle, Vegetables, and four other perishable items badly needed to bring down prices in the domestic market.

Report in Pakistan media that India was delaying the exports to press for its demand to fully open up the Wagh border and transi rights to Afghanistan. But the real politic in the was the divergence of views of commerce minister Humayun Khan and PM Shalat Aziz Khan son of former ISI general who openly opposed trade with India without progress on Kashmir appeared keen not to implement such plans.

The Hindu reported on April, 15, 2005 of more Kashmir related CBMs in the offering promoted more of opening of trade routes along the LoC. Dr. Manmohan Singh had tabled for talks there opening of Jammu – Silakat highway.

Both the reports stated that the India is pursuing import of natural gas The Hindu coverage of identified more areas in India – Pakistan trade. The industry boldly favoured early simplification of the visa procedure besides step to legalise the unofficial trade and further boost trade and commerce between both countries. Pakistan should also grant the MFN status to India.

The decision to open up truck service between Musaffarabad and Srinagar could be the beginning of the transit trade and the Hindu clearly cites that this is evident from his explanation posted on the official web site of the Presdient General Musharaff.

The New Indian express gives importance to nitty – gritty of relationships that surfaced during the opening of the roads and services. The marriage of Bashrat, who came in the first Musaffarabad – Srinagar bus, was solemned with his first cousin Jaima Hayce at his native place of Bandipora in Baramullah district. (The New Indian Express, May 2, 2005)

The proposed multi-billion Iran-Pakistan – India gas pipeline project will become a reality, The New Indian Express reports the New Indian Express quotes the plan as envisaged by the petroleium and natural gas secretary S.C. tripathi. It may take at least there years to complete the project as hard negotiation begins for one year, followed by tapping financial resources for the project and next year completion.

The Hindu gives coverage of the trade fair organized by Pastagear Artisans Welfare Association (DAWS), with a host of traders from all over the country. The participation by the Pakistani traders and craftsmen is an extension of the peace process started by two countries.

The Hindu coverage of the 100 member delegation of the six day tour of Pakistan holds no barred approach to trade barriers, especially the FICCI is dismantling trade and tariff barrier would enable south Asioan giants to reap the benfits and the study identified seven areas that need to be tackled upfront. These include de-freezing of the list of items (now limited to 768 items) importable from India, liberalizing business visa regulations, opening up trade in services, highway linkages, linking rail service, road route via wagh border and dismantling of trade and tariff barriers. (The Hindu, May 28, 2005)

The New Indian Express, Pakistan is seeking more times to firm up its commitment to a particular pipeline. Whether players like it or not, the US will loom over the pipeline. For obvious reasons the US will put its money behind the pipeline that does not go via Iran.

Indian oil Corporation has offered to sell 8,20,000 tonnes of diesel to Pakistan via the Wagah border at discount.

The Hindu coverage of the issue of re-opening of the trade route as also the kailash manosarvar road would be taken up with China. Since our relations with China are improving re-opening of the old trade would be taken up with the Chinese government.

The Hindu coverage of Mr. Aiyar arrived in Tehran on a three day visit will focus on a 25 year old on the purchase of five million tones of Iranian gas annually. The $40 billion gas deal with Iran is complex as it allows Indian Companies to operate in Iran's oil and gas sector, and gives them a direct foot hold in the area. India's long term purchase of natural gas has been tied up with its participation in developing one gas field and two oil fields in Iran. As part of the deal, India's ONGC Videsh Ltd will get 20% share in the development of yadavaran – Iran's biggest onshore oilfield.

The New Indian Express quotes though India finalized a 20 billion – doallar deal to import (LNG) from Iran beginning 2009 – 10 to meet its energy requirements, Condoliza Rice east week made out a strong case for Islambad not to violate the Libiya and Iran sanctions act of 1996 of US (ILSA), which forbids more than 20 million dollars investment in oil sector.

The Hindu, recuniting the PoK refugee after five decades to given three decked head line with much bold type shows the concern of the media in portraying the gesture extended by the government on either side in bringing the people more closer.

The New Indian Express, Pakistan does not want to import diesel from India for the Indian diesel cost US 3 – 4 Higher per tonne than from Kuwait and other arab countries, if India reduces the price, the import of the diesel from New Delhi via land route is not possible in the forseeable future.

At the end of first day's discussion of (JWG) on pipeline, there was some on technical issues between India and Pakistan. While The New Indian Express quoted that JWG will look at options of financing the project in the back drop of US sanctions against Iran. India and Pakistan decided to appoint separate financial consultants for the implementation of the $7 billion Iran gas pipeline. Once operational Islamabad would begin with importing 10 million standard cubic metre per day. India is looking at importing of 60 MMS CMD, increasing the quantity to 90 MMSCMD in three years. (The Hindu, July 12, 2005)

India – Pakistan trade has registered a 146 percent jump in April – November 2004. Total trade between the two countries stood at $380.79 million, up from $ 154.95 million in April – November 2003 – 04.

Pakistan's exports to India rose from $ 72 million to $155 million in the last financial year, registering a growth rate of 115%. The New Indian Express coverage of the trade equation shows the boost in trade during the course of composite dialogue.

On the pipeline project as reported in both the NPS, the left parties will not to the line of UPA government when Dr. Singh signalled that the project was fraught with difficulties. This is an acid test for the UPA government or it renege on the independent foreign policy. (The Hindu, June 24, 2005)

The pipeline is fraught with difficulties as it needs an international consortium banker to underwrite this project and make it viable. The union petroleum minister did not want the project to be abandoned and quipped that the project is not grounded as to obtain nuclear technology and fuel from the US for power generation. But, The New Indian Express report had Aiyar's acerbic attack on the UPA government that PM had slowly pulled the rug under the feet, of a project which was sincerely been carried out for the part 18 years. The report also stated that India's nuclear deal with the US was not not "quid pro quo" to abandon the $7.4 billion Iran – Pakistan – India gas pipeline.

In the wake of controversy triggered by PM Dr. Singh on the risks involved Pakistan will go ahead with the project, by an overland gas pipeline from Iran or Turmenistan, undersea gas pipeline from Qatar and import LNG. On July 8 Pakistan and Iran signed a memorandum of understanding (MOU) to carry forward the talks about the multi- billion dollar from Iran – Pakistan – India gas pipeline.

In sharp contrast to the rest of J & K which eagerly awaits the opening of a shorter trading route and softening of borders with the PoK, this part of the state desires the early re-opening of historic trade routes with the Chinese – occupied territory these routes traditionally kept these remote areas in contact with the outside world for several centuries and what enthuses the Ladkis is the recent assurance of PM Manmohan Singh that he would take up the re-opening of the Denkhok – Kailash Manasarovar road with the Chinese government the Hindu coverage of the report gives enough background details to the bureaucrats responsible for speedy redressal of trade in these areas.

The economic co-ordination committee presided over by PM Shakat Aziz has lifted the four year ban on Sugar import as a part of the strategy through the wagh route which was closed after 1965 war.

The New Indian Express, New Delhi seems unwilling to enter into an agreement with Iran on the long delayed $7.4 billion Iran – Pakistan – India gas pipeline until its security. Concerns are addressed. (August 7, 2005) Iran wants the project structure to be in place by December end and implementation mechanism and project financing model by April next year so as to begin work on the pipeline. And the next day the The New Indian Express headline read "India my join Iran, Pak to build pipeline". But the Hindu emphasized the role of Iran willing to go ahead with pipeline project with the euphoria over the project ceased to exist especially after the US showed flexibility over. Pipeline to the nuclear question the US assistant secretry of state Christina rocca video conferencing session with a group of Pakistani journalists on investments in oil and gas sector in Iran received a severe backlash from the US for Iran had violated its obligations under (NIT). The New Indian Express absolved the report on the US stance on investments in the Iranian oil and gas sector, which would attract sanctions.

It has been found that fresh fruits, carports, salty tea, sufferon, 'bhabe' beans, basmati rice, hearbs such as dhania and even spices such as tea ginger and garlic can be exported. Raw material such as willow and saffron would reach the Punjab markets in Lahore and Rawalpidi, while goods such as rock salt, raison, apricat area other dry fruit would come to the state from the neighbouring Punjab province. (The Hindu, September 5, 2005)

The New Indian Express coverage of Pak commitments on Iran – Pak – India, gas pipeline has received impetus from Iranian secretary National

Security Council Ali Carijani Pakistan supported efforts to resolve the issue of Iranian nuclear programme through negogiation and opposed the use of force against the gulf nation. Pakistan was against nuclear proliferation but at the same asserted that every country has the right of peaceful use of nuclear energy in accordance with (IAEA) rules and regulations. Pakistan wanted that Iran – US nuclear difference should be resolved peacefully with the efforts of the European union troika. (The New Indian Express, September 8, 2005)

The New Indian Express reported that talks were last held in December 2003, to resume talks. Both sides agreed on point-to-point flights and over lights facilities only Indian airlines and Pakistan international airlines were allowed to operate between the two countries.

The New Indian Express, forging an open sky policy with India and endeavouring to liberalise its Visa regime for businessmen and other communities at the FICCI interaction which would eventually fortify commitment to the January one, 2006 deadline for (SAFTA) would also remove restrictions on stringent tariff regime. The Hindu, denoted statistically in the business page of Pakistan exports to India in the period April – June had gone up by 150%. In the same period, India's exports to Pakistan had gone up by 8%.

The Indian Minister conceded that South Asia had not been able to enjoy the fruits of regionalization while individual countries like India were trying to take advantage of globalisation.

The first consignment of onion arrived from Pakistan and the cabinet secretary reviewed the situation with the senior officials of the Department of consumer affairs, food and agiculture. This has been reportedly more vicacious headlines in the Hindu with The New Indian Express failing to forge the reality. The keenness in reporting facts to liquidfy the on-going conflict is a great leap for the govt. of Pakistan and India. (The Hindu, October 26, 2005)

Surveying the whole spectrum of economic areas in which the countries could co-operate, India was ready to look at non-tariff barriers within the ambit of joint study group. The Pakistan government and the business have in the recent past complained about the adverse impact of 'non-tarrif' barriers on trade with India. In response to pleas from India for the conferment of MFN status accorded to Pakistan by India unilaterally, Islamabad has argued that despite the MFN status its trade with India has been negative due to non tarrif barriers. For instance, he said, India could look at importing power from Pakistan, if the iatter was surplus in it, while Pakistan could export cotton yarn, textile fabrics, surgical instruments, sports goods, electric fans and water coolers to India.

The New Indian Express, shipping officials of India and Pakistan agreed to amende the protocol permitting shipping companies of the two countries to transport cargo to any third country, allow third country vessels to paid up cargo from their ports. The agreement also helped to repeal the articles of Pak – India shipping protocol 1975 to make it up to date with the current needs of regional and international markets.

India and Pakistan agreed to begin construction of the over $ 7 billion Iran – Pakistan – India gas pipeline by mid 2007 so that the first gas would flow by the end of 2010. India would draw 60 mllion standard cubic in per day from the over 2,100 km pipeline project and ramp it upto 90 mm second in the next 2 – 3 years. While Pakistan would start with 30 mm screened and double its off take by 2013.

The India – Pakistan joint study group to promote trade and commerce worked out a road map to finalise a 'mutual recognition agreement' merit. (The Hindu, March 30, 2006) Both sides agreed to form two working groups on standards and conformance, sanitary and phyto – sanitary within the subgroups on non-tariff barriers (NTBs). The MRA could pave the way for enhanced trade. Pakistan has been complaining of its negative trade balance with India despite the latter gaining the MFN status to the former. Pakistan has argued that it is not able to enhance it exports to India due to a number of NTBs.

If the sub-group on customs co-operation and trade facilitation measures there was concensus on measures to explore the possibility of a bilateral arrangement on customs co-operation, to exchange information on the certificates of the origin, import and export declaration, customs laws and procedures, valuation, trade statistics, to encourage exchange of information electronically between the customs of two countries, and to identify areas of mutual technical assistance and capacity building. (The Hindu, April 8, 2006)

India and Pakistan agreed on a number of proposals at the end of third round of composite dialogue. A joint statement welcomed the ratification of the south asian free trade agreement (SAFTA) by all (SAARC) member countries. With the operatisation of SAFTA from July 1, over 4,000 commodities would be open for trade compared to less than 1,000 under the India positive list maintained by Pakistan. A new shipping agreement would be signed in the near future. Talks on air services agreement would be concluded expeditiously. The existing deal was signed before the era of private air lines.

The joint registration on Basmati rice, IT-enabled medical services, optical fibre, liberalization of the visa regime, mutual co-operation in capital markets has been conveyed by the securities and exchange commission facilitate trade including export cargo of Afghanistan.

The New Indian Express reported that Pakistan foreign minister Kurshed M. Kasuri said that Pakistan has no plans to abandon the Iran – Pakistan – India gas pipeline project despite strong objections from the US. Composite dialogue was moving in the right direction. India demanded "practical pragmatic approach" for resolution of issues.

Pakistan had taken the position that full fledged trade relations to India via wagh border were not feasible, pending resolution of the Kashmir issue.

The New Indian Express also reported the US has offered funding and security guarantees for $3 billion Turkmenistan – Afghanistan – Pakistan (TAP) gas pipeline if Islamabad abandoned the IPI project. (April 22, 2006)

Pakistan maintains that it is still weighing options to chose among IPI, TAP and a pipeline from Qatar, but no discussion has been taken so far.

The meeting between deera, Amarnath Khan Jadoon of Pakistan, Kazam Vazori of Iran attending a three day international energy forum had agreed to go ahead with the pipeline proposal despite the Iranian nuclear controversy.

Under the SAFTA agreement signed by the seven South Asian countries in January 2004, Pakistan negogiated a 'sensitive list' that would apply to India, but in explicably has now ordered that trade would be governed by the existing bilateral arrangements. (The Hindu, July 31, 2006) Under SRO No. 695(1) 2006 dated July 1, regarding tariff concessions for SAARC, goods could be imported into Pakistan under the agreed SAFTA tariff concessions. SAFTA operates on the basis of agreed sensitive lists. SAFTA has little operational meaning if member (countries do not honour their commitments in letter and in spirit.)

Coverage of Human Rights Issue

There were 47 stories in The Hindu and thirty five stories in The New Indian Express.

The Children were not carrying torches, as is the norm, hence they were mistaken as militants, challenged and fired at by troops at the ambush point. The National human rights commissions has asked the defense ministry to send reports after taking suo moto congnisance of media reports. The report also stated that counter - insurgency measures should not undermine democratic values, violate human rights, subvert the rule of law or kill civil liberties.

The New Indian Express and the Hindu has reported that the army assured all help to Kashmiri militants ready to shown the path of violence but warned of an iron first to deal with foreign ultracs operating in J & K. (June 10, 2005)

The hard line faction of APHC led by Syed Ali Geelani, the militant outfit Alumar Mujahedeen, M Mufti Mohammed Sayeed, Opposition national conference Omar Abdullah, CPI (M) state general secretary M.Y. Tarigani, Hizbul – Mujaheedeen Supreme suáeme commander Salahuddin, People conference chairman Sajjad Lone, separatist leader Javed Ahmed mir who heads the JKLF all condemned the Pulwara Act. (The Hindu, June 12, 2005)

APHL chairman syed Ali Shah Geelani, Shabir Shah were detained today at different places to maintain law and order as the situation in the town was surcharged following the blast which left its people dead, the The New Indian Express reported.

The Pulwama blast was condemned by Janata party president Subramaniam Swami and urged the centre to send Air Force planes to bomb the 17 known camps in PoK (The Hindu, June 15, 2005). Cross - border retailitary action was permitted under united national resolution.

Despite the Indian governments offer to release five members of a Pakistani family imprisoned for visiting Taj Mahal without proper Visa, Pakistan has failed to formally confirm their nationality as required under relevant laws of the two countries for setting them free. Officials at the helm of affairs in the ministries of foreign affairs and interior are unmoved by the miseries of the ill fated family despite the passage of several months. The New Indian Express report has made the issue more relevant to be taken up by the other members by clearly stating the names of family members.

A dedicated band of believers in Indo - Pak friendship including eminent journalists Kuldep Nayar, Vinod Mehta, Actor Nandita das, and politicians like former union minister Sukhdev Singh Dhindsa and other peaniks started from historic Jallian Wala Bagh after paying victims of partition arrived at the wagh border (The New Indian Express, August 16, 2005). There was also heavy weight delegation from Pakistan comprising human rights violation. Asma schangir, and members of Pakistan National assembly Itizaz Hussain, RSI Aziz Ullah Khan, and chowdhry Manzoorf Ahmed. But reports of the nature went unrepoprted in the Hindu which shows the spirit of bonhomic in spite of the constant bickering among nations.

Mr. Singh, a resident of the border village of Bikhiwind, went missing in August 1990, apparently when he inadevertently strayed across the border with Pakistan. Mr. Singh was mistaken for research and analysis was agent

(RAW) and taken into custody for allegedly masterminding a series of bomb blast in Lahore (The New Indian Express, August 22, 2005). Islamabad may consider any clemency appeal made by the relatives of Sarabjit Singh. When a group of members of Parliament met Prime Minster Natwar Singh, the PM assured the delegation that he would speak to Pakistan President Pervez Musharaff.

Moving beyond terrorism and drug trafficking, Indian government discussed the prisoner's issue (The New Indian Express, August 7, 2005). There were 1,348 Indians in Pakistani jails, - 923 civilians, 371 fishermen, and 54 prisoners of war. This year, Pakistan granted access to Indian prisoners in January, February, June and July.

The JKLF leader criticized the government that Mohammed Afazl who facing death sentence in the parliament attack case was innocent and needs to be acquitted (The Hindu, August 28, 2005). The new Indian express expressed that when Indian High Commissioner to Pakistan Shivashankar menon spoke over phone to Mushahad Hussain Sayeed, Secretary General of PML's readiness to release the prisoners. He however complained to ruling party leader that Pakistanis foreign office was not responding to the Indian offer of realising Pakistani prisoners.

Youth in jail despite POTA panel advice, tells as of the status quo of courts and denial redressal when other bodies feel that the prisioner can be freed with impunity. When there is no incrementing evidence against, those languishing in jails, the court has to implement its decision faster in the matter of release of prisoners. Sheik Moraj Hussain, 25 years old Kashmiri youth continues to languish in the meerut jail more than three months after the central review committee (No.1) on POTA (prevention of Terrorism act) recommended the withdrawal of POTA. Charges against him and asked the UP government to issue appropriate directions to the public prosecutor. The POTA review committee, chaired by justice P.N. Nag held that it was prima facie case against Aizaz Hussain Jan and Sajjad Hussain Jan bat there was no prime facie lase against sheirkh miraj hussan. (The Hindu, August 24, 2005)

The review committee in its order detail May 5, 2005 instructed the public prosecutor to file an application for the withdrawal under section 321 of the criminal procedure without delay and asked the special court to dispose of the application as early as possible. (The Hindu, August 24, 2005)

The POTA review committee asked the UP Government to issue appropriate orders to the public prosecutor to comply with the order of the review committee. The public prosecution has not filed an application for the withdrawal of charges against Miraj Hussain. Such stories failed to surface in the new Indian Express.

In the Sarabjit singh's case senior officials admitted that the tremendous pressure being mounted by television channels had forced the Indian government into raising the issue with Islamabad again and again. The Indian high commissioner in Islamabad show Shankar menon had taken up the matter with Pakistan foreign secretary Riaz Mohammed Khan for the Second consecutive day (The Hindu, August 25, 2005). Though India has not publicy requested that Sarabjit Singh had not granted claimency, the suggestion that things move in a positive direction reported the Hindu.

India denied the proposal of exchange of prisoners for the release of Sarabjit sentenced to death in Pakistan for his alleged involvement in bomb blasts in 1990.

Pakistan should first seek clemenly for Kashmiri youth Mohammed Afzal Guru before India seeks the release of Sarabjit Singh, whose death has been upheld by Pakistani supreme court for his involvement in bomb blasts in Pakistan, the chief of United Jihad council Syed Selahuddin. (The Hindu, August 29, 2005)

India and Pakistan do not inform each other when citizens of their countries are caught on different charges (The Hindu, August 28, 2005). Under the current practice information is provided only in respect of those detainees who have completed their prison terms. In December last the foreign secretaries of the two sides had agreed to provide consular access to all prisoners irrespective of their status but the understanding is not being honoured.

Conularr access is the fast stage, which enabled the mission officials to establish contact with the prisoners and establish his/her identity. After taking a photograh of the prisoners, the officials seek details from the detainee that would enable them to establish identity.

Under the Pakistan law Mr. Singh has been convicted by courts at three different levels including the Supreme court on charges of murder and terrorism.

Though the apex court held his death sentence, he could file review petition. If the apex court decides not to entertain this petition, Mr. Singh would file a mercy petition with Pakistan president. Under article 45 of the Pakistan constitution the president has powers to commit any punishment awarded by any court or grant pardon (The Hindu, August 30, 2005). The Hindu gave a detailed coverage of the consular access but never disclosed anything on the blind FIR filed.

While the The New Indian Express resorted to define Sarabjit Singh by magnifying the controversial blind FIR filed before the magistrate in 1990, at

Indo-Pak border near Kasur by Pakistani security officials nine days later as 'Manjit Singh' (August 30, 2005), the Hindu did not emerge with such story. The controversy gained momentum and neddle of suspicion pointed towards Pakistani security officials as soon as slhangity wrote in an article cited "Sarabjit suffers for Manjit" in local daily dawn. He was awarded death penalty by the anti terrorist court in 1991 based on the original confession he had made before magistrate. The case highlighted the need for India and Pakistan to do away with capital punishment and agree to a protocol to release each others nationals held by two nations. The investigative nature of The New Indian Express emnates. The New Indian Express further adds onto say It would be too much to expect legal reprieve for sarabjit in a country that had hanged Zulfikhar Ali Bhutto, a former head of the department (August 28, 2005). Diplomatic straight jacket will not offer an easy way out for either Musharaff or Singh. Only statemenship backed by wise third party counsel can stop the fuse from blowing.

The identity of Sarabjit has come to matter little in the murky world of international explonage in which there are no sinners and saints No government owns up an undercover spy or a cross border terrorism. To the anti - terrorist court in Pakistan, Sarabjir Singh isManjir Singh. No one would really know whether he was spy or a victim unless he lives to tell his own story.

The Sarabjit Singh episode provides the government and the people of the two countries an opportunity to pondeor over the price that the two sides have been paying for their deep mutual districts. Many of them are not spies, cross border terrorist Raw or ISI agents. Fishermen straying into one another is border is a common occurrence.

Many, overstaying their welcome in the host country are detained, interned on mere suspicion of spying. That the case of Sarabjit Singh came to public light after 15 long years, that too following the persistent efforts of Canadian human rights group is an eye opener (The New Indian Express, August 28, 2005). That the independent media in both countries had no knowledge of Sarabjit Singh long travail is equally troubling.

Daljit Kaur, said that she would go to Delhi again to urge former PM A.B. Vajpayee to use his rapport with Pakistan government for the cause of saving Sarabjit's life. She would also meet BSP president L.K. Advani in Delhi to build pressure on the Union government to take more steps for her brother's release. (The New Indian Express, August 31, 2005)

After consular access and other enquiries India conveyed to Pakistan, that Sarabjit sentenced to death for his alleged involvement in the Lahore bomb blasts in 1990, is an Indian national. The new Indian Express has another sapnner on the main story to explicate the criminal of the charge stating that quotes of one of the main witnesses in the Lahore bombing as saying he was not sure whether Sarabjit was involved.

Terming the attack on parliament as an unparalled assault on the Supreme seat of democracy, the court had said that there was clinching evidence against Afsal regarding nexus with the Slain terrorists who carried out the terrorist act of diabolical nature (The New Indian Express, September 6, 2005). Though the apex court had absolved Geelani, it had observed that there was a needle of suspicion on him regarding his role in the diabolical act of attacking the supreme seat of democracy but there was no direct evidence to convict him in the case(The New Indian Express, September 6, 2005). Afzal filed a petition seeking review of the August 4 judge ment of the apex court confirming the verdict of the trial court and the Delhi High Court awarding death penalty for the December 13, 2001, attack on parliament (The New Indian Express, September 6, 2005).

The New Indian Express, The Hindu reported that, Amid emotional scenes, India and Pakistan scripted history by repatriating 583 prisoners, the largest mutual exchange during peace time. Following simulataneous repartriation authorities detained the released prisoners for questioning for couple of hours. Relatives were then summoned to identity the released person before allowing him to walk free. It was day of major disappointment for many others, especially the families of 54 pow who were believed to be held in various pakistan's jails since the 1971 war one realizing that their relatives were not among the repatriates their distrakght families were joined by others in an imprompted demonstration (The Hindu, September 13, 2005).

Pakistan ruled out swapping sarabjit singh sentenced to death for alleged spying and bomb blasts, with some of the Pakistani prisoners housed in Indian jails saying that it had no spies in India. Pakistan also procliamed that all the 587 prisoners released by both the countries at the wagh border were civilians and not security prisoners.

Detailed and elaborate coverage of the supreme court dismissing apolice petition seeking a review of the judgement upholding the acquittal of Delhi university college lecturer S.A.R. Geelani and Navjjot Sandhu alias Afsan Guru in the Parliament attack case. A bench consisting of Justice K.G. balakrishnan, and Justice P.P. Naolekar detained to interfere with the August 4 judgment by a bench comprising justice P.V. Reddi and Justice Nokekor. The trial court on December 18, 2002, awarded the death penathy to Afsal, Shukat, and Mr. Geelani while sentencing Ms. Guru to five year imprisonment. On appeal, the High Court on October 29, 2003 upheld the death penalty given to

Afzal and Shakat but dismissed both Mr. Geelani and Ms. Guru. While Afzal and Shakat filed appeals in the apex court against the death sentence, the police appealed against the acquittal of the other two. The apex court acquitted Shakat of the charge of involvement in the conspiracy but held him guilty under sec. 123 of the Indian panel code for concealing knowledge of the plot (The Hindu, September 23, 2005). The apex court did not find any reason to interfere with the High court order acquitting Mr. Geelani and Ms. Guru.

The agreement between the Indian coast guard and Pakistan maritime security agency in setting up a hotline to miligate the woes of fishermen arrested for unintentionally transgressing the maritime boundary of the other country, will only partially tackle the problem reports in The Hindu (October 5, 2005).

A large number of fishermen, mainly from India, who are attracted by the catch on the other side, are jailed for long spells. The maritime boundary is national and positioning of markers is impossible on the high seas. The fishermen, who cannot afford costly direction finding equipment, stray into the maritime zone of other country. At the time of arrest, they do not understand the gravity of the crime.

A buffer extending upto five milies into the maritime zone of both countries, where common fishing is allowed and flag meeting abroad ships on the Indo Sri Lanka pattern will obrate arrests.

The hotline would enable informal repatriation" from the other side. Two coast guard stations near the Pakistani coast could send vassals to escort back arrested Indian fishermen instead of Pakistani agency handing them over to the police. More Indian fishermen commit boundary infringements because the sea on the Pakistani side has more maritime life.

The decision followed the agreement between India and Pakistan as a part of the ongoing composite dialogue process. It was agreed to provide consular access to all persons within three months of arrest and release of prisoners immediately after completion of sentence and nationality to release all fishermen and civilian prisioners who have completed their sentence and whose nationality has been confirmed. (The Hindu, November 10, 2005)

The New Indian Express, Rajya Sabha MP Jaya Bachen has lashed out at Pakistan for denying human rights to residents of (PoK) and warned against attempts to misinterpret the right of self determination to undermine the territorial integrity of the state (The New Indian Express, November 10, 2005). Pakistan should stop pretending to be protector of human rights in J & K while denying such rights in areas of state occupied by it.

The New Indian Express, the Handwara killings echoed at the round table conference on Kashmir being chaired by PM Manmohan Singh. The enquiry set up by the army are non-transparent and there his been no result of any magistrial enquiry constituted by the state government since last four years.

The family of Indian prisoners Sarabjit singh whose review petition against his death sentence was rejected by the Pakistan supreme court has threatened to commit suicide if the government failed to have him repatriated within a week Before takingany extreme step the family would sit on a hunger strike.

India and Pakistan agreed to expedite disposal of pending Interpol references in each others country which included the under world don Dawood Ibrahim. India has sought Pakistan's assistance to hand over about 100 people wanted by the CBI while Islamabad claimed that 70 of its wanted people were in India. (The New Indian Express, March 23, 2006)

The release of the prisoners is in pursuance of the understanding reached between India and Pakistan during the recent Home secretary level talks. India repatriated 38 Pakistani civilian prisoners, while Pakistan released 19 Indian detenus at this border check post.

Coverage of New Stores on Different Political Parties and Their Notion of Peace

During the period of study these were serves stories in The New Indian Express and nine in The Hindu.

BJP the major political party severely criticised the Hurriyat leaders visit to Pakistan without passports would help the terrorist to more across. The RSS had also criticized the BJP for allowing the Hurriyat leaders to Pakistan without Indian passports which will later pave for the movement of terrorists across the nation. The Hurriyat leaders did not represent the whole of J & K did prominently figure when president Musaharaff did accuse of the BJP of making such statements.

The Hindu reports the paradigm shift in India - Pakistan ties, with the joint statement issued by India and Pakistan has evoked an all - round welcome from across the political spectrum with congress lauding the government for having the confidence to push through the CBMS. The BJP party president L.K. Advani also welcomed the move as the whole process which was initiated by the previous NDA govt. and the joint statement is moving forward. The joint statement of January 2004 had stated that Pakistani soil would not be allowed to used for anti-India terrorist activities.

The CPI (M) general secretary Prakash Karat said that the party welcomed the outcome of the talks stressing more on the Siachen dispute.

The CPI secretary D. Raja, it was good that leaders solve problems by strengthening CBMS, diversified people-to-people and economic co-operation. The congress spokesman, Anand Sharma, the party had consistently maintained the dialogue should continue irrespective any situation that may prevail in the society.

The New Indian Express reports that district was the main issue that hampered the ties of both nations.

The New Indian Express and the Hindu reported the former PM Bhutto, it would be never meaningful if democracy was restored in her country and elected leaders represented it in the dialogue process. She favoured opening of routes between two punjabs to facilitate people-to-people contact. Cricket matches and opening up of more travel routes were helping the process of normlisation of relations between the two countries. (April 2, 2005)

The New Indian Express reports pays were attention to the arrival of ministers, and like from Pakistan who do willingly promote the peace process.

The Hindu the delegation was hosted by none other Lalu Prasad Yadav then Bihari warmly greeting them a lunch on provided for them. The former PM of Pakistan PML leader Shakat Hussain even went on to say that even if Lalu lost in Bihar, he can very well context from Pakistan. (April 2, 2005)

The Hindu, Mufti Mohammed Sayeed has welcomed President Musharaff latest proposal of maximum self - governance to resolve the Kashmir issue. Geelani leaders of the Hardline Hurriyat he decided the fate of people is decided forever by plebiscite, DFP leader Shabir Shah, that he would organize debates for the propose in all the 14 districts from May 25, 2005 to enlist the opinion irrespective of their ideology and party affiliation. (The Hindu, May 22, 2005)

The Hindu coverage of thousands throng the festival of the Buwani mata in the valley, shows for the last few years it has become permanent future to receive thousands of Kashmiri pandits. Though pandits were assured of their rehabilitation, they feel that it should happen with the consent of the majority community and not by settling in the government constructed cluster (The Hindu, June 17, 2005). The Hindu coverage of the CM Mufti mohammed sayeed asking the gun weeding youth of Kashmir to see writing on the wall and give up arms is a seminal message to adopt a holistic approach to the on going peace process and eventually wriggle out of the dragnet. Youth to work in tandem with the peace process is to foster the strength of the divided minds. (July 10, 2005)

The first ever intra Kashmir dialogue went unreported in The New Indian Express. The delegates made an impassioned appeal to all the different groups including Radha Kumar the Delhi policy group, Imitiaz mir layer from doda, Syed Afshana, teacher at Kashmir university, siddique wahid, head of gulab singl chair at Jammu university rights, activist blaraj puri, ershad mehmood of the institute of policy studies Islamabad, all alleged for reconciliation. To people like Neazi, Chairman of the coalition of civil societies, peace was a comprehensive ideology. (The Hindu, July 31, 2005)

The dialogue was jointly organized by the council for dialogue and reconciliation (CDR), Dlehi policy group (DPG) and forum of regional voices (FRV). The delegates asked the governments to cover all citizens of the former state, including Gilgit - Baltisan and urged to have Gilgit - Baltisan the same administrative status as other parts of the former state. It asked militant groups operating in Kashmir and the government of India and Pakistan to enter into a ceasefire. It urged India and Paskistan to reopen other routes linkng Jammu and Kashmir to the outside world. This is for the first time people from Northern areas have come to Kashmir. The The New Indian Express story had a reference to the strong protest registered by retired PoK chief justice Abdul Majid Malik against the Hurriyat leadership for not visiting Gilgit and Baltisan during their recent visit across LoC. The New Indian Express News story also that Hurriyat leaders expressed resentment over the recent statement of PoK PM Sikkander Hyat Khan in which he had said that moderate faction was not representative of all sections of people.

Subramaniam Swamy opposed the current peace talks with Pakistan saying a plan to withdraw from Siachen, and thereafter Sir Creek, was in the offing in the name of CBMS. The army which was resisting the plan was being pressured to accept the withdrawal of the jawans from the Siachen glacier. Far from being of "zero" strategic value, control over the Siachen heights enabled army to monitor the infiltration of terrorist. The cost saved in with drawing would be offset by the increased fighting of the ISI - led insurgency. Dr. Swamy also opposed joint survey by both sides in Sir Creek, saying it should be undertaken only when the course of the river that divides the area changed westwards again. (The Hindu, October 29, 2005)

The New Indian Express, Omar Abdullah, National conference leader who attended the pugwash roundtable conference on Kashmir, endorsed on the view of president Musharaff's proposal on joint management of J & K. without changing the sovereignty. If first involved devolution of maximum power to the state government on either side and then create a group with India, Pakistan and representatives of either side of Kashmir monitor it. (November 4, 2005)

The restoration of Kashmir's autonomy to the position,where union of India has jurisdiction only over foreign affairs, defence, currency. (The New Indian Express, March 15, 2006)

Coverage of Separatists Among Themselves

The New Indian Express had four reports where else The Hindu had six.

The New Indian Express reported that the united Jihad council chairman supreme commander of the Hizbul mujahedeen Syed Saladuddin had cleared to back up the dialogue process. The leaders stand always formulated the non implementations of the UN resolution which did not won the favour of the lot even among the separatist. Manwaiz offer of division along geography received severe rebuttal among the separatist elements who wanted the separation of the land on religions grounds. The Hindu has decidedly given a portion of this struggle to high light the point of difference even among the separatists wing. The separatists may come under one umbrella again in the valley as a council one - on - one between heavy weights syed ali shah geelani and Miswaiz Farooq is on the cards to bring the Hurriyat flock under one banner. Geelani who walked out of the amalgam in September 2003, has been maintaining that his faction was the real and purged Hurriyat. (May 5, 2005)

The New Indian Express reported the crucial executive council meeting of the Mirwaiz Omar Farooq Hurriyat Conference remained in conclusive, as the amalgam received an early set back when its former chairman maulana Abbas Ansari said that the people are having divergent views and they can never meet. Moderates had differences with hardliners led by Syed Ali Geelani, the former Hurrriyat Chairman as Geelani says talks with India are fatile and instead should be held with Pakistan. (May 10, 2005)

The Hindu reports that a day after Pakistan asked the All parties Hurriyat conference to get united Mirwaiz Umar Farooq offered to step down with both factions be disbanded and the erstwhile alliance of seven members be restored.

Mr. Geelani's faction had constituted a five member committee to talk with the other group on the unity issue. The new Indian express that the Hardline faction of Geelani suffered a setback ahead of the crucial meeting of the advisory council meeting to decide on the invitation to visit Pakistan as (JKPL) one its constituents would abstain to protect against the Hurriyat's inaction following the arrest of JKPL chairman shekh Abdul Aziz. The New Indian Express coverage of PWO Pakistan leader and his three associates were suspended from its advisory council, deepening issues among the separatists. The action against Geelani came in the wake of his associates was prompted by the fire brand leader asking them to play a leading role in the separatist struggle. (The Hindu, May 11, 2005)

The Hindu reported that the Jammu and Kashmir national front and a fraction of the people's conference alleged that the alliance was being dominated by the Tehreck - e - Hurriyat - e - Kashmir. Other parties were being side line, did not consult them before leaving for doda. Constituents not being taken into confidence while taking vital decision and fails to garner the support of the party.

The New Indian Express, the party leaders met at Raj bagh headquarters under the chairman ship of Ghulam Mohammed Khan supari and decided to snap relations with Geelani and pave the way for greater unity. The national front headed by Nayeem ahmad Khan joined the Hurriyat conference led by Nuz Amar Farooq, while Ghulam Mohammed Hubbi merged his faction of people conference with its parent organisationled by bilal lone. (jum 17, 2005)

But the Hindu report criticized Mr. Geelani the moderate faction of the Hurriyat conference at a seminar "is there any substitute to right of self - determination organized on the eve of Pakistan day (March 24, 2006). he also added that those who engaged in talks with New Delhi had violated the Hurriyat constitution which stressed the right to self determination in accordance with the UN resolution, there was no question of Surrender but we will fight till we achieve our goal.

Coverage between Centre and the State

During the period of study there were twenty stories in The New Indian Express and forty – five stories in The Hindu.

The New Indian Express (April 6, 2005) reports said that reports to the Union Home Ministry by central security Agency alleging short comings of the Jammu and Kashmir police while performing the supervisory role of anti - militancy operations within Srinagar city. There were instances wherein the local police has not responded to the intelligence winports from various sources.

The Hindu coverage of BJP president L.K. Advani the non-acceptance of Hurriyat as the sole representative of Jammu and Kashmir as the dialogue has to include the people of Ladakh. Jammu and the Pandit community which migrated from Kashmir valley. He blamed Jawaharlal Nehru for committing two historical blunders by giving separate status to the Jammu and Kashmir under article 370 and secondly, by taking the issue of the state to UN. (April 17, 2005)

The New Indian Express reported the sending of NSG bomb experts to Srinagar to tide over the situation.

The New Indian Express cited instaces wherein the infiltration which remained lull during the months of April has gained ascendancy in the month of May 2005. Defense ministry spokesperson also cited instances of infiltration of militants across theborder as launching pads and training camps are still functional. Their has been frequent moves to stop the bid of infiltration by endording the January 2004 statement of President Musharaff not to use his country soil to sponsor terrorism. India vehemently rejects the signing Nuclear non-proliferations treaty stating it is discriminatory in the present south asia context. (April 17, 2005)

The Hindu and The New Indian Express repeated that a castle force to be constituted to prepare a long term plan for the social and economic development of Jammu and Kashmir (April 22, 2005). The report further states the task force to Sarabjit a report within six months and the final report within one year.

The Mufti government made it amply clear in the legislative assembly the emerging situation in the state has closed the option of the game as a means to resolve problems and dialogue has taken a center stage. The violence as an option to press one's point of view has lost support all over the world was fast dawning upon those who used the gun in the state for furtherance of their agenda.

The task force submitted its interim report within six months outlining the strategy to improve infrastructure, tourism and the creation of employment opportunities in the state.

The state has taken unique role in restoring the property left behind in the state by people who migrated to Pakistan and assured them that they will not be disposed of their property.

The issue of former state subject and present day Pakistan resident reclaiming their lands is not that easy as the state law draws its constitutional sanction fom sec 6 of article 7 of the constitution (April 22, 2005). The constitution authorizes the state assembly to enact a law to grant Indian citizenship to permanent residents of the state, who after migration to Pakistan, return under a permit issued by the state authority. According to entry 17 in the seventh schedule of the constitution, citizenship is a union subject.

Article 11 makes the power of Parliament to exact laws on cititzenship on this subject absolute. Parliament passed the citizenship act in 1955, which is equally applicable to J & K. The act does not make any separate provision for theose persons who went to Pakistan in 1947. (The Hindu, April 24, 2005)

As the resiedient of the state became citizens of Pakistan, they ceased to be citizens of India and could be granted citizenship by the central government alone.

The New Indian Express though J & K Government promises migrant pandit safe shelter, the estates department has ordered that pandits be evicted from government accommodation. In 1990, when militancy erupted in the valley most of the pandits migrated to Jammu. The families who stayed back in the city were moved to metro hotel and then to government - owned Buddha shah flates. For security reasons. The estate Department calls it unauthorized occupation and asked the occupants to vacate the flats. (May 19, 2005)

The Hindu, the Jinnah and Kashmir Finance minister and congress MLA meet the joint administration of J & K and PoK by India and Pakistan by empowering the autonomous regions. These autonomous regimes will fulfill the aspirations of the respective assemblies (June 24, 2005). A conference of intellectuals an politicians from both sides would be created to discuss the future of the state without preconditions. The differing views of minister regarding administration of the multi ethnic, multi- cultured multi - lingual was reported.

The New Indian Express and the Hindu explained the possibility of two - page letter to Dr. Singh by Mr. Vajpayee regarding the avowed interests of Pakistan government objecting to the growing demand for trilateral talks, international guarantees for the settlement of the Kashmir issue and travel of Hurriyat leaders via Samnagar - Musafarabad bus to Pakistan without Indian passports. The Pulwara incident is slip out of the commitment it had made in the January 6, 2004 statement. (June 17, 2005)

The Hindu coverage of the one day Seminar on impact of turmoil on quality of life in Jammu and Kashmir organized by the J & K regional chapter of Indian Institute of public administration tells Mufti advocated self rule type of governance and the experiment of creating autonomous Hill development councils in Leh and Kargil. 'Self rule' or 'maximum autonomy' did even catch the imagination of many including CMs (June 26, 2005)

Gandhian and President of Akil Bhartiya Rachnatmak Samaj (AERS) also demanded that the dialogue is the only way out for solving Kashmir issue. Bharatiya Janta Party President L.K. Advani on the attack at Budhat Chowk in Srinagar lasted for 24 hours with intermittent firing from militants holed in the walls and described it as an act of desperation terming it as sneak attack" It is matter of concern for the entire country (July 23, 2005).

The New Indian Express, with the deadline for the transfer of power in Jammu and Kashmir, pressure was momented on Sonia Gandhi from CM sayeed not to replace him. The fragile peace process between India - Pakistan and the congress - PDP coalition would come to a stand still if the mufti is replaced. Mehbooba mufti also lobbied with the centre for her father continuation as the CM.

The New Indian Express, the union Home Minister Shivraj Patel during an international worleshop : Diaster risk mitigation : Potential of micro finance for Tsunami reovery proposed to give a free hand to newly set up national disaster management authority to change policies in relief operation. The NDWA was given statutory powers which the planning commission does not have.

The Home secretary V.K. Duggal accompanied senior security and home officials to review the security scenario following the killing of the minister of state for education Ghulam Nabi lone.

The New Indian Express title read that "Mufti may step down paving way for Azad" while the Hindu title read "plan for change of guard in J & K says Azad" (October 22, 2005).

The congress had its own dilemma in deciding what the change of guard in J & K would bring in especially after the October 8 earth quake. There has been speculation on whether the reins of the state administration would pass on to the congress as was agreed upon when it inked its power - sharing deal with PDP after the assembly elections 2002 (October 23, 2005, The Hindu). The congress refrain had been that it had not discussed the issue since relief and rehabilitation was its top priority. Also there was a feeling within the congress, that a will not anger well for the party to be seen wrangling at this juncture. Many prominent academics and representatives of civil society organization came out in support of the continuation of Mufti Mohammed Sayeed as J & K chief minister, where the signatories were of the view that "India's national interest would be best served by his continuance in office as CM so that he consolidate the forces of peace, democracy and development that have been set in motion".

The congress will take charge of the J & K coalition as CM Mufti sayeed will step down by the Nov. 2 deadline (October 23, 2005). The party is taking over the reins of administration after 30 years. In 1975, it handed over the power to Shekh Abdullah following an accord with Mrs. Indira Gandhi, then PM.

The New Indian Express, Opinion is divided on his 'healing touch' policy aimed at weaning youth from militancy observes find that Sayeed could not make much difference on the Human rights front as allegations of violations were the highest during the regime compared to the previous 12 years during the outbreak of militancy. Sayeed's reported reluctance to implement the wazir commission report on delimitation of assembly constituencies and reorganization of districts had annoyed the coalition partners whose member hail from Jammu.

Many people in the state trace the origin of the Kashmir problem to the regional conflict existing between Jammu and the valley. Political factors were at the root of the problem and it needs to be solved through the democratic and political means.

The problem started immediately after 1947 - 48 when monoarchy came to an end and a transition of power took place from a Jammu - based ruler to the new political elite of the valley. This transfer of power was far from smooth: 1953 an agitation started in Jammu directed against the valley's hegemony, even unnerving the first PM, Jawarharlal Nehru, who said "for the first time, I am worried about the future of the state" (The Hindu, October 30, 2005).

The change will satisfy the political aspirations of the people of Jammu, besides strengthening the secular identity of the region and making it a healthy link between the rest of the country.

Analyst believe that Mr. Azad will have to maintain a fine balance between Kashmir and New Delhi. It might be more forceful in advocating talks with militants / separatist or pursuing bigger issues such as opening of the srinagar / musaffarabad road was done by his predecessor. The editor of the mass circulated weekly chattan, Tahir Mohiddin said that it is not difficult for him as he belongs to the national party and Mufti is headings a regional party.

The national security Advisor M.K. Narayan along with chief of the army staff, Gen. J.J. Singh, Director of intelligence bureau ESC Narasimhan visted the state and apprised the situation along the Loc and infiltration bids, which had reportedly increased in the last two months. They were assured that the militants had only changed their tactics and were engaged in targeted activities.

Asked about the demand of RSS leaders for abrogating article 370, Vajpayee said he favoured this, scrapping Article 370, of the constitution that gives special status to J & K (The New Indian Express, July 8, 2006).

Patil congratulated the people of J & K and Mumbai for putting up a united face against the terror attacks which claimed 8 lives in J & K and 183 lives in Mumbai.

There was no apparent evidence of co-ordination as grenade was used in J & K and RDX probably in Mumbai.

H, APs Abdul Kalam unfolded his nine - point mission for the prosperity of J & K and advocated state - level movement to eliminate terrorism and setting up of an economic zone near the LoC (July 29, 2006).

Separatists Leaders and Centre

During the period of study there were forty four reports in The Hindu and Thirty - five in the New Indian Express.

The separatist leaders had two rounds of talks with the NDA govt, followed by meeting of leaders in Pakistan, PoK and the follow up talks with UPA govt. also has found prominance in the leading leaders. The separatist felt that people honoured the political approach than the military solution. The The New Indian Express highlighted the services of the congress leader saifuddin soz, layer Ashoka Ahan, Press Shankar Sha, bureaucriat Wajabt Habibullah who is close to 10 sampath as go between. The democratic factors forum chief shabir shah, PDP Mehbooba and NC chief omar Abdullah openly acknowledged the kind of talk undertaken by Merwaiz would find a solution.

The Kashmir committee that figured in reports failed to play a pre dominant role as the disputation within the union government on the mechanics of dialogue reflects larger langer divisions within the policy. Policy establishment on the ongoing talks with APHC.

Even Mufti showed reluctance to accept the union government's role in avoiding major political parties in the constituted committee.

The report both in the Hindu and the The New Indian Express of the visit of moderate faction Hurriyat leaders to Pakistan, PoK proudly claims formal inclusion of Kashmiris in the dialogue process for the resolution of Kashmir issue. They also promised that they would visit Ladakh and Jammu regions to take people into confidence. The Hurriyat will also make efforts to bring back Kashmir pandits whofied the valley in early 1990's.

The separatists the Hurriyat conference led by Mirwaiz under Farooq along with Abdul Ghani Bhat, Moulis Abbas Asnari and Bilal Gani lone will be meeting the president Mushrarff on April 17. But even before that they planned for scheduled talks with PM Dr. Singh before April 17. The centre had conveyed a word that they could meet him on before April 14 or 15 as they are available in Delhi on April 17. Geelani faction also could meet the Prime Minister (April 14, 2005, The New Indian Express).

The reports in the Hindu state the joint declaration by India and Pakistan to further the agenda of CBM has generated cautious optimism among the people of Kashmir. Militant organizations and the hard liners Separatist camp have reacted strongly to the development.

Calling him "kargil hero" four militants outfits Al-Wasihreen, save Kashmir movement, Al Arifeen and Ferzander - - - millat - termed the progress a sell out The head of united Jihad council and HM Supreme commander, Syed Saluddin were severely criticised in the wake of President Musaraff's visit to India. Mr. Geelani, the hardline faction leader was appreciated and Geelani termed the summit as highly frustrating, The New Indian Express and the Hindu.

The Hurriyat leaders apparently changed their mind after consultation with Pakistani establishment. The Hurriyat had adopted a similar approach at the time of the Agra summit in 2001.

The Hindu and The New Indian Express repute the Pakistan's radial shift in the Kashmir policy, had make Geelani to make the felt need of the day that the core issue between the two countries and out-of-box solution was unacceptable (April 21, 2005). The U.N. resolution should form the fundamentals of a solution. The Hindu reports the lathi charge teargas shlls resorted to disperse and - e- milad procession by DPM, a constituent of the Geelani led HC (April 23, 2005). But there were differences in thenumber of 70 separatists being held. The twice offer by the HM chief operational commander Gazi Mrs. Bahuddin through the Kashmir news agency that it would seriously consider any truce offer by New Delhi to put an end to 15 year old blood shed in Jammu and Kashmir brings hope more hope to the government which has been waiting for similar such proposals from both the militants (The Hindu, April 24, 2005). But such open and can did remarks were unheard of in the not too distant future. The bus service was only a ploy to divert the attention of the people. The Hurriyat was keen on entertaining the pandit community back to Kashmir and they feel the whole of Kashmir would be incomplete without it (April 26, 2005). This was announced during the meet of syed salim Geelani, in charge of public relations wing of the moderate faction of the Hurriyat led by merwaz Umar farooq.

Geelani expressed that conspiracy was hatched to kill him in order to stop him implement the UN resolution on Kashmir (The New Indian Express, May 3, 2005). The New Indian Express coverage of international Kashmir alliance (JKA) an amalgam of overseas Kashmir separatists outfits that the talks between separatist from J & K was credibility test for Pakistan which has always created impediments in such peace moves. In view of the long history of Pakistan abuse of the Kashmir case in general and the muslim sentiment in particular, your government shall cease to pass the credibility test (The New Indian Express, May 9, 2005).

The separatists people conference leader never shared the same solution as suggested by the moderate faction of the HC mirwaiz farooq, for he believed that ascertaining the wishes necessary for a permanent and lasting solution to the Kashmir imbroligo (The Hindu, May 23, 2005).

The Hindu and The New Indian Express (May 28, 2005) a high delegation of Hurriyat conference will visit Pakistan and PoK. As per the understanding the permit was not supposed to be for other parts of Pakistan. The visit of the Hurriyat beyond LoC was termed negative by the centre and would be contrary to the understanding reached between New Delhi and Islamabad. The Hindu the BJP party was very stiff of allowing the Hurriyat leaders travel to Pakistan outside PoK without passport and Visa.

The JKLF chairman Mr. malik was not optimistic with the movement of people across the border the united jihad council and supreme commander of the HM group syed salahuddin did not find the move of the government encouraging (The Hindu, May 27, 2006). Mufti Mohammed Sayeed opposed the move of HC beyond PoK. The moderate faction of HC took the cause more seriously than the rest of separalist leaders and acted. More decisively The New Indian Express quotes that Pakistan expected the Hurriyat in Islamabad when they visit the part of Kashmir under its control they were asked to fill in the travel documents when they enter Pakistani territory during their visit across LoC.

The centre also rejected the passport and travel permit of the DFP chief shabir Ahmed shah to Pakistan and PoK on the grounds that he had specified Kashmiri as his nationality on the application forms. The DFP delegation will not board the caravanof peace in protest against the centre's decision.

The Hurriyat, delegation leader Mirwarz Omar farooq that time has to move beyond the united nations assembly resolution body which has failed to implement them for 57 years. General Musharaff has aimed similar views asking people not to stick on to the earlier resolution but explore other possibilities especially the post 9/11 scenario. (The Hindu, June 9, 2005)

The Hurriyat also assured for negogiation as long as the exercise did not mean continuation of the status quo and conversion of LoC into a permanent border. The New Indian Express (June 12, 2005) expressed that mirwaiz umar farooq in organizing united states of Kashmir. The Hindu and the The New Indian Express that the week long visit of the Hurriyat faction to PoK and Pakistan has roped in reconciliatory measure during the course of their talks.

After having had a parley with the Pok and the Pok government, the moderate faction sought the call of the Indian goverhment to hold talks. During the second day of the people - to people contact programme in handwara toure of north Kashmir Morwaiz said that the Kashmiris had finally been accepted as the principal party to over 57 years dispute involving divided parts between India and Pakistan (The Hindu, July 10, 2005).

The New Indian Express that Hurriyat leaders are ready for talks with the centre as soon as PM Manmohan Singh, decides the dates (June 17, 2005). Senior leader of the conglomerate Abdul Geelai Bhatt denied that the Hurriyat visit to PoK and Pakistan were to ascertain the opinion of the people (July 4, 2005).

The moderate faction of the Hurriyat leader Mirwiz Umar farooq while addressing a symposium on "Kashmir, looking towards the future: propounded a new concept for resolving the Kashmir issue, one of the united states of Kashmir in which people could move freely.

Conversion of the LoC into a permanent border or statesquo was not acceptable shows the reluctance of the moderates to be more pro-India and not rewarding to India.

The Hurriyat moderate faction paid tributes to Martyr's of 1931 a day ahead observing everyyear on July 13. It was an July 13 in 1931 a number of Kashmiris were gunned down by Maharaja Hari Singh's police (The Hindu, July 13, 2005).

After nearly 16 years for the first time an inter active session with the Pandit community and the Hurriyat leaders began in Hurriyat headquarters in Raj Bagh the Hurriyat leaders stressed on the return of the migrants to their original homes and not security clusters built by the government. This reveals that more amicable solutions were on the way to resolve the difference. The pandit leaders rejected any offer of talks with the Hurriyat as the Hurriyat wanted to establish secular credentials world over. Though the pandits yearned to return to the home land they were seen as outsides and never welcomed by the terrorist organization, J & K government.

The BJP led NDA government had fixed two round of talks but the UPA did neglected with the PM's call for dialogue in his I - day speech.

The abrupt call for dialogue without a date being fixed has sent wrong signals among all separatists including Malibr Abbas Ansari, DFP President Shabir Ahmed Shah, Hardliner Syed Ali Geelani.

Mr. Jaiswal, the union minister of state for home on his two day visit to srinagar has expressed the desire to resine talks if Hurriyat came forward. At aninteractive session, few people could have imagined that a mainstream party leader in Kashmir would draw cheers from the audience when sharing the dais with for midable separatist leader on the question of what could be the future of the state. Mr. Abdullah threw a challenge that if anyone from the separatist camp convinced him of a better solution in Kashmir other than autonomy he would willingly join their ranks. Mr. Malik reiterated the stand of complete independence from both India and Pakistan.

UN government's special representative W.N. Vohra apprised PM Dr. Singh on militancy - related and political developments in the state. Hurriyat's desire to hold talks with centre figured in the discussions. The new Indian Express observed every cue of the centre with regard to the talks the centre announced for the Hurriyat to hold talks especially after or delegation of the conglomerate returned from their trip to Pakistan.

At an extra ordinary meeting, the Hurriyat executive, the leaders discussed the details of recent meeting between Hurriyat chairman Mirwaiz Omar Farooq and centre's special emissary wajahat Habobullah (The Hindu, August 30, 2005). Sources close to the Hurriyat said that Mr. Habullah had sought to for convenient dates for a possible meeting between PM and Hurriyat leader. The Hurriyat wants to resume talks with centre but if only an invitation is extended from the PMO's office. Though the leader of the moderate faction of Hurriyat conference was invited for talks, no formal letter by way of invitation has been sent to the Hurriyat leadership (The Hindu, September 1, 2005). Nor there has been any fixed agenda as reported in the Hindu and it is learnt that whereas the internal security bureaucracy was unexcited about any dialogue with the separatist leaders, the decision was handled at the political level. The moderate faction of the APHC led by Morwaiz Umar Farooq formally accepted the invitation extended by PM Manmohan Singh for talks with the government (The Hindu, September 2, 2005). The allegations on DFP leader shabir Ahmed Shah denied police allegations that he was involved in a hawala case (The Hindu, September 2, 2005).

On the eve of the talks with APHC mirwaz said the dialogue process had come a full circle (The Hindu, September 5, 2005). First wehad two rounds of parleys with NDA, then with the leadership of Pakistan and PoK and now we are holding talks with the UPA government. But The New Indian Express where the Hurriyat wouldurge the PM to take four steps to create confidence and demonstrate to the Kashmiris that a ground level change talking place. He would seek a reduction in the paramilitary and armed forces in the state, the issue of human rights violation, ask for dilution of the special powers given to the armed forces and urge the government to release prisoners languishing in jails. Geelani's strong disapproval of the talks with PM Manmohan Singh got widely reflected in the Hindu. Marvaiz does not represent the freedom loving people of Kashmir has been the constant strain from the hardline separatists. Mr. Geelani did not spare Pakistan either that they have shifted from the earlier stand on Kashmir. The on going struggle is not for status quo, converting the LoC into IB or the return of 'peace and nomalcy' but for the righteous cause of the right to self - determination (The Hindu, September 6, 2005) JKLF chief Mohammed Yasim Malik, DFP Shabir Shah did not turn up for the conference.

The new Indian Express coverage of following up on round one of talks with PM Dr. Singh and Hurriyat leaders, the centre had asked the J & K government to review cases of those detained under the (PSA), the now defunett (POTA). However the union Home secretary U.K. Duggals letter to the state chief secretary to this effect came the day the J & K state government booked Dukhtarn-i-millat (daughter of Islamic nation) Chief Asiya Andrabi, eight of her party members and driven under th PSA. All nine women were arrested for alleged hooliganism and harassment of women, under what they have called moral clean up campaign. Besides allegedly motivating youths to join Militant ranks. Mirwaiz told express "It was just hours after the PM detainees will be reviewed. Why did the government choose this moment? (September 8, 2005)

Mirwaiz team numbers speculated that it was designed undercut the Huyrriyat moderates. Mufti government had admitted that 560 persons were held under PSA in a report tabled in the assembly two years ago. The home ministry will recommend cases to the screening committee totake a final decision to grant relief to political prisoners and those not suspected to be involded in terrorism.

A move for triparitate talks mooted

Both the Hindu and the New Indian Express expressed their desire that Hurriyat wanted the Kashmiri leaders to be associated with the talks which has not happened as yet but the fact that both Dr. Singh and Gen. Musharaff are talking to them shows that Kashmiris are being indirectly associated with the dialogue (September 18, 2005). He kept the amalgam's view point before the Pakistan president while terming the meeting as a Hurriyat effort of having a triangular dialogue on Kashmir. Simultaneously with India and Paskitan. This emerged in their third interaction in five months, Hurriyat chairman Mirwaiz umar farooq met Pakistan president Pervez Musharaff here and extended full support to th India - Pakistan dialogue process but expressed reget onver the slow pace of the peace process (September 18, 2005). The Hindu Mirwaiz Umar Farooq chose the platform of organization (OIC) of Islamic conference to demand the list of CBMS which were demilitarization of Kashmir, repeat of PSA and AFSPA laws, dismantling of bunkers from villages and towns and tangible action regarding disappeared persons. The two day conference, heart to theart being organized by the panthers party, brough leaders and intellectuals from PoK and Jammu and Kashmir together on one platform for the first time. The PoK delegation was led by senior leader sardar Abdul Quayyam Khan After the opening remarks by the panthers party chief bhim singh, Dr. Abdullah said Pakistan conferred him as its enemy number one."

Dr. Abdullah expressed the hope that the conference would arrive at a solution and save "the best possible solution in my view is the safe borders between two parts of the state without altering the status quo. The part in

India will remain with India and that with Pakistan will remain. But the movement along the borders will free people.

The prime minister had deputed, the senior most congress leader saffudin siz to bring the Mirwaiz Umar, Farooq - led Hurriyat to the negotiating table as the centre's interlocaters had almost failed to persuade the separatist leaders to resume the dialogue (The New Indian Express, September 21, 2005).

The New Indian Express, JKLF Chief Amanullah Khan who was keen to attend the intra - JK heart - to heart talks was not granted visa as Interpol had issued a red corner alert against him for his alleged involvement in the assassination of Indian diplomat Ravinder Mathur in UK. Indian government could not issue him a visa as the local court in srinagar had also issued a warrant against him. (The New Indian Express, September 21, 2005)

The Hindu has Reported that

The Chairman of the moderate faction of Hurriyat conference Mirwaiz Umar Farooq demanded that relief workers from J & K should be allowed to go to the other side of the L.O.C. to provide assistance to the earthquake affected people living in PoK (The Hindu, October 15, 2005). and this issue which is strictly humanitarian, the Pakistan political establishment should not have any objections to it and should not delay the process. The Mirawaiz family is one of the few in Srinagar what has relatives in Musaffarabad, the capital of PoK.

The New Indian Express, the centre involved sajjad lone for the talks, as the intention of the centre is take the dialogue process beyond the HC. The Vajpayee government was the first to initiative talks with the Hurriyat conference in 2004. Vajpayee government came to power on 1999 with K.C. Pant as the inter locator in 2000. Three years after his initiative in 2003, the centre appointed former Union Home Secretary N.N. Vohra as its interlocutor (January 11, 2006). Vohra did not send any invitations but advertised in news papers in J & K asking groups to come forward and hold talks the Hurriyat rejected this move also. The Hurriyat entered into parleys with the union law minister Ram Jethmalani - who had launched a private initiative called Kashmiri committee. Though the initiative was not given any support by the centre, the Hurriyat still continued to hold talks with Jethmalani's Kashmir committee. The ambit of dialogue with separatist after the composite dialogue with the militants. (January 11, 2006)

Top secret meetings with they figures involved in J & K conflict were held by Dr. Singh and National Security Adviser M.K. Narayan before he left for US on November 28, 2005. But the Substance of the talk was not disclosed.

Regular meetings with Farooq Kathwari, a well connected ethenic Kashmiri businessmen, (Kashmiri study group) (The Hindu, January 25, 2006)

The ongoing discussions also had Vijay Sazawal on Jan 11, 2006 to discuss the involvement of the pandit community.

Mr. Syed Ali Geelani was permitted with visa to visit the Haj and the consent PMO office held discussions with HM leader Mohammed Yash Shah. Mr. Malik as an undertrial and as recent filtration with LET traces the property of the PM holding talks with him. The report states that though the meetings illustrate the seriousness with which the PM treats the dialogue process, the secret negogiations are not without critics.

The New Indian Express, come took a strong exception to these uni-dimensional talks and hit at the conglomerat's assertion that it represented the people of Kashmir. Chairman of people conference Sajjid Lone refused to part of a joint dialogue with New Delhi with the other separatist leaders. He reiterated his call for making the dialogue inclusive with all "relevant actions" on board, even militants.

The New Indian Express, The Hurriyat under the leadership mirwaiz decided to start the first ever intra - J & K dialogue to arrive at a consensus approach to the Kashmir solution. Its objective to rally the parties and province people who have been traditionally septical of its ideology around new Kashmir resolution ideas of demilitarization and governance. (January 29, 2005)

The New Indian Express, Geelani was insisted to participae in the second round table conference on Kashmir in May and the PM Dr. Singh had extended to talk to the hardline Hurriyat chairman separately. (April 9, 2006)

The New Indian Express, the moderate faction of the Hurriyat conference, which obstained from the centre's round table conference. Conference this year, would take a decision to participate in the second such exercise next month after a through deliberation with amalgam. The report also stated that the difference in the stand how different sectionare represented. People of Jammu, Kashmir, Ladakh, the Kashmir under pakistan's control and northern areas might have their own perception of the Kashmir issue. From the report the Hurriyat still fails to emerge unified voice as J & K, instead denotes it as the Kashmir under Pakistan's control.

The New Indian Express, the separatists groups in J & K did not have a 'veto' on the 'success or otherwise' of the second round table conclave.

National security Advisor M.K. Narayan also said that the success of the round table does not depand on the attendance of any group A, B or C, and at the same time maintained that the efforts were to tell the separatists to recongise th validity and utility of participation, in the meeting to be presided over by PM Manmohan Singh on May 25 (The New Indian Express, April 24, 2006). The first round table conclave, chaired by PM was held here on Feb. 25. Founder member of JKLF Hashin Qureshi was the only separatist leader present at the meeting.

The Hindu (July 31, 2006), Senior supreme court lawyer and track III activist Ashok Bhan held separate meetings with Hurriyat chairman Mirwaiz Umar Farooq, Abdul Ghani Bhat, DFP Chief Shabir Shah about the recent set back to Indo - Pakistan talks and conveyed that the government did not want to close the chapter of dialogue with them.

The much awaited talks between the separatists and PM Manmohan Singh was givena warm welcome by Mr. Azad. Mr. Azad even suggeste a mid - term poll if the separatists wer willing to contest. At the same time the Hurriyat should join the elections and test their popularity.

On self rule, it means electing people of your choice and as far as the elections - particularlythose held in 2002 - are concerned about by the world community.

The mainstream political parties paid tributes to those who sacrificed their lives fighting the Dogra rule on July 13, 1931. But chairman of the all party Hurriyat conference mirwaiz unar farooq in a veiled reference to the NC alleged that the mainstream group was exploiting the stentiments of Kashmiris by celebrating martyr's day, humiliating the grand scarifies made for the liberation of Kashmir from alien rule.

Coverage of Waller Barrage / Tribal Project and other Related Stories

During the period of study there twenty two reports in The Hindu and eleven reports in the New Indian Express.

Swiss expert appointed by the world Bank made an inspections of the controversial baglihar dam with Pakistan commissioner headed by syed Jamaitullah shah and Indian team headed by D.K. Mehta. No significant changes did arise during the course of secretarial level talks were reported in the Hindu expecially in the course of ongoing composite dialogue. The reports in the Hindu dated June 21, 2005, Baglihar, Pakistan's demand rejected". Raymond Lefitle, neutral expert appointed to give his opinions on the Baglihar dam on the chenab river, has referred to accept Pakistan's demand that India stop work on the project till it gives a verdict or whether or not the dam confirms to the Indian water treaty. Pakistan raised the issue of suspending the work as the project till neutral experts came to the conclusion on the technical aspects of the dam.

Mr. Lafitte took the view it would be too expensive to suspend work on the project and then commence it again if the verdict went in Indian's favour. The report also laments the need to reschedule the talks on Tulbul navigation project as Pakistan has never invoked the Indus water treaty, letting the issue languish since India has made no move to resume the construction of project. Date's for the rescheduling of the talks were for 10th round of such of parleys since 1988 after the arise. The Indian side will by headed by water resource secretary J. Harinarayan and while Pakistan's secretary for water and power Ashfaq Mehmood will lead the delegation ofhis country (June 29, 2005). The New Indian Express quoted that Pakistan president Pervez Musharaff has said that "we cannot resolve these smaller issues like the Baglihar its puts into our mind our capability of resolving the very complex major dispute".

Extensive reports in the Hindu July 26, 2006 a team of Pakistani experts visited the baglihar hydel project Media personnel were not allowed inside Pakistani team objected to the height of the days. But on the same day the new Indian express failed to highlight such issues.

The Hindu delibeated in its report of Islamabad objections to the design on the Kishananganga project under the Indus water treaty 1960 - involves the diversion of waters of a tributary Kishanganga in India Neelam in Pakistan of the river Jhelum another Tributary (Bunar Mandhumathi) near Bandipore in Baramulla district India will return the entire volume of water used back into Jhelum on weekly basis through willarlake. Pakistanhas expressed reservations about the design of the dam, the inter-tributary transfer of waters, as well as sought the existing land uses. India has sought quantitative technical substantiation of its objections from Pakistan. The world bank has recommended the appointment of a neutral expert as desired by Pakistan. The role of the world bank is delineated wherein the dispute to be resolved is passed on to the neutral expert. The first question is to resolve the dispute through the Indus commission itself.

The question is not resolved there then it is taken to the neutral expert to be appointed by the two countries or by a third party agreed upon by the two countries. In the absence of such an agreement, the WB, in consultation with the two countries would make the appointment of the neutral expert. The decision of the neutral expert is final and binding.

Two management by the WB of a trust fund to meet the expenses of the neutral expert. Three the role of the WB in the establishment of a court of arbitration. If the difference does not fall within the category of the neutral expert, the difference should be treated as a dispute then court of arbitration would be established. The role of the world bank, along with other institutions such as the secretary general of the united nations, is to participate in the selection of three appointees in the seven person court. The parties to the treaty each select two members of the court. The world bank itself plays no part in the actual hearing or determination of the issue before the tribunal. The Hindu reported the matter in more descriptive manner to make the issue more clear to the public, and the bureaucrate alike. But such reports were absent in the The New Indian Express.

Both the newspapers have reported that Pakistan has given a heavy nod for the results of the NE on the subject. The increase in height in Mangala Dam by 30 feet at a cost of Rs. 62 million, including Rs. 26 billion in compensation. The project envisaged compensation of Rs. 15 million for the land to be acquired for the project, Rs. 5 million for the houses and resettlement works of Rs.6 billion. The embankment of the bank will be raised by 30 feet, providing capacity to raise the existing level by 40 feet owing to the slopping design, while the spill way will also be raised by five feet. There were reports in the Hindu regarding the assurance by New Delhi on Buglihar by New Delhi is ready to accept any change for the modification or the technical flaw it can be identified in the project. This was announced during the recent visit of Pakistan PM Aziz to India.

The Hindu reported that of the Baglihar phase I, wherein 70% of civil works and 81% of electro - mechanical works have been completed in Phase I of the Baglihar hydro electro project. The Pakistan government third to stall construction of the dam involving Article 9A of the Indus water treaty. The Indian government has consistenly maintained that the dam was strictly under the ambit of the treaty and that there was no violation of the treaty. The project envisages a total cost of Rs.4,000 crore of which Rs. 2,700 crore has been incurred so far A total of about 7,000 people are working on the project including skilled labour and engineers.

The New Indian Express coverage of the Kishnaganga project wherein Pakistan objects to Kisenganga project was the 21 km long underground canal envisaged by India, it claimed was the violation of the treaty a time bound resolution of the differences on Kisenganga through bilateral talks failing it would approach the world bank as it did in the case of Baglihar for international arbitration.

The New Indian Express also quoted that Pakistan Indus commission commissioner Jamat Ali Shah that would contemplate invoking the article 9A of the Indus water treaty for a time bound solution of the differences of the Kishanganga project.

The Hindu repeated after two days of haggling, India and Pakistan signed on the minutes of the talks on Kshanganga Hydro power project and the preparation of the draft was decayed due to objections raised by the respective parties.

The Hindu gave enough authentic the world bank reasons recently appointed Raymond to Lafitte, a swiss national civil the engineer, and professor at technical details swiss federal institute of technology in causnne, as the neutral expert at Pakistan's request. India has indicated its willingness to Pakistan to consider on technical grounds the issues relating to provision of low - level spill way crest to a higher level and reduction of the free board level of the dam without compromising on the hydro-electric generation. There is a possibility of silt accumulation in the dam and the free board is meant to cushion the dam from being damaged by the waves effect.

A situation like this arose in 1988 with the Bhakra dam in Punjab. The treaty allocates 33 million acre feet to India from eastern rivers as against 135 million acre feet allocated to Pakistan from western rivers. The baglihar dam in Doda district of Jammu and Kashmir will be lead by India's water resources secretary S. Hari Narayan eminent lawyer Fali S. Nariman would present India's case, along with shamkar das, a specialist on international law The two day meeting discussed six issues on the kishanganga dam which was an inter tributary project on the river Jhelam. When both sides were reaching an understanding on four issues, the two most contentious issues of inter-tributary transfer and protection of the existing agriculture and hydro electric uses could not be taken up as the Pakistan side cut short the meeting.

The four issues that were discussed were on 1. The flood value in the design of the dam 2. the location of sedimentary studies, 3. The water intake level and 4. the release ofwater downstream.

The professor, the neutral expert at Swiss federal institute of technology will give an equal hearing to both sides and would confirm to the provisions of the treaty and there would be no financial determination.

Raymond Lafittee appointed under the terms of the treaty gave opinion as the Baglihar dam dispute on the Chenab proposed a site visit on mutually convenient dates.

The New Indian Express, quoted that failure by his country and India to agree on Baglihar hydropower project in Jammu and Kashmir is an irritant in the quest for a wider agreement on Kashmir issue. Baglihar dam on the chenab river would deprive its main agriculture province, Punjab, of water for irrigation. The Hindu coverage of Pakistan approaching the world bank for the appointment of a neutral expert to resolve the differences with India on the design of th Baglihar project and on May 10, the Bank appointed Prof. Raymond Lafitte of the swiss Federal Institute of technology at the neutral expert.

Pakistan objects to India's construction of the Baglihar project, when started in 1999. While Pakistan has raised objection of the design of the dam saying it would affect down stream flows, India has maintained that it had not deviated from the provisions of the treaty. India is reported to have offered to make changes in the design to accommodate Pakistan's objections without compromising the safety of the dam or the benefits of the project with Baglihar India did evolve strategies to solv the dispute unlike the Siachen glacier where India failure to take note of the 1989 agreement.

The Hindu, reported that of the Baglihar dam wherein Mr. Dasmunsi confirmed that he undertook the trip to acquaint himself with the status of the project with the adjudication by a neutral expert appointed by the WB to resolve the differences over Pakistan and India. India has already invested more than Rs. 2,500 crores of the total of Rs. 4,000 crores an the project is said to be halfway mark. The media reports that India is well placed to defend its case.

The resumption of talks between the water secretaries of two nations the Indian side headed by J. Hari Narayan while Pakistan headed by Ashfaq Mahmood ended in conclusive. India insisted on the revival of the work conceived in the 1980s and work began in 1984. It was stopped midway in 1984 after Islamabad raised objections. To sustain navigation in Jhelum river perenially, it is considered necessary to maintain a minimum depth of water, which will permit movement of boats. The tulbul project is a navigation - cum-control structure at the mouth of wullar lake. It envisaged regulated water release from the natural storage in the lake to maintain a minimum draught of 4.5 feet in the river up to Barmulla during the lean months.

This is to ensure round the year navigation from Anatmag to Srinagar to Baramulla, a distance of over 20 kms.

The treaty also allows either country to have restricted access for domestic and agriculture use, generation of hydro electric powe through a run-of-the-river project and non-consumptive use including navigation provided the same quantum of water is returned to the river.

The Hindu and The New Indian Express reported the state owned power development corporation has suspended after 150 - 200 m of the 550 m long diversion tunnel number 2 had been washed away. The New Indian Express, as the water level in the dam reservoir rose alarmingly to following tunnel collapse, a red alert was sounded in doda district. The Batote - Kishwar

NH has been flooded and blocked, andmany wooden bridges in the area have been damaged, cutting of links with remote areas.

A technical team from Pakistan, comprising of civil and water engineers would reach India on July 23. It would first visit Roorki near Jammu where the model of the project is kept and then visit the actual site.

The Pakistan Indus water commissioner syed Jammat Ali Shah, who recently led a team to Baglihar hydro power project site has sub mitted his report stated "Indian violation of the Indus water treaty in the project's design. After Pakistan submits its case to the neutral expert India will submit a counter case. If it was adjudged, dispute, then the WB and other international bodies would form a court of arbitration.

The Hindu reported that the WB appointed swiss neutral expert, who is adjudicating differences between India and Pakistan will be accompanied by India and Pakistani experts in India from October 1 to 7. Pakistan in its memorandum to the expert, primarily raised the issue of power in take level, the height of sluices and the size of pondage. The paper work on replies and rejoinders is stated to be completed by December and both sides will rest their case by January end. The three member Swiss team accompanished by six Pakistani and four Indian officials visited the lowest level of the dam where the submerged gate spill ways were constructed on the right bank. Pakistan alleges that the Indian design is a gated spill way located at the lowest level and will allow India to control the water flow, which is violative of the Indus water treaty The 1086 km Chenab originates in the Kulu and Kangra districts of Himachal Pradesh and is feel by tributaries Chandra and Bagha as it enter Jammu and Kashmir. Flowing through the hillybelt of the state along the Pir Punja, it enters silakot district in Pakistan and is a major source of irrigation in Pubjab. India states the gated spillway have been constructed on the chenab to prevent silt deposits. Baglihar engineers point out that spill ways with channels are constructed to remove the silt deposited in the dam and have nothing to do with controlling the waters of the chenab.

Pakistan also alleged that the reservoir stores water beyond the limit of the Indus water treaty set for power generation. It claims that the reservoir will deprive Pakistan of 26 to 28% of water in winter and affect the continued rabi crop season.

The programme of Mr. Laffitte was rescheduled as he expressed a desire to spend more time at the site where two diversion tunnels of the dam structure were installed. The issue in hand was the diversion of the natural flow of the chenab as according to Pakistan two tunnels were constructed to divert the water thus violating the Indus water treaty. Pakistan's case relies on articles III of the Indus water treaty which states that Pakistan shall receive all those waters of the western rivers which India to under obligation to let flow. Besides this article 4 of the treaty signed in 1960 states that each party will use its best endeavour to maintain the natural channels of the rivers, as on effective date, in such condition, a will avoid, as far as pratiable any obstruction to the flow in these channels likely to cause material damage to the othe party. India's case is based on the word 'restrictive use' of the western rivers which substantiated in Annexture D of the same treaty.

This says that India can store water on the chenab for generating hydro electric power.

Accordingly to India, the storage is a non - consumptive use that does not affect the water flow.

The New Indian Express, India accepted the Baglihar dam under the 1960 were treaty between the two countries and it had objections only on the height of the dam. There were slight changes after the composite dialogue in the way the news was reported.

Islamabad announced the postponement of the talks with India on the waller / tulbal navigation project will rescheduled shortly owing to pre-occupation of the Indian water resources secretary with other business. India and Pakistan have been engaged in India to resolve the issue for 15 years.

India and Pakistan began the 11th round of talks to resolve the dispute over New Delhi's plans to construct a barrage across the wuller lake inJ & K. The issue under discussion is the Tulbal navigation project, which Pakistan refuses to as wullar barrage, and dates back to 1984. India proposed to build a barrage at the mouth of the waller lake where it meets the shelum to reduce the natural dipletion of water in summer and make the river more navigable in the day season. India began construction work on the project but halted it in 1986 following objections from Pakistan. Pakistan says the construction amounts to storage of water of the man Jhelam river and is thus violation of the 1960 Indus water treaty Both sides unhopeful of major progress which is taking place under third round (Secretary - level talks of the composite dialogue.

Coverage of Siachen Issue

There were twelve reports in The New Indian Express and twelve reports in The Hindu.

The Hindu has covered the Siachen issue using very bold types of headline in the front page covering almost half of the newspaper. The headline make "siachen peace mountains : manmohan" Existing boundaries cannot be changed because these are for our protection. Cites the fitting reply given to

General Musharaff and Pakistan. Manmohan Singh became the first PM to visit the trip to the glacier at more than 12,000 feet above sea level. Indian express has also taken up a very detailed issue of the whole issue with entire bold type headlines "make Siachen a peace zone" Pak the Prime Minister has allowed a CT scan and two Home theatres on the mountain. The Hindu has 4 decked head line of the progress that has to be initiated on the mountain. The redeployment of the forces can be carried only after mutually determining the actual (AGPL) ground position on Siachen. The report also stated that India favoured plotting the further course of the LoC which flops at NJ 9842.

The New Indian Express (April 20, 2005) reported that the left parties demand a urgent solution to Siachen. The New Indian Express suggested that India was keen to settle Siachen issue with PoK for maintaining troops on the glacier was costly proposition for both countries. The two leaders have instructed that the existing institutional mechanism should convene discussions immediately with a view to finding mutually acceptable solutions. The Hindu & The New Indian Express the Indian delegation led by defence secretary made it amply clear that commitment to re-deployment of troops only if both sides agreed on methods for authentication of current troop positions (The Hindu, May 27, 2005). While the Pakistani team, led by defence secretary, Tariq Wascemghazi insisted on the withdrawal of troops to the pre - 1984 position as per the 1989 "agreement" without any pre-conditions. Despite eight round of talks differences persisted on the interpretation of the 1989 pact. India maintained that the understanding, not an agreement clearly stipulated the authentication of troop position, Pakistan proclaimed that agreement was unconditional. The New Indian Express (May 27, 2005) quoted that Pakistan would have to authenticate the 110 km (AGPC) on the saltro ridge to safeguard India's future interest where else the Hindu stressed more on redeployent of troops. No breakthrough in the talks and ended in conclusion except for the follow. Up talk on Sir Creck issue. It was the ninth round of talks on Siachen after both sides arrived at an understanding in 1989 and second after resumption of the composite dialogue process initiated by the Vajpayee government. In the siachen glacier, though there has been no cross fire since November 26, 2003, the weather conditions are very horrible (May 28, 2005). The report got an insight into the multi dimensional working of the engineering unit which provides logistical support to the last paot in the northern glacier which has one of the highest peaks in the world. The engineering unit is working day and night to provide the best facilities to the soldiers posted at a height ranging from 10,000 to 21,000 feet above sea level. Most of the problems are due to low oxygen levels which are 50% of the normal availability.

Long staff Arthur Henced and it sings by both British national discovered the 12 km long siachen glacier at the height of more than 20,000 feet above sea level in 1909, would have never though about humans whould come to inhabit around the year. The Hindu coverage of the ordeals of the soldiers tells us in the endurance and for bearance of soldiers who get acclimatised at a few kilometer ahead of the base camp which is also 20,000 feet, the tallest peak of the glacier. A soldiers gets 15 days to get used to low oxygen conditions and the cold (The Hindu, July 27, 2005). This is familirisation session. The army doctor say the usual consequences are low oxygen levels and the cold are nasal bleeding, breathelessness, loss of appetite, mountains sickness, High altitude cerebral odema which is potentially fatal. During the 15 day acclimatisation period, soldier are taught the basic skills to brave the weather. Allteration is also given to to guarding the skin as the main problem reported while on the glacier are related to frostbite on the nose and chin. Even decaying feet is common.

Training is provided in the use of equipment including special clothing to combat cold. Helping cope with health problems relating to low - pressure condition is another feature of the training. Training in the use of pressure bags is provided. These can beused in contingency situations to create normal atmospheric conditions to help a suffering collegues. There were spots wher one has to climb on 200 feet of snow along 90 degree ingredient access to the glacier from the Indian side is more difficult compared to the Pakistani side. There are posts that take 21 days to reach and are situated a few metres from the posts of the Pakistan troops. (The Hindu, July 29, 2005)

The Hindu coverage of the biodegraders tells us of the move to address growing Pakistan on the sicahen glacier of burning human wastes. The pro-digesters are carried to an altitude of 21,000 feet by air and surface transport. (The Hindu, August 26, 2005)

The New Indian Express reported that PM statement of turning Siachen into a mountain of peace has fine tuned its proposals on Siachen. On Siachen, this will mean using satellite imaging to fix troop positions. On siachen, New Delhi knows that Islamabad does not want to exchange the maps denoting the Indian and Pakistani army positions on the saltoro ridge that flanks the 1 km long glacier as a precursor for disengagement. But it has now conveyed to Islamabad that it is ready to use satellite imagery to fix army positions on the grid (September 13, 2005). Thereafter the troops from both sides can disengage once political decision is taken on Siachen, the two armies can prepare a roadmap for disengagement that addresses the asymmetric deployments. The new Indian express coverage of the proposal to send a joint Indo - Pak expedition to the world's second highest peak, 8,611 metres high mount k2 towering over Battoro glacier, the second largest in the Karakoram after Siachen had been submitted to the (IMF) and to the defence ministry. Even before reaching an agreement on demilitarization, such ventures prompt others to ponder whether the unending dispute could be resolved in a sportime manner, a psychological pursuit. (The New Indian Express, September 26, 2005)

India and Pakistan would have to arrive at an understanding on what would be done with the area where the troops were currently deployed. Redeployment of India and Pakistani troops in the siachen will bepossible provided the two sides agree on the current actual ground position line the sources indicated that India favoured plotting the further course of LoC, which stops at point NS9842 Pakistan president, Pervez Musharaff during his visit to New Delhi in April, agreed that their should be some form of verification of the AGPL.

The Hindu reported, Siachen, considered a double CBM is bogged down due to differences between Islamabad and New Delhi on the conditions for the withdrawal of troops from the glacier as per the 1989 understanding Indian insistence on the demarcation of areas under control by both sides is disputed by Pakistan on the plea that withdrawal had to be unconditional and it was not prepared to certify Indian "aggression" The latest understanding is to take an integrated approach involving six identified issues related to the glacier and work towards a common understanding before Siachen is taken up as one of the eighth subjects under the third round of composite dialogue. The six areas are, from where the troops are moving, to where would they move, how to define the areas of disengagement, a regime to monitor the implementation of disengagement, verification mechanism on do's and don't on the glacier and what is to be done about NJ 9842. (October 5, 2005)

The New Indian Express, reported that India and Pakistan are inching closer to an understanding on withdrawal of troops from Siachen with Islamabad inclined "in-principle" to acknowledge current positions on the glacier. New Delhi, on its part, will need to be more flexible on the distance to which troops will pull back. When Pakistan president Pervez Musharaff visited India last week both the leaders had directed either officials to expeditiously find a mutually acceptable solution to Sir Creek and Siachen issue. It is learnt that the acknowledgement of troop positions in Siachen will be done in the withdrawal plan attached to the main attached to the agreement document.

India had been existing on recording and registering positions for authentication purposes. But the withdrawal plan will positions from which th Indian troops will pull back and also where they will be stationed after that autonomy to automatic acknowledgment.

This was the most controversial element of the settlement envisaged twice earlier in 1989 and 1993. Once the acknowledgement of positions is agreed the withdrawal plan will be formalized and siachen will stand demilitarized. On withdrawal of troops, however, the army feels Pakistan is at an advantage of the terrain on its side allows easier and faster access to the glacier thanit would be formthe Indian side, So it argues that the Indian troops should be displayed closer from the glacier than Pakistan troops to ensure that time taken by either side is the same.

There are differences on this issue but sources point out that India would need to be more flexible given its position will now be acknowledged. Once this is done, a verification process can be put in place.

In the final stage, both sides will, by way of joint survey mechanism, delineate the LoC north of NJ9842. This was the point up to which theceasefire line in 1949 and LoC in 1972 were drawn. The Karachi agreement of 1949 mentions NJ 9842 as the terminal point and states "there north to the glacier" (The New Indian Express, March 25, 2006)

India suspected Pakistan of cartographic aggression in the 1905 when it backed the mountaineering expedition region. In 1984, India sought to preempt any such designs and gained militarycontrol of the area. It has since argued that the line north of NJ 9842 would move along the Saltoro ridge while Islamabad maintains that the line move s last of Karakuram. The New Indian Express, reported that the two countries have agreed in principle to demilitarize the world's highest battle field but Indians insist onauthentication of current positions held by respective forces to while Islamabad has not agreed so far. Top defence officials of both countries would meet in New Delhi on May 23, and 24 to discuss solution to the Siachen issue. (march 28, 2006)

The Hindu reported that the JD part presented Subramanian Swamy demanded a white paper on a Siachen talks. He expressed opposition to any pull out of troops from the area (April 8, 2006). The New Indian Express, emphasized India and Pakistan are 'closer' to a 'final point' Siachen problem and talks are on for finalizing modalities for authentication of present troop positions that can pave the way for demilitarisation of the world's highest battle field.

New Delhi has also asserted that it was keen on having iron - clad guarantees from Pakistan to avoid a scenario in which India will have to reclaim the position it now occupies in case a need arises. (April 21, 2006)

Coverage of Report on Sir Creek

There were 5 reports on Sir Creek in The New Indian Express and only two in The Hindu.

An extensive report in the Hindu on Sir creek, but mere details were reported in The New Indian Express. The bone of contention between Sindhand the Kutch ruler of the coastal strip of the land and the talk were inconclusive. This is the light round of talks and the second under current round of composite dialogue. The demarcation has been a bone of contention for several decades (22 years). The issue dates back to 1914 where an agreement was signed between the then government of sindhu are Rao Maharaj of Kutch. According to the agreement both sides agreed to a line running through the middle of the creek, but Pakistan claimed that 17 creeks of the Sindh coast belongs to it, while India maintained that almost half of the area of Sir Creek belongs to it. India wanted Pakistan to accept land delineation on the basis of joint survey conducted in January to determine the pillars installed in 1925 (The Hindu, May 29, 2005). The Indian delegation headed by Additional surveyor General M. Gopal Rao and additional secretary Pakistan's ministry of defence Alisan-ul-Haq chaudhary said both sides had agreed to meet at a later date.

The New Indian Express quoted that an agreement on Sir Creek would help both countries to finalise their respective exclusive economic zones in the coast between Gujrat and Sindh to file their claim before the UN convention of law of seas. The Hindu and The New Indian Express this is the eight round of talks on the subject so far in bid to resolve mutual claims on Sir creek. The disputed Sir Creek, which runs along the Rann o fKutch in India and Sindh in Pakistan is at the centre of a 22 year old dispute between two countries (The Hindu, May 29, 2005).

In January, both sides had deployed eight teams each for the survey of the horizontal segment of Creek. The decision to carry out the joint survey was made at the last meeting between the two sides in December 2004. Sir creek is part of the eight point agenda of the composite dialogue. The survey results will be very useful in resolving the dispute related to the demarcation of the boundary in Sir Creek, a 96 km long strip of water between the Rann of Kutch (in India) and Sindh (In Pakistan). The joint survey conducted in January this year to identify the boundary pillions installed in 1924 to demarcate the area. The demarcation of the boundary has been a bone of contention between India and Pakistan for several decades. In 1914, an agreement was signed between the then Government of Sindh and Rao Maharaj of Kutch. According to the agreement, both sides agreed to a boundary line running through the middle of creek as a border between two states. The final demarcation was completed in 1925 in which the boundary was shown by a "green line" depicted on the castern side of the creek. On one side of the

Creck is under Pakistan's control whereas there are Indian naval installation of the other side Pakistan lays claim to all the 17 creeks of the Sindh coast while India maintains that almost half of the area of Sir creek, the seventeenth one, belongs to it.

The contention is that the "green line" was simply an indicative line and the boundary line should be defined by the mid channel of the creek as shown on the map of 1925. But Pakistan rejected the Indian view on the grounds that the notion of the mid channel is applicable only to navigable channels and says this channel is not a navigable channel.

India has proposed that pending formation of the boundary in Sir Creek, the two sides could consider the delimitation of the India - Pakistan maritime boundary from seawards, by commencing exclusive economic zone (EEZ) limit and proceeding landward up to a mutually acceptable limit as per provisions under technical aspects of law of sea (TACOS). (The Hindu, May 29, 2005)

The Indian Express reported that, the seaward approach is based on internationally accepted principle and will benefit both countries for the exploitation of resources.

India has also come out with a more acceptable proposal on sir creek Pakistan is willing to accept the horizontal line (defined by 38 pillars called the western terminal) that meets the head of creek. India is prepared for adjustment of boundary within the creek without changing its stand on wartime boundary, including the industries economic zone. New Delhi wants to define the maritime boundary by drawing a line from the southern most tip of creek. Both countries realize the urgency to resolve the sir creek issue because of the final date for submission of proposals on the UN convention on law of the seas is 2009. (The New Indian Express, December 13, 2005)

Foerign ministers held technical level talls to discuss methods for the first ever survey of the sir creek by both countries.

Whole the dispute has been continuing since Independence, there has never been an objective survey of sir creek, with both sides relying on documents. Dating back to 1914. These were arguments basically reached by princely states and both countries have been disagreeing on the intre pretation of these in the current context.

With pressure mounting to settle maritime boundary by 2009, the two countries decided to take a joint survey of Sir creek for an updated version of the ground situation given that the creek is a shifting geographical body. India and Pakistan have already carried out a survey of the horizontal line and even identified many boundary pillars erected well before 1947. The survey of the creek now will provide the basics for future negogiations for the settlement of the dispute.

The exercise will also determine the ground terminus from where the maritime boundary can be ascertained India had proposed earlier that both sides first agree on the maritime boundary and once it as done, new Delhi may be flexible drawing the territorial boundary.

Aslam has reported that efforts underway to iron out differences on Sir creek, a small strip of marshy land in the Gujarat cost which the two countries have been trying to resolve. ON Sir Creek there is agreement on joint survey. However modalities have to be worked out since technical experts who met in December could not arrive at an agreement, these issues would be discussed at great length in the talks scheduled that would take place in New Delhi on May 25 and 26. (The New Indian Express, March 25, 2006)

Coverage of Reports on Third Party Mediation

The New Indian Express had ten reports on third party mediation wherelse the Hindu, only seven.

The first report in The Hindu, wherein Dr. Manmohan Singh made it a point wherein he can sensitise the international community on India's plight relating to terrorism in the G-8 meetings at St. Peters Burg.

The Hindu also reported on the Sep. 11, 2004 meet between PM Dr. Manmohan Singh and the President Pervez Musharaff and Condeliza Rice proclaimed their support in resolving the bilaterial trade. General Musharaff condemned the stance of cross - border terrorism for he was well ahead of firing the border with Afghanistan. The New Indian Express reported that stage has been reached where solution to the core issue of Kashmir needs to be discussed. Kasuri briefed Bush on the latest developments in Indo - Pak relations, incuding the visit of Kashmiri separatist leader to (The New Indian Express, June 12, 2005) Pakistan. The Chinese ambassador or sun yaxi opined that peace process between India and Pakistan must resolve the issue among themselves and if needed china can contribute their might in resolving the issue.

During the visit of the Italian Ambassdor Armillini, in India, and action plan for economic and strategic relations with India was being finalized by the European union. India was a major player in south Asia and thrust will be given on infrastructure building and Agro industries He also suggested that on his five day visit to Kashmir was a fact finding mission for him. The travel advisory issued by many western countries including Italy not to visit Kashmir has to be obliterated and confidence to be instilled in the minds of the people regarding the initiatives taken by the J & K government. The visiting dignitaries always emerged with an upbeat move to restore ties with the Indian government.

During interaction with Mr. Bush Foreign Minister Khurshed Mehmod Kasuri, briefed on the latest developments in the Indo-Pak relations, including visit of Kashmiri leader to Pakistan and emphasized that the stage has reached when thecore issue can be discussed.

The extensive coverage with Bold headlines in both the papers expressed the shrewdness and anxiety extended by the super power in dictating terms to the world globally for Bush insisted on the sanctity of line of control (LoC) (The New Indian Express, July 19, 2006) to be maintained which determined the sovereignty and integrity of a nation.

Mr. Bush also took the PM and the newspapers into conficence while acknowledging the fact that the earlier stand taken by president Clinton on Kashmir is honoured even by the present government. The New Indian Express (July 19, 2006) reopened the topic of NSS (Next step in strategic partnership, the Hindu blankly reported with the issue of nuclear technology. Bush also ruled out mediation in the bilateral dispute. But he promised that he would act as a facilitator among the nations. Rejecting Pakistani's demand for parity with India in accessing civilian nuclear technology (The New Indian Express, September 10, 2005), the united states has said the land mark accord with new Delhi was a mechanism to deepen further India's commitment to international non-proliferation.

Before meting PM manmohan singh Pakistan president pervez musharaff sought the U.S. help in presiding India on area - specific troops reduction in J & K (The Hindu, September 15, 2005) Pullout of troops from certain areas in J & K - later identified by Ambassdor Jahangir Karamat as Bramulla and Kupwara would be a definite step towards meaningful progress. (The Hindu, September 15, 2005)

The New Indian Express also reported that India know - tows the US and Jettisons Pakistan to effaced the tendentious campaign would be unleashed in the US to misrepresent India position on Iranian nuclear proliferation (September 18, 2005). A series of articles and editorial in the mainstream American Media have trusted India position on Iran beyond recognition. The Washington times even accused India of nuclear collaboration with Iran. Washinton post suggested it was India's opposition in Vianna that led Washington latest decision to postpone a vote on the Iran question at the International atomic energy agency. The new York times refused to mention that India supported the European initiative on Iran. (The New Indian Express, September 18, 2005)

This public campaign suggested India is the biggest obstacle in the attempt to bring Iran to book at a time when washinton is trying hard to sell the nuclear pact with Delhi (The New Indian Express, September 18, 2005). By putting India's Iran relationship against the Indo - US nuclear pact the campaign has aligned the liberal Arms controller who were expected to oppose the pact with realists in the US congress who were expected to back it. The focus on Iran has also neutralized the traditionally pro - India jewish lobby on the congress.

As Musaraff flaunts his new Israeli connections in the US, Singh confronted the problem of managing the dynamic inter connections between different strands of Indian foreign policy. But he has to recongise that musharaff is making some big advances in Washington. To ensure relations with the US and Pakistan are managed properly, Singh might have to stop defferent parts of the government from running separate foreign policies. (The New Indian Express, September 18, 2005)

The Hindu reported that US President George W. Bush ruled out forging an accord similar to the civilian nuclear deal Washington clinched with new Delhi. The best way of solving the issue was through dialogue between New Delhi and Islamabad.

Mr. Kasuri told the American journalist That there was lot of 'misinformation' about Pakistan in the western media on cross border infiltration and appealed to him to reflect the Pakistani perspective. He justified that despite the presence of 1.7 lakh American troops in Iraq there were bomb blasts and violence everyday and it certainly does not mean that US hesitates to track down the culprits, Another remarkable instance like the presence of 17,000 American and NATO troops in Afghanistan and an additional 19,000 Afghan troops, the problem of terrorism persisted.

With PM Manmohan Singh rulingout reduction of troops in the Kashmir valley tell acts of violence and terror continued, Pakistan's National Security adviser Tariq Aziz has rushed to Washington to press India demonstrate more flexibility. (The New Indian Express, September 17, 2005)

The New Indian Express reported that Pakistan has formally approached the nuclear suppliers group seeking a similar to the one between united states and India to produce nuclear power, saying it needed more atomic power plants to meet future energy requirements. Though initially different to approach the US to seek a deal, like the one struck by PM Manmohan Singh visit to Washington, due to relevation of proliferation by its disgraced nuclear scientist A.Q. Khan, Pakistan is recent weeks stepped up campaign to secure advanced nuclear technology.

Pakistan wants 13 nuclear power plants against India's request of six and has given the details to the US and some other western countries of its requirements.

The visiting British defense secretary John Reed asserted that the fight terrorism has to be 100 percent (The New Indian Express October 6, 2005). Backing India's moves to find a political resolution to the Kashmir issue, Pakistan had to adhere to UN conventions on terrorism.

Saudi Arabia King Abdullah Bon Abdul al - Aziz is trying to moderate between India and Pakistan to resolve their differences on various issues. India has maintained it is against any third party mediation to resolve all differences, including J & K with Kashmir (April 20, 2006).

But the Hindu reports of India and Pakistan, The Bush administration under the present circumstances must be on the evidence of who or what groups may have been behind the blasts (July 19, 2006).

The New Indian Express identified that the Hurriyat trip to PoK did embarrass the PoK top leadership and identified that there was a lot of plain speaking from the separatists amidst their week long visit to erstwhile pricely state of J & K This time compared to the previous trip.

The New Indian Express Geelani accusing Pakistan tocing the line of dthe US and now their turn is to rope in Kashmiris leaders to make the US plan a success.

Coverage between Separatist and Pak Government

The report both in The New Indian Express and the Hindu made wide coverage of the espousal of the camps in the other side of LoC. Mr. Yasin Malik JKLF leader who had been assisted by Pakistan information minister sheik Rasheed Ahmade to set up a large militant camp for infiltration into India in the 1990s has given the government an opportunity to stress on the issue in the context of peace process. The Hindu reports also stated on 'Malik Relevation Serious' and special note to be taken as they occupy high position in Pakistan. Both the NP, The New Indian Express and the Hindu revealed the deal of the Hardline faction leader of the Hurriyat conference and his deadline of offer of travel to Azad Kashmir The rigidity in his stand is unequivocal stand of the Hardline faction of Hurriyat conference leader as they fully believe that Pakistan has sabotoged their dreams of self - determination and autonomy by conceiving with the Indian government by showing more flexibility on the Kashmir issue Geelani is prepared to visit Pakistan as a free kashmiri and accuses centre of going back on its promise of plebiscite.

The Hindu reported that during his visit to India, Mr. Geelani who led an five member faction of Tehrek - e- Hurriyat was the first to get the audience with Gen. Musharaff. According to Geelani, atrocities are still being committed on the people of the state by the security forces. He claimed that between January 2004 and March 2005, 786 people hid lost their lives, 2,526 were injured, 2322 arrested and 196 local disappeared. Both the hardline faction and the moderate faction demanded the inclusion of Kashmiris in the dialogue.

The Hindu reported that the militant turned separatist leader was not allowed to pay visit to Pakistan president Musharaff. Both the hardline faction and moderates faction of the Hurriyat conference were permitted entry but Mir was asked to wait. Mir had to beat a hasty retreat within minutes of making the entry.

The Hindu as well as the The New Indian Express reported wanted the Sharade Peeth in PoK to be removated as the pilgrims can visit the ancient temple of heritage and learning.

General Musharaff has sought the early inclusion of Kashmiris in the dialogue rocess.

The foreign secretary Shyam Saran approved of the meeting of the president General Musharaff and the Hurriyat leader, for India being a democratic country, there is a possibility of a relationship between the two countries.

The Hindu & The New Indian Express Hurriyat faction was asked to meet the general a day after Manmohan Singh government announced his decision to meet the Hurriyat leaders. A visit to Pakistan by the Hurriyat was allowed by the Pak government. The passengers were allowed to travel within the erstwhile princely state of J & K. General made very clear his proposal not to insist for a present. Triartie dialogue at The New Indian Express quotes that India's reservations were ignored, Hurriyat leaders will travel to Islambad from PoK and then to Pakistan. They will arrive in Islamabad or June 4 for talks with Musharaff, Aziz and other leaders. The Pakistan government considered the of visit by Hurriyat leaders very important since Islamabad has been demanding the involvement of Kashmiri leaders in the current process to find a solution to Kashmir issue. The moderate faction of the Hurriyat which stepped on to Pakistan soil expressed hope that no solution is possible without the involvement of Kashmiris and declared that all past accords failed due to as they were reached without ascertaining the wishes of the people.

The New Indian Express relates the cross over as described by Mirwiz Umar as a 'big step' in the peace process which could form the basis for a triangular dialogue between India, Pakistan and the Hurriyat conference.

The Hurriyat during the visit to PoK demanded the Pakistan to shed notions of romanticism associated with the struggle of the Kashmir, and Mr. Yasin malik openly blamed the leaders of PoK for the death of 80,000 Kashmiris. The Hindu reported that the PoK president Sardar Mohammed Anwar Khan that LoC is not the solution to the Kashmir dispute and regretted that the UN failed to implement its resolution on the lingering dispute. The Hurriyat still requiring more time consultation draws closer home that the meeting did endin impasse with Yasin Malik not participating in the talks and Aziz giving a vague reply to the journalist waiting outside the PM house though Mirwaiz Farooq was hopeful during most of the occasion. The new Indian Express, the visiting Kashmiris leaders went on sight seeing tour of Lahore and met with political leaders and ordinary people (June 7, 2005). They later prayed at the famous Islamic shrine of Dalta Durbaer and visited Minar - e- Pakistan built to commemorate the formation of Pakistan. The New Indian Express after returning from Pakistan, the unfazed leader of the opposition over the hackles raised by the sangh parivar made it amly clear that apart from sentimental values to the country of his birth, the objective of historic was to promote the peace initiatives launched by the NDA government for Indo - Pak peace process (June 7, 2005).

There were differences on the headlines indicated by the Hindu and The New Indian Express. After the arrival of Hurriyat delegation in Pakistan Morwaiz Farooq did proclaim the erasing of the borders irrelevant whereelse The New Indian Express that Hurriyat backed up Generals views on Kashmir (June 10, 2005). The 1948 UN resolution on Kashmir envisaging plebiscite do not provide for an independent option. The right to self - determination is limited to joining either India in Pakistan. The latest move is aimed at strengthening the campaign for independence (June 10, 2005).

The New Indian Express quoted the Hurriyat leaders favoured division of Kashmir not on religious grounds but on-geographical grounds.

The Hindu coverage of the JKLF factions come together headed by Yasin Malik and Himanullah khan have agreed to bury their difference (January 12, 2005). A seven member committee headed by Mr. Haider was constituted to restructure the party.

The New Indian Express, the moderate Hurriyat faction giving a tacit backing to Pakistan President Pervez Musharaff reported autonomous Kashmir formula sans independence, complete independence for Kashmir will not be acceptable to India and Pakistan.

The New Indian Express (June 17, 2005), Malik blames the Pak media for distoring the text for he confessed that that when they were disowned by

Pak, and PoK, they were given food and shelter by the Pakistan information minister Sheikh Abdul Rasheed in 1990, Rasheed, being a Kashmiri helped us by providing shelter and food to about 3,500 Kashmiri youth at his residence and farm - house.

Even the Pakistani government has extended invitation to moderate faction of the Hurriyat to attend the OIC meet in Yemen inked the hardline faction of the Hurriyat for they were being sidelined (The Hindu, June 29, 2005). Even the Pakistan government has used its good office to recognize the moderates as the sole representative of the people of J & K. While the express denoted the move of two separatist leader for the talks (Shabir shah DFP & Mirwaiz omar Farooq) and it was vague. Theban of ANA (All party National Alliance) an amalgam of several political outfits in PoK, Gilgit and Batisan has challenged the decision of the Pakistan government for imposing a ban in their participation in the local elections. The new Indian Express quoted that APNA leaders flayed the Hurriyat conference's visit to PoK and questioned the visit to Pakistan via PoK. Such issues did not get prominence in the Hindu.

Mirwaiz Omar Farooq has deputed Ashraf Sarafi, Musuf Naseen and Fayaz Nashbandi. Though Mirwaiz has an Indian passport and goes to attend conferences on Kashmir, this time he has chosen to send a delegation. SKLF chairman has nominated his Islamabad - based associate Altaf Quiri and DFP president Shabir Ahmed Shah has given his mandate to his Musaffarabad lieutenants Mehmood Ahmed Sagar. The New Indian Express did not elaborate on this feature.

The hard-line separatist leader Mr. Geelani in a scathing attack against the OIC demanded that they had shown flexibility vis-à-vis India towards Kashmir (The New Indian Express, December 13, 2005). Hurriyat Conference also on that it had failed to represent the aspiration of the Kashmiris and criticized Saudi King of Shah Abdullah's decision to preside over the republic day function.

The Hindu report stated that a three member delegation of the moderate faction of the APHC, chairman Mirwaiz Umar Farooq to left to Pakistan to express solidarity with the victims of the October 8 earthquake and study the progress of the peace talks (January 1, 2005). The Hurriyat met Gen. Musharaff in New Delhi on April 17, June 7, when Kashmiri separatist leaders crossed PoK, on June 2 Srinagar - Musaffarabd bus, on Sep of they interacted again in New York and on December 8, 2005 Mirwaiz briefed Gen. Musharaff about his proposals for the establishment of a "united states of American" self - governance and demilitrisation of J & K. (The New Indian Express, Jan 7, 2006)

Hurriyat had fully agreed with the approach adopted by Pakistan for the solution of the Kashmir issue. He appreciated Pakistan's suggestion of demilitarization and said if implemented, the proposal would be would very important milestone in the ultimate solution to the Kashmir issue.

Coverage of Army

During the period of study there were eleven started in the Hindu and 6 reports in the New Indian Express

Border security forces operating in the valley have received orders to withdraw from counter – terrorist operations in the city. The central reserve police force in co-ordination with Jammu and Kashmir police will be solely responsible for the security of the state capital. BSF troops were sent to Srinagar in 1990 after the state police and the CRPF failed to contain violence wince 1990, BSF has eliminated 2,653 terrorists, among them the architect of the 2001 attack on parliament house, shalibz khan. (Sep. 11, 2005, The Hindu) Critics allege that the failure of the CRPF to contain the attack on the tourist reception centre in April indicated its weaknesses. CRPF officials say all forces operating in Jammu and Kashmir had there share of failures. Compared with the communication intelligence infrastructure of the BSF, which enable it to track terrorist communications, the CRPF technical capabilities are rudimentary. Nor does the CRPF have a chain of informers and moles, in contract to the network run by the BSF's 'G' bracnch.

After playing a vital role in fighting militancy, the BSF pulled out the last of its five battalions from Srinagar and four from Anantnag handing the charge to the central reserve police force. Four battalions had moved out of Anatnag and the de-induction from other major towns such as Bermulla, Pulwara, Sopere, tral and Badgand would take place. The de-induction had no link with the recent talks between PM Manmohan singh and the Hurriyat conference. The central reserve police force which took charges of counter – insurgency operation is confident of dealing with the situation. The CRPF had fought militancy with Jammu and Kashmir police. In 1990, the CRPF was in the forefront of the fight against militant. (Sep. 13, 2005,The Hindu) The press reports were part of a 'disinformation campaign' launched against our force by vested interests.

Engaged in massive rescue efforts in J & K, the army has offered helicopters to Pakistan for relief and rescue operations in PoK. The offer was made during the several contacts that took place between senior commanders of both the sides. On a request made by the Indian side, Pakistan agreed to overlook the movement of Indian army helicopters in the border areas of Uri and Tanghar for rescuing troops and civilians. The army and the airforce operating together under 'operation Indad' (Succor) continued their operations for the third day, readjusting their efforts according to the directions issued by defence minister Pranab Mukerjee and army staff J.J. Singh. (Oct. 11, 2005, The Hindu) The armed forces have been told that the first priority is to some lives followed by providing sustenance to the affected population and restoration of infrastructure.

The army denied reports that some of its troops crossed the LoC to help rescue Pakistani troops and rebuild their brokers destroyed by the Oct. 8 earthquake. (Oct 14, 2005,TNIE &The Hindu) As there was a lot of destruction on Pakistani side a patrol party came to the LoC and asked for showels and pinnacles. Indian soldiers gave the personnel some implements, with which they dug up earth, looking for servivors. They retrieved some weapons and returned tools.

TNIE reported that the General officer – in – commanding its corps, it Gen. SS pholloon stated that the srinagar – musaffarabad road is badly damaged at several segements. A 10 km streets of the Shekum valley road is badly damaged due to landsides, triggered by devastating earthquake that hit J & K and its neghbourhood on October 8.

The army's director – General of Military operation, madan Gopal stated the two militant organizations from PoK have suffered heavy losses in the October 8 earth quake.

The HM and (CeT) have lost several activists but both the organizations continue to be active in J & K. The first publicly revealed assessment of the army talked with that by other intellgence agencies. As in the case with the army, other agencies are not stating the number of terrorist killed by the quake but assert that several of the 50 permanent terrorist training and communication camps in Pakistan had been damaged with HM being the worst hit. (Oct 16, 2005, The Hindu) In fact, the terrorist organization attempted two major infiltrations soon after the quake struck in an effort to capitalize on the disruption caused by natural disasters. But these were detected and neutralized by the security forces.

The Hindu reported that two jawans of the terroritorial army were killed, injuring seven others when the ultras opened fire on a column of about 40 – 50 soldiers of the battalion who were returning after their morning exercises in Kali Bari in Kathna. The central reserve police force had deployed five companies for relief and rescue operations in the earthquake ravaged Uri, tenghar and other areas of J & K.

Brushing aside apprehensions that the opening of the LoC would provide newer channels for Pakistan – based militants to cross over into

Jammu and Kashmir, there were fewer incidents of violence, the basic aim was to provide succour to the quake affected people in PoK. Ct. General Madan Gopal, DGMO announced that there in no question of the entire LoC to be opened up, but the details have to be analysed. (Oct 20, 2005,The Hindu)

The army was readyto implement any decision of the government on Pakistan's offer of free movement of Kashmiris across LoC, the troop fatality rate had dropped by 40% due to acquisition of modern weapons an better information being provided by the in house and other intelligence agencies. The army was now focusing on reducing deaths and injuries due to non-combat reasons. Apart from implementing and refining the recently unveiled octrine by conducting exercises, the army was also framing separate doctrines for low intensity conflict operations and the united nations peace keeping operations.

The army Ahead of the opening of quake relief centres along the LoC reopened the road connecting Srinagar and Musaffarabad. Braving rough terrain and lanships, army and BRO workers finished the work in record time.

The army opened up Kaman post and the Silkat point in the uri sector was planned up to be opened.

The army opened up the Kaman post and has taken initiatives to open up the Uri sector. The Pakistani and the Indian army had fought great battles here in the year 1971. While the roads are being opened and bridges reconstructed, the biggest challenge before the army is to make it mine free.

The army authorities temporally closed a military run school for villagers at Anagam, after Lashkar terrorists threatened the students parents. Residents of the mountains above bendpora have reported an increased terrorist presence. The government run higher secondary school in the area was also forced to relocate, after the Laskar claimed that Co-education violated the Islamic Principles.

While senior army officials insist that the heightened infiltration is not the consequence of failure in policing LoC, Indian defences do seem to have suffered some degradation as a consequences of the earthquake. Several dozen bunkers, essential to positioning troops on the high mountain for counter infiltration patrols were destroyed along with considerable stretches of counter infiltration fencing.

TNIE, there has been steady withdrawal of army, 5,000 troops from J & K as violence decreased. It is not withdrawal but redeployment of forces from J & K to the NE as violence level comes down.

There was serious warning on custodial deaths. Lt. Gen. Dhillion is said to have told the meeting that 'error of judgement in soldierly actions is acceptable but error of intention will be viewed very seriously.

The army staged a flag march following clashes between muslims and Buddhists triggered by reports alleged descreation of the Quran at a mosque in Kargil. Clashes exempted between Muslims and Buddhists at Budh Kharboo in Kargil area after some unidentified persons allegedly tore off pages of the holy book in a mosque there.

The seizure of huge quantities of arms, ammunitions and explosives in the recent past in different parts of Kashmir did not suggest any let-up in the designs of militants and in efforts from across LoC. (March 24,2006,The Hindu) The diary recovered from the hideout of a top HM militant had the details of money spent for processing high quality explosives. The army recovered a cache in the Trehgam area based on the information provided by locals.

TNIE reported that the army ignored specific information on Pakistani movements in the Kargil area of J & K leading to bloody clash in 1999. Doval who headed the IB in 2004 – 2005, termed it as national of intelligence failure' there was communication sent to the people concerned. The only defence given by certain agencies was that it was marked to a person and perhaps it did not reach the person sitting on the other side of the table. Pakistan's intentions has become clear June 2, 1988, the government agencies were alerted nine months earlier. The communication on Kargil was signed personally by the then IB Director Shyamal Dutta. This in itself was unusual as IB directors normally don't sign such documents. It was sent personally by him to the defence minister, to director general of military intelligence, and various officers. All it said was it was not marked to Dumon, it was marked to the DGMO. Lamenting that there was no 'response' to Dutta note, Doral said that if the agency provides the information, the user agency must invariably provide the feedback. (April 11,2006,TNIE)

Army chief, General J.J. Singh declared the Tithwal Made village open and dedicated if to the residents. The dedication of the village marks the culmination of the massive rehabilitation and reconstruction drive undertaken by the army under 'operation sadbhavana. (June 23, 2006,The Hindu)

Coverage of Militancy Related Stories in the State.

During the period of study. There were forty three stories in The Hindu and sixty three stories in the New Indian Express.

The Hindu reported that militants slit the throat of five men of Bihamdhoka village in Rajaori district and in a similar fashion killed the resident of saglnue village. The mujahideen was responsible for such heinous act. There were reports in both the newspapers wherein militant killed one person and injured 14 other including seven journalists. The militant outfit al

Mansooran and Jemat – Ul – Muja hidden have claimed responsibility for the attack security forces foiled an infiltration bid in Jammu and Kashmir killing its militants and four army personnel wherelse such reports were absent TIE. In another encounter on the same day Ibrahim Dar a key Hoz – Ul – Mujahideen operative, the architect of a alliance between high and (LeT) cadre in srinagar organized a high profile car bombing and suicide attacks was killed. Many coloumn of news study in the Hindu reflect the security forces having been doing even though stray incidents of Human rights violation gets reported. Such reports did not find a highlight on the next day TIE. The hindu as well as TNIE reported in extra large bold type headlines of the bomb blast by an unidentified bomber, killing 4, and leaving it more injured. Hiizbulla Mujaheen Group was responsible for such heinms act. The suicide bomber rammed the explosive ladden car into the army vehicle, but subsequent investigation revealed that the attacker had just about managed to escape from the scene shortly before the blast. Both newspapers that such acts were perpetuated to derail the peace process. The Hindu as well the New Indian Express reported on July 10, 2005, the largest infiltration since India – Pakistan peace process was initiated 19 months ago. In a 100 hour army operations between the army and militants nine militants who had crossed the LoC on the other side of the border of Gurez sector of North Kashmir. The report also stated the army had killed 52 militants during 14 infiltration attempts since April in the Kashmir valley alone. (July 16, 2005, The Hindu) There was extensive valley alone. There was extensive coverage of reports on Lashkar hand such in Ayodya Attacks in both newspapers by TNIE failed to give much importance to crossing over the border by the militants. Though the Hindu reports did not show much apprehensions of Prabab Mukerjee earlier it was prompted to high light the course of infiltration as soon as the large bid to taken infiltration across the border. The reports denied the attempts were not significant like kargil.

The Hindu revealed at much later date that the new Indian Express of the ploy used by militants to sabotage on going peace process.

The 11 Hizh-Ul-Muoagudeb nukutabts were hired by top Hizh-Ul-commanders to hurd grenades, in crowded places, as wals pard Rs. 6,000 for killing borther of minister of state for Home A.R. Veeri. These militants were allegedly responsible for killing of chief minister mufti Mohammed Sayeed's nephew. But the New Indian Express did not cover all the militancy related news stories. Militants lobbed the grenade on a security patrol at south Kashmir Bijohare township o Anantanag district 55 kms. From Srinagar – Jammu National highways causing splinter injuries to 19 pedestrians and a Jawan. But such reports were not highlighted in the Hindu.

The Hindu as well as the Indian Express had given a wide coverage to militant attack on the tourist reception centre accommodating 24 passengers a day before the bus to Musaffarabad is to be flagged off. The venue is hardly a few meters from Sher – E- Kashmir stadium where PM, Manmohan Singh is to flag off the bus. The four militant organizations Al – nasireen, save Kashmir movement, Al – Arifeen and Farzarden – e- Millet have owned responsibility for the attack. The government is firm on not letting militants derail the peace process and the bus did leave for Musaffarabad as per schedule. A high level meeting presided by Home Minister Shivraj Patil, home secretary U.J. Duggal, Director Intelligence Burean E Narshim and special secretary (Internal Security) Anil Chowdhry. (April 7, 2005) Despite the governmental efforts to tackle the peace process,the militants have taken efforts to derail the process every now and then. But this attempts is failed by the boldness with which the Indian government is creating a conductive atmosphere for peace.

The separatist leader Syed Geelani declared that the bus to Muzaffarabad was not a significant step towards peace in Kashmir, but an attempt to make the line of control the permanent border and maintain a status quo. Mr. Geelani demanded that Pakistan had been trapped by India and united states and instead of furthering the cause of Kashmiris was helping India in its agenda of continuing with the status quo.

The bus passengers were unfazed 24 of the 29 passengers crossed over to the other side of the LoC in spite of the threats from Al-Nasheen. The report further stated that people have shown courage in the face of struggle. The congress party Sonia Gandhi, the communist part of India (Marxist), CPI (M) general secretary M.Y. Tariamit, the CPI national secretary D. Raja all condemned the attack. Both the newspapers consistently supported the cause of the passengers as well as the honourable step taken by the respective governments.

The Hindu reported that the people have come out to greet the bus after a mood of reconcilation after a day – long conference of CM's. On Internal security and law order Dr. Singh wanted the terrorists to grasp the mood of the people.

The infiltration across the border has increased though a thaw in bilateral relations is mooted. The terrorist activity was in lull for a period of 4 months and it has once again raised its hood was told by the union defence minister Pranab Mukerjee at the conference on "peace perspectives on south and south – east Asia : Prospects and challenges at the Punjab university there was interview coverage in TNIE of the double standards on terrorism and there was a need to have political courage and statesmanship within the region to grasp new challenges as well as opportunities for peace in the sub continent. (April 15, 2005)

The TNIE , The Hindu had word coverage of the car bomb blast killing army men.

The Hindu report that of army men were killed, 20 injured while TNIE quoted 6 army men and injuring 19 others. Though their were differences in the number being quoted both stated the militants detrioated the IED planted in a car parked on the road hit the private bus carrying the army men proceeding on leave. The Hizb – ul – mujaheedeen have claimed responsibility for the attack. This is the third car bomb attack by militants in the past two months and second within 11 days. (June 25, 2005, TNIE) Deputy Inspector General of Police Central Kashmir range said that car was probably packed at the site earlier and the bomb detected with remote control.

Army camps have constant target source of attack for the militants two persons including Jaish – e- mohammed militant and the Jem militant Aftab Ahmed, a resident of Doda district were killed. In Search operation, troops found and defused two detonators with 1.8 kgs of RDX in a hide out. (April 19, 2005, TNIE)

Even as the (CBMS) were taking a gigantic leap, militants callously treated such mometous beginning as well as renewed threats to derail smoothening of the peace process. The militant groups Al-Nasrem, Al-Arifeen, Farzade-e-millit and the same Kashmir movement have posed new threats to bus passengers with hilarious. (April 3,2005,The Hindu) Statements like they have the list of the bus passengers in their hands and would turn time "into coffin" the militant attacked the village defence committee members who were returning after the work killing four members of the family. The victims were not carrying any firearms with them. But it went unreported on the same day in TNIE.

The increased security from Srinagar to the last point along the LoC, militants triggered a landmine at Hanjiwara near pattern when workers were busy repairing the roads. Similar story appeared in the new Indian Express when seven persons were injured in the IED explosion. (April 6, 2005, The Hindu)

Both the Newspapers mentioned on the threat issued to passengers and there has been a source of worry for many passengers whose relatives live in areas that are not directly connected with Musaffarabad. The passengers were asked to meet their relatives to take the Wagh border.

The PoK based Hurriyat, headed by Farooq Rehmani has decided to boycott all the programmes chalked out by the government to celebrate the starting of the road link across the LoC. (April 6, 2005, TNIE) But such reports were missing the Hindu. The presence of second list of passengers with the militants contradicts the claims of Kashmir CM an there was no leakage of information from the government. (April 14, 2005, TNIE)

The Hindu reports, that a top – Hizb commander killed when president embarked a his two day visit security forces achieved a major success by eliminating the top commander of the pro- Pakistan Hizbbul-mujhideen and his body guard in his little village. (April 17, 2005, The Hindu)

The militants beheaded a policemen and shot dead an activist of the resulting PDP while five others were killed in separate incidents with strong protest in the Niskht area condemning the killing of the Assistant sub-Inspector Ali Mohammed Rah. Such reports were missing TNIE.

The Hindu reported death of the Nephew of Mufti Mohammed Sayeed by militants, when he was coming out of the mosque in his hometown, Nijibe hara. But no such reports found prominence in The New Indian Express. The Al-man sooreen militant outfit owned responsibility for the attack. (May 4, 2005, TNIE)

The militants took the initiative of killing the J & K civic panel chief, pattan Municipal council president Mohammed Ramzan Main and three other police body guards. One of the four militant outfit Al- Arifies claimed the responsibility for the attack.

Like the unfolding of a thriller, the New Indian Express gave a full account of the first major attacks of the militants after a new season of bonhomic began between India and Pakistan. A man lying in mangled white Maruti Gypsy was waving his blood drenched hand – collegue Harrinder Singh, blood oozing out of dozen of wounds across his chest, a woman running on the road splashed with pieces of windscreen, a bunch of injured CRPF men were trying to pull each other up, the shops around were in a total mess, and much more that meets the eye was the first – hand account of the balst by express reporter.

The Hindu and TNIE covered return of violence grenade attack near the school killing two women, 60 persons, including 25 children were injured. Home bound students of the Tyndale Biscoe school along with pedestrians, bore the brunt of th blast an unidentified militant threw a grenade at a security force on Lal Chowk around 2.40 p.m. (May 13, 2005)

TNIE and The Hindu quoted police arrested former NCA and senior National conference leader Gul Rafeequi for allegedly escorting a top militant commander in his official car to Amritsar. Goel Rafeequi was booked under relevant clauses of the criminal conspiracy and unlawful activities Act. (May 21, 2005)

The Hindu that a total strike was observed in Kashmir valley in protest against the alleged descration of the quran by US soldiers at Guantaname Bay, and the police achieved a major success with the killing of the HM Commander Mohammed Yusuf in an encounter in Kawoosa. But TNIE news story failed to indicate the death of the militant instead a high light the after shocks in J & K to Koran descration. (May 28, 2005)

TNIE after a brief lull, the militants detonated an explosive laden car in Anantnag town and hurled a grenade in the Dalgate area of srinagar, wounding nearly 40 persons. The blast was detonated by a remore control device when an armoured vehicle of the (CRPF), its apparent target was passing by the blast injured 13 civilians and seven CRPF personel. The wounded layin a pool of blood. (Aug 22, 2005 TNIE) One foreign militant was killed in Kupwara district while the body of a special police official Reyaz Ahmed shah was fished out of Jhelum after he was abducted 11 days ago. A woman, Zenifa Akhtar, was abducted by militant in Handwara and later killed.

The Hindu five top militant were killed when Rashtriya Rifle accompanied by special police officers, launched a search in the Mukhi Forest area on information that five commanders all foreign mercenaries held meetings when security forces caught them by surprise.

The militant group Jihad council chairman Syed sulahuddin made but right statements regarding the announcement of ceasefire when General Musharaff proposed the borders are to made irrelevant long as the Indian troops are stationed in Kashmir. TNIE and Hindu wherein the militants attacked shopping complex, a school and post office were situated in the area where the car was parked. The explosive was RDX and weighted not less than 210 kg most have been kept in the car along with an improvised explosive device. The tour wore a deserted look and police and paramilitary forces were deployed to maintain law and order.

The Hindu coverage of different set of training camps is proliferating on this side of (LoC) to train local population against militants who have come here to fight in the name of Jihad. The people are trained in elementary use of weapons for self defence.

Locals learning to use weapons is the way of survival. The dangers of militant attacks increase as the passes open up with the melting of snow and the militant descend to lower attitudes. The first village defence committee, formed at Marrah in surrankate, was instrumental in fighting militancy. Now Youth from this village are training people in other hamlets. The locals are trained in the basic technique of fighting with weapons, mostly 303 rifles through demonstration. (Sep 25, 2005 The Hindu) The stress is on co-ordination and using the combined fire power to repulse a militant attack. Though peace has returned, many areas are still militant infested. Measures were taken from local villages to protect their life and property though security arrangements were beefed up every now and then.

The Hindu coverage of troops foiled yet another incursion bid from across the border and five members of the militant's family were wounded while security forces seized RDX and rescued persons from the clutches of ultras overnight.

The police arrested four men allegedly working as conduits for terrorists outfits in Kashmir at the behest of (ISI) inter services intelligence. The Hindu reported that police recovered arms, ammunition, fake currency, a sketch of the palam air force station and army combat fatigues from them such frequent arrests only denote that there has been cross – border infiltration But TNIE headline specified the target of the militants unlike the Hindu. The headline read "Bid to attack Air Force station" where else the Hindu did not boldly identify the target of the militants. It leaves the public misinformed like any other report on without any sign of consciousness.

The Hindu reported that the IED, planted on the Bumbi – Supore road in north Kashmir's baramulla went off ministes after the ministers cavalde. went past at 4.15 p.m. The J & K ministers, purzada mohammed syed and G.A. Mir and two legislators escaped a bid on their lives. On June 27, Jammu and Kashmir minister of state for Home A.R. Veeriescaped an asssination attempt when the police arrested an armed HM minutes before he was to address a meeting in Anantnag district. The report also cited the killing of 10 persons including seven militants.

The Hindu the increase in militant activity across the border has increased with 6 militants being killed in an encounter in Keri sector of the Rajori district, though constant vigil and combing operations are being held along the LoC, by the village defence committee (VDC). A VDC of 15 Gujjar muslims is collaborating with VDC's comprising members of the minority community in the same Kalkute belt.

TNIE and The Hindu that the six heavily armed terrorists stormed the high security markshift Ram temple were killed in the encounter before they could damage the Shrine. The makeshift temple had come up the day the disputed Babri Masjid mosque was demolished 13 years ago. Almost all leaders including the separatists leader condemned the attack for the fragile peace process may stand liquidated.

The fourth infiltration attempt along the LoC in the past two weeks had killed four soldiers, a subidar while trying to foil an infiltration bid along the

LoC. Four Lashar - e- Toiba were killed in the battle and failed intelligence reported the arrival of Abu Hanzala, divisional commander and Abu Ahmed responsible for several attacks.

The security forces defused an improvised explosive device found planted on the Amarnath Yatra route near nandari, to protect more than 3,959 registered pilgrims flagged off by Mangat Ram Sharma at 5 a.m. Evidences recovered goes to prove that terrorists commit collateral damage on every occasion in spite of the vigilance deployed every where.

TNIE had a extensive report of militant training camps in Pakistan, with instances drawn from the Pakistan Herald magazine in its cover story exercised that afte a period of lull, one of the country's oldest militant training camps at Manshra in the North west frontier province (NWFP) is bursting with activity. Though there are officials denials by the Interior Minister Aftab Khan Shrpao, militant outfits like Hizbul

The Minister for state for Public health and engineering syed Bashir Ahmed escaped inherit when around 5 p.m. militants in Budsha chowk area fired at the minister's car as it passed by. The Hindu report never mentioned that he was at the residence of CM Mufti Mohammed but the new Indian Express made a mention that he was at CM, residence and the militants fired at the vehicle. The ambiguity in report is found in the news report other than the fixed structure of the News story.

Deputy director of the soil conservation department in Srinagar who is a HM militant as well as Hawala operator has been arrested for illegal activities. The special staff of the SW Delhi police in Co-ordination with military intellgence arrested four alleged militants working as conduits of Pakistan's ISI.

Foreign secretary, Shyam Saran that training camps continued to exist in Pakistan.

The Hindu coverage of 13 militants infiltration into the valley in Keran and Uri sectors, nine militans were killed at chotari in the Uri sector, North Kashmir, and another four militants killed in the Kiran sector of Kupwara indicates the spurt in infiltration after a brief spell of lull. The army and the security forces aren't inert, but routing militancy in every possible way. The report also states that nine bodies were found dead after 100 – long – hour battle.

TNIE coverage of the ruling PDP leader Moulor Iftikhar Hussain Ansari had a Narrow escape as police detected an IED planted by militants on a road in Bulgara district just before his visit to the area. Some civilians were injured when militants tossed a grenade towards a security patrolling party at Koil' muoch – Kulgam in Anatang district.

Mujahideen, Harkaul Mujahideen Al – Badr Mjahideen, Lashkar - e - toiba and Jaish - e- Mohammed managed to stay in touch with the cadre in 2003 – 04. The report on the regrouping of the militant group comes amid the composite dialogue process.

The camp rejenuvates the deactivated in the events following 9/11 2002, and entertained new recruits in the age group of 13-15 years. Official funding to the militants continued as the Musharaff government has permitted them under a regime of "controlled freedom". The recruitment was being done through man-to-man contact programmes. But detailed reports were not found in the Hindu.

The Hindu coverage indicated a stern warning to Pakistan government refrious activities by hinting on the attack on the eve of imagination of the Srinagar – Musaffarabad bus service on April 6 and the recent one on Ayodaya could have bearing on the dialogue process.

Repeated terrorist attacks had the political to disrupt the peace process with Pakistan, the PM statement of June 6 is a clear indication of the governments unequivocal stand on the on going composite dialogue.

Security forces arrested five more militants in the wake of Ayodya attack, who were planning to trigger explosions in different parts of J & K. The Le-T module posted indicate the continued bid to disrupt normal life.

The infiltration bid across the LoC was covered by two different newspapers in their own way. TNIE, headline read 'Pak violated ceasefire twice. India, whereelse the Hindu indicated that "Pakistan alleges ceasefire violation followed by another new story India denies allegation". The question of person being abducted during the search operation along the LoC is a matter of buffeing to every keen reader, as the reporters have stated the Poonch sector of LoC as he may fail to tell exactly the place of intruder.

The Pakistani foreign office summoned Indian deputy High commissioner I.C.A. Rahavan and handed a demarche (protect note) on the alleged incident Mr. Raghavan reciprocated the claim stating that there was no evidence in it. Pakistan government pays too much attention when a PoK man was being abducted but the laxity on the cross border infiltration is left.

The army denied that they violated the ceasefire agreement for the troops stopped firing as soon as there was no firing from the other side. Such claims are fallacious for there was firing from the Pakistani side. An explosive laden car driven by a suspected militant on the srinagar – gulmarg road was cornered by the Budgams police and averted a major tragedy Militant had put a fake Delhi registration number and two persons carrying pistols jumped out of a vehicle, the driver too sped away but the police chased on a motorcycle later discovered that the car had RDX weighing 100 kg.

Militants slit threats of 6 villagers road the horrendous story of the Hindu, I Biramdhoke village in Rajori district. (Oct 11, 2005) The militants abducted the men in the morning and after six hours in carpentry slit their throats though the village has 30 village defence committee numbers. The HM are responsible for the gruesome act. Wherelse TNIE the story readers five massared in Pre –dawn attack in Rajouri district" killing five hindus but the Hindu' reported that the throats were only slit.

Around 5 p.m. when Buddhieh chowk area was bustling with life, the militants hurled a grenade on police vehicle which caught fire. As the city reverborated with sound of gunfire, people ran hilter skelter. Both the newspaper made a very prominent coverage of the incident, but TNIE even had a road map showing the route of the militants and their hideouts. In the discriminate firing that continued seven journalists were injured.

Even in the militant related activities om Srinagar, the Hindu reported Gunfight ends in Srinagar" wherelse TNIE reported "38 rescued in Srinagar reveals how headline need to be better focused not told in implied manner. It's title that provokes the reader to gave a glance. The Hindu indicated the figure rescued to be 72 which contradicts the number told in TNIE. With the heavy presence of police and BSF, life in city centre of Lal Chowk and Budhah was disrupted as the gun battle between forces and the militants took a centre stage. While the Hindu reported that it 24 hours, TNIE indicated it 21 hours. The Hindu reported that our men drilled holes to drop grenades, TNIE reported that they were using slab cutters to drop hand grenades to flush out militants. Militant group, Al mansoorian and Jamiat – Ul – Mujahideen claimed responsibility for the attack.

Both the newspapers have very often reported stories of camps in PoK and detailed report describing the gamut of the militancy groups. In the 742 Km long LoC, the army is faced with a spiraling cycle of infiltration and violence. Between January – July 2005 there have been 139 infiltration cases, as compared to 356 in the same period in 2004. But in July 2005 there were more than 15 infiltration attempts, with 58 militants killed. The groups infiltrating are led by the HM, followed by Let and JeM. Express was witness to an operation at Natu Post in Poonch sector, where the 93 Infantry Brigade ministered movements of suspected militants in two houses just short of the LoC, and under the shadow of a Pakistani army post. Army sources estimate nearly 700 militants are waiting in holding camps in PoK, in order to be thrust into J & K. While the army says there are 53 functional camps across the LoC, captured militants

The New Indian Express, four militants of HM were killed in a gun battle with troops in Poonch district of J & K.

Have only confirmed being trained but provided no details of camp locations. Top army officers say there are 28 control stations functioning in PoK, these are intend with as many as 1,113 radio sets in the valley alone. This does not include satellite phones used by top Laskhar militants. Helped by the Multi-tier fencing on the Loc, the army has been able to push back many infiltrators. Yet, efforts to plug the flow of funds to the militants hasn't been so success ful. According to estimates more then 533 lakh passed through Hawala channels into militant hands between January July 2005. The figure for the first seven months of 2004 was Rs.409 lakh. In short, militant infrastructure is ticking away across the LoC, despite pakistani's repeated commitment to the contrary.

Huge cache of arms and explosives including 1,572 rounds of ammmunication and 2.5 kg RDX have been recovered form there militant hideouts in Rajanuri and poonch district of J &K. The Poonch and Rjuri district have always served as militant hideouts as reported very often by In the parliament attack case, the Hindu read 'the apex court upheld Geelani's acquittal" whereas the PTI report of TNIE had diametrically opposite heading "Afzal's counsel says SC should have threatened him like shakut".

The Upholding the supreme courts judgement is widely been appreciated by the Hindu but TNIE feels that the co-accused in the plot to be has to be dealt afresh as he was not given the privilege of representative in the trial court. The court prejudices and inadequacies were highlighted in the TNIE. Geelani address to the press on the unfair trial meted out to Afzal found highlights in TNIE but not the Hindu.

In audacious none calling a shook at the authorities, militant have put up posters in a government school in Jammu region announcing cash rewards to people providing information about security force personnel and their informers. In the posters, the outfit declared a Rs.1 lakh award to a person who helps in the killing of an informer and Rs. 2 lakhs on the head of a security peson and his rifle, while Rs. 50,000 would be given to those giving information an informers to security forces.

Threats loom large from militant outfits such as LeT, HM, JeM, who have sent a wave of panic in the tours ahead of the independence day celebrations in srinagar. A good number of foreign militants were roaming around in the city and all roads leading to the stadium have been sealed and traffic diverted. But TNIE had a file photo and not even whimper of rumour reported.

The Hindu coverage of the forward belt of Kargil, particularly the Balatik sector which has a ethnic mix of Butta, shmne and purry speaking areas has been the direct victim of shelling across LoC for several decades. The normal functioning of classrooms, the classes which were earlier held in the underground bunkers in a suffocated environment are now held in open. Two years ago, the pass percentage in the school was 30% and now 75%.

In a strike ahead of the Independence day celebrations, militants killed five Hindus an injured nine others in vilapur district. The militants 20 in number attacked 2 UDC numbers and opening fire indiscriminately. This provoked US to say that every national day celebration has to be carried out only after beefing up security or within the folds of the army. The Hindu reported that this was the second time that Shaja village in Udampur district had been attacked two were dragged out of their houses and killed and another villagers tongue was chopped off before he was released.

An improvised explosive device (IEd) planted at the adjacent park and fitted with a time device, burst an hour before CM mUfti Mohammed sayeed arrived at Bakchi stadium. Militants made an attempt in pattern Baramulla, compare to disrupt the independence day celebrations.

The Hm, Al-Mansooreen and the Islamic front have claimed reponisbility for the attack. Such repeated incidents go to tell the hindrance created by the militants to shatter normal life in the area. Flats for migrant pandits intending to return to the valley brings surface but, adding it at the end of the news story IED blast near Srinagar I pay venue TNIE either indicates the lack of space to the story or of slightly treated of a rehabilitation measure.

The new Indian Express has unearthed more evidences behind the Ayodya attack. They have traced the story in such a manner to identify the denominations to which the terrorists belonged, either to JeM or LeT. They also have identified the kind of transaction that emerged during after the attack. This tells more on the investigative nature of the news stories than the Hindu.

The militants attacked another nearby camp with grenades and automatic wapons causing injuries to two security personnel and three civilians. Militants beheaded a man belonging to the nomadic Gujjar community on the outskirts of a village in Udampur district. They also wrapped the head in a police of cloth with warning support security forces and face death on it. Mohammed Amin who once belonged to Harket – Ul – Jihad – e – Islami disclosed that at present there are more than 5,000 boys who are being trained in various terrorist camps across LoC and they were paid a sum of Rs.2,000 every month as an allowance to meet their daily needs. Intially he was used as a helper in the camps and later on sent to fight the troops. The disclosure made by Amin pint to new routes being taken up by militants.

Two militants challenged the security forces guarding the theatre as soon as minutes after Manir Khanappeared on the seen as "Mangal pandey'. An alert policeman shot dead one of them while the other feed and took refuge in an adjacent house. The militant's intention was to storm the CPRf camp near the Cinema hall. The identity of the militants, believed to be foregners, wasbeing ascertained. Three hardline rebel groups, the Harket Mujaheedeen, the Jaish - e - Mohammed and Al-Mansurain claimed responsibility for the attack.

Six members of special police officers family, including four children were killed when militants of the Hizbul Mujahideen attacked their house in Udampur district of Jammu and Kashmir. The family is undaunted and determined to continue the fight against terrorism. The militants opened fire from the maize field adjourning the officers house. The Hindu gave the fate report on of barkat's family a glimpse of the difficulties endured by villagers who refuse to support the Jihadis. According to Burkat, the militants threatened his family with dire consequences if the male members did not joint the outfit.

Barkat and Rafiq joined the police force as special police officer on order to defend their family.

When militants ambused their convoy near Awartipureon the Sringar – Jammu national highway five soldiers from the Rashtriya Rifles were killed and seven others injured. Three jawans were killed instantly after two militants hiding in a bylaw opened discriminate fire on the convoy and labbed grenades. Searches were launched to nab the militants responsible for the attack. The Pakistan based LeT claimed responsibility for the ambush.

Both the The Hindu and TNIE reported that the army in now facing a new breed of militants armed with hitech devices. The disturbing discovery was made after the army seized a huge cache of fire arms, ammunition and a compact disc (CD) in the remote Gurez sector along the LoC. The CD has formulae and manuals to assemble IEDs, bombs and rockets. It contains an arms training manual and bomb making techniques the army claimed that besides the CD, explosives 50 – 100 car bombs were recoverd. Pre-fabricated boards, printed circuits, RDX circuits, detonaters, battery operated IEDs and large number of remote control devices. The arms and ammuniction were buried in the eight – meter – long natural cave in the rugged mountains of Gurez close to the LoC. The recoveries were made after the army got a specific tip-off.

The Hindu reported on the disturbing trend after the withdrawal of troops from areas of in northern J & K, there are warrying signs that terrorist organizations are upgrading their offensive capabilities. A haul of over 2,700 kg. of explosives in the Kashmir valley and new bombing tactics along the LoC are also major sources of concern for Indian security officials.

Most of the recoveries consisted of freely available chemicals such as potassium permangate, aluminium powder and terrorists drove cars fitted with explosives along with regular traffic thus evading patrols intended to detect roadside mines and improvised explosives devices.

Where militants were killed in separate incidents in J & K, and an abortive attempt was made to blow up a police station by firing rockets into it. Rashtriya rifles was reported in the Hindu, and the police acted on the tip off and two militants were killed in the encounter. The Hindu reiterated the need to contain, the battle between the militants and the security forces is for from over in the remote areas of Jammu and Kashmir along the Ar panjal areas

Till april 2003, the villages were at the mercy of LeT. This zone had the maximum concentration of militants, as the area was trategically located, provided access to other parts of the state. The hikes were in accessible, in the absence of roads. When the locals picked up weapons to fight back, militancy received a jolt all over the state.

A strategic base was list, when more than 100 militants, most of them foreigners were present. Knowledge of the terrain and their stamina gave the locals the cutting edge in counter military operations. But the terrain provides a number of entry points through dense forests. The local youth enlisted as special police officers were sent to the Jiwali ara to search for militants. There is an excellent rapport between the spos and the sikh troops, thanks to linguistic affinity. Gojri, Spoken by the locals, is similar to Punjabi spoken by the such soldiers in 16 Rashtriya rifles. The disengagement of th spos, when their lives are at risk, has put them in a quandary. Another sore point is that not a single gallantry award has come their way.

The Hindu has cited instances wherein this is the only place in the state, where woman have picked up weapons to protect their families and even confronted militants. This time there are women, including those who lost their husbands, who have been trained in the armed warfare and they are ready to battle it out. Till recently the women knew only how to handle the archaic 303 rifles but now some of them have been taught the use of automatic weapons such as the 47 or even the SCR given to special police officers. Apart from physical security, the immediate challenge before the community is to improve female literacy, which dropped because of militancy. There is no proper education system in the hamlets, particularly for girls. Even now government teachers coming from an elite background from nearby areas play truant Women turning strong hold in the fight against militancy.

The grenade exploded killing 20 people near the Jehangir chowk near the assembly complex around 7p.m. when there was a heavy rush of people at the exihibition crossing as the only flyover in the city war kept out of bounds.

Minor explosions in the state, were boldly reported in the Hindu, but TNIE has neglected such reports.

15 militants and four army personnel were killed in separate militancy – related incidents as security forces failed an infiltration bid in J & K. Another militant was killed in a separate operation by security forces at wailoo in the district.

Ibahim dar key HM operative who commanded the recent bombing offensive in Kashmir was shot dead by the J & K police. Dar organized a service of high profile car bombing and suicide squad attacks, the architect of an alliance between High and LeT. Dar was arrested for a 1996 murder and while in prison he found a mentor in the senior Hiz commnder, Hashim Javed Iqbal. Under Iqbal's tutelage, Dar allied with Srinagar – based elements of the Le-T and Al – Umar to form the save Kashmir movement (SKM).

Though the infiltration level along the LoC has declined compared to last year, the militants communication link continues to pose challenge for the security forces. The communication equipments installed along the LoC intercepts messages between militants and their operators in PoK.

The intercept threw lights on the presence of militants in the state and their support structure in PoK. The most active communication tower of the militant outfit is in Nraiyal techsil (PoK). The exchanges start from 8 p.m. and continue till 10 p.m.

Most of the messages are in Punjabi dialects (hinting at the ethnic origin of the militants) and are in codes, which keep changing. Hence the information gathered is never precise the network cannot be jammed, as it can surjeh over ito other frequencies.

TNIE reported that is quick to decipher that major militant outfits running training camps in (PoK) has bun damaged according to security sources due to earth quake. The camps of militant outfits like Kaish-e-mohammed, Lashkar—Toiba, Tehrek-Ul-Mujahideen, HM and Al-Badar had been damaged to a great extent. All these areas fall within a radius of 10 km from the epicenter of weekend's tremor.

Militants have made about five infiltration attempts smee October 8 earthquake, but the security forces were ugilant an alert to foil such attempts.

The government had also received reports of militant capability being officiated by the people.

About 25-29 of them have been killed and some of them wanted to take advantage of the disturbed situation.

The communication among the militants has been a cause of worry as read in "The Hindu" but TNIE leaves everybody at rest after proclaiming the hideouts that were shattered after the earth quake suggesting no more fear can erupt at least for some time.

TNIE, A prominent CPM leader Ghulam Nabi Ganai was shot dead outside a local mosque near his bouse at Seer – handen village of matter which he was taking some villages.

J & K minister of state for education Ghulam Nabi Lone was shot dead by militant while CPI (M) state secretary My Tangami escaped an hurt in a similar bid in the high security area Tulsi bugy. The militants opened free leaving lone dead and two civilians in a pool of blood.

When the militant challenged the security guard Abdur Rasheed, the militant hurled a grenade and fired indiscriminately. The real target could have been Mr. Targami whose associate Ghulam Nabi Genai was gunned down by militants in South Kashmir.

The Hindu, has taken prompt initiatives to report on the infiltration bid thoroughly wherelse the TNIE gives importance only to when prominent personalities are killed or abducted shows that common man's dilemma often ignored.

Hours before Ghulam Nabi Azad was sworn in as CM of the J & K a militant blew himself up in an explosive – lader car on the outskirts of Srinagar. The suicide bomber was proceeding from south Kashmir on the Sringar – Baramullah highway and TNIE states that the militant gave the security men a chase before detontiny improvised explosive device (IED). The blast took place near the private residence of sayeed. The police had apprehensions about militants strike the city in view of the swearing – in ceremony taking place.

Three BSF personnel, including a head constable were critically injured in a grenade attack. The incident took place when they fired grenades inBSF firing range at kletch. Several militant outfits have condemned such acts for they were either anti-human, anti-Islamic. The first to condemn the attack was LeT elements. The lashkar does not believe in carrying out terror attacks targeting children and women. Several other militants ruled out their hand behind the Delhi blasts.

The Hizbul Mujahideen, Al Badr, Al mansorian, the moderate fartion of the Hurriyat all condemned such acts.

Two heavily armed militants, believed to be part of a fidayeen squad attacked the CRPF bunker in Lal Chowk with hand grenades and resorted to indiscrimate firing. The attack was soon repulsed but not before one CRPF

Jawan died. The CRPF personnel returned the five and in the gun battle which initially lasted for two hours, left two civilians and another CPRF jawan dead.

TNIE had also detailed account of the Al-Mansoorian which has claimed the responsibility for the attack.

Former J & K tourism minister, Senior PDP member ecaped an assassination bid with a minor injury at a public meeting at tangmarg. The Hindu reported 40 sustained injuries while TNIE quotes it to be 60. TNIE reports that Al-arficen was responsible for the attack, the Hindu did not mention anything specifically.

Security forces killed a militant holed up in the hotel bringing to an end the 24 hour long stand off whichbegan the attack on the CPRF.

Another militant moving suspiciously near another hotel was captured. Bhat according to DGP admitted that he was involved in the attack. His accomplice, identified as Furquen of Pakistan gave a tough time to the forces and was finally eliminated by a crack team of police and the CPRF in the basement of th hotel.

The Hindu reported that intelligence and police authorities in J& K had identified a srinagar resident tariq Ahmd dar alleged to have organized the New Delhi serial bombings under survilliance six months ago. He was arrested for funneling cash from Saudia Arabia to the Let in J & K. As new priorities emerged the Dar operation was relegated to a low priority. Thus it found that the militant were actively funded from UAE. The Hindu news reports have analysed the funding agencies for the militants.

Both the Hindu and TNIE for the third consecutive day militants strike in Kashmir – by Parking an explosive laden car outside the gate and was probably detonated by a remote controlled device. As the official car of the former minister of state M.L.A. was directly hit with bruises on the face and his security guards were injured. The Hindu quotes 45 injured wherelse TNIE –40.

The story quake came as a boon for cash as a boon for Lashkar leadership had three sub-headings.

(1) Mission of glory (2) In search of heroism (3) diminishing returns provides an insight into the life style adopted by the terrorist.

Lasker strategists think that high profile terror strikes will allow them to harvest the good will generated by their well funded and organized relief efforts. The death is not the objective of the Lashkar's fidayeen attacks but explicit instructions to fight Indian forces for as long as possible – but to attempt escape if defeat became inevitable. The motivations for joining the jihad in the state appeared to be the prestige and status it brought among the peers rather than affiliation to or an understanding of the Lashkar's ideology.

The news report in The Hindu have go – on to trace the ideology that held the terrorists together but much significance of the ideological framework in their news report are treated very casually.

Contrary to public perception, fiyadeen strikes have yielded only very limited returns, in military terms. In 1999, the year fidayeen attacks began, terrorists dominated 17 Indian police and military performed losing just five of their own cadre. Though the report Sanguine of the result, for thereaders baffled by the numbers being killed by the militants out number the secretary forced that the security forces have to improve their mancover ability.

But by the last year as the Jammu and Kashmir police grow increasingly skilled in storming techniques the figure had reversed 26 terrorist were killed as against 21 force personnel. However pro-jihad magazines in Pakistan including several affiliated to the Lashkar accord a peace of pride to the Fiyadeen – a term used by describe warriors driven by the love of God. Strikes in Jihad press regularly assert that fiyadeen attacks have killed Indian troops by the dozen.

The Hindu has reported that a large scale build up of Lashkar – e – toiba cadres in the mountains above the Bandipura area north of Kashmir has sparked off fears of major escalation. Many Laskhar operatives involved in these attack appear to have infiltrated in the wake of October 8 earthquake, using the opportunity offered by the disruption of the Indian border defences. On November 16, the Jammu and Kashmir police arrested Lashkar operative Samimullah A haus, who had been asked to execute strikes in the state's writer capital, Jammu.

Large scale effort by Jihadish groups had made contact with several top politicians including J & K minister for consumer affairs and public distribution, Yasin and obtained identification from the NC to place operatives in J & K political system. Although there is no evidence that Mr. Yasin or other politicians contacted by Bukhari were aware of his work as a Lashkar organizer or knew of his real objectives, Bubhari testimony has high lighted the vulnerability of J & K political system to penetration of terrorist groups. Using cash – coercion, and common political interests, terrorist groups have long sough to build affilications which can protect their most critical assets, overground sympathesim operating under cover of legitimate businesses and political affiliation from targeting Indian forces. In at least some measure, however, support for terrorism seems to be paid in cash, rather than won at gunpint – a method, intelligence servers, refer to as 'active mesures' The troops from the army's south Kashmir – based victor force counter terrorism formation recovered diaries and letters recording the financial activities of the

Hizb's. Kulgam districtunit. The documents show that that the Kulgam unit alone received over Rs. 4.5 million a staggering amount given that the organization has no more than a few dozen armedoperatives active in the area.

The Hindu reports have unearthed over all affliatory nature of the terrorists and the surplus of initiatives to corroborate the former has been made relevant but TNIE fails to give raise nad 'etre' of the connivance of the terrorists with the political system.

A letter written to the Kulgam Hizb commander, Khurseed Ahmed Shekh by still un identified operative code – named Rahmullah showed much of this money was used to purchase good will. Rahmullah's letter asked shiek to make several monthly payments to sympathizers. For example, Rs. 2,500 was to bepaid to a local notable, code named 'boss' while Rs. 4,000 was to be given for being sent to a girl's school run by local Islamists. Hizb finances were also committed to south Kashmir Islamists bitting the influence of the CPI. The generous funds send to the Kulgam Hizb were both reward for such operations and special assistance to help the unit recover from a series of blows delivered to its command structure.

Forces operating in J & K have long complained of lack of an adequate legal framework for action against those who harbour and handle funds for terrorist.

The new unlawful activities act which has provisions to facilitate the prosecution of overground supporters of terrorism, individuals who do not actually carry out acts of violence but are critical to their execution. The test of effectiveness lies in how it is implemented.

TNIE reported that one of the major network of the LeT a module arresting one of its militants was busted by the state police, including the man allegedly responsibly for the attack on the rally addressed by PM Manmohan Singh.

In a major security breach militants blew up a Sumo vehicle near the entrance of the highly fortified old airport in sringar where fighter jets were based. As no one was injured, the attack was merely carried out by militants to get publicity.

Four militants, including two Pakistani commanders of Al Badr and L–et outfits were killed and four policemen injured in gun battle in J & K. Acting on specific information about the presence of the militant in a house at boatmen's colony, the police assisted by thearmy and CRPF cordoned off the area.

The peace activist Harmeet Soodan was abucted in Iraq, it meant sleepless nights for relatives far away in J & K's Buramulla and Pubjab Mohali.

Soodan been to a sikh family in Baramulla immigrated to Canada but kept the connection with his homeland alive and the valley is chipped into secure his release. The srinagar based citizens forum coalition of civil society had launched a campaign for his safe release.

Militant forced upon a joint patrol party of J & K police and security forces at Jugal – Sakhimalan resulting in the death of (SPO) militants later managed to escape under the cover of darkness. (January 1,2006 The Hindu)

The character of militancy in Jammu and Kashmir was changing with the militant cadres, though reduced in number, demonstrated greater strike capability a higher academic profile and with reach the governor sinha critical the Pakistan establish ments silence over the activities of the terror outfits and the enlightened modieration which the US or the western world thinks president Musharaff is practicing received much flak. (January 1, 2006 The Hindu)

The security forces gunned down the HM batterlion commander in an encounter at Aragam Bandopura in North Kashmir, killing three militants. The security forces retaliated and four soldiers including a (SCO) were injured in the clash. Militants hurled a grenade on a police patrolling party wounding three policemen and six pakistanians. Militants outfit S – E M claimed responsibility for the blast.

HM militant, special police officer mehra ed – in safi, VDC member Bansi Loc were among three killed in separate incidents in J & K.

HM Chief syed Sahabuddin ws arrested in Musafferabad along with Ghulam Hasool shah abas GeneralAbdullah ofS – Ul – M, Mufti Rauf of Sem, Zakir – Ur – Rehman, Let, TiK along with several other top kashmiri militant during a demonstration.

Pro-Pakistani HM Uttars an explosive driven car when a army convoy was passing the old airport road. The explosive car was blown toprocess

Suspected Let militant be called a man and threw his body ina village and the note recovered from his body of the victim that deceased was an informer.

The HM ultras had sized the place of worship (mosque in Akura village) in anantanag district of J & K was shot dead by security forces.

The Hindu ensures on the changing vistas of the terrorists target which is a reminder to improve fudddy – duddy ideas on security infrastructure and callowness of the tactics adopted by security establishment.

The militant huled a grenade at the house of derishAbdul Ahad in Muribag locality seriously injuring over 20 persons. (June 23, 2006 The Hindu) This is the first such attack on the dervish in Kashmir. The attack on Ahmed sahib has strong reaction from political parties cutting across party lones. CM Ghulam Nabi Azad, Former CM Mufti, Hardline Hurriyat Conference leader Syed Ali Geelani, National Front Chairman Nayeesn Khan, Democratic Liberation party chief Hashm Questhr, PCC president Perrade Mohmmed Sayeed, Opposition NC< HM Condemned the attack.

The dervisls being attacked has received much support from all party circles but other issues go neglected.

A series of grenade blasts in Jammu and Kashmir killed at least 25, persons including 10 security men.

The recent wave of violence along the fringes of the Pir Punjal range in southern Kashmir may be linked to a power struggle within the HM ovr the proceeds of the orgnaised crime style extortion operations the police eliminated Bhat, Hm commander, Anantnag district, and his diaries record raised an estimated Rs. 5,95,000 no small amount given that the Hizb active cadre strength in Kulgam and Anantnag is put under 50 men.

Investigators believe that the massive is though to have been intended to compel local contractors to make direct payments to the terrorists rather than to his district and divisional superiors.

TNIE reported that militants lobbed a grenade at a CRPF predict outside a building housing the 'charri mubbrak' the holy make of 'Lord shiva' killing one person and injuring ten persons.

Self styled district commander Nissar Ahmed safi alias Tarabi and his deputy sarafiz Ahmed alias safi were killed in an encounter at Mirbah area of the district. Extortions of money from local contractors gave become the order of the day.

Troops of 16 sikh regiment shot dead eight LeT terrorist who were attempting to cross the LoC at Hema inKeran sector, dispute the successful interdictions of of the the lagest cross – border infiltration attempts in recent months. The terrorists have subsided in cutting thebarbed wires fencing

Year	-	*Terrorists crossing across LoC*
2001	-	2,417
2002	-	1,504
2003	-	1,373
2004	-	537
2005	-	Rising because of the degradation of Indian forward defences
2006	-	597, lower than the 2005 figure

along the LoC, but were then detected with thermal imaging systems and interdicted. Terrorists have also improved their fencing. Penetration skills.

The Hindu reported the precise determination of successful infiltration is near impossible official estimate suggest that it has been on a steady decline.

India has rejected Pakistan's call for a reduction of troops in the region, pointing to continued across – border infiltration.

TNIE reportes stated that victims huled grenade at a vehicle carrying terrorists near suttan Bakery at dal gate.

Killing five persons, injuring 12 others. This was the sixth attack on tourist in the Kashmir valley since the beginning of the tourist year.

The J & K police gunned downone of the utters who master minded the attack on NC MCa salema itto.

The Hindu reported that the police have succeeded in eliminating 44 commander Riyaz Ahmed Bhat less than two days after an attempt on the life of the former J & K minister, Salima Itto. Bhat was responsible for murder of several political activists, including CPI (MX) members, non political civilians.

Eight persons, including five tourists from west Bengal were killed, 37 injured. The motive behind the series attacks that lift eight persons dead was to terrorise people, hit soft target to get maximum publicity. Over 10,000 tourists from different parts of the country are presently in Kashmir the panic among tourists was evident in Samnagar, even when they were enjoying in places like Gilmang, Pahalgam and Sonmarg.

TNIE reported that the earlier blasts had hit tourism to a great extent, but whatever had remained disappeared with recent attacks.

Pakistan maintained that the international terrorist was not units soil, he would be arrested straight away if any proof of his presence was given. Interior minister Aftab Ahmed Khan sherpao quoted that Pakistani had been playing the role of frontline state in the war against terrorism.

The militant outfit, HM, has indicated that it will play a political role in solving the Kashmir issue without reneging on its armed struggle. This was disclosed to in an interview to KNS, a local new agency, by Hiz chief syed saluddin with analyst attaching much importance to his statement.

The chairman of UJC, a musaffarabad based grouping of 13 militan outfits also stated hat ceasefire should not be made a pre-condition. Armed confrontation would acts matually recale as he dialogue process moved forward. Writer Zauf Ahmed Zarif has observed that the militant organization talking about donning a political role will certainly help in making any process a success.

A recent conference in Islamabd organisedby Puwash demaded the inclusion of militants on the dialogue process.

Development in the state during the course of composite dialogue

During the course of study there were five stories in The Hindu and two in the New Indian Express

The coalition partners in J & K are locked in a tassel over the self rule and demilitarization proposal mobile by Pakistan president Pervez Musharaff.

The congress and the PDP have expressed their divergent stands. The PDP has come out openly in favour of self rule with deputy CM and PDP leader Muzaffar Hussain Baig who a reportedly differed with the party, had come out with a signed, full page advertisement in the local daily supporting the self - rule proposal.

The demilitarization proposal has received a set back from the congress led government for there was no army in the three towns but either the CRPF or the state police who were carrying out anti-terrorist operation. With regard to self rule the congress led government with Mr. Azad as the CM, the people of the state elected their representatives to the assembly and self rule has become norms under the Indian constitution.

The friendship between Mr. Azad and NC is a open secret. NC president Omar Abdullah has indirectly rejected the self - rule proposal.

Quoting the PM, Azad said he is invited for talks not only the Hurriyat and other separatist groups who have not so far participated in the elections, but also mainstream parties who have taken part in elections and received people's mandate.

The decision of J & K CM Ghulam Nabi Azad to contest from Budherwah assembly segment will have a long term impact on the politics of the state. The report stats that, these 'days of power' may help the part consolidate further. But the real test will on 2008 when the assembly elections are scheduled to be held. (The Hindu, March 5, 2006)

CM Glulam Nabi Azad kicked off his election campaign from his Balderdash hometown by asking militants to shun violence, surrender and join mainstream. (The Hindu, March 9, 2006)

The PDP and the NC - J & K two major main stream parties appear to be at their competing best in rallying behind Pakistan president Pervez Musharaff proposal for self - rule for Kashmiris on both sides of the LoC.

While PDP has passed a resolution in favour of self rule at Party's central Working committee through Mufti had passed reservations over the issue at a time over the proposal.

The former J & K CM Farooq Abdullah visibly felt upset over the timing and handling of the February 25 round table conference as it was agendless. Shivraj Patil had gives a consent over the organising of the autonomy committee. Dr. Abdullah said the autonomy was within the Indian constitution and we do not know any thing about general Musharaff proposed on demilitarisation and self rule. Where else Ms. Mebooba Mufti has called for 'self rule' concept which would address balanced development and stabilization in all three regions of the state. (The New Indian Express, March 28, 2006)

The panum Kashmir convenor Agni Shankar said there should be a free flow of Indian constitution in the valley and the Indian sovereignty must not be diluted. He also rejected the proposals of self - rule and demilitatrisation of J & K.

However today he demonstrated that 'self rule' was an ideal solution to the Kashmir issue and even suggested a conclave of academicians from universities at Kashmir and Jammu to evolve a consensus on the proposal.

NC Chief Omar Abdullah refrained from using the term 'self rule' one may call it any name, the sum and substance of the peoples demand is an urge for the independence of thestate within a prescribed framework to which India herself has been signatory (on which) Pakistan has now shown a conspicuous shift in the policy.

The former CM Mufti Mohammed Sayeed has declared that the Hurriyat body represents classent and need to put across their point of view.

Coverage of Report Justifying and Glorifying The Past

There are five reports in TNIE where else there were no reports in The Hindu.

TNIE reported that, coverage of report justifying and glorifying the past there are five reports in Advani who had to step down from the presidentship of the BJP following his controversial remarks in Karachi on Pakistan founder Mohammed Ali Jinnah, does not regret describing him as a secular person. Statement on Jinnah was made out of coviction and it was a mistake. To have withdrawn his resignation on return from Pakistan.

Worried that his wavering stand on the issue of Jinnah by first resigning and then with drawing his resignation was because the party passed an unanimous resolution asking him to take it back. Thus Advani cleared his proclaimed stand. The new Indian expres that reported Mr. jaswant Singh visit to Quard-e-Azam Jinnah's mausoleum and his political biography.

It is through posters, bill boards, and wall writings that senior BJP leader L.K. Advani were making their resentiment against him a when you eat this country is food, why sing paens of the Pakistan founder. (The New Indian Express, April 9, 2006)

The documents pertaining to the All India Muslim League from 1906 to 1977 were with the family of late Muslim league secretary sham - ul - hussain they had initially been left behind in New Delhi and were shifted to Pakistan in large steel boxes after the 1947 partition of the sub continent in the direction of Jinnah and remained in the custody of the Hussain family as a private collection. (The New Indian Express, April 22, 2006)

The military enthusiasm was more evident in Pervez Musharaff at the failed Agra summit with PM Vajpayee. According to Jaswant Musharaff second not to understand the debilitating impart of the Kargil conflict had on the atmospheres and his rhetorical overstatement caused deep embarrasement to India and placed a strain on negogiations. In his new book Jaswant "A Call to honour : In service of emergent India" Jaswant Says, the greatest irony was Musharaff ending as the largest gainer from the misadventure as he removed PM Navaz Sherif from power. (The New Indian Express, July 22, 2006)

Coverage of Other Stories

During the period of study there were forty two stories in The New Indian Express and seventy three stories in The Hindu.

The report coverage in the The New Indian Express how even after a host of CBMS the Pakistan government was reluctant to cut this year's defense budget of Rs. 233 billion saying the outlay was necessary to ward off a patent threat from India. Former chief ISO chief Jawed Ashraf Quasi told opposition not to be carried away by the peace process.

Even after the various blasts in and around Kashmir, Yahaan is the first ever movie made in ever - before - seen location in the state.

The Hindu cites that thousand of pilgrim throng the sufi shrine in Jammu and Kashmir in spite of the miilitant threat. The gesture of presenting president Musharaff his birth certificate, and the Pakistan first lady found some time to reflect on a bond that has linked the two countries. Thc parliamentary Affairs Minister Chulam Nabi Azad had very thought fully sent boxes of the choicest peaches from his own garden and naturally when they telephoned him to thank him for the tempting gift, Mr. Azad took the opportunity to ask them to attend the House for passing of the Finance bill.

The Hindu that ties with Pakistan vital, says Mamohan for the peace process is irreversible only if the Actual ground situation with regard to cross-border infiltration is checked. The New Indian Express quotes anti - united states demonstrators as normal life was paralysed due to general strike in protest against the alleged descration of the Holy Koran by troops in Gunatanmo Bay.

The J & K government nor the army had not made arrangement for the media during the coverage of the visit of Hurriyat conference and other separatists leaders to PoK. This amply suggests that the media was largely ignored. The Hindu coverage of the former J & K CM Farooq Abdullah that the state had lot potential for promoting golf.

The Advani trip to Pakistan and the warm welcome accorded to Advani brings home to few facts more closer how Musharaff and Aziz were also the alumni of St. Patron Heralse The New Indian Express coverage of Advani trip to his house in Karachi, and the population has grown by 3307. In 1947 the city had 400,000 people - it is believed to have crossed the 100 mark.

The Hindu coverage of the movement of Bakerwal families along with their sheep moving from low to high attitudes areas in the Pir Panjal range in Jammu and Kashmir.

The Hindu reports, the Sri Lankan chief of Defense staff of Sri Lanka, Vice admiral D.W.K. Sandagiri visited the forward position along LoC.

J & K government is gearing for the Amarnath Yatra which could extend for two months.

A Hindu wrote Pakistan's first national anthem, written by Janannath Azad, a Lahore based Hindu, who write Pakistani's frist national another. Karachi girl fine after heart surgery shows finer moments with people exchange across LoC.

Wildlife enthusiasts are happy, thanks to ceasefire tiger has strayed from PoK.

The Baba Chambliyal Shrine is near the zero line on the Indian side of the Ranbir singh para section and rangers participation set to add colour to the event thousands turned upto watch chambliyal festival and shows that a relaxed atmosphere is an indication of the ongoing peace process. Various such significance reports were found more in the Hindu compared to The New Indian Express predicts the sample interest taken by the Hindu to show the mood reconciliation.

The Belganmyouth repeats feat reaches Srinagar after 34 days of cycling in the Hindu and this short account of bewitching beauty his suggestion that should form anybody's destination leaves anybody hard pressed for travel reach and enjoy the spot harbours sweet memories who plan a visit (The Hindu, June 29, 2005). Two party members from J & K defected from BJP to SP, Sheikh Abdul Rahman (BSP) and Ram Prakash Sharma (BJP) and welcomed at a function here by the party general secretaries, Amar singh and Ram Gopal Yadav and Rajya Sabha member Jaya Bachan (The Hindu, July 1, 2005). The cultural exchange between India and Pakistan remained grim albeit of trade boost as a consequence of the on going dialogue process. Pakistan has banned import of films made or developed in any form, according to the list of 30 banned films. (The Hindu, August 1, 2005)

Another news repoint of the Hindu coverage indicated that two F-165 for Pakistan. The white House had announced plans n March to sell F-165 to Pakistan. The sale had been blocked for 15 years to punish Pakistan for its nuclear weapons programme (The Hindu August 1, 2005). The New Indian Express news story where the rape of a woman allegedly by Pakistani army officials have set off tension in PoK. As the news of the rape spread, united Kashmir people's national party joined the villagers in protest. The New Indian Express in the sale of F-165 to Pak, the US administration promised sale of \$1.2 million military equipment to Pakistan early this year, had notified support of two used

The Hindu, the temple officials reported that over 47,000 pilgrims visited the Amarnath cave in the past 10 days. The five day theatre workshop in Gulmarg, organized by the Yakjah (which means reconciliation and development network in collaboration with the Delhi based pandits is a grim reminder of how Kashmir pandits were murdered by militants. The objective was to build bridges and remove stereotype which have taken over the real picture. Such ventures stand to promoe consensus among linguistic, ethnic and religious diversity of the different geo-political entitics of J & K.

Hindu coverage of putting Kashmir back on the tourist map is laudable measure by the union tourism minister Renuka Chowdhry with an sanction of Rs.40 cores to boost tourism industry.

According to the News Story, "Lofty attraction", the 500 km. plus line of actual line of control (LoAC) separating this part of Jammu and Kashmir and the Chinese occupied territory is no mere barren mass or cold desert. This street was till recently closed to foreigners on account of its sensitive and strategic position. (August 13, 2005)

Such stories depict the isolated areas in the country which can boost the country's tourism every year. The Hindu coverage of the Chinese delegation, led by senior col. Awang Duriji, was received by Brog: Manvender Singh of the Indian team was organized in Eastern Ladakh on the occasion of the independence day celebrations. Iqbal, Pakistan's national poet belonged to anantnag district. For the first time on an independence day, songs sarac Jaban se acha were sung at the Jammu University Auditorium. (The Hindu, August 16, 2005)

Lt. General P.R. Gangadhar took over as the colonel of the Jammu and Kashmir light infantry (JAKLI) regiment at the 16th Biennial Battalion commanders conference held at the regimental centre. JAKLI had added to its credit by producing the first param vir Chakra winner of the regiment, subedar major and Hononary Captain) bano Singh, who did a splendid job at Siachen glacier, highest battle field in the world (The Hindu, August 20, 2005). L.T. Triveni Singh who fought a Suicide squad of militants at the Jammu railway station was also from the JAKLI and was posthumously awarded the Ashok Chakra.

The Hindu coverage of the amaranth Yatra where about four - lakhs devotees visited the cave and 57 died due to poor weather conditions and deteroting health and other reasons. More than 10,000 personnel of the police, fpara military and military forces were deployed. (The Hindu, August 21,2005)

A brother finally speaks to his sister after 58 years reminds as of the softening of the (LoC) in this belt is not only imperative for the divided families to be united but also important to heal the partition wounds which remain afresh.

Pakistan deliberate attempt to force on India was hatched even without sharing with other wings of the armed forces came to light in starting disclosures in an interview to the English daily Dawn by Air Marshal (retd) Khan. Air Marshal (retd) Asghar H Khan, while over the command to Nurkhar had not briefed. Him about any impending war because he was not aware of it himself. So in order to double check, Nur Khan called on the then commander in - chief, General Musa Khan. When questioned Gen. Musa admitted that something was afloat. A still highly sceptical Nurkhan was then asked to meet Lt. Gen. Akthar Hsasan yalik, GoC Kashmir, the man in operation Gibraltar, for further detailes. Gen. Malik told him not to worry, because the plan to send in some 8,000,000 infiltrators inside the occupied territory to throw out the Indian troops with the help of the local population was so designed that the Indians would not be able to retaliate therefore the air force need not get into the war made (The Hindu, September 1, 2005). The performance of the army did not match that of PAF mainly because the leadership was not as professional. They had planned operation Gibraltar, for self glory rather than in the national interest. And they misled the nation with big lie that India rather than Pakistan had provoked the war and we were victims of Indian aggression. The Israel governments cautioned its nationals avoid visiting the valley as it is very high concrete threat. The non binding travel advisory issued by the Israel's national security council's counter - terrorism unit attached to PMO's and does not seem too excited about Israel's warming with wish Pakistan.

The New Indian Express of the sheep imported from India have fallen sick and Pakistani importers are planning to send them back at the wagh border. (The New Indian Express, September 10, 2005)

The New Indian Express, the J & K police has banned unauthorised use of press stickers on vehicles and also warned all cyber café, hotel and restaurants owners to dismantle 'cabinet system' to check immoral activities and waywardness. The information department issued now stickers to the accredited journalists and only those will be authorized to use press stickers on their vehicles (The New Indian Express, September 12, 2005). The move comes close on the heels of a sustained campaign launched by a women's outfit Dukhtaran - e - milant against the increasing menace off flesh trade in the valley.

Pakistan President Pervez Musharaff got into a heated argument with a group of human rights activists who referred to his recent interview to an American daily wherein he quoted as saying that women exploited rape to get visas. The latest row occurred at a conference organized to discuss issues related to women of Pakistan. According to Pakistan English daily Dawn, pandemonium broke out at the meeting organized to promote Pakistan's soft image when after a confrontation with human rights activist an irate president declared that those who opposed his policies was the enemies of Pakistan. (The New Indian Express, September 19, 2005)

The New Indian Express, pregrent workers were forced to deliver without any medical aid whole innocents juveniles were subjected to torture and harassment by Pakistani security forces in northern areas of Gilgit and Balthisten (The New Indian Express, September 19, 2005). The New Indian Express, the former PM remarks came while he released a book on the life of 93 old amla, who has represented the state in Parliament for 21 years. Had the government in 1980 headed public voice, there could nothave been so much blood shed. Amla opposed the dialogue between Raji Gandhi and Farooq Abdullah (in the 1980s) He believed that Farooq Abdullah couldn't be trusted, particularly in the backdrop of the still fresh dismissed of his Farooq) Government by Indira Gandhi.

The earth quake that rocked Jammu and Kashmir billed 200 people and injured 100 people. More than 2000 houses were damaged. The full impact of the quake could not be known as roads to many of the affected villages remained inaccessible due to land slips. No contact could be established with many villages and people protested against the poor response of the administration. (The Hindu, October 9, 2005)

The earthquake that hit Muzaffarabad in PoK, sending shocking waves across north India was the biggest to strike the region in the past 100 years.

The previous record was in 1943, when a quake with a magnitude of 6.7 on the ricter scale hit the region.

The centre offered all assistance to quake hit northern areas directing ministries, the army and the air force to restore power and other essential services and render full help in search and rescue operations.

The army launched large - scale rescue operation "operation Indad" in aid of the earth quake - affected people in J & K (The Hindu, October 9, 2005). A total of 19 army personal cost their lives. In the army swung into action after the earthquake and provided relief in Uri, Rampur, Baramullah, Naogron, Tangdhar, Ponch and other areas. PM Manmohan Singh has sent a message of confidence to Pakistan president Pervez Musharaff following earthquake, which has caused heavy causalities in Pakistan.

The New Indian Express, the role of the army differed where the army is reported to have seized Uri and barred the media from entering the town of Baramullah district in J & K even as the injured were being evacuted. The reason for the recent tremor was cited in The New Indian Express. Over centuries, the Indian plate one of the 13 that make up the earth's crust - has been moving towards the adjacent Eurasian plate at an average speed of 4 cm per year. This movement has cracked the Indian plate into several faults slowly building up stress in the faults and in the plate boundaries. The stress can only be relieved through the great quake reported an internationally renowned quake specialists Roger Bilham and peter molnar of the university of coherado, Boulder, USA and Umod K. Gaur.

Special reports on the faultline areas in The New Indian Express gives new insights in the nature and tenure of earthquake. The science and technology ministry thinks scismic microzonation - assessment of ground shaking at a particular station to construct better quake resistant structures is the only way ahead to predict the time or location of earthquake accurately. (The New Indian Express, October 9, 2005)

The ministry has completed the seismic microzonation of Delhi and is planning to cover all areas falling within 200 km of the Himalayan faultline in future seismic microzonation involved recording the response of soil layers and the variation of ground movement in areas where quakes have occurred It yields a separate map showing the effect earth quakes might have on different areas, which are classified as low, middle and high intensity zones. seismic microzenation is done using ground motion recorders. The main indicators are soil layer thickness, natural ground frequency, shearwave velocity and amplification factor. India offered Pakistan all help and assistance it may require in the wake of massive earthquake which caused widespread death and destruction.

The death toll in the powerful earth quake in J & K has risen to 927, including 619 in Baramullah and 301 in Kupwara (The Hindu, October 11, 2005). The number of injured has now crossed 3,000 and 4,597 houses have been destroyed. Protests were held at various places on the Rampur. Barmullah national highway IA people complained of inadequate relief and security of tents even in Uri town.

Teethwal Village, divided by Kishnaganga river (Neelam in Pakistan) which runs along the LoC has been practically wiped out and 90 bodies were recovered. Before partition, teethwal was part of Muzaffarabad and the ruins of a bridge that connected teethwal with PoK still stands on Kishvilangaga.

The New Indian Express, panic gripped valley as almost all major mosques announced that another earthquake is likely to hit the area. As rumour spread, people rushed out of houses. Many spent time in the open and a few preferred to stay in the mosque. The New Indian Express, the problem with VIP visits is that they ironically serve as distraction in rescue and relief operation (The New Indian Express, October 11, 2005). Visits by personalitics like the PM, the congress president Sonia Gandhi and BSP president to the quake hit areas means shifting of the administrations

Focus to Protocol and the Security of the Highly Protected Leaders

As Sonia visisted Uri to assess the damages caused by the quake an elaborate paraphernabi of state government leaders, including CM Sayeede, offered down and security arrangement. This involved the several helicopters and thousands of army and police personnel. The report states that people here point out the official and security apparatus involved in the arrangements could be better utilized to rescue people who may be verified under the debris, arrange medical treatment for those injured by immediate evacation and provide relief to other needy people.

All Congress CM and PCC, AICC team were dispatched to the affected areas to co-operate the party's relief and rehabilitation work (The Hindu, October 14, 2005). Congress - ruled states adjoining J & K have been asked to send relief material.

The poor relief mechanism and chilly conditions pose serious challenge to over lakh of people affected by earth quake in the Uri belt. In Uri alone, 10,223 persons (official figures) are without shelter. Temperatures have been plummeting every night, falling to degrees celcius. The tents provided so far cannot shield the people from cold.

Uri is the last Indian post to the north of Pir Panjal. In 1948, Governor - General Louis Mountbatten asked the Indian troops not move beyond the

Uri. A ceasefire line was drawn. It divided every home. There is not a village that does not have family member across the LoC. The BSNL opened special lines in Uri town. But it has made little absence of direct telephone line to PIL, communication has been rendered impossible and people have been forced to move but of their homes. In 1948, local recall, Khnda Bakish, the last degree General ternied the delineation of the LoC as a blow to the Pahari muslim in both political and humanitarian temrs.

Delhi hama has donated Rs. 1 crore to Jammu and Pakistan to help survivors of earth quake.

The New Indian Express, the tremors have rendered many survivors in need of psychiatric help as each time a tremor strikes, it resurrect images of horror and destruction among them. What makes the effort defeating, is a series of aftershocks that have joited the region for the last Six days, bringing back pain and fear of the devastation unleashed by the October temblor (October 15, 2005).

A full academic year would be wasted for thousands of children in the quake devastated areas. As both Uri and tanghdhar belong to the winter zone, the final examination are held in the last week of October. Already eight board examination of students of quake devasted areas has been postponed (The Hindu, October 16, 2005).

Earth quake casualties in Poonch which adjoins the LoC are matchless compared to those in Uri and Tangdhear to the north of Pir Panjal but the number of people would have become shelterless is no less. The ceurpean commission decided to allocate another. 10 million urws for the victims of the quake a week after the killer tremblor devastated parts of Inida and Pakistan. The 10 million Euro in new finding would target such sectors as food, drinking water, shelter, and medical materials, medicines.

The New Indian Express, the J & K council of ministers month's salary towards the CM relief fund to help quake victims. The minister have also advised all MLAs, and MLCs. to make their contribution.

The Indian Red cross society has been in the forefront of providing relief material to the earthquake victims (The Hindu, October 16, 2005). According to Murali S. Deora, vice President of the international federation of Red Cross society and Red crescent socities more than a lakh blankets, kitchen sets and tents have been dispatched to srinagar and Jammu for the victims.

In view of the massive damage caused to Uri - Musaffarabad road, the (BRO) has sought more time for making it motorable. It was difficult for the workers to clear the area quickly, as the landsteps triggered by the earthquake covering entire formations.

Not withstanding the hundreds of truckload. Of relief arriving here, many affected families in llanghdhar town and adjoining villages have been neglected they go Teetwal and other areas as they see no damage outside. Influential people have devoured most to the relief and those living in inaccessible areas are still suffering.

Though the exact dates for facilitating co-operation between India and Pakistan in providing relief to victims of the earthquake are still to be decided, many divided families who came across the LoC to meet their relatives have retured home disappointed. Practically every family in the belt along the LoC inhabited by Gujijour and Pohari - speaking people have been divided. Little contact has been possiblehere as there in no direct link of the telephone lines to PoK.

Olympic council of Asia vice president has writtento the Olympic countries of SAARC countries to support India is bid to host 2014 Asian games. If 2014 games take place in New Delhi, it will be less expensive. The SARRC countries will also have the opportunity of technical officials to be inducted by the Indian Olympic association.

The New Indian Express Mushtaq Ahmed Geenai, filed an PIL in the state High court accusing the head of J & K accountability commission justice R.P. Sethi's son Anil of taking Rs. 5 lakh from him in connection with the Panchayat Ghar electrification scam to ensure the commission's judgement went in favour of the accused in the scam. Gnani, himself, an accused in the scam said he had annexed to the PIL, a nideo footage a local hotel. The conduct of the rural development minister prima facia saflects the casual approach adopted by him in according his approval, which ultimately resulted in huge financial loss to the state and benefited some unscrupulous officials.

Pakistan secured over $5.4 million in pledges from 50 delegations from 50 countries in the form of grants and soft loans during a day - long conference organized by Pakistan to raise money for reconstruction and rehabilitation of 3.3 million affected by the quake (The Hindu, October 18, 2008).

The outcome of the conference will be shot in the arm for Pakistan president who is under flak from within for the weak response from the west for earthquake material despite Islamabad unequivocal support to the international war against terrorism. The decision of the opposition parties to boycott the conference in protest against the alleged reluctance of the government to take this on board in the relief and reconstruction efforts did cast a shadow on the high profile event but failed to have any impact on the enthusisatic donars in expression their solidity. The single largest donor country was availed states, which pledged $ 510 million, Sudia Arabia pledged more than $310 million, china $300 millicn and Iran $200 million. The pledges outweighed the initial reconstruction cost put at $5.2 million.

The temple has a special significance in the evalution of the people of Kashmir as an intellectual identity and it was an ancient site of learning in the sub continent. The indigenous script of Kashmir has been named after the presiding dirty i.e., the goddess Sharda. The members of the Kashmir Pandit community have been demanding that they be allowed to visit the place. (The Hindu, February 5, 2006)

The right wing women's outfit Dukhtarian - e - milat raided a number of restraints and gifts shops in Srinagar to stop young boys and girls from celebrating valentines day. This shows the remonstrance of the reflected by the Muslim fundamentalists group in the state and their steady influence in the state. (The Hindu, February 15, 2006)

A special TADA court issued non-bailable warrants against the former J & K minister Ghulam Mohammed shah and senior or separatist leader Syed Ali Shah Geelani and Mohammed Yasin Malik in a case showing disrespect to the Indian constitution and torching the national tri colour 18 years ago. Police had registered a case against 24 people, including Shah, Geelani, Malik, and Khan for showing disrepute to the Indian constitution and torching the national flag during a public meeting organized by the now - defunct Muslim united found at Iqubal Park on August 20, 1987. (The Hindu, February 10, 2006)

A soldier from the Chaotic days of militancy a retired NSG commando major A K Ravindran got back to the valley, not with gun with a film crew (The New Indian Express, March 19, 2006). Major A K Ravindran is unspooling his memories into reel Kiti Chakera made in Malayalam, will tell the forces story, first - hand .

A Kolkota based theatre group is set to explore Shared Cultural hand by staging plays in Pakistan highlight the themes of globalization and minority bashing. Faced with the problem of providing fresh vegetables to soldier in high attitudes areas, including Siachen, the government was developing transgenic tomatics which could grow in the cold environment of the Himalayas. (The New Indian Express, March 31, 2005)

In a development that would strengthen the lobby in Pakistan demanding lifting a ban on screening of Indian films, the Lahore high court has dismissed a petition seeking a direction against screening of Indian movies (The Hindu, April 28, 2006). If Pakistan's ideology and culture were not affected by the exhibition of films from Holywood and other countries, how could the Indian films cause any danger to the ideology and culture, the court held.

The New Indian Express, the Pakistan government initially denied noted poet and film maker Javed Akthar permission to visit Karachi for Mugah - e-Azam premier but later cleared it (The New Indian Express, June 25, 2006). The belated clearance of the visa clarified that our purpose of going there was not commercial but to participate in a noble gesture on the part of Akbar Asif who wanted us to attend the premiere to generate funds for the earthquake victims of Pakistan.

6

Editorials

Editorials Covering Eco and Cultural Co-operation

The visit of the former PM of Pakistan to India has been stressed by The Hindu.

The five member delegation of the Pakistan government with PML leader and former PM Shakat Hussain to India the ironing out of differences catapulted to a better beginning. The visit took the sheen of the memotics of the dead past reviving more hope among the people. For the first time in 57 years a ceasefire has been held for 16 months. "Bold Decisions" were the suggestive steps churned out Pak leader Shakat Hussain during his eventful stay in India, thus formulating a new polices to settle the core issue of Kashmir.

Dr. Singh and General Musharaff set a new date for the resumption of train services between Rajasthan and Sindh. The proposal to strengthen the activities of the private sector and joint business council.

The soft borders are clearly the way out, the frequency of the Srinagar-Musafarabad bus service has to be increased.

The editorial of The New Indian Express gives a compelling note on Pakistan's refusal to grant MFN status to India has been a sticking point and threat of Indian foods flooding Pakisthan causes great disquiet across the border (The Hindu, April 15,2005). Pakistan complains that it has not benefited from the MFN status granted to it by India because of tariff barriers, India has similar complaints which it comes to items like tea. While the annual demand for tea in Pakistan is estimated at 140 million kilograms, India's share at present is only around 5 million because 30% tariff imposition. But the Hindu editorial were vague on the same day without any specific aspect of the trade being suggested and the demand and supply of the market was avoided.

But, on the other hand, The New Indian Express, it is unfortunate that the Pakistan government restraints the travel ahead of politicians waiving off politicians to travel across the LoC has created furor and the politicians feel let down instead of being treated on par with other public. The bus service is anointed only for the divided families across the border, reuniting the divided families, the singular motto of the such service. The segregation among the passengers sends wrong signals across the border thus violating the need of such service (The New Indian Express, April 4, 2005). The countries are shedding decade of maximalism to keep the bus moving for the normalization of ties and but by bit crubs of the movement crubed.

The trade routes between India and Pakistan has been opened up to all goods from either countries.

Pakistan has not granted the MFN status to India which has been a sore in the eyes, as Pakistan believes that this has not been to India, as Pakistan companies are not able to sell fruits and textiles to India (The Hindu, July 30, 2005). In order to provide access and improve bilateral trade with Pakistan, India has to offer unilateral concession to Pakistan.

The unloading takes place across the border and they are then shifted to another bus, to take up the initiative. The load is unloaded on either side of the zero line. The porters from either side load the items into trucks. Thus there is no licensing, tax laws, or any other paper behind the whole issue.

There is huge improvement over the situations where an Indian exporter of vegetables could only hope to send the consignment by train on specified days the rail service was available.

Nevertheless The Hindu editorial also feels that the Indian establishment has tended to see borders as sites of tension danger rather than as windows of opportunities and promise. The mind set is changing but the peace has to be stepped up.

The Hindu paper also clearly warrants on good polictics by creating shared economic stakes and mutual dependencies.

Another project that has become the cynosure of all eyes is the Iran – Pak – India gas pipe line which can reverse the trend of the economy

The Hindu editorial reported Dr. Manmohan Singh answer to the opening up on Iran gas pipeline project the Washington Post is fraught with risk and uncertainity. The editorial is bound to question the vacillation in the mind of PM whether the stance was taken to appease the Bush administration or he has failed to negotiate the viability of the project which would bring in laurels to the whole community. The Iranian gas pipeline and to utility cannot be mistaken for the left are more concerned with the commitment of pursuing the independent foreign policy, but slowing down the entire project in exchange for nuclear co-operation promised by the Bush administration.

At stake is not the foreign policy but the energy security concern of this country is demanding the media proposed Kudos to Mr. Mani Shankar Iyer for recognising the externalities of the gas pipeline which should be constructed and the inclusion of China is being explored by India and Iran (The Hindu, July 25, 2005).

The paper mooted the conscious decision of the Indian government in proclaiming to the whole world that India is a sovereign republic to take up an independent decision. Media instigates the Indian government to carve a niche for itself in the international forum.

The editorial in The Hindu commended Dr. Manmohan Singh for displaying clear sightedness and resolve to flag off the bus service to Musafarabad. The editorial apparently praises the grit shown by the passengers who kept cool their tryst with Musaffarabad.

In refusing to let bureaucracy and formalism stand in the way he two countries addressed a pressing humanitarian issue.

The proposed for a bus service across the LoC was a non-starter so long as the two countries could not agree on travel documents that passengers must carry. India and Pakistan had reason to believe that their positions and claims on Jammu and Kashmir territory controlled by the other would be affected if passengers used passports to cross the LoC. In the longer term, if people – to – people contacts developed helped in easing tensions.

The editorials states that people to people movement will affect the movement for 'self' determination.

The editorial pipeline, lifeline, The New Indian Express, July 15, 2005 is a very remarkable headline to be reckoned with for it propels more on the significance of such project for improving the depleting zones of economy and which in turn the encourages the role of government in transforming south Asia's geopolitics. At the same time, The New Indian Express has speaks volumes on the Independent foreign policy adhered by the UPA government. The editorial delineates the broad frame work that was worked out between India - Pak joint working group and finalisation on the financed and technical details. Negotiation on the price of natural gas and the transit fee that is required to bring it through Pakistan will be a long process. The safety of the pipeline through Balochistan and the Islamabad opposition to overland transit for its good and people to Iran Afghanistan, Central Asia will be quid pro quo the ensuing demands.

The pre-eminent visit of Pervez Musharaff has its own advantage in its economic gain like the Srinagar - Musafarabad bus service than the safe building of gas pipeline.

The New Indian Express estimates put the potential for bilateral trade at 10 billions by 2010. Editorial instigated both the governments to address the issue of tariff barriers and logistical impediments.

The Hindu editorial cited the positive outcome of the Manmohan - Musharaff summit is the decision to set up a joint business council. India has been demanding most favoured nation stakes to get the road blocks to flur trade removed, Pakistan has been on tariff and non-tariff barriers (NTB).

The President Onkar. S. Kanewar, 'Federation of Indian Chambers of Commerce and Industry has promptly focused on the limited list of items that Pakistan has so far been willing to import from India. Travel volumes to cannot build if a huge list remains banned. The editorial of the Hindu welcomed the move to encompass trade services as India could offer expertise in areas such as health, IT and its related service.

Signing of the deal on gas pipeline project with Iran and America with nuclear deal have affected India perceptions internationally (The New Indian Express, September 21, 2005). During a course of interview with the Foreign minister Natwar Singh at New York to the NDTV has made remarks with fairly dangerous implications. The editorial to quick to highlight whether he is suggesting foreign policy is no more than the extension of domestic politics.

The editorial pointed out that it is not wise to give up the hand of friendship with Iran. But it must convince Iran to stick to nuclear non-proliferation treaty which that country is signatory of. The editorial forms a broad framework wherein they can pursue an independent foreign policy, irrespective of the ordeals on the way. The question of reference to Muslims cannot appease the world community of Muslims and it is not leverage for an independent foreign policy. More of gumption and ingenuity play the roles in framing an independent foreign policy.

Editorial Covering CBMs

The editorial of The Hindu suggest that though the opening of the other two routes Srinagar- Musaffarabad, Delhi - Lahore which are comparatively longer than the Amritsar - Lahore, the potential for people to people interaction could be enormous especially since the new bus service will cater primarily to Punjabis who are well known for their exuberance and skill at networking.

The editorial stressed that both the governments of India and Pakistan must give Visas at Lahore and Amritsar since the processing of the application forms at the national capitals to acquire Visas is a needless irritant (The Hindu, December 19, 2005). The editorial further that enhanced people-to-people exchanges appear to provide the most constructive means of allaying the deep rooted suspicion that each country harbours towards each other.

Pilgrims would get a chance to pray at shrines that many might not have able to visit since partition Businessman on either side of the border who have been pressing their respective government to lower trade barriers are likely to make full use of the new opportunities provided.

Editorials on the Art of Diplomacy

The Hindu carried two editorials on the art of diplomacy out of editorials which appeared during the period of study and the New Indian Express carried 8 editorials on the art of diplomacy out of ..... editorials which appeared during the period of study.

The soft borders has acquired a sinister design. There is a free movement of goods and services. Free movement has also helped terrorists across the border. The Indian express has also claimed the activities the militants and also reports palasthan dissingenous such claims.

The editorial also pinpointed the restraint shown by India can not be taken granted by Pakistan, Man Mohan Singh may show reluctance to visit Pakistan (The New Indian Express, August 20, 2005). The Indian Express vehemently opposed inflicting needless harm on Kashmiris. Pakistan is the cynosure of the west as Pakistan militants are alleged to have links in London blasts.

The lack of progress on the New York meet between president Musharaff and Dr. Singh, has created bumpiness on the road to peace and the Indian Express editorial denoted that it has entered a dangerous moment (The New Indian Express, August 20, 2005). The peace process is compared to cycling. The faster you pedal, the faster the changes or else it becomes more dilutory.

On the question of reduction of troops and internal ceasefire, the hardliners in Delhi wish that extended commitment on the part of Pakistan will augur the process. Failing to act at this moment will only give credence to those in Pakistan who agree that India will never respond to its gestures on terrorism and that removing the gun will leave India with no incentive to talk on Kashmir.

The editorial from the New Indian Express still longs for a commitment from the Indian government but the Hindu seems to trust the role of the government in controlling terror and reduction of troops.

The New Indian Express states through factors like soft border, cross border terrorism militancy on the issue of Kashmir the dialogu process that has siphoned major attention of the public and the similar or dissimilar diplomatic linking that kept both the government at tethered ends.

But the Hindu editorial on the Similar meet cautions every time President Musharaff and Dr. Singh meet it is unrealistic to expect change in relationship.

Even after two round of talks between India and Pakistan, the main issues of contention has been settled.

During the third round of discussions to be held in January 2006, the major issues to placed under settlement. The specifics of the four hour long meeting between the leaders of India and Pakistan was not provided (The Hindu, September 17, 2005). Dr. Singh made an indirect reference to Islamabad on meeting Mr. Bush that the Pakistan still controls terror and it must stop the inflow of terrorists. The infiltrators are trained to move across the border and explosives are manufactured from local material. Indian media still wary whether under these circumstances Dr. Singh would respond to Pervez Musharaff request to withdraw troops from Kupwara and Baramulla.

A modest role has been effected from the transfer of duties from the BSF to CRPF. But the media still insist backup role to played in protecting the interests of Kashmiris.

The editorial of The New Indian Express is still cynical about the attitude of the Indian Government downplaying the issue of Kashmir in the international arena.

Though the composite dialogue has given more leeway, the progress of talks, president Musharaff seems dithering on all occasions and prolonging the peace process underway. The "concrete proposals" were never spelt out, but instead it is more or less wavering (The New Indian Express, September 17, 2005). Raking up Kashmir issue in the international arena has been his hocus - pocus for long and other issues get stymid. The end to cross - border terrorism has never been promising. Modus operandi is encouraged with rigour even if the counter measures are taken up to debilitate the forces. Unfazed by criticism the training for terrorist received new fillip from various sources. General Musharaff high lighted the fact that Kashmir has never been mentioned by India in the international arena and they have done it to show flexibility on their part.

The decade long conflict will not find a hub and raison - de - tre if the aggressors are still buying time to resuscitate the issue for ages.

Peace process is compared to a tight rope walk (The New Indian Express, September 20, 2005). As both sides cannot say to the people that they have gained so much in the encounter or proportional division cannot be spelt to the public of both nations at large.

In the bargain, India may not of accede for any territorial adjustment and the readjustments had to spring from Pakistan. In the bargains, they have used violence to pursue political goals. Overtly and covertly the editorial opined that peace can be brokered if only Pakistani establishment can be made to realise what can be gained out such an outcome and satisfy people at home that they have not lost but also gained.

The new Indian Express has offered the initiatives of diplomacy in suave manner through at time cynical to the way diplomacy prevailed when power sharing groups brokered peace and eventually ended up in not high lighting the rich dividends that the disputant may fail to perceive.

The New Indian Express has been more aggressive in relying on the equations that emerge after every cycle of talks leaving more room for thought and the sagacious role any government can rope in.

The general does not shirk difficult issues, an extra ordinary capacity for turning things, and Musharaff is clearly positioning himself as a moderate mediator between tradition and modernity, fundamentalism and progressing Islam and Israel, terrorists and peaceniks (The New Indian Express). Normally being charming is not a virtue associated with battle hardened generals. The old saying "the problems can itself be the solution", could well have been written with the general conception of Pakistan in mind. The Kasuri – Natwar Singh meet did not bring about a store off in the ensuring dialogue process, the talks did receive a jolt at New York between Mr. Singh and President Musharaff.

The external affairs minister Natwar Singh consolidated gains have recently emerged danger to the peace process. The inability to talk on Kashmir (Pakistan) and the cross border terrorism (India) has brought about a change in order of happenings. The problem of movement across the border has not been resolved by Natwar Singh. The joint statement by Natwar Singh. The joint statement on Siachen glacier and the Sir Creek mission no in forward.

There is no saying that Kasuri - Natwar Singh talks did not receive elan due to the truncated talks of Singh and Musharaff in New York. Bargaining chip was terrorism and Kashmir through a shilbboth of CBMS were achieved during the talks and not much (The New Indian Express, October 5,2005).

India bargained for credible assurance to end cross - border terrorisms and followed by reduction of troops. Pakistan insisted the reduction of troop world improve the political climate in J & K. The latter's plan cannot materialise unless the former ensures trust from the Pakistan government.

As the Indian express editorials though relied much on the deliverance from the Indian government, later were found to be more suggestive of the trust that can be garnered from the Pakistan government.

There had been much debate on the dialogue process and The Hindu editorial suggests that New Delhi has to open the doors not only to the secessionists who have been vying for long but also others opposed to ethnic Kashmiri succession. This category includes players like the CPI, Mufti Mohammed Sayeed, National Conference, the congress which have future equity in the states future.

The editorial has examined whether it is the dilution of the dialogue process to some extent it is yes - but also no. The dialogue has wrought some changes but a definite U - turn will depend on the new ideas that emerge hopefully during the meet.

APHC is not the sole spokes person of the multi cultural linguistic ethnic Kashmiris as they have not put an end to violence (The Hindu, January 17, 2006).

Pakistan President Gen. Musharaff's has not demonstrated his strength to quell the Pakistan based terrorist groups, nor there is a lack of seriousness in his decision of demilitarization and self-rule.

The editorial plainly indicated that dialogue cannot be the sole parameter but only a tool to bring to an preconceived end. The Hindu editorial is eluserve of the other tools that can be employed in a democratic setup to iron out differences among different groups.

General Musharaff insistence on involving Kashmiris in the dialogue process need not sent India shock to Indians establishment which has consistently stuck to the bilateral talks.

The intervention of international guarantee sent only positive signals for prymatism shows that they needed a third source when striking deals (The New Indian Express, May 26, 2005).

India, too, with its bitter memory of Pakistan walking away from the Simla agreement of 1972, might find it worth while to have international endorsement of the settlement of J & K.

The Indian Express also says it does not mean internationalisation of the issue.

But pointed out that Musharaff shifted emphasis from maximum self-determination to self-governance, Indian government should cash in on such recourse.

The Hindu has navigated on quitessence of the dialogue process wherelse The New Indian Express wallows on the achievements that heralds beyond semantics.

There were two editorials in The Hindu but no such editorials in The New Indian Express.

The Hindu has given an amicable solution to the Siachen but though The Indian Express has sat aside this issue.

The high attitude, cold temperature, and treacherous terrain of the glacier region have taken far greater toil of human lives than the artillery shells skills fired by the Pakistani army. India approved of the defence secretary level talks of 1989 where the two armies should re-deploy to positions each held at the time of simla agreement The Indian army insists that it should not be made to vacate the saltoro ridge that it currently occupies and it is worried that Pakistan might be tempted to re-occupy the posts, unless there is no bilateral agreement on Actual ground position line. At the sixth round of talks held in 1992, Islamabad indicated that AGPL could be demarcated on an annexure to the main agreement. But since this annexure was envisaged as a document with no legal, moral or political implications the proposals falls short of what the Indian army wants (The Hindu, June 15, 2005).

New Delhi and Islamabad tend to make an integrated approach to the six facts of the dispute so that progress gets underway in 2006.

The newspaper hinted that,

1. They will need to pinpoint positions currently held by the two armies.
2. Arrive at the definition of the area of disengagement.
3. Create a regime to monitor the pull back.
4. Set up a verification mechanism to rule out future violation.
5. Settle the alignment of LoC beyond the gird reference point WR 9842.

If they can agree on the mechanism that will verify the compliance with the agreement, the certification of the actual ground position line, a tricky process, may not be necessary.

New Delhi wants Islamabad to certify that the Indian army held the saltoro ridge before the pull back Pakistan has refused to do so on the ground that it would be tanta mount to 'aggression' (The Hindu, October 6,2005).

The editorial of The Hindu demanded that the army as a professional institution, in a democratic system to take lead from government of what is at stake.

Editorials Suggesting Terrorism

There were of fear editorials in The New Indian Express but there were three editorials in The Hindu.

The rumpus over Kashmir militant turned politician Yasir Malik visit to Pakistan and the reference made by him, that once the information minister ran camps for the militants sparkled off controversy at home (The Hindu, June 28, 2005). Malik then clarified that camps were being made ready to house the victims of J & K violence failed to patch-up the claim that he made earlier.

Rasheed, I & B Minister of Pakistan was refused travel in the Srinagar-Musaffarabad bus for organizing terrorist camps.

The editorial in The Hindu has broader framework publicised that the arrival of many others who supported separatist violence for discussion in India sooner or later. New Delhi has to frame some kind of consensus to accommodate such leaders who dictated terms from the other side.

Bestiality Exposed by the Terrorists Demanded.

Terrified children, abandoned school books, the sickening cry of children, the world over, has condemned the incident. New Delhi has taken over by some extra effort to keep the saboteurs at bay.

The The New Indian Express editorial opined that this needs to be nailed before militant groups eager to fan disaffection at a time when a semblance of normalcy has returned to the valley and to deflect any blame that may come in their direction to ensure it becomes incontrovertible truth. Where else The Hindu has re-examined the unanticipated move of the suspects.

A Brazillian electrician London neighbourhood was targeted by the police and innocent children of Kashmir became a target on the pretext that they ran away without proving their identification.

Some of them do not stop when challenged and the suspects though being innocent are victimised. The lapse of security focus in both countries is very well identified and the police do little to assuage the outraged public opinion. The media has lamented the scourge of state terrorism (The Hindu, July 26, 2005).

The editorial of The New Indian Express justified that unwarranted act of the security by calling a spade, a spade for when we set up inquiry commissions to investigate shoot - to - kill orders that go terribly wrong and demand measures to insure that such tragedies, the public should take cognizance of the great stress and tension under which those placed in charge of security have to operate. Britain was one among the nations which accused of army excesses in Kashmir, today Britain has realised the dangers fraught in which security forces operate. The Hindu lamented that a system that rationalized horrible human right offences by claiming that the only way to protect citizens lives from terrorism is to take out suspects can be characterised as not worth having. It also calls for strengthening human rights act 1993.

Similarly, the story of Rasheed, Information Minister editorial ending violence. In The New Indian Express, candidly states that individuals are being named, suggests the issue of terrorism cannot be swept under foggy abstractions. The compromising stands of the Indian government is very welcome as the Indian leaders were denied the Visas. It is also argued that General Musharaff during Kargil, have been complicit in violent artivities in India. If for the sake of peace process we are willing to engage with them, why single out Rasheed? Shiekh Rasid has to convince the Indian government that whatever his past record, he now genuinely disavows support to terrorism and the claims are general innuendos not specific allegations. Both the editorials abhorred misgivings on the same issue.

Editorial with Precautionary Note on the Evolving Peace

The editorial in the new Indian Express contemplates a multi-pronged strategy to tackle the bid of infiltration especially after the lull in April 2005. This is one of the rising challenges amidst all initiatives to keep the peace process gaining momentum.

Audacious infiltration across the gurez mountain in J & K have served some petty compulsion. On the issue of terrorism and other threats to national security the UPA government is yet to demonstrate a convincing resolve (The New Indian Express, July 16, 2005).

The editorial dared to demonstrate a convincing resolve for the ill thought out revocation of Pota or misguided courting of dialogue letting down of the guard of Vis-a-vis intransigent ULFA, the message that is going out is of a government in denial or unwilling to take a threat head on. The emphasis is to take a few pointers from Great Britain government which lost no time after the London blasts to embark on systematic operation that is devoid of a remarkable populist political pasturing. No government can allow terrorism to become a rountinized thing easily diverted by political calculations. Preponderance of such vehement editorials abhorring condemning terrorism were found too little in the Hindu.

The Pakistan president Pervez Musharaff who is asking India to reduce the troops in urban centers in Kashmir should give assurance that the withdrawal of troops will not augar for the spirit of militants and counter productive.

The Pakistan soil is not devoid of terrorist camps is not damning of evidence of India alone (The New Indian Express, September 5, 2005). Recently there are reports from US and other countries that the soil holds terrorist camps.

Singh is meet Hurriyat leaders and the meeting with President Bush later, this month may bring about a change in the internal dynamics of the states. It will supplement the ceasefire line between India and Pakistan in J & K, ease daily tensions in the valley, give Kashmiris a stake in the Indo - Pak dialogue process. The paper has vehemently supported the cause of that Singh should not lose the opportunity in easing the tensions across the two nations. Though there were predictions that if should be a bilateral process the media has created a broad frame work that the people should be engaged in the dialogue process. A tripartite challenge will being about a semblance of justice to the ongoing struggle.

The caveat initiated by media is laudable for suggesting that India need not gloat over the pressures exerted after the London blasts and bombings in Egypt and tremendous pressure created by the world community at large. The mounting pressures on Musharaff must help him to tackle terrorism.

A framework is created my media to engage Pakistan to help them root out terrorism with the help of India. Such candid gesture by India stands to tell the world community at large the memance of terrorism by India and the scourge of terrorism can be tackled Pakistan's ambiguities on terrorism are rooted in the strategy Musharaff adopted after September 11, 2001. While giving strong commitment to the US on rooting out the Al-Queda in Pakistan, Musaraff has sought to protect the Pakistan army's long standing political investments in Afghanistan and Kashmir from global war on terrorism.

In the short term India remains the best bet but for engaging Pakistan (The New Indian Express, July 29, 2005). In the longer term his failure to nudge Pakistan towards political moderations and social modernisation will only add to India's challenge in the region.

A close look at home at Pakistan reveals that Madrassas have become breeding ground for the Jihad factories (The Hindu, August 5, 2005). In order to deflect the criticism of the west, Musaraff had to venture for talks with religious heads who don't approve of such intrusims of the government.

But in the social context, where the state educational systems is dysfunctional, there is no identify political alternatives to madrassa, which offer a measure of literacy and learning.

Editorials Covering Cross-border Terrorism

Newspapers attitude toward tackling of terrorisms and the failure of the security agencies.

There are six editorials in the The New Indian Express and four editorials in The Hindu.

The Editorial in The New Indian Express endorsed the view that General Musharaff has promised India all help in tracking down culprits – a cyclostyled resolve that is reissued each time there is a Islamist outrage on the planet (The New Indian Express, November 3, 2005).

Across the LoC, a united states helicopter carrying the relief material was fired upon. This cannot be explained a way with the act of desperation of the terrorists as Musharaff had very often reiterated that after the January 12, 2002 a month after the parliament attack, he famously vowed to dismantle terror, reform madrassas, drive out foreign Jihadis.

The paper has termed his reference as LoC irrelevant, and also justifies that the real test for Musharaff lies in showing courage to lead his troops into Mudrike and The New Indian Express intimidated that, otherwise the world awaiting to do the job for him.

The editorial in The Hindu examined that there is truth 'deficit' in Pakistan as declared by Manmohan Singh to end cross-border terrorism.

Manmohan Singh has declared that there is truth 'deficit' in Pakistan to end cross border terrorism (The Hindu, November 17, 2005).

Ever since 1980, the Indian establishment has vowed to take action if provided, mostly recently in 2001-02. Ever since the Delhi blasts, with the identification of the Lashkar-e-toiba, there have been growing calls to take a tough line against Pakistan.

The editorial applauds Musharaff for part delivery of justice. By 2002, there was steady decline in but the months of August to November 2005 saw steady decline compared to the saw month in 2004.

But in spite of these the editorial also evaluated that peace process has yielded rich dividends. It is askance to tell that Pakistan has not still removed the terrorist infrastructure from its soil that still continued run terrorist camps, recruit cadre, raise funds etc., Pakistan should not be permitted to negotiate peace process with gun tucked under the arm emphased the editorial in The Hindu.

The violence in the state has been in steady decline after the crisis of 2001-2002, was diffused. Though Pakistan seems to have realized that the Jihadi's elements pose a threat not only to India but also to Pakistan, an end to violence can not be anticipated if the Pakistani army and Islamist alias give a fillip to low-grade covert warfare to secure concessions (The Hindu, December 13, 2005). Stripped of political legitimacy within J and K, terrorism cannot survive as they cannot deliver even a limited descalation claimed the editorial in The Hindu and this assumption is a flaw. As dialogue with APHC is stalled the organization has no authority over terrorists group. The editorial in The Hindu reiterated that a broad based dialogue is no substitute for fighting terrorism resolutely. The terrorist group are able to unleash terror owing to growing technological sophistication like phone-based communication technologies where else the Indian Intelligence organisations lack operation infrastructure. Investments in modernizing the intelligence bureau's communication capabilities and a computerized online record base on suspects for J & K police must be made to fighting violence more intelligently.

The editorial of the New Indian Express spills beans on the various attacks that coomed large in the major capitals like Mumbai, Varanasi, Bangalore, Delhi, Diwali Killings after many Kashmir killings (The New Indian Express, July 12, 2006). The terrorists are targeting the major economic strikes in the country which is palpable after the major strikes. Tourism is the only economic activity of the state of Kashmir which have come to a halt and Kashmir's local economy is hopeless minus terrorism.

The editorial also pointed out the administration has become a mute spectator and vents its ire on inent domestic intelligence apparatus

The editorial in The New Indian Express delineated that the security agencies due to the lack of political direction, the terrorists have outwitted the US using Indians to strike India's major economic targets Delhi, Bangalore, Mumbai.

The editorial makes more paradoxical statements that if terror was communalised once, the current fashion is communalising anti-terror policy - by using Indians to strike major economical targets in the country (The New Indian Express, July 13, 2006).

More sagacious and outrageous comments hailed in the The New Indian Express.

The Mumbai blasts has evoked strong criticisms and the failure of Pakistan government to abide with the January 2006 joint statement(The Hindu, July 13, 2006).

The editorial in the Hindu condemned the disingenous nature of the Pakistan government and has entogised the ministry of external affairs which has gone publicly urging Pakistan to dismantle the infrastructure of terror and act resolutely against individuals and groups who are responsible for terrorist violence and to draw back from making any links between resolution of bilaterial disputes and terrorist bombing.

The future India - Pakistan detente process will depend on the public good will. Which will dominates with each terrorist strike.

The editorial claimed that the refrain of Pakistan that they are no more training forces has grown thin with evidences hailing from other nations.

Shazad Tanwar, has bombed the London underground system in July 2005, Assam Hammond, a lebanese national arrested in beinut this April for planning to bomb new York city, Lebanon's counter terrorism organisation, the internal security forces, Hammond was intending to travel to Pakistan in the nearfuture to undertake a training course - all reveal that the Pakistan has been training militants on its soil as the endorsement hails from citizens concerned globally.

The editorial re-directs the PM to use this leverage of growing international outrage to compel Pakistan to deliver on its repeated promises to end terrorism. It is possible that no level of international pressure will deliver the result India seeks.

The editorial drew a robust resolution on the exercise of international community cannot change the mind set as the defiance of US editcs by Iran and South Korea that there are limits to vests coercive powers and jihad against India can be pursued and altered.

The Hindu editorial relies more on international pressure but The New Indian Express suggests on the failed commitments and unresolved Kashmir issue.

The New Indian Express editorial reinforced the message that terrorism has percolated to most vulnerable targets, i.e., from Delhi to Doda and Bangalore to Benares. This was aimed at provoking communal violence (The New Indian Express, July 13, 2006). Pakistan foreign minister Kasuri suggests that terrorism in India will not cease without the resolution of J & K question, Kasuri has only "read aloud the writing on the wall" that the UPA government refused to read.

Pervez Musharaff has been seen in India as someone it can do business with But he has failed to keep his word in ending cross - border terrorism. Musharaff has lost his sheen as a credible interlocutor, that India should openly support democratic movement in Pakistan.

The editorial in The Hindu has substantiated the war on terror by premising on examples garnered with the arrest of Let of trained different nationals in the Pakistani soil, while the New Indian express speaks of the disadvantage at home where Dr. Singh is not able to get co-operation from the opposition and fellow politicians. The editorial of The New Indian Express spoke ill of the holistic approach of the UPA government, from upgrading elections surveillance systems, improving ground level intelligence. But fails to underscore the present juncture as a strategy to compel Pakistan to inflicting terrorist activity on the soil (The New Indian Express, July 15, 2006).

The Narendra Modi as an icon for anti-terror march in Mumbai, the HRD minister Arjun Singh, Minority affairs Minister Anthulay are doing no favour to the Muslim community has been focused on obliterating the kind of succour that be guided at this moment from the international community to sabotage the furthering of terror across the border.

This reminded Pakistan that the détente process between India and Pakistan will be a dissimulation if Pakistan satisfied the condition that its territory would not be used to sustain terrorism. Wherelse the Hindu was not much conditional.

The New Indian Express editorial demanded the need for preparing a dossier that could argue its case before the world. Whenever Pakistan demanded evidence the dossier would be quid pro non to satisfy their interest (The New Indian Express, July 22, 2006). The presence of Dawood Ibrahim, much wanted for prime target in the first serial terror blasts on Mumbai - which took over 300 lives. Ditto People like Masood Azhar and Ahmed Umar Sheikh who were released at Kandhakar after hijacking of an Indian Airliner, both found their way into Pakistan and threw themselves into activity.

This also suggested Pakistani complicity and as for infiltration from Pakistan into J & K, has continued through all these years.

The editorial in the Hindu reiterated the need for Pakistan to stick to January 20064 commitment and vehemently the need for settling of the issues bilaterally.

The international community as a whole is less than satisfied with Islamabad's counter - terrorism record (The Hindu, July 18, 2006). India is trying to side step talks on the contention issues and is concentrating on CBMS can make little sense.

On the trade benefits accured by both the nations after the CBMS came into full swing and disapproved of India's supposed foot dragging for not delivering on the counter - terrorism measure that Pakistan need to take in its own interest

Editorials Coverage of N - CBMS

The New Indian Express has delivered more number of news stories, editorials, features to enlighten common man to be cognizant of such oddities.

The bottle neck for expanding India - Pakistan nuclear framework is sub-continent's enduring insecurity rooted in the political nature of Indo-Pak relations. Each nation may inevitably get what the advanced nations have in their arsenals.

Paens of non-proliferation treaty by Washington have made defense of nuclear establishment India - Pakistan into unaccountable enclaves.

In Pakistan A .G. Khan set up a nuclear smuggling racket and in India they have turned into scientific ghettos.

Having cornered the lion share of the country's research and development resources since, independence, the nuclear and defence establishments, the incontrovertible truth of being unaccountable received a lot flake form varied media (The New Indian Express, August 13, 2005).

The major challenges that confront the N (CBMS) are anomalous status vis-à-vis global nuclear order and two nuclear stability with Pakistan. The first one is achieved when Dr. Manmohan Singh visited the US and civilian nuclear energy programme was initiated (The New Indian Express, August 5, 2005). The second one needs the support of the first policy. As if the sensible policy must not end up with only nuclear non-proliferation alone but also prudent management of nuclear relationship with Pakistan.

The nuclear CBMS was first initiated by India in Lahore 1999 and then latter found that Pakistan has to slow down the strategic restraint regime which it wants to continue further Pakistan too wanted the inclusion of cruise missiles but Indian government has gone too far in reviving the technical details of the launch of ballistic missiles. Which may not augur well in the upcoming state of developments. The editorial reiterated the need to corner the political mandate in the game and not stick on the incongruities in the launch. The nuclear CBM has received enough attention in The New Indian Express compared to The Hindu.

Editorial on Sir Creek

An exclusive editorial on Sir Creek were never found in both the newspapers, but Sir Creek mission was found as an appendage to "title heartening progress on siachen" so very little could be gleaned on Sir Creek from the nps as both lacked the vehemence of the aspect in the composite dialogue which gave the insinuation of government lethargy or inaptness in assessing the situation.

India and Pakistan appear to undertake a joint survey and consider options for the delimitations of the maritime boundary. The two sides are unclear whether they have applied international law in this case (The Hindu, October 6, 2005). They have made effect to mitigate the hardship fishermen undergo on account of the non-demarcation of this boundary by agreeing to set up a hotline between Indian Coast guard and Pakistan maritime security agency. India and Pakistan should abandon the practice of arresting fisherman who inadvertently cross into their territorial waters and instead institute mechanism for the informal repatriation of these innounts.

Editorial on The Composite Dialogue

There was one editorial each for the composite dialogue on the Hindu and The New Indian Express.

The editorial on the third round of composite dialogue diminished the hope of machievellian plot of the Pakistani government. Though number of rail, road and other opening points received much endorsement or approval from the Pakistan government, the crucial issues still staggering.

Pakistan still views that CBMS are only platform for the Indian government to sidestep from the core issue of Kashmir (The Hindu, January 26, 2006). Pakistan government seems to "squaring the circles of the views on Kashmir". Cross border terrorism is employed to exert pressure on India. Though both sides paid obeisance to the long list of statements of measures which had their origin in 2004, the editorial lacked that widely spoken about or disturbed area of the cross border terrorism had not been given broad space as it is deemed to be.

Moreover the editorial blods the Indian government to seek an early solution on the Siachen issue, though there has been more developments on this front, withdrawal of troops by both the governments. Though much attention was paid to third round of composite dialogue, it was devoid of the anticipated move.

The editorial in the The New Indian Express, stated the spell of silence maintained by the members before the round table conference ensued in memory of the four boys killed in the "Crossfire" in Kupwara's Handwara town suggested.

That the though the dialogue was more representative turned out to be roll call for key absentees (The New Indian Express, February 27, 2006).

The Hurriyat has expressed their non-attendance with most ringing statement of insincerity came from Mirwaiz oma Farooq who heads a band of men self professedly committed to dialogue and resolution.

The new Indian express editorial hinted on the constant refusal of the Hurriyat to putting its popularity to the test of elections. The editorial also states stated that the Hurriayt's refusal to attend either to score a point or consider the meeting as unrepresentative. The course would be to strengthen the dialogues Hurriyat's absence would only tell on the absentee's sincerity.

Editorial on Third-Party Mediation

There was one editorial in The Hindu on third party mediation compared to the New Indian Express.

The editorial stand on third party medication in Pakistan where President Bush frankly refused the civilian nuclear energy co-operation with Pakistan, strategic partnership with Pakistan was the least that the President had to deliver to the hosts. Bush also insisted publicly that Pakistan has to do more to combat terrorism.

Bush formal statements either in Islamabad or Delhi revealed that there was no shift in eitherthe nuance or the emphasis in the remarks on Kashmir and Indo-Pak relations (TNIE, May 6, 2006). India has never been objective in the Indo-Pak relations given its historic fears about Kashmir.

A sustained American engagement with Pakistan has the potential to meet some of India's own real objectives.

Editorial on Factors Affecting Delay in Conflict Resolution

There were two editorials that appeared in The New Indian Express but only one appeared in The Hindu.

The editorial of the New Indian Express suggested that the peace process with Pakistan has began to stall. The editorial regretted that even after a year Pakistan President Pervez Musharaff visited India, the PMO cannot even set dates for a reciprocal visit (The New Indian Express, July 1, 2006). Nearly seven months after external affairs minister Natwar Singh was forced out of office, the grand old party cannot find a suitable candidate to replace Natwar Singh. A frustrated foreign minister of Pakistan, Kushad Mahmood Kasuri, went about asking if there is any one in New Delhi he can speak to.

The editorial admonished the in eptness of the government that the longer the PM, who is increasingly burdened with complex management of domestic politics, avoids appointing a full-time foreign minister, the greater would be the damage to India's long term interests.

The Indo-Pak peace talks after the Mumbai blasts veered on the semantic used by the Prime Minister and the foreign secretary that composite dialogue is not cancelled but postponed indefinitely.

The editorial suggests that the local dimensions defind by both the society and politics. India unfortunately has strike the local factors too (The New Indian Express, July 17, 2006).

The intelligence agencies did not receive the kind of boost from the government. The editorials have given much importance to the active intelligence agencies. But the operations can succeed if it does not vary with the politics of the day. The editorial has targeted the muslim community in unbecoming terms, condemned them for not utilizing the available resources in the country like the inaptness political leaders who do not communication the strong desire for education an jobs. The editorials detrops the false destinction of the Muslim problem as special and considers it as anathema for India's biggest political and social challenge.

But the Hindu veered on Pakistan's inability to fight against terror groups operating on its soil, is used a leverage to extract concessions on Kashmir has become more obvious, especially after the Mumbai blasts which is a part of the long battle ahead.

The postponement of the composite dialogue will do little to change them from their disingenuous machimations and disjointed attitudes (The Hindu, July 17, 2006).

Editorials Suggesting the Views of the Political Parties Opposing Peace Process

There are two editorials in The New Indian Express but no editorials in The Hindu

After all it was the Vajpayee government which boldly made the arrangements in the Indo-Pak peace process. Under the current dialogue their has been a nit-picking by the former PM for political scores.

Even during Vajpayee's government the Hurriyat leaders made frequent trips to Pakistan and the moderates among the Hurriyat were allowed to interact with Pakistan leaders. As the main opposition party they would critique the government policy but seemed not to cite instances to merit diversion (The New Indian Express, June 23, 2005).

The New Indian Express has apt as a moderator or mediatory role to clear the impasse.

The editorial of The New Indian Express eulogized the role played by Atal Bihari Vajpayee in the Indo-Pak engagement but the letter to the Dr. Manmohan Singh reflected his inapt sagacity to deal with such situation especially when their was a change of the ruling party differs. Instead of nit-picking their should have been multi pronged policies that will mollify the issue.

The confusing trend shown by President Musharaff had helped the media men discuss the various interpretations that he suggested to dispense doubts put instill fear in the minds of all men.

Maximum self-governance and more buses across the border making it rather irrelevant or soft across the LoC. Followed by bizarre statements he spelled that J & K as seven distinct region and spoke of contiguity between regions (The New Indian Express, May 23, 2005). All these related developments touches for dithering and insidious attempt to paralyse the peace process which is gaining momentum.

Editorials on Hurriyat

The Hurriyat has failed to contest in the state and local elections of Jammu & Kashmir which is untenable fact of its own identity as a political entity which is at lurch. The voice of Kashmir or the representative of the people of Kashmir is rediculous to justify owing to non-compliance in a democractic set up.

The hurriyat conference visit to Pakistan has made them realize the harsh realities with much élan as anticipated in changing gwo-strategic reality (The New Indian Express, June 18, 2005). There has been fractures between the moderates and the hardliners, which becomes obvious especially after the present trip to Pakistan.

The hardliners like Syed Shah Geelani and Yasin Malik are swayed by the old idea of Kashmir. The moderator like Bilal Lone nor Farooq feel that they have paid a heavy price for violence parpenetrated.

The New Indian Express editorial is critical of the vehement role played by the Hurriyat Conference and the ambiguous reply by Pakistan has eroded the image of party. How can it hold stakes during the current peace process when their image is undermined. The recent visit to Pakistan has over shadowed the trust placed by the UPA government. The Hurriyat leaders have to disarow terrorism and settle for talks with New Delhi without preconditions. Hurriyat has to still restructure and rejuvenate its party members before they seek a seat in the on going dialogue process. No full blown support is bestowed by the print media for the Hurriyat though they seem to play an active role in ironing out the differences.

But The Hindu has made a demanding enquiry on the visit of the Hurriyat Conference to Pakistan which has belied expectations of both governments. Pervez Musharaff has always stressed the need for the involvement of the Kashmiri people in the dialogue process. But this time cut short of this. Musharaff earlier demand of offering seat for the separatist during the discussion on state future discussion.

The Pakistan side feels that though they conceded too much on the normalization process there is no change of position from New Delhi (The Hindu, June 10, 2005). But, the statement described by the Pakistani side is untrue.

Though Pakistan violated the intra bus agreement the peace process is on. Earlier arrangements have to be made that there is a lot of clarity before. It is better to think and talk than not talking. The mistake committed by the NDA needed not be repeated by progressive government.

Editorial of The Previous Govt. Vs. UPA Government

The Hindu editorial Vajpayee government has accused the Manmohan Singh government by turning the already settled peace process into "Kashmir Centric" The free movement of Hurriyat leaders into Pakistan without passports showed the diabolize process through which the whole issue of travel is manipulated. The inter national support that is garnered by the different factions of separatist leaders for the trilateral talks "International guarantee" Sabotaged the much laboured achievements of the previous NDA Government. The other issues which provoked the previous government are the Siachen glacier, Sir creek mission, economic and friendly issue, Iran-India-Pakistan gas pipeline which needs better institutional framework and authorities to work for.

The Editorials portrayed the allegations of the UPA government of disturbing the peace process. The Vajpayee government promoted more of CBMS. Thus Kashmir was set aside of the whole issue (The Hindu, June 21, 2005).

The free movement of Hurriyat leaders into Pakistan has made the event retrograde in the relationship for such attempts were the kind of real polities of the separatist leader or the gimmick to bring umbrage in the relationship

Pak visit of Mr. Advani who welcomed the visit of Hurriyat leaders to Pak raised the eye-brows of many in the BJP party. The editorial supported the initiatives and the paradigm shift of Manmohan Singh and in detente of relationship asking him to move forward with better political calculation. The policy of Dr. Manmohan Singh is found to be eminently sound can argue for more political space.

Editorials Covering Separatists Peace Process

The editorial underpinned the necessity of the latest round of talks of Hurriyat with Dr. Singh and Pakistan President Pervez Musharaff. It brings home three facts. The politics of symbolism who talks to whom first, often dominates substance. The Hurriyat who is now more uncertain about what it wants from the dialogue process. The Hurriyat is also uncertain it stands vis-à-vis Pakistan. The editorial cited that where they were finally insisted fortalks, they gave the impression that they wanted to talk to General Musharaff first and then backtracked in meeting PM Dr. Manmohan Singh on the dates proposed.

Editorial for Progress of Peace Process

The Indian Express editorial reflected on how best the issue of travel by the Hurriyat leaders the bureaucratic set up could bring about semblance of progress on peace process.

It is Pakistan which has raised objections to passengers who travel to Pakistan territory without passport and how it is up to the govt. of Pakistan to decide.

Earlier, the Vajpayee government has permitted the travel across the border by the Hurriyat after the Kargil war and allowed the Hurriyat to consult the centrists. Editorial further called in for talks there talks with the separatist on the other side of the LoC and help further peace process in the region.

The meeting of hurriyat leaders and the Kashmir pandits and the new rapprochement among them goes to the unity forged for the well being of Kashmir. The pandits were very much targeted over, they were made to flee.

The internal dimension of Kashmir problem is changing. The legacy of bitterness runs deep but if the coming together can create and aura of happiness, Kashmir can envisage a new vision for itself (The New Indian Express, July 21, 2005).

The cynics may think that the Hurriyat is craving for political space.

The steps engineered by the Hurriyat leaders to bring all the fractred sections together may help to build a strong Space for their unification. The editorial stated that the reconciliation shouldnot always be mediated through state but by bringing all different group together.

The editorial in The New Indian Express suggested that the suicide attack on the state road transport corporation office in Srinagar must serve as a reality check of the changing matrix of peace relations. The terrorist plans is clear. Thwarting the bus service is key to re-igniting the kind of alienation that gives them and their cause of oxygen. Between the people and the government and Alienation between the two governments. The onus is on the two governments is to provide security and do what can be done to restructive militancy.

The role of hardliners as obstructive, counter productive and dangerous. Mirwaiz took care not to name anybody in his crique but it is obvious that the foens of his attention was really the Tehreek-e-Hurriyat chaired by Syed Ali Shah Geelani which has acted as a consistent spoiler ever since the Hurriyat split in 2003. Mirwaiz became the first Hurriyat leader to participate in direct talks with PM. Hurriyat, it should persist with its approach of offering a ceasefire within J & K. (The New Indian Express, September 12, 2005)

Detente process in Jammu and Kashmir is speeded up with Manmohan Singh and Hurriyat Conference agreeing on common ground to ease tension among nations. APHC leaders have promised to put forward, a plan for step by step resolution of the conflict in J & K (September 7, 2005). In turn the APHC will demand the reduction in counter - terrorism charges and release of prisoners held on terrorism charges. The limited fall back of troop in 2004 did not bring about reciprocal decline in jihadist violence, there is relectance to repeat the exercise as by the Indian military officials note.

The editorial seems to pin a new kind of relationship that will help yield common formula to subserve several problems of the people of the state, not just the abstract entity called Kashmir problems.

New Delhi orchestrated free envoys like the official interlocution, N.N.Vohra, the congress politician Safifuddin Soz and the bureaucrat wajat Habibullah have caused more apprehensions than warranted.

Finally the Jihadist violence can be contained only with the engagement of India and Pakistan.

Notwithstanding the decline in violence at least five people die everyday.

The editorial resents on the dialogue process being an idea to delivering peace on ground.

Coverage of the Role of the Army

The stupendous role of the army (operation Indad) being conducted by the Indian army in the areas of devastation, round the clock facing all odds needs approbation

The army movement role when civil administration would not scale much is also common commedable The army men are scopping up bodies and survivors from the debris with their bare hands.

Even in the midst of such catastrophe, the militants have attacked two families in the Rajouri district leaving ten innocent people dead (The New Indian Express, October 11, 2005).

The editorial The New Indian Express pointed out the terror amid disaster that are the terrorists are brutalised people awaiting for any loophold to decimate innocent people. The men in the alive green are known for their consummate skills and the relentless effort have to conquer terrorists, in the after math of devastation which stands tell that they construction to be welcomed as a force for the good of the people.

As the government of J & K was trying to cope up with the fallout of October 8 tragedy, the terrorists group have demonstrated their lack of humanity (The Hindu, October 19, 2005). The outfit killed the minister for state for education, Ghulam Nabi lone after it was thwarded its attempt to assainate the intrepid secretary of the state committee of the CPI, Yusuf Ali Tarigami. The srinagar attack and the murder of another CPI(M) leader in Paligham indicated that the tactical approach agamst leaders and members of political parties that subscribed to constitutional scheme.

The Indian army had made some hardway in winning the hearts and mind of the people, the militants evidently wanted to arrest the process of reconciliation between the people and security force. The militant groups active in Kashmir continue to take guidance and instruction from people across the LoC. The transfer of power of the BSF to CRPF have provided some space to militants.

Editorial on Pok

Number of Editorials that appeared on PoK were meagre. But The New Indian Express has only one editorial but there was no editorial in The Hindu.

The New Indian Express drifted to the so many inner contradictions in Pakistan's position on Kashmir which was never difficult to comprehend. Since the Simla Agreement of 1972, India had gone by the assumption that the Kashmir dispute was by and large settled. As a consequence it had ignored the decision in Islamabad to separate Gilgit and Baltistan from the PoK and keep it in constitutional limbo (The New Indian Express, June 14, 2006). It also refused to react to the developments within PoK and expected Pakistan to do the same on J & K.

The New Indian Express focused on PoK, Gilgit and Baltisan created a more balanced negotiating framework with Pakistan.

1. This should help India raise the national awareness on the many ignored dimension on Kashmir and educate international community on the complexity of the dispute.
2. It sends out a long - delayed message to the people of Gilgit, Baltistan and PoK that India will not be mute spectator to the injustices perpenetrated on them by Islamabad.
3. Many ills of Pakistan's rule in PoK, India should not, however become complacent about its own constitutional and political obligation to the people of Kashmir.

Both NPS had expressed more or less similar linking onthe political scenario in the aftermath of the composite dialogue where The Hindu had three editorials wherelse The New Indian Express had two editorials.

Political Scenario in the Aftermath of Composite Dialogue

The Hindu in its editorial has identified the contours of politics in the state with statistical data.

The congress party known for self-abnegation must renounce its claim now. For the change of leadership will strengthen anti-India sentiment in the valley on the emerging power equation in the state.

The PDP is not the sole representative of the ethnic - Kashmiri region (The Hindu, October 25, 2005). The NC won 34-90% of vote polled in the Kashmiri valley against the PDP's 25-80% and the congress 14.8%. The earthquake in J & K must have increased the activity of the people. Not sharing the coalitional governed PDP may also prove to the disastrous for the Congress. The success of Ghulam Nabi Azad lies in ensuring a corrupt free government, the need to strengthen the peace process by initiating a broad based dialogue with the ethnic – religious communities.

Both the PDP and the Congress need to demonstrate to the people of J & K their future lies in co-operation, not chauvinistic rivalry.

But The New Indian Express,

Gulam Nabi Azad assumption of office cannot be termed as historic for J & K has an array of ministers such as Shiekh Mohammed Abdullah, G.M. Sadiq, Mir Quasim and Bakshi Gulam Mohammed who were corporeal manifestations of the centre.

The challenges before the new regime to break away from the Fiefdom model has characterised J & K since independence. Though Mufti was tall leader there are several lapses which needs rectification is the absence of single debate in the cabinet regarding any vital issue. The questions of regional autonomy, the contentious dispute over who constituted the permanent resident, the creation of new administrative units the expansion of secondary schools, education were all carried out by bureaucrats or by the ministers. Limiting the size of the ministry, anti-defection laws, National rural employment guarantee act were unheard of in the Ministry proposal. Deinstitutionalising democrcy after two decades may be apipe dream but the government of the day was given mandate and the voters still long the pledged to be redeemed (The Hindu, October 29, 2005).

But The New Indian empress, the congress under Ghulam Nabi Azad will be required to perform in government while keeping a watchful eye on its coalition with the PDP.

The challenge of governance is so great in Kashmir that the ruling coalition cannot afford to let any inner faultline show. The Congress can either win peace and erase of the already blemished image on its record.

Such a wary, approach guided by The New Indian Express in the wake of Azad taking over the reins of the government is a kind of a grim reminder to the taste of sharing power.

Azad must utilize the advantage that he has with the centre for the welfare of Kashmir. But policy of governance and policy making lies with Kashmir (The New Indian Express, November 3, 2005). He must not do so in ways which do revise memorise of puppets in Srinagar and masterminds in New Delhi. The Congress scared record of politics in the state still a live score in the state. All regions, all sections in the state will benefit from a federal and decentralized system in Kashmir.

There appeared no editorial in The New Indian Express but The Hindu their appeared only one editorial.

Editorials of Human Rights Violation

The media expressed no qualms of doubt of the inapt handling of the prof. S.A.R. Geelani's arrest and acquittal, The Hindu has strikingly explored leads to violation of human rights. The erstwhile Vajpayee government had initiated the special cell to bring quick results. Though the special cell used all the finesse to track the culprits, they safely pruned it down on the four conspirators instead of treating them as mere preliminary investigation and leave terrorists at large. The government of the day demanded instant results and if there had not been POTA, it is possible the special cell might have investigated the case more thoroughly and identified the real conspirators. The privilege of POTA may not be efficacious but may not help in unlocking of the crime.

Given a terror of such magnitude, the five armed men had planned to kill ministers and MPs and blow up parliament. Fingerprints samples were not lifted from the car, the terrorists used to enter the complex. The police had failed to identify the five faces, disfigured in the shoot out, because the investigators were carrying all fake ID cards.

The investigating officer revealed during cross - examination that the police made no serious effort to trace the identity of the numbers in Dubai and Pakistan, the terrorists dialled before launching attacks. Sat - phone number are not easy to track, but after the Sep 9/11 attacks the FBI has assured to help the Dubai - based handlers.

Editorials on Justifying the Past

There was one editorial on justifying the past in The Hindu compared to The New Indian Express where appeared two editorials.

Advani though seen as a hard liner always has stood for better conventions than any in the party. He never slipped away the - Convictions that he has always stood for either his unflinching commitment to Hindutva or his fanatical defence of Narendra Modi. The editorial feels that he has taken an edge. over others in promoting peace and friendship with Pakistan. So much so, the "Ultra nationalist" whose jingoism once pushed India to brink of war with Pakistan today stands accused by Party and Parivar of betraying India on Pakistan soil (June 9, 2005).

The media has acknowledged his paying obeisance to the Mnsolem of Quaid - e - azad as a very bold step and with his own hand described Jinnah as a 'rare individual' who created history indeed who stood for secular Pakistan. In the context of his talk he made a reference to the August 11, 1947 speech in the constitutient Assembly of Pakistan that the founder of Pakistan envisioned a state that guaranteed equality for all citizens in the eyes of the state and freedom of faith for all citizens. A substantial constituency for India has been won by Advani is what the media has termed his visit which triggered the imagination of many kindling hopes of softening stand.

The Editorial clarified the stand of the BSP President L.K. Advani and his entourage in Pakistan re-engaging the whole framework of which has sent flutters to the party as well as the RSS ideologue eulogizing Jinnah in Pakistan of continuing an ideal state - one which guaranteed equality and freedom of faith to all its citizens. The party President received much flak of criticism from the BJP and the parivar. What ever the notions of the ideal state Jinnah has proposed Pakistan was always theocratic and non secular (The New Indian Express, June 13, 2005). The idea of two nation theory was propounded by none other than Parivar's ideological guru and propounded of Hinduvta. Vinayak Damodhar Savarkar

Addressing the 1937 session of the Hindu Mahasbha in Ahamadabad he said India cannot be assumed today to be a unitarian and homogenous nation the Hindus and Muslims in India. On August 15, 1943, he clinched the issue, I have no quarrel with Mr. Jinnah's two nation theory. We Hindus are nation by ourselves and it is a historical fact that Hindus and Muslims are two nations. Will the parivar follow up with a resolution extolling savarkar's two nation doctrine.

Leaders of the major political party though anchored in have taken pains to construct a new identity for the leader the architect of Pakistan. Recalling such episodes may help him consolidate the ruptured feelings.

Advani though held for Babri Masjid demolition, but for ensuring the premature and unproductive end of Agra Summit proved brave when he had to confront a hostile press and public (The New Indian Express, June 3, 2005). This statement of a national consensus and his unequivocal support to Indo-Pak peace process irreversible protends the sustainability of the present Indo-Pak relations the space he created on his good will gesture to Pakistan, showcases that the abrasive political position undermine the broad appeal that the exercise of power at the top demands. The New Indian Express editorial feels that he wanted to crush his personal image of himself and re-define his image in the present context.

He wanted to convey the message that it is deliberate attempt on his part to lay claim to the Indo- Pak peace process, to see it as a legacy of the BJP rule.

The editorial of The Hindu had very little to say on the entourage of Mr. Advani and the amazing role of Mr. Advani as a peacenik. Both the NPS have unfailingly supported the entourage of Mr. Advani.

The BJP leadership flayed Advani for having apologised in the enemy's soil for Babri Masjid demolition has caused embarrassment to Sangh Parivar and condemned his act as treacherous. Mr. Advani's refrains on the tour was that the BJP was not against Pakistan the backlash from Parivar shattered the myth.

The Print media especially The Hindu held the sole authority of peace momentum did not hail from the successive governments in power but gained momentum on it own show how impartial and not prejudiced its approach towards peace has been.

Advani visit to Pakistan is vied both by the media and the general public. Advani acted as a perfect peacenik but it was emotional trip for him. The BJP especially the Sangh Parivar didn't find his trip bringing in hopes for he had proclaimed in the Pakistani soil said that the demolition for the Babri Masjid was unpardonable and Jinnah to be a secularist.

Advani merit attention with efficacy with which he portrayed the man in Jinnah more than a leader. Advani statement was a reminder that Indian history is not simple black and white story of herocs and villans, Jinnah was at one time considered an ambassador Hindu - Muslim unity.

This open pronouncement from the leader of the opposition L.K. Advani has been termed to be a far greater achievement than the Sangh Parivar.

Advani has done the histories of India and Pakistan a great service by re-opening the Jinnah question (The New Indian Express).

The Print media hailed Advani as an intellectual in spite of the fulminations against him by his own Sangh Parivar.

Newspaper Attitude (Ed-stand) Conflict Management

There are four editorials in The New Indian Express and three editorial in The Hindu during the period of study.

Musharaff plan of sending relief through the LoC is termed as gimmick diplomacy for it had been carried out within 48 hours after the earth quake if would had weight.

For three days there was no LoC and Jihadist have taken advantage (The New Indian Express, October 20, 2005). Even amidst death and destruction they have established their trade mark of ferocity by killing Hindus earlier in the week followed by the assassination of the state education minister.

The LeT has outpaced the activity of helping the quake hit victims than the Pakistan's army. This goes to till the clout LeT has on its soil even during distraught times, the editorial feared what will be theier hold during normal times.

The newspaper also refused the opening of LoC and they may appear as the Trojan horse through the openings of the LoC with the absolute governmental sanction leaving mere innocents at their peril. India cannot be emotionally black mailed into accepting an open LoC as a fait accompli.

The terrible tragedy (the massive earthquake) measuring 7.6 on the rictor scale with its epicenter in the Hindukush mountain exhibited all three characteristics. The tembler devasted parts of Pakistan, PoK, India and Afghanistan. The tragedy may have tacken place in disputed territory but has united the two parties. The devastation in PoK which has rendered many die and lift many homless and the united nations office for the co-ordination office of humanitarian affairs relief operation remained struck mainly in the life saving mode.

A mere exact casualty figure and a better and more detailed assessment of the condition of survivors will arise only after Pakistani soldiers, relief workers and volunteers are able to reach the areas still remained cut off.

But it can be hardly compared to the scale of devastation in Pakistan, where authorities still feel a second wave of death due to difficulties in reaching the survivors and treating the wounded.

India had offered relief and rescue operation to Pakistan, and Islamabad has accepted the goodwill gesture extended by India. The political sensitivities involved proclaimed by Musharaff halted the procurement of Indian Air force planes and pilots stated the editorial in The Hindu.

The opening of the LoC can help the divided families come together and in the hour of relief and calamity to be given an opportunity to connect each other (The Hindu, October 21, 2005).

The decision at the last month after gap of six decades, to open up five points on the LoC for quake relief did appear to be historic one. The editorial The New Indian Express has suggested that much of the delay in distribution of quake relief material has to be laid on Pakistan's door. The inept handling of the relief measures on the Pakistani side has compelled the Pakistani to open relief both side of the LoC.

The editorial The New Indian Express suggested that low level of political magination has tied up the process. But given the magnitude of destruction on both sides, India must fond ways to go back and forth the dividing line (The New Indian Express, November 8, 2005).

India's offer of help to Pakistan seen with circumspection is not surprising. The cruel irony of the situation is that the tragedy has struck the place where that has been most marked by political tension between two countries.

The foreign assistance is well received by President Musharaff cannot oblivate the fact that he is not able to help a part of Pakistan which is at the mercy of Pakistan government cannot be read lightly for he has gone to say to the world community of Pakistan's weakness, when a part of Pakistan defacto government is facing the biggest catastrophe (The New Indian Express, October 11, 2005).

Ministry Umar Farooq, the moderate Hurriyat chairman appeal to the people on both sides to alleviate the suffering of the devastated victims is aplaudable.

New Delhi's offer of relief and rescue operations was made just hours after the earthquake hit the area. If India and Pakistan had agreed to co-ordinate their disaster relief operation, such mutual assistance would have constituted an important CBM.

But Islamabad is worried about allowing the Indian army for relief and rescue operations in PoK. Given such apprehensions, may be far too optimistic to expert that the earthquake will pay large peace dividend. (The Hindu, October 11, 2005).

7

Features

(a) Features Covering CBMS

During the period of study there were fourteen features in The Hindu where else there were three features in The New Indian Express.

The feature in The Hindu proposed that the bus is a model construct that should guide the future course of India-Pakistan relations. First proposed in October 2003 by then External Affairs Minister, Yashwant Sinha many felt that the bus would never get moving given the fears and reservations in both sides. These fears were proved wrong when External Affairs Minister, Natwar Singh, clinched a deal on beginning the bus service in February with Pakistani leadership. The BJP flayed the United Progressive Alliance government for allowing the passengers to travel to (PoK) Pakistan occupied Kashmir and Pakistan without passport; the use of passports to cross into territory which India claims as its own is not without implication — for New Delhi's national position on PoK. Mr. Natwar Singh speaking in the Lok Sabha on March 21, 2005 claimed that if you consider (PoK) Pakistan occupied Kashmir as part of India how do you expect that we should have a passport to come to our own country from our own territory.

The feature also insisted that the course of travel within Jammu and Kashmir is made possible only by permits and Azad Kashmir is to cross (LoC) Line-of-Control will be issued a permit by the Regional passport office Srinagar.

To the dismay of the press, the (LoC) Line-of-Control was manned by security men on either side which defeated the very purpose of the bus journey. The streets to the airport wore a deserted look with shops closed and the anticipated cheer among the public. The same venue where the Prime Minister highlighted the measures for development did not kick start the public at this stage.

The euphoria aired by the electronic media nationally and internationally stands to tell whether the production was managed to bring the people away from the venue into confidence. The attack on the tourist reception centre on the previous day has sent shivers down the spine of the public which had forced them to remain indoors.

There is a strong rebuttal of claims made by the print media after having witnessed stark reality on the way from airport to the venue or from the venue to the airport. This outbreak of the strong sentiment expressed by the people on both sides of Line-of-Control cannot be choreographed by some agency at this hour to distance the claims made by the terrorist after the attack on tourist regional centre.

The strong indications of the changes that have occurred after the tourist reception centre being bombarded by militants targeting many millions. The coming together of the two Kashmiris on either without prejudice in history has taken a new framework for the first time.

The cautions framework with determined approach would not help realize the ground situation wherein Geelani school of thinking felt highly critical of non convergence of the public mood with emotive symbolism of the bus service. The railing establishment in Pakistan is wary of the painstaking effort taken at every juncture to restore confidence with Pakistan occupied Kashmir.

Alienation in Kashmir is still a question to be determined by all right thinking citizen. Cumulative dissatisfaction is the genie which leaves them undeterred and fall in line with much wont patronage of Pakistan in near future. Pakistan's minisele involvement in Kashmir freedom movement cannot wean away the separatist tendency among the militants. Pakistan has miserably failed in proxy war and cannot win much across the table had been a proper insignia to the Kashmiris and anticipated protracted aid from the rival camp.

The sentimentality of the much heralded bus service can vouch for a new U turn to the issue. The feature in The Hindu leaves more room for thought regarding alienation. The aftermath of alienation sapped the confidence of being a part of the Indian republic.

The government of India and all Party Hurriyat Conference (APHC) had two memorable encounters with the Pakistan between Prime Minister and the Kashmir outfit could be prove to be third time lucky though the erstwhile BJP government that had arranged the Hurriyat for talks, the BJP approach towards Kashmir question was too rigid to allow any meaningful outcome.

It was Mr. Advani who was the interlocutor during the course of talks with Hurriyat was predictably unhelpful, as the only in alma mater to discuss was the evolution.

Though the talks were held between two sides nothing emerged as the result of the talks. (The Hindu Sep, 2005)

Then and now (India and Pakistan peace process had a different U-turn but alternatively the ongoing at Rasina Hill has changed from the past.

The bus service plying between Srinagar and Muzaffarabad, the plying of trucks on the same route, the Pakistani journalist travel to and from the past between boundaries, the intellectual forum the Pakistan occupied Kashmir meet to finalise reconciliation in intra-Kashmir talks.

Militancy and infiltration contribute at lower level through desperation of those that would gain continues near public schools and often public places. The breakaway Hurriyat leader Syed Geelani too remains significantly a fly in the ointment as he has a large following.

Zero - level tolerance towards human rights violation against civilians dies in where the Patibal - Prechithan militant where they were killed in cold blood.

The print media widely criticized the terrorist killing the civilians and the Huriyat maintain a silence and disingenuously try to blame the government.

The NP stressed that the Hurriyat must convince the Pakistan establishment that they allow greater freedom of goods and services, trade and commerce across the border and telephone services could be liberalized so that communication could be quicker and cheaper.

Protests and rallies are in exigency and legal revenues must be enforced to delegitimise violence and bring about peace rallies.

The latest is Kashmir. The border is an accident of history and not the making of the people, nor is it their choice. To make it soft after five decades is nothing but opening its sluice gates for the movement of jihadis. The Al Queda which is holed up in Afghanistan and a headache for Musharaff will have easy access to the hills and valley of Kashmir once the bus traffic becomes frequent and the minder because less vigilant. Travel based on identity cards is fraught with danger. Subversive activities, encouraging disaffection, will increase and make the task of the security forces more difficult. The fall of the Berlin wall has not improved the lot of the east Germans. Nor are the westerners happy to accommodate the poor cousins.

The feature in the Hindu stated the difference between the two governments in facilitating CBMS.

The Vajpayee Government in 2000 and 2001, and had made arrangements to bring about a change in the composition of the Hurriyat and neither allowed the Hurriyat delegation to visit Pakistan. The present government allowed the Hurriyat to travel by the Srinagar - Muzaffarabad transit facility but also the Hurriyat used the facility to travel to Pakistan proper, the media deemed it as win-win solution for though they were allowed to travel to PoK with passports signed by the Pakistani side or not, the Manmohan Singh government can fend off critics whether they were all owed to travel to Pakistan with passports lies in the hands of the government concerned. The Hindu feature quoted that Hurriyat visit to Pakistan is a major and dramatic confidence building measure. Such ventures may help in talking the Pakistani public on the new line of thinking on Kashmir both the governments evolved late.

The launch of the bus service across the erstwhile Pakistan has been applauded by Mirwaiz, Ansari, Bhat, but how they will respond to the leaders across PoK is a test of their leadership credentials. The political relevance will be felt only if the issue on borders becoming irrelevant can be pushed further (June 2, 2005, The Hindu).

The gains from the visit is very evident, but the question of Hurriyat leadership onward journey to from PoK to Pakistan is treated as a controversy? The suspicion that arose during the course of the travel from Pakistan and PoK, and if Mirwaiz remains true to the sentiments as honoured today, they will support the peace process now underway.

The feature in The Hindu is highly critical of the outcome of the visit with coming back of the Hurriyat leaders to Srinagar. They are sharply divided after the visit Mr. Mirwaiz opened, that the visit is historic and the solution on Kashmir is imminent. Yasin Malik and his followers do not mince words to say that the visit is merely historic (The Hindu, June 16, 2005).

Mirwaiz is of the opinion that the coming together may create a reconcillatory atmosphere. Yasin Malik does not support the triangular process as initiated by Omar Mirwaiz Farooq. Mirwaiz proposal to work beyond the UN resolution of 1945 and adapt to the changed realities of September 9/11.

Musharaff during the press conference at Canberra wanted 'Kashmir to be autonomous' Dividing Kashmir is not the locustandi of the Musharaff. Bilal Lone one of the Hurriyat leaders has made it mandatory that the viable peace process can be made clearing the period of Musharaff as he is the commander in chief of the armed forces.

The feature in the New Indian Express went to the extent of eulogizing the NCMBS. The one and only formal nuclear CBM between India and Pakistan to annually exchange a list of national nuclear facilities was initiated by the PM Rajiv Gandhi during the visit of President Zia-Ul-Haq to India in 1985. Talks between India and Pakistan over the last decade and a half have only produced two conventional military CBMS. Prior notification of army exercises of the certain size near a border and commitment by the two air forces not to violate each others airspace. India proposed a broad package of conventional military CBMS that would lead to greater contact between two military establishments. But for inexplicable reasons, Pakistan has been unwilling to accept even the simplest of Indian proposals, for example, one on regular talks between two armies led by vice - chief of staff. Even harmless interaction between India's institute of defence studies and analyses and its counterpart in Islamabad has not found favour with Pakistan (Aug. 8, 2005; The New Indian Express).

The feature provided three new factors facilitate a forward looking approach to Indo - Pak military.

The objective reality of nuclear parity with India should reduce Pakistan's fear that India will use its alleged conventional military superiority, to the extent it exists. A ceasefire between two militaries had held since the end of 2003 along the LoC. It is time now to bring military predictably and tranquility to Indo-Pak frontiers.

The feature in The Hindu examined a new fillip to the peace process. The proposed re-opening of the Karachi consulate and revival of the rail route empowering Sindh and Rajasthan would ample shift in the peace process towards south Pakistan and help redress the grievance. Both will be a boon to Sindh province and the port city of Karachi which account for 90% of Indian visa seekers from Pakistan. The MQM, an influential political party shares power at the centre as well as the province of Sindh lobbied to get the establishment to give into the strong sentiments of the people and paved the way to make the consulate and the rail link a reality (The Hindu, Dec.16, 2005). Millions of post partition migrants living in Karachi have suffered in maintaining ties with their families in India. The problems are not confined to an expensive journey to and from Islamabad, finding in the capital, and waiting in the long queues. But, also harassment at the hands of the local police. The citizens of Sindh can look forward to a less cumbersome way to obtain Indian visa with the re-opening of the Karachi consulate. The proposed revival of the Kolarapur,

Munabo rail route linking Sindh and Rajasthan will provide the shortest possible route to the people of the region to meet their relatives and friends in India.

The rail route was shut down after the 1965 India - Pakistan war. Though both sides restored bilateral ties and communication links after the 1965 and 1971 wars for a variety of reason, the rail link would not be restored. As a result, for the last 40 years the people of Sindh who wanted to travel to Rajasthan by land had to take a circuitious route via Punjab.

The feature stated that the Pakistan's establishment was not very enthusiastic about more links with India, on the ground that (CBMS) for the people of greater people - to - people contacts have to go in tandem with progress on Kashmir.

The charm of the Kashmiris generated with the plying of more buses across the border is away, by the increase in the fare and the restrictions placed on visa by both countries. The one way fare of Pakistani Rs. 900 and Indian Rs.700 for the less than 45 km. travel between Amritsar and Lahore and of Pakistani Rs.1200 and Indian Rs. 1000 for the just over 100 km. Amritsar and Nankana Sahib route reflected the anti-poor mindset. The regularisation of visas between Amritsar and Lahore and vice versa, one has to travel all the way to New Delhi and Islamabad to get his or her visa. So far, there is no proposal for visa facility in Lahore, Arnritsar or other invitees. In majority of cases, visas are granted to only those who have relatives or friends with verifiable address. Any person, irrespective of the status intending to visit either India or Pakistan for the first time, is entirely at the mercy of the intelligence agencies for clearance (The Hindu, Dec. 23, 2005).

The feature suggested that if Pakistan is not ready for liberalized visa regime, India should take the lead which ease tension among the public but it may add to the woes of the intelligence agencies to identify the culprits.

The rail link between Sindh and Rajasthan would facilitate the reunification of families can be made more easily linked provided the great Pakistani port to which they were connected before 1947 be opened to provide a less circuitious route. The editorial also suggested that such large opening would help only if the catchment area is wide. In future, for example, the two governments should look into the possibility of running passenger trains between Mumbai and Karachi as well as Delhi and Karachi (The Hindu, Jan. 10, 2006).

The editorial suggested a rational visa policy which can mitigate the suffering of people across the border.

The journey of the express across the international border was an occasion to unwind - let loose pent-up emotions. The Thar express was flagged off by the Sindh governor, the scene was no different at the Hyderabad station though it was 2 a.m. when the train pulled in. The feature said that the people wanted to know why it took 40 years to restart the service. They also wanted an assurance that it will not be sacrificed yet again at the alter of India - Pakistan tensions. It was clear that people on both pre-post partition Sindh have been eagerly looking forward to like for years (The Hindu, Feb. 22, 2005).

After the first year of its inaugural run the bus service has received a severe jolt. The first and foremost impediment is the travel document form itself. Even mainstream NC leader Omar Abdullah who had gone on to attend the Pugwash conference in Islamabad had found it very difficult to fill the form the intelligence agencies of the two countries were suspicious. 35000 trained forms have been distributed in the past year and 2,000 are still waiting for the clearance. The five points that opened across the LoC for people to move about and help on another in the hour of grief culminated to adopt the same procedure followed in the case of Srinagar - Musaffarabad bus. Unless the political establishment of India and Pakistan work to change the mindset of the security establishment the best of political initiatives can yield little (The Hindu, April 8, 2006).

(b) The Feature in The Hindu on Trade

Pakistan's trade with India would continue to be governed by a positive list, which allowed only 773 items to be imported from India. India also wanted Pakistan to give it MFN status. That would become a non-issue had Pakistan implemented SATFA fully. The State Bank of Pakistan, the country's central bank has reported that between 2003 - 2004, that are after excluding the items that are positive list for India, 45% of the items could be imported by Pakistan at lesser cost from India that the current cost of import from the rest of the world.

The tariff and non-tariff barriers in India that discourage Pakistani exporters despite India having given the MFN status to Pakistan as far back as 1996. (The Hindu, July 31, 2006)

The feature pointed out though equal treatment gender SAFTA would not be possible, until there is progress towards resolution of some political disputes between the two countries including the Kashmir issue.

(c) Feature Predicting the Peace Process with N-CBM

The US sale of F -16 to Pakistan has raised a controversy over the sale deal providing more weapons to India also highlights that peace in the sub-continent is sabotaged. Left intellectuals still believe that the sale of F-165, F-185 to Pakistan is but a ploy to destabilize the peace process in progress which comes in the wake of bus service between Srinagar and Muzaffarabad. The visit of Rice to India with sole motive of re-writing the power equation in south Asia. But earlier when F -16 was granted to Pakistan it was done with a premise of vacating the communist regime in Afghanistan, whole India found shelter under the rival camp (the communist).

The prevailing situation Washington is the supply of arms to both Israel and Egypt on the hope their would be parity. Both Egypt and Israel favoured mediator. But Pakistan is an aide of Washington whereas India loathes such mediators. The American official caricatures Pakistan 2020, which reveals the Indian intelligent system fails to perceive the guide in the transfer of hardware which usually precedes compliance. American policy shift toward Pakistan need not be lampooned for the tie-up with Musharaff is not only trace Osama-Bin- Laden but also retrieve a nation from a impending quagmire.

Mediation is a no-no in the equation and especially the powell-Rumsfeld reinforced, India - Pak take a new relationship is being hailed. The New Indian Express has taken painstaking efforts to unlacing the controversy snow balling around F -16 the Hindu either has restrained itself or seem to abhor the critical note behind the sale of F -16 or F -18 or more to India and Pakistan in the so called nuclear flash point of the sub-continent which even the super power feels the grandiloquernt steps that can be taken to stymie the onset of another nuclear holocaust with much imbalance in South Asia. The New Indian Express has also carefully orchestred the role of India in the global market and the unrelenting efforts of the US.

(d) Features Covering the Economic Co-operation

During the period of study there were two features in The New Indian Express where else there only three features in the Hindu.

The visit of President General Musharaff to India, with the green signal given at the political level to remove all barriers to trade between India and Pakistan i.e., has set up a new quantum leap in imports and exports (The Hindu, April 20, 2005). During 2004-05, exports from India are expected to reach $440 million while imports from Pakistan are to be about $60 million. Commerce and Industry Minister Kamal Nath, we will remove any trade barriers to imports from Pakistan. The Pakistan President is believed to have been circumspect about the prospect of giving (MFN) to India, mainly because of the trade imbalance between India and Pakistan. It is to be seen whether bilateral trade flows which have already doubled from $1,250 million to $500 million over the last three years rise with the same speed.

The pipeline which needs the co-operation of Pakistan when seen through a prism can be divulging many solutions. (The New Indian Express, October 1, 2005)

The UPA government needs the pipeline to keep the leftists happy and therefore they have no hesitation in exploiting the compulsions of India's domestic politics for their own commercial interest.

Pakistan too needs the gas pipeline for domestic and political reasons. This will stabilize the kind of relationship with India especially on the economic interest. Both the TIE and Hindu editorials economic feasibility to build the pipeline does cast more on Pakistan's exchequer and they will not defy the US president in building a safe pipeline without India in the deal.

But, for India this singular exercise is to appease the leftists liberals and Dr. Manmohan Singh's UPA not to renege on the independent foreign policy manifestos which stands to tell on commitment.

This was the logic which India's original negotiating position was built, that if Pakistan want the pipeline, they also need something in return, this was not additional assurance on terrorism it was something as small as limited transit rights to Indian goods by road to Afghanistan.

The way the pipeline in structured, if would first runs along Pakistan's western coast, enter India for a short distance in Gujarat and then loop into Pakistani soil to enter into India at some point much later. (The New Indian Express, July 30, 2005)

The BJP started off the gas pipeline. The voters stole it from them and gave it to Congress.

The New Indian Express portrayed that should Pakistan ever want to cut off your gas supplies you could do exactly the same to there by blowing up the little loop in Gujarat. The tit-for-tat business really sometimes would not iron out. The left has shown a great defiance to America. India must now build the pipeline that it must defy Washington. Musharaff is not the one to join any alliance to spite the different forces especially the yanks? If he really had the intention to call a spade a spade he could have resorted to removing them forcefully from their airbus? The hub of the issue is that Iran as well as Pakistan need to presence of the gas pipeline. But American interests needs to be safeguarded, India and Pakistan into economic interdependence and also strengthen a religions moderate and unabashedly pro-American regime in Pakistan.

Pakistanis have emboldened their stand on not allowing the transit rights to Afghanistan whereelse India permits them dollar million for the pipeline they have designed. When India wants to be sent a some high protein food biscuits to Afghanistan they not allowed to pass through.

A consignment of buses and other biscuits have been turned back by the Afghanistan. They have been shopped to Mumbai shipped to Bandra Abbas in Iran then driven back to 2000 km into Kabul.

The complexity of regional relationship thus pipeline isn't merely a project of economic gain or strategic defiance, the media makes it amply clear and logical of that a go-ahead for the pipeline to be carried away, politically, economically and strategically.

The Indian Express also convinced the Indian government to defy the US like the North Korea, Iran and Venezuela. Both papers seem to goad the government to an conscious independent decision to prove to the world that they are independent sovereign republic much capable of taking worthy decisions whatever may be the imponderables.

The domestic ideological foreign policy of the UPA government has come in for severe criticisms thus when the leaders more on ideological fault lines, they may get entangled in the framework finding it difficult to come out with their own decision, thus paying the price for being party to the so-called contract. The New Indian Express highlighted the vagueness of the 250 - word common minimum programme which abhors the much prominent aspects and not straightjacket, minimum worded manifestos.

The flexibility shown on nuclear question to Iran gas pipeline which has changed the much desired the proposed gas pipeline project which could meet the necessary gas requirements of South Asia.

The nuclear framework or the energy received from nuclear power may be 4%, even by the optimistic prediction India may get a boost of 20% our energy needs by 2020. Dr. Singh's policy of appeasement like - about becoming dependent on Pakistan, paying transit fees to the Musharaff regime, wanting reverse transit rights, safety and security is like walking away from the project. When US Secretary of State Condoleza Rice was in New Delhi in March in proposing an energy dialogue with India showed flexibility on the nuclear question to the Iran pipeline. Though they received a rebuttal from the NDA led government, a lot has changed since then.

Though India had forced for an alternative choice Man Mohan Singh government showed a new willingness to engage America's strategic agenda in Asia. The new nuclear framework is to take shape, India will have to nudge with US on test ban concessions.

But the energy deficit in India cannot be circumvented with nuclear energy which provided, only 4% of the energy needs. The onward crunch in energy may serve some 20 % of our energy needs. The media bemoans of the remaining 80% which may leave us in lurch if demands are not met.

Piped gas from Iran is a low cost source but even this would need to be supplemented by gas imports from Myanmar, Qatar and central Asia. Importing gas in liquefied form is an option but the costs are much higher. Security of transit through Pakistan but there are a number of political and financial solutions available including the involvement of China as the end point of the pipeline. US opposition to the pipeline is not of antipathy to Islamic regime but it will undo all the efforts it has made to dominate the transit route of Asian energy. Losing interest or not looking in potential investors may leave the country in state of 'energy crisis'.

The Americans oppose the gas - pipeline deal on several counts (The Hindu, August 25, 2005). It is, the Americans are concerned about the bonanza that oil rich - countries, including Iran, are reaping due to sky rocketing of prices. Secondly, the pipeline would set a dangerous precedent for other countries to follow. Iran is suitably placed as natural transit corridor for the transport of Capsian Sea oil and gas. The U.S. has therefore, gone overboard to draw transit; routes for cap.m oil that by - pass Iranian territory. The prime example of this approach has been the construction of the Baku - Ceyhan oil pipeline. In this case the Americans made an extraordinary effort to route the pipeline towards the Turkish part of Ceyhan, so that Iranian territory was avoided.

In this Politically driven deal, the companies involved had to spend millions in extra cost to construct the pipeline through unfriendly terrain and conflict prone zone.

Thirdly the most important, the pipeline would anchor, friendly ties among Iran, Pakistan and India. This would greatly undermine US strategic leverage with India and Pakistan against Iran in the future.

(e) Business Ventures

Both the countries have joint stake in the development of Chah Bahar part with Jebel Asir in Dubai fast growing over-crowded, Chah Bahar is ideally located as a future - shipping hub for facilitating east-west trade. Once endowed with sufficient warehousing facilities, Chah Bahar can be used fully for promoting trade with land locked Central Asia. Besides Chah Bahar is also geo-strategically significant as it stands at the gates of the Gulf of Oman and the Arabian sea, over looking vital shipping lanes emerging flows Persian Gulf.

But the The New Indian Express stated that Prime the Indo-Pak gas pipeline is on cards especially after the EAMS with Iran (The New Indian Express, September 9, 2005). The trade routes with this country is improving provided that there is free flow of goods and services.

Amritsar to Kabul would take only 24 hours. It all depends when Islamabad allows transit. The business potential in Central Asia is limited because lack of access. Investment of $600 million at least are required to build rail links (via) Iran to central Asia to develop business potential. A road link from Chabhar part to Afghanistan is underway.

The feature in The Hindu understand that Pakistan Prime Minister Shaukat Aziz after the 'big date with Mr. Bush' on Jan. 21, 2006 deviated from its earlier stand on the gas pipeline which would boost the economy and meet the depleting energy demands of Pakistan owing to the UN sanction imposed on Iran (The Hindu, January 26, 2006). This is very much reminiscent of PM Manmohan Singh's statement in Washington in July 2005 about the risks and uncertainties involved in the project.

Pakistan did have an eye on the Indo-US nuclear deal, and therefore played a stepmotherly attitude towards the pipeline project to appease the US. Thus would eventually serve as a better bargaining position to reap rich dividend; from the US or safely bracketed like India.

But the New Indian Express feature emerged with the post 9/11 U-turn by Musharaff who wanted to protect the nuclear arsenal, his regime and ensure spare for Pakistan in a post - Taliban Afghanistan. The enthusiastic support to the US "War on Terror" would ensure future influence in Kabul, it was calculated. But the US has now made it clear that it is the country for a long haul. This created nervousness in Islamabad.

(f) Coverage of Features Reduction of Jihad after Composite Dialogue

During the period of study there was only one feature in The Hindu and no such features in The New Indian Express.

After the third composite dialogue the feature in the Hindu examined on the Jihadist forces who sought asylum from the Pakistani establishment. After the visit of president Bush in the sub-continent, Pervez summed to back the US policy for the extension of civilian nuclear energy and on Kashmir. The various intelligence sources said that the military communication between the Pakistan and the commanders is still prevailing. The unprecedented hunger strike observed by at least top 15 Jihadi commanders indicate to protest what they see as Pakistan president Pervez Musharaff decision to abandon the Jihad in J & K (The Hindu, March 13, 2006). The feature suggested that Lashar chairman Hafiz Mohammed Saeed, Jammat - Ud - Dawa leader, Zaeem Qadri, a functionary responsible for public relations with former PM Nawaz Sharrif, Pak, Mantana Saifuddin Saif, the secretary general of the MMA criticized Musharaffs policy of succumbing with the international pressure.

Gen. Musharaff position is stated to be precarious for his predecessors like General Yahya Khan, Gen. Ayub Khan, Gen. Zia-Ul-Haq were deposed, by place reveals and who know will Gen. Musharaff may have to meet the same fate.

The distancing of Gen. Musharaff from the Jihadists force was perceived when the chairman of the Hardline Hurriyat faction went public with outrage on January 28 that Pakistan president had no mandate to propose a political solution acceptable to the people of occupied J & K "It is the Kashmir freedom struggle" "not the president Musharaff". The feature deterministic of the concrete proposals of the Pak government to quick terrorists.

(g) Coverage of the Dialogue Process after the Third Round of Composite Dialogue

During the period of study there were three features in The New Indian Express where else there were only two features in The Hindu.

The feature in The Hindu determined the break through that the Delhi conference on J & K offers the prospect of a dialogue with the wide section of the public but a break with a flawed history of back - room deal making (The Hindu, February 23, 2005). The feature claims that APHC to be non representative as they have failed to legitimize it through a democratic test. APHC moderate chairman Mirwaz under Farooq said "It believes that a permanent resolution of the Kashmir crisis, the government of India and Pakistan shall have to essentially deal with those people who have been treating J & K as a disputed territory". But the APHC in November 17, 2004 met President Pervez Musharaff and prime minister Shaukat Aziz in PoK without a whimper of protest. Not only the APHC has shown reluctance to attend the Delhi conference but also other separatist leaders like Yasin Malik, Shabbir Shah, Syed Ali Geelani and the U J C. The feature questioned the credibility of the APHC which expressed no qualms in meeting the anti-India elements to the leaders who are committed to the state's accession to Pakistan. The National Conference has expressed the desire for greater autonomy while the Congress was not while the LUTF wished direct administration by Delhi.

Leaders like Maulivi Abbas Ansari, Bilal Ghani Lone, Mohammed Nayaeem Khan, Age Sayed Yassan and Faze-Haq-Qureshir spoke against the Delhi participation for it would be futile without proper agenda and would arose mistrust and suspicion. The APHC and other secessionists believe that it is ploy like the Srinagar-Delhi axis, a replay of the New Delhi - Srinagar pacts. The feature also claimed that though the NC, Congress and the PDP represent a substantial section of the people and accepting a plurality of is pre-requisite for a meaningful peace.

The Delhi conference was noted for carelessness and haste.

The conference on Feb.14 excluded Panthers Party which has significant presence in J & K. Ladakh UnionTerritory front leader Thupstan Chhewany was invited but the region's Congress unit was not.

The idea of a broad based dialogue had its origin in 2003-2004, and in 2005 a blue print for such a dialogue had been drawn up. National security advisor JN Dixit played a key role in these preparations with foreign secretary Shyam Saran, its director Ajit Dorai, secretary of the research and analyse wing Vikram Good.

After Dixit's death, the successor rule, Narayan addressed the external dimension to the conflict more than to the discussion among the political actors.

The meeting between PM Manmohan Singh and Mirwaiz took place with the pressures of the US and M.K. Narayan was omitted from the decision making process and nothing was gained from the meeting after /Mirwaiz Farooq failed to call for an end to terrorist violence.

During a visit to Pakistan New Delhi was in turn unwilling to meet APHC demands for prisoner release and reduction of Indian forces in Srinagar. Though the dialogue failed to garner the support of the different conflicting parties with its vested interest, the feature has suggested more democracy within the state.

To initiate substantive dialogue on the constitution amendment orders, which eroded the substance of article 370.

2. J & K political parties need to spell out their vision on greater federalism.
3. End to the central civil scheme pretence to consider if denying state citizens umon goverment jobs in J & K best interests.
4. Financial autonomy.
5. The demand that J & K citizens be protected by state specific fundamental rights rather than those granted by the constitution of India.

The Delhi conference cannot bring about an end to violence, but its progress could force an end to the evasion and polemical grand standing that has characterized the dialogue process so far.

The feature in the New Indian Express cited that the Hurriyat promptly attended pugwash - a European think tank which is into conflict resolution in South Asia on March 9 which will be chaired by the Hurriyat, the mainstream parties, NC and the centre's interlocutor with Kashmiris N.N. Vohra for the meeting. But the refusal of the Hurriyat to attend the conference sends wrong signals to the centre.

Lack of an agenda and the lack of consultation with PDP and Ghulam Nabi Azad on the round table showed an unplanned meeting. (The New Indian Express, February 27, 2006).

Though there were few men pressed into service for the task hardly their names found prominence. If the purpose of the round table is to show president George Bush arriving in India on March 1, the progress on Kashmir front has turned out to be counter productive.

There was no dialogue between the emergent forces and the locus of the political authority at the centre. The round table talks may help to cover this hiatus if taken seriously. (The New Indian Express, February 27, 2006) On the eve of Bush visit to India and pigwash in Islamabad. The climb down of Gen. Musharaff from his earlier stand on plebiscite and self -determination is notable.

Dialogue being tool, enough home work has to worked out before the commencement of any session.

For the round table in Delhi junior officials of the IB invited the Hurriyat, but they refused PM Sayeed was no taken into confidence for he was not personally invited (The New Indian Express, March 20, 2006). The round table conference by pugwash in Islamabad, had large number of audience attending so unwieldy a crowd and that they could not get a conference note at the end of the table. The national conference harped on autonomy, the PDP positioning itself between independence autonomy - calling for self - rule mainstream parties clamoring for both 'autonomy' and 'self rule'. The separatists were found to climb down from the goal of independence the way out for them has to be the hub for discussion and cleverly positioning them.

The feature on The Hindu further stated in the walk of PM Manmohan Singh's round table conference on J & K, the long established hierarchies of power between religious groups, ethnic communities and regions were relaying with one another to establish their identity.

The opening of the trans-LoC routes to Gilgit and Skardu will help diminish the region's economic independence on Srinagar.

Gujjur and Bakerwad communities consigned to the margins of both politics and development use lingering for a share in the onward gain for power.

BSP represents the Jammu regional sentiment which will capitalize on the appalling status of 1,20,000 partition refugees who are still not given state- subject rights essential to their acquiring property rights in J & K. They also have the hope Kashmir pandit community, displaced from their homes by Islamist terrorism in 1989 - 1990. The prediction in feature indicate that chauvinist disintegration is looming large. (The Hindu, March 30, 2006)

NDP voicing for autonomy, PDP asserting self rule, M. Aslam authority on Panchayat Raj system believed in strengthening local institutions holds the key.

India-Pakistan detente then is transforming not just the relationship between the two states but transfiguring the political life of J & K itself.

(h) American Interests over Kashmir (F)

Dming the period of study there were two features, in the New Indian Express and no such features in the Hindu.

The feature in the New Indian Express examined the rich dividend American on focusing on Kashmir.

Historically the Kashmir issue has been one of the major sources of discord between the two largest democracies. The US has demonstrated its keen interest to initiation mediation and peace - building efforts to further its interests in the strife torn region, which is important for economic resources and markets. The Kashmir dispute has wooed United States policy makers ever since 1947. Americans have pursued a variety of approaches to Kashmir problems (The New Indian Express February 26, 2006). They have often prescribed unilateral, bilateral and multilateral initiations under the United Nations umbrella.

There has been much international drama at the end of the cold war to bring most of the countries including India and Pakistan under the umbrella of the Nuclear Proliferation Treaty. The strategic perception by Washington is that global terrorism stems from this region. The United States is in search of strategic partner to combat Islamic terrorism. It seeks access to control Asian oil reserves and hence needs Pakistan, the moderate Islamic state to balance the fundamentalist regimes and secure oil pipeline access through Afghanistan and Pakistan. The United States policy makers have followed behind - the- screen facilitation, routine offers of the request of peace formula, semantic diplomacy in New Delhi and Islamabad.

Pakistan preferred wooing American intervention and mediation as a strategy to internationalise the Kashmir issue to wrest away rather than go for a mutual settlement with India. American attempts and offers of mediation have been at the behest of Pakistan. The United States has also been nurturing a 'third option' on Kashmir via 'the wishes of the people'.

The feature of The New Indian Express is very suggestive of the comments made by President George W. Bush at the Asia society wherein though the tailored speech failed to discriminate the conflict to be resolved on 'both sides' then corrected 'to all sides' indicated the fallacy in the merging trend of the conflict on retrogressive step towards the conflict. The Americans have not yet moved away from the concept of India, Pak as well as citizens of Kashmir (The New Indian Express, February 26, 2006). This watershed in the development on Kashmiri dialogue process as the American still harped on the citizens of Kashmir. As Bush prepared to visit the sub-continent, the Pakistani's will raise the rhetorical demand for American mediation on Kashmir. The feature is afraid of the number of political errors that may emanate if President Bush is allowed to' speak more on Kashmir.

The successive Pakistan government wants the ember to simmer, to get political and domestic advantage. Secondly the terrorists outfits feel all the more advantageous in destabilizing the peace in the region.

The Americans attitude towards the Indian establishment or south Asia has to be looked up with a skewed policy. The sale of F -16 to India was the announcement by the (IAF) though their was market for 126 fighter jets. The F-16 are being made in Fort writh, Texas but for the orders from the Indian sub-continent the factory was going to layoff about thousand workers. Hence it is in the interest of the military - industrial complex in America to have South Asia afflicted with inter state acrimony. America may lose leverage if there was no tension there and Advani struggled to declare Pakistan a terrorist state during the tenure of the National Democratic Alliance (NDA) government.

The paper also cited that Indo-Pak relations will improve if the proposed gas pipeline carrying Liquefied Natural Gas (LNG) from Iran to India is built.

We cannot be sure that the pipeline project will go through if America persisted its objection. Unless there is a turn around in relations between Iran and America, the America companies can get contract for building and managing the pipeline, the Bush administration is unlikely to change its position. Such related developments were absent in the Hindu.

(i) Newspapers Attitude Towards Peace Process and Conflict Resolution

During the period of study there were several features in the Hindu and three features in The New Indian Express.

The feature in The Hindu determined the kind of suspicion that prevailed in the vitiated atmosphere and the trading of charges that has kept the peace momentum at a abysmal condition.

A day before the December 25, 2005, Bangalore attack, the (MEA) Ministry of External Affairs had to defend the human rights violations in Balochistan where the violence is quelled by bomb shells, grenades, etc. (The New Indian Express, January 13, 2006). The feature delineated that such reference to the incidents in Balochistan goes against the commitment of the Indian Government Dr. Singh went public in Dhaka in Nov. 13, 2005 where he declared that he is not ready to choose his neighbour. Purport of any bilateral talk will meaningful only through dialogue with government. The question of Balochistan does not fit into the paradigm. The General did accuse India providing economic support to anti-government elements in Balochistan for fomenting trouble.

The General had sent an invitation of sorts for the cricket match and also blamed that "now if he comes here we do nothing about the peace process, I am afraid we are past wasting time".

Regarding issues on demilitarisation self-governance in Kashmir, the general is frustrated with India's attitude and approach. The Indian government rejected the plea at 10 p.m. on January 7, 2005 stating that "I would love to say, that any demilitarization or redeployment of security forces within the territory of India is a sovereign decisions of the government of India and can not be dictated by foreign government. "It ought to be clear that concepts such as joint control or joint management, which is an integral part of India, cannot be on the basis of settlement of the issue of J & K."

The newspapers attitude towards peace especially after April 2005 where India and Pakistan expressed peace process which was irreversible, has taken a hit with all these pot shots. If the leaders remain serious about the peace process being irreversible, they need to take charge of what is happening under its umbrella. "Solemn commitments continued in the very bilateral joint statement issued on April 15, 2005 have not been implemented yet.

The babus have shown little urgency between April 15 to Dec. 31, 2005 in meeting the deadline in the bilateral agreement.

The overt and covert activities of the terrorist groups like the (Let) Lashkar-e-Toiba, (Jem) Jaish-e-Mohammed responsible for several attacks, has become a cause for worry for India. The September 11, 2001 attacks has changed the mindset of Pakistan as the United States deplorably needs them in the war against terror. The peace process has become a statement with increased terrorist activity across the border. The feature finally determined that the trading of charges will not save the impasse.

The feature The New Indian Express has hailed that even after January 4, 2004 comitment President Musharaff seemed failing to keep up the commitments, so India considered that Musharaff increasingly has become part of the problem and his credibility as an interlocutor for India is rapidly eroding.

Though the Hindu promptly noted the Mr. Singh's comments on Balochistan after he failed to keep the Dhaka commitments, the feature in the New Indian Express adduces that the democratic force has to be adhered to in the neighbourhood and instigated that New Delhi must develop a long - term strategy for encouraging democratic forces in the region.

The feature in The Hindu illustrates the covert negotiation on Kashmir becoming evident and examined whether this jigsaw puzzle will take place with the secessionist groups in J & K. India has for several months pursued an energetic secret dialogue on J & K involving interlocutor from the state and the United States - based members of the either Kashmiri diaspora.

On January 25, the Hindu broke the news of these meetings. Incensed by such publicity Mr. Malik in a press conference in Srinagar publicly admitted that he had met the PM in 2001 and 2003, but insisted that talk of meeting (secret) circulating in the media is nonsense. (The Hindu, February 4, 2006)

The national security adviser to the government Mr. Narayan met Farooq Kathwari, a United States national who is a significant contributor to the Islamist organisation. Prime Minister himself held a meeting with Vijay Sazawal, United States based Kashmiri pandit leader.

The travel document was issued to Syed Geelani toward Haj and during the course of the extended travel, it was ploy used by Geelani to hold discussion with Pakistan based Islamic leader Mohammed Yusuf Shah and Islamist leader Ghulam Nabi Fai.

World wide covert services conduct negotiation where political principals fail to corner. The feature amply illustrated that Israel long -running secret talk with Palestine Liberation Organisation, Central Intelligence Agency cold war dialogue with Soviet Union committee for state security, the (KGB) have actively engaged in bringing about detente among nations.

The feature also explored the possibilities of not having men driven with wearing the mantle of power to execute certain strategies like Arjun Singh who presided over the execution of policy objectives of Prime Minister Rajiv Gandhi in Punjab, or the late Rajesh Pilot vigorously engaged secessionist in J & K, the feature deplored that Indian spies have thus stepped in where its politicians have failed.

Though they are just manifestations of an underlying malaise - political New Delhi seems to have no real idea of what it actually wanted in Jammu & Kashmir.

The med between Mr. Kawari United States and Dr. Singh strongly indicated the kickback for United States pressure on Pakistan to de-escalate violence. The feature suggested that the only way out is that the hide bound, dissent allergic intellectual establishment that informed policy in Jammu and Kashmir demonstrated will and dissent. The inclusion water resources Minister Saifuddin Soz to begin result oriented dialogue on federal autonomy.

With the course of composite dialogue, the hope of self governance in Kashmir and even asked the government that there is no dishonour in exploring the flexibility and leeway provided in the constitution to satisfy the aspirations to the people of Kashmir (The Hindu, April 26, 2006). The average turnout in the four bye - elections is reported to be more than 50% and the people of the troubled state are expressing their faith in democracy.

The Prime Minister scheduled to hold a second round of talks across the table with various Kashmiri groups in Srinagar on May 25. But the New Indian Express stated that the Hurriyat will not attend it. They had boycotted the last one held in Delhi, which was called without adequate preparations. Having held a round table conference with the mainstream parties in Delhi, perhaps the Prime Minister should hold another one with the separatist leadership, this should include, the Hurriyat, the outfits like Yasin Malik, Shabir Shah, Sajjad Lone and Syed Ali Shah Geelani. Whether Geelani or not/ he should be invited.

The resistant to peace process halts from three varied sources.

1. NDA and its loyalists.
2. The unreconstructed right which joyfully prescribed to a theory of inevitable hostility with Pakistan and Islam.
3. The ubiquitous agencies which have strong institutional stakes in conflict with Pakistan. Untrustworthiness and deep distrust of Pakistan army's Jihadi links and ideological hostility towards India. identified in the feature in the Hindu. These are the recently factors.
4. National security has been elevated as the most sacred mantra and reluctance among the political, bureaucratic and armed forces leaders to think innovatively beyond cliches and prejudices.
5. Indian nationalism and statehood no longer need sustained hostility with Pakistan for our collective equanimity.
6. Peace with Pakistan will have massive peace dividend in both countries, and South Asia region, opening up trade and economic co-operation.

7. Mobilising the democratic voices and sentiments in favour of a workable accommodation with Pakistan.
8. It is necessary to spell out openly and boldly what India is prepared (and not prepared) to do in the cause of peace.
9. The Prime Minister is yet to put in place an empowered negotiating structure, too many peace makers are at work, and this does not add to the governments reputation for competence.
10. The people of Pakistan, including the military establishment, erratic political leaders, political parties, should feel that it is new India, democratically, self assured and economically forward looking that is offering reasonable terms of friendship and reconciliation.
11. And the people of J & K too, feel accommadative potential of Indian democracy.
12. Peace need not be a frightening prospect.

The New Indian Express stressed more on Intra Kashmir dialogue organised by the centre for dialogue and reconciliation (CDR) in Jammu which brought together eminent personalities from both sides of Kashmir, including Northern areas, and third such meeting and showed that the consensus of developing on a host of issues - like an endorsement of Indo-Pak dialogue, condemnation of violence of all types, a realizations that the solution will not redraw boundaries, or alter the sovereignty of India and Pakistan. There is also growing awareness that the solution would have to involve all sections and regions if old Jammu & Kashmir and could not be valley centric. (The New Indian Express, April 24, 2006)

The feature in The Hindu suggested that after the elections the people preferred administrative-building acumen are more important to Jammu & Kashmir voters than questions of ethnic - religious identity. This is another changing phase during the course of the composite dialogue (The Hindu, April 25, 2006). Though religious parties, different political parties, leaders sang poems of ethnic diversity, the electorate has demonstrated that the population still feels the necessity of democracy.

The feature in the Hindu suggested that there was no progress especially after 7/11 Mumbai blasts. Mr. Kasuri remarks and the lack of Foreign Minister compounded the problem further. Though the officials planned July 20 - 21 to take stock of third round of composite dialogue and for the fourth round was not cancelled but postponed indefinitely. Pakistan expected quick deal on Kashmir, but India deplored the process of ending cross - border militancy and terrorism.

The peace process has diminishing returns though the votaries of the peace process like Talat Masood claim that as far as substantive issue are concerned no breakthrough has been expected. Even a breakthrough in Siachin has failed.

The feature pointed out that President Musharaff as per analysts feel that the best way to find peace in the region, is that time is running out. He has failed to match action with words and can India succeed where super power could not succeed, the argument goes on 'commitment' to war on terror. The trust deficit is palpable after three rounds of composite dialogue. (The Hindu, July 14, 2006)

The MMA which holds power in the North West Frontier province (NWFP) that endorsed President Musharaff controversial referendum in 2002, is angry with him for his pro-United States war on terror in Afghanistan. Musharaff walks the thin line between keeping the United States happy and the religious group at home satisfied.

The gains after three composite dialogue have been very little, people to people contact, the creasefire along the Line of Control, back channel motives, but the feature suggested that there are silver linings and trenchant critics would not deny this.

The feature in the New Indian Express felt proud of the contribution of the security agencies, for they have excelled in their performance compared to the Federal Bureau Investigation, Central Intelligence Agency (blessed with multi million dollars) budgets.

Who could not identify middle eastern Muslims instead targeted the Latin American Roman Catholics.

It is rather absurd to throw the onus on to the already burdened machinery which suffers from ennui the risk of encouraging publicity - hungry cops dosing silly things. Research Analysis Wing track record may be poor but has performed better than the over funded Central Intelligence Agency. Inter State Intelligence has done little in Pakistan but persecuted people in other countries. But the feature (The New Indian Express, July 17, 2006) admonished the media, to be stoics to checkmate collective adversaries, deny them sweet success of public visibility in contrary to the views of the feature in the Hindu which has painstaking effort to identify the roots of the terrorist and the background of their support.

The feature in 'The Hindu' has expressed outright limits to tolerance and the options that are in store. The non-commitment to the January 2004 joint statement and Pakistan which had more often than reneged on the promise failed to convince not only the Indian establishment and security agencies but has slammed public good will. The Foreign Minister of Pakistan Mr. Kasuri's remarks linking Mumbai with unresolved bilateral dispute, Kashmir at this juncture provided ample room for thought for the Indian intelligentsia to arrive at innocuous conclusions like 'no unresolved dispute' no human right violation can ever give an individual - even if he or she happened to be a victim of injustice - the right to blow up innocent civilians on a train or elsewhere. The feature referred to the 'Hawkish' operation of Parakaram and the 'mawkish' operation of Lahore the erstwhile, BJP government has remarkably navigated to find a solution. The feature harped of the futility of the military action and it is absolutely whimsical to hold the composite level or secretary level talks.

Three factors were identified by the feature in the Hindu which surfaced before the identity of the perpentrators of the Mumbai blasts were established.

Speculations were rife in air as the Al-Queda which is with as much war with Pakistan can extend the same to India, foment communal backlash by giving a leverage to the Sangh parivar and derail the peace process. The ultimate Indian response may be giving veto power to terrorists on the going composite dialogue. (The Hindu, July 17, 2006)

The JeM and the Let although banned in Pakistan exist under different names and with collusion with the Pakistani establishment may derail the peace process as they are dissatisfied with the peace process, to extract more concessions. If at all, after the Mumbai blasts, India may not reciprocate the same or it is incredible that India will offer such help.

The feature dictated the need for forsenic, swift and professional investigation. The feature suggested for a long-term strategy towards Pakistan is more important than the prospect of two foreign secretaries talk.

The New Indian Express feature pointed out that the international community gathered in St. Peterburg strongly to condemn cross - border terrorism against India, and it is unwise that New Delhi at the drop of the hat can gainer inter- national attention every time.

India will find it hard to threaten a full scale war every time like at the end of December 2001 and in the middle of May 2002, the US jumped into Indo-Pak conflict to present into escalating to nuclear level. (The New Indian Express, July 25, 2006)

The feature has stressed for reactivating the dialogue with Pakistan, a long term strategy needs a serious face - to -face conversation between General Musharaff and Dr. Singh, and India has to delink the peace process from cross border violence, the Hindu, also augurs for not holding the peace talks back.

(j) Features Covering Terrorist Growth Activities and Related Developments

During the period of study twelve features in The Hindu and four features in The New Indian Express.

The feature in The Hindu views on the modus operandi of various terrorist organisations.

The story of Laskhar-e-Toiba and its pan-Indian destruction became a part of the long read story (The Hindu). The student of medicine had been a central figure in a Laskhar-e- Toiba operation attack the Mumbai stock exchange using car bomb. Had the operation succeeded the death toll might have well have made the carnage caused by last week's bombings in Delhi appear trivial.

A long term Lashkar operative, Chillo detained by the Jammu & Kashmir police in 2006, on suspicion of ferrying funds to the terror group but was released without charge. He subsequently moved to Pune to pursue studies but spent much of his time on building pool of contacts for the Lashkar. Chillo was contacted by the Srinagar area Lashkar commander Sheikh Ahmed, who was sent to co-ordinate a joint assassination squad set up by the Hizbul Mujahideen and Lashkar. He turned now to Chillo who already had a cell in place. A carefully crafted intelligence bureau which also led to controversial elimination of a woman Lashkar operative Raza in an encounter at Ahmedabad eventually led to the detection and exposure of the 'Zulu cell'.

Understanding the Lashkar position requires an engagement with its core position, that the Jihad in Jammu & Kashmir is not a battle over territory, but part of an irreducible conflict between Islam and unbelief. Committed to the eventual creation of caliphate that would rule over all the world's Muslims, the Lashkar asserted that 3 Jihad without end must continue "until Islam, as a way of life, dominated the whole world and until Allah's law is enforced every where in the world. As a noted scholar of Islam Yoginder Sikand perceptively pointed out the Lashkar vision of Islam is one that leads to represent the Quran itself as a manifesto for Jihad.

The terrorists protest against cannot be demand heinous, dastardly, as they are cliches to be no more of use (The New Indian Express, November 4, 2005). The terrorists cause may them and is not easy to decide their unusual acts. The perpenetrators and collaborators have to be solely responsible for this.

Even nation like Israel and the United States could not contain this act of violence. Terrorism can be acted upon only with intelligence. We should not object to terrorism as is ideologically bound to act.

The steps to be taken are not only adhere to Prevention of Terrorism Act but also which is more appealing to our sense, but tackle it with law enforcement agencies.

In the long term terrorism can be denoted by shared common interests. At every international forum that all talks on terrorism is an ritual enactment.

There are global checks on nuclear proliferation, inspection, international audits. Time is now ripe for setting a strong cell to contain this irrational act everywhere.

Various terrorist group in Jammu & Kashmir are using an alarming number of children as "terror tools". The children are used as spies, porters and as guerilla's who throws grenades and plant Improvised Electronic Device.

The children (some barely nine or ten years) are even used as shields encounters and deployed in operation against Indian security forces. The children are waylaid during their return from school and caught unawares. Most of the children picked by terrorists are from remote areas of Rajouri, Poonch, Doda, Udhampur and Kupwara and belong to very poor and illiterate families. In fact, the Jammu and Kashmir police has noticed a clear trend since 2004 - more and more children go missing from remote areas. (The Hindu, November 20, 2005).

The children confessed to the army how they are being caught and used for their purposes for instance Akram was on his way from home when he was stopped by terrorists and part Rs. 500 to throw a grenade in the local market. He had no choice but to meekly accept what was being directed. Gafour was recruited by terrorist from Udampur village and used for operations against security forces.

In another instance the army found Iqbal 11, working as a porter, guide and part - time guerilla. The security forces claim that along the Indo-Pak border, Pakistan boys as young as 13 - 14 years carrying deadly weapons were being trained. They revealed that they had been trained at a madarassa in Pakistan and were being sent to the Indian territory.

There were elaborate features and reports of the existence of the Lashkar operative and how they execute their sting operation. Many who were cornered and interviewed especially aftermath of the October 8 earthquake revealed the existence of Laskar operative.

The enormity of the natural calamity did not sabotage the dreams of the terrorists and their infrastructure, but the Laskar aided funding relief operations in the devastated Pakistan occupied Kashmir have rejuvenated the moribund citizens (The Hindu, December 8, 2005). The Lashkar have gained a new clout in Pakistan occupied Kashmir and has taken every step to abet terrorism. The story Bukari in the Hindu amply demonstrated the odds faced by young men who give up their life and profession to serve the Jihad. Investigations have found that even as terrorist activity in Jammu & Kashmir went into decline after the India - Pakistan near war of 2001 - 2002, the Laskar focused its energies on building up successive rings of highly organized covert skills, drawing on individull with high levels of education and technical skill.

In 2002, Bkazi befriended a north Lashkar based Lashkar operative Abdul Wahab, a resident of Multan in Pakistan, educated at the International Islam University after abandoning his career as a chartered accountant.

Bhukari drew inspiration from Wahab who had abandoned life and profession. Bhukari and Wahab developed an intellectual relationship reading the Islamic tracts that both the traditional rites did not exist and quiescent Islamic practices were a failure.

After Wahab's death, Bhukari moved for full time Lashkar operative; Bukari purchased a white Maruti Jeep like the JK police, allowing for the easy transport of weapons and Lashkar operative. Funds and operational instructions of Bukari cell were provided by the Lashkar commander who had replaced Abdul Rehman, a Pakistani national known only by Multiplex aliases 'Bilal Haider', 'Salhuddin'.

The new formidable challenges ahead of the Indian policy markers are 1. The Laskar has demonstrated the ability to recruit either Kashmiri cadre - individual, moreover with significant education and technical skills.

Secondly the infrastructure of the LeT is intact and the Pan-India operations after the October 8 earthquake, the Diwali serials blasts in New Delhi showed that the Lashkar has a safe rapport with the Pakistan military establishment - allies whom the Pakistan president is either unable or unwilling confront.

Thirdly the Indian counter infiltration position along the Line of Control has weakened after the October 8 earthquake the newly inducted Central Reserve Police Force has to raise up to the occasion.

The feature in The Hindu has traced the ideological social and economic background of the militants.

Ezaz Ahmed Bhutt, who threw a grenade at police personnel near the palladium cinema in Srinagar. Lal Chowk was no more than an average South Asian teenager. He hid in a hotel and after the ambush with senior official killing two (CRPF) Jawans and two civilians was later arrested by the police when he was on his heels to escape.

The newspapers have forthwith publicized one face of Lashkar highly educated, impeccable bourgeois terror cell organizers like Tariq Dur, the pharmaceutical firm executive who helped funding the Diwali bombings, Belkari, the Kashmiri law student.

Bllt there are other forces from middle class backgrounds Butt's journey into Laskar rank illustrated that while an ideology of religious hatred drove among the Islamist terror groups, poverty plays not a small role in helping them build their armies (The Hindu, December 9, 2005).

But lost his father when young and then had to shoulder the responsibility at home which his income was not sufficient for. His incident meeting with a young Faislabad resident who joined the Lashkar some ten years ago arrrived on the scene worked as a recruiter for the Lashkar. This appeared to be a golden opportunity to Bhatt who plunged into the profession on the money and comforts doled out to the activists.

A former Pakistan army soldier Javed Iqbal taught several dozens recruits basic combat skills, including use of pistols, grenades and assault rifles. Iqbal focussed on improving the physical skills of his students through long distance hikes and drills.

To sociologist who have studied recruitment into urban gangs, the phenomenon will be familiar - as will its outcome.

The feature in The Hindu has an in depth analysis on the origin and the pan - Indian style of functioning of the Jihadist forces across India. Mere shoot out in Bangalore may not disturb the investors as large numbers are lost in fatalities due to terror strike globally. This is done in difference to Pakistan strategy to avoid war.

The feature also quoted the histrionic behind such performance of the terrorists. The quotes of scholar Stephen Cohen stated that "the goal of the terrorist is to use an extreme act to change the way in which this group (and society) sees reality. Thus terrorist is literally bad actor, a bit player in a drama that seeks to change reality by a theatrical performance of increasingly unimaginable horror (The Hindu, January 10, 2006). As in the case of violence in literature and films, the level of horror has to increase over time to attract the attention of by standers, who have their own mechanism of coping with the awful.

Hassan Ibu al-Sabbah, the brilliant 11th century mystic who founded the fidayeen as a means of resistance against anti-Shia chauvinism, understood that terror was not just means, but an end in itself. For these early terrorists, the Historian Amin Maeloaf has perceptively noted "murder was not merely a means of disposing, an enemy but was intended primarily as a two fold lesson for the public. First the punishment of the victims and second the heroic sacrifice of the executioner.

The feature also warned Jihad will vanish from the surface of the earth, like the Seljuk empire which never recovered unity. It is precisely this bond of outcome that Lashkar hopes its jihad will one day bring about.

The feature denoted the ways and means of controlling terror groups. Improved policing and intelligence are the components of India's war against terror. The feature of optimistic about Jihad's doomsday and anomalies are drawn from prototypes that existed during the much earlier periods. (The Hindu, January 9, 2006).

The feature in The Hindu has delineated the nature of terrorists on the Indian side of the (LoC) Line of Control and on Pakistani soil.

The terrorists in the Indian side of Line of Control have powerful reason to fight on: hard cash. The estimated 1,500 ethnic Kashmiri men in jihad camps across the Line of Control may have begun to tire of war without apparent end. There are several men who escaped from Pakistani jails and surrendered to Indian forces.

There were instances where the Mustaq Ahmad Mih area Hizb Commander had spent the last hours of his life was killed in a March 10 encounter, head issued 58 receipts to the organization local financiers, the main businessmen, fruit traders and contractors. From the Kulgam area alone then Mir had raised a more - than - respectable Rs. 1.5 million for the Hizb unit. The recruitment is taking place from the ranks of the rural poor who migrate to the plains of Punjab for six months. (The Hindu, March 28, 2006).

South Kashmir's apple trade, train routes construction and flowering business provide easy pickings to terror groups such as which in turn pumps back the cash to its overground operatives.

The feature suggested the role of different political parties in bringing about a ceasefire. The feature suggested that the All Party Hurriyat Conference chairman called on New Delhi to declare a unilateral cease fire in Jammu & Kashmir, saying he would persuade the Jihad organizations to reciprocate. People Democratic Party, National Conference have argued that India needs to move towards withdrawing troops and paramilitary forces from Jammu & Kashmir.

The Hizbul Mujahideen Chief, Mohammed Yusuf Shah, and its operational commander, Mohammed Shah Nawz had said in a recent interview that they are open to a dialogue as long as the Mujahedeen they command are the principal interlocutors New Delhi and Islamabad engage.

The feature in The Hindu identified how Madarassa have served as vassals for the terrorists.

The Harkut-ul-Mujahiddin which thought to be defunct has been reborn after the March 17 Ahmedabad encounter. (The Hindu, March 24, 2006)h

The commander of the first Harkat terror cell Imran Shahzah Bati was shot dead along with lieutant Mohammed 'Furkhen' Iqbal, two longstanding ethnic Kashmiri Harkat operatives, Mohammed Ayub Butt and Madassir Rather. Much of Bhutt network was set up by Bhutt under the pretext of fruit seller Bhatti was introduced to friends as a business associate. But Iqbal, who had long been one of the Harkat commander's most trusted Lieutenant was able to make contacts with newly recruited associates in New Delhi, Goa, Gwalior, Agra, Kota. Madassir Rather succeeded in Obtaining admission to a Madrassa near Southern Gujarat town of Valsad on the Mumbai - Ahmadabad route. So Bhatt rented the Ahmedabad apartment.

Does the rebirth of H-Ual have state patronage?

It has become increasingly clear in recent weeks that the Pakistan President Pervez Musharaff finds himself in increasing conflict with some of his one - time allies, notably Islamist hardlines in the Lashkar. As such, Pakistan covert services could be throwing their weight behind the Harkat as a counter weight. On the other hand, the Harkat revival could be part of a generalized Islamist offensive leading into 2007 elections in Pakistan, in which pro-jihad clerical parties hope to acquire power. The feature leaves a dreaded note that "What is clear, though, is this, Pakistan's Islamist armies have no intention of joining in a detente with India that promises them only their obliteration.

The feature in The Hindu even identified the strong alliance of the mainstream parties (PDP) People Democratic Party with Hizbul Mujaheedin.

The People Democratic Party alliance with the Hizbul Mujaheedin became evident on April, 17, 2006 when the state police arrested Shabbir Ahmed, a terrorist - turned politician activist who had taken a Rs.1, 190 sft contract to arrange the assassination of four politicians. The relationship soured when it became clear the PDP could not deliver in promises to ease security force pressure on the Hizbul Mujaheedin. (The Hindu, April 28, 2006)

The feature of The New Indian Express has identified major factors during the previous National Democratic Alliance Govt. and the present (UPA) United Progressive Alliance government of tackling terrorism.

While it is premature to ascertain who was responsible for these blasts there is either little doubt that terrorists once again sensing a political vacuum and lack of resolve in the top echelons of government (The New Indian Express, July 13, 2006).

The National Democratic Alliance government's anti terror policy was a combination of formalism draconian powers to the state and political overreaction. Its legislative interventions like (POTA) made it susceptible to the charge that it violated the civil liberties. Instead of targeting terrorist, it started making terrorists to create an atmosphere of anxiety.

The United Progressive Alliance policy was do away with all strong signals to terrorists, for fear of political over reaction, prevent tough scrutiny of groups that may be out to do harm.

The feature pointed out to the fortitude and patience of Indian citizens provides enough resistance to terrorist designs. The government trying to engage in a political strategy it does not have the power to execute a security strategy it cannot have for fear of political consequences.

The feature of The Hindu has cited the structure of the origin terrorist forces and the modus vivendi of their operation. They had traced the identity of the culprits and the style of their functioning was derived from the composition of the making of a bomb with local materials which made them ascertain that the materials must have dispatched by the LeT terrorists or amateurs. On the other hand the feature in The New Indian Express cited examples from the peace accord inked by Rajiv Gandhi, immediately after the assassination of Indira Gandhi and the Operation Blue Star. Though peace accords often followed after a sweep of changes peace never returned to the state for the first time, but only when the state had the strength to fight, and ultimately prevail because of its vastly superior resources and will power, whatever the immediate score in teams of bodies on the ground. The model can be traced to events of this kind to quell terrorism (The New Indian Express, July 15, 2006). The government's inaptness in handling nazalities of the AP, Assam have paved the way for a rare soft phase in India's history of fighting terrorism. The feature also reminded that times and climes have changed since and now.

The earlier periods were very complicated but as of now more of peace making umbrella prevailed by and large with Pakistan.

In spite on the active surveillance, pro-active counter terrorism, no compromises, the feature demanded the United Progressive Alliance government to provide cart blanche for the security apparatus and intelligence agencies.

The feature in The Hindu suggested that especially after the Mumbai blasts, there has been newer emerging trend in the nature of the terrorism across the country which became evident from the chemicals that go into the composition of the bomb like (Potassium permanganate, RDX) indicated that the operation would been facilitied by local operations of these terror groups (SIMI) Student Islamic Moment of India, enormously dangerous movement of small number of recruits into the ranks. Some networks extend across India.

The Lashkar has attempted to tap the estimated 3,000 seminaries in Maharashtra, where an estimated 2,00,000 students study (The Hindu, July 12, 2006). Investigators believe that he also attempted to recruit for cadres for the Lashkar among seminary students in Gujarat but with little success. Islamic mobilization in Bangladesh is a source of considerable concern for the West Bengal government. Local politics have long complicated counter - terrorism work in the state of Uttar Pradesh that needs to be addressed. The Kerala government believed that it operated through 12 frontal organization engaged in a charitable work.

Former (SIMI) Student Islamic Moment of India have played key role in several major strikes in northern India, as investigations into the July 28, 2005, bombing of Shramjeev express at Jaunpur and Varanasi serial bombings of March 7, 2006 demonstrated.

The former report in The Hindu suggested that the bombs with explosives could have been manufactured by Student Islamic Movement of India groups, the latter feature pointed out that the bombs were not made by amateurs.

Investigators were unable to establish, after the arrest of Badroo who had been tasked with picking up Rs. 3,00,000 payment for the Lashkar, Ramzan and Lone had been asked to transport circuit and detonators to contacts in Mumbai whether the explosives needed to build a device had been brought to Mumbai by separate Lashkar courier.

Despite the threat of an India - Pakistan war forcing a reduction of levels of violence within J & K, the Lashkar was looking to take its jihad to a new level. (The Hindu, July 13, 2006).

In1998, serial bombings of Mumbai, the largest ever terror strike, Pakistan's worth west frontier province, Mafioso Dawood Ibrahim smuggling networks are being used again to pump in large flow of explosives. Evidence exists that Dawood Ibrahim's mafia shared ideological affinities with Islamist terror groups.

The feature still doubts the veracity of the weapons shipped, who fabricated them and whether Lashkar in J & K based operatives had a role in organizing the bombings, though not clear, the happenings in Mumbai indicate that is a grand design of the protracted war.

Where else the feature in The New Indian Express cited that terror is indigenous and communal backlash.

The apparent lack of link between the serial blasts in Mumbai, with the epicenter of militancy has thrown up new challenges for security agencies, especially as it substantial the viewpoint that an autonomous network has finally come up in the country outside the borders of Jammu & Kashmir.

The security agencies have ruled the hand of an outside element and insisted on the worrisome involvement of a local cell made up of men with normal lives and a clean crime state" (The New Indian Express, July 22, 2006).

The feature also pointed out the emergence of indigenous terror cells among Indian Muslims is certainly a culmination of a process that has its roots in anti-Muslim state and subsequent communal polarisation.

The blasts at Varanasi on the eve of Diwali, Id festival in Delhi aimed at sharpening the existing communal division and thus creating an atmosphere conductive to future recruitments.

The feature also suggested that Indian Muslims share ideologically with Kashmir Muslims but statistics show that only a staggering figure of less than 50 have joined the cluster militancy group of Jammu & Kashmir. Youth from other parts of India like Uttar Pradesh, Bihar or Gujarat have failed to join the ranks.

The feature has traced the origin of the terror cells with the Jamat-e-Islami organized after partition of 1941 by Maulana Abul Ala Moudi. When Jamat-e-Islamic was introduced in Kashmir 1951, its affinity was always with Pakistan chapter rather than Jamat-e-Islami (Hind). The Jamaat-e-Islami has remained as an apolitical organization with unflinching loyalty to Indian motherhood. The Indian Prime Minister had boasted there was not single recruit in the Al-Queda, he was absolutely right.

Security agencies, in Kashmir have traced new trail in terrorists hide out who prepare themselves to avenge communal violence against Muslims and the recruits are the victims of communal blacklash.

Chand Khan who joined the Jihadi groups after Gujarat role, Gehauri, his close associate Karim Tana set up a proper terror network for the Lashkar for avenging the communal riots, the doctor Jakes Anjari decided to leave his job and plant bombs after the Babri demolition, joined Tehreek - Islam Maslimeen (movement for reform among Muslims) have taken steps to avenge communal violence against Muslims.

The feature drives home the issue of the emergence of indigenous terror cells among Indian Muslims is certainly the culmination of process of alienation that has its root in riots.

The feature insisted that though many terrorist organizations were banned by the Musharaff regime, many still are alive under different guises.

The Lashkar-e- Toiba has assumed a new role like doing social service within Pakistan, though considered an outlaw by the government. The JUD cannot be banned as told in half hearted jobs by a former Chief of military intelligence is that the United States knows that it can push Islamabad on this only at the risk of further alienating the people from President Musharaff (The Hindu, July 17, 2005). The feature takes it more emphatic that President Musharaff is sending out the message that of the peace process with India is seen as failing to deliver the result Pakistan wants, he has not given up the "unconventional military option".

(k) Diplomacy Fails

During the period of study The New Indian Express had one feature where diplomacy failed but The Hindu had no such feature entirely to be discussed in diplomacy.

The outcome of the changed heart of President Musharaff and the question of trust that he tried to personify should be seen through a prism (The New Indian Express, May 16, 2005). Never has been a change of tone in the voice of Pakistanis nor they cannot be trusted at all cost and history is replete with such instances of unprecedented attack. The New Indian Express further intensified the question of trust, "isn't diplomacy really war by other means, a lull in proceedings where you put charm offensive. So that you can rethink your strategy.

The feature also stated boldly that "we cannot make any concessions at all". Our stand on CBMS, territorial adjustments etc remain the same the question of peace process is incompatible with tough line on security. Kargil did not happen as we trusted Pakistan, but we were sleeping over the watch. The question of trust hovered around the whole feature wherein our trust cannot be mistaken or it was illusion, but matter of fact a concrete, conscious attempt to chase the erase the scars. The feature at length discussed on the hawk or the nature of hawkishness that is found in diplomatic circles. We have never used low - level insurgencies the way Pakistan has used and hence forth. The support for Pakistan is at harvest inside Kashmir has become the main stake. The Islamisation can bring about internal strife and the difficulty with many of our so called realists is that they do not think about the long term changes, they are imprisioned by short term logic. Peace won through honour will safeguard the interest of the nation and the people. No compromising on our military security or vigilance on our core principles". The question of trust need to be debated or you will be deceived, and if you don't trust you will be condemned to live in torment.

The distorted version of the attitude of Pervez Musharaff after his change of heart will be a pipe dream, unless the basic tenets should not be diluted for their will be any unpremeditated intrusion. 'Trust' did not figure much in the Hindu or they were less tempted to attempt on the constant dithering attitude of the President and the policy vis-a-vis India.

National Security Advisor M.K. Narayan was amazed at the categorical denial of Pervez Musharaff on the table of his decisions not part with the information of Kashmir. The general has not come up with proposals on Kashmir. The Indian government did not wait for chances but deputed Satish Lamba for back channel diplomacy to ascertain from General Tariq Aziz the purport of his visit and talk. Mr. Tariq has promised to disclose the matters before the General's arrival.

The national security advisor M.K. Narayan made attempt to deliver the message that the Hurriyat is the sole representative of J & K and did not know what are the demands Hurriyat conference.

Mr. Narayanan failed to see accommodation of Pakistan professed concern only in the size of the security presence in Jammu and Kashmir. The level of violence has to come down and the infiltration has to stop, in order to bring about a concrete solution in level of employing of security.

(I) Feature Covering Peace Process and the Related Developments

During the period of study there were five features in The New Indian Express on peace process and related developments compared to six features in the Hindu.

The partnership on ground for peace has become the larger initiative as efforts to involve secessionist leaders in peace have guided little as they have sought to rope in militants. The trust to be reposed on militants in Kashmir and Muzafarabad has failed (The Hindu).

The Hindu feels their need not be intermediaries for they can involve the boys who have been direct source of trouble.

The upsurge of violence in the state was abetted, aided by the local youth and the paper demanded the involvement of youth in the peace process. The militants wish to be in the peace process provided the security in the barracks, return of the boys from wilderness and cessation of violence. The Hindu at length discussed on the cessation of hostilities with a composite package with the following, considered, open up dogged channels to provide better opportunities to understand the issue involved and a dialogue process with Kashmir militant towards creation of a rehabilitation council for the youth. The rehabilitation council should assemble data on numbers of youth who committed themselves to violence, the number still active, the numbers across the border, the numbers in jail, the numbers missing or dead, the economics status of those that do not fall in the above categories; ascertain the plight of kith and kin of the dead militants.

The Hindu cited that the country has to demonstrate that it cares and can embrace those willing to mend their ways. Rehabilitations work did not gain momentum in the past due to bureaucratic limitations and political manoevrings.

The history of both nation cannot be rewritten. The South Asia can be made more free and prosperous, as long as the borders are kept irrelevant and free movement of trade, ideas, people and services gained more momentums. (The New Indian Express, April 24, 2005).

The crackdown on terrorists in Pakistan and Pakistan occupied Kashmir will help the Indian public fully acknowledge that Pakistan has co- operated very much in seizing the moment does really work for the concern of the Indian sub-continent.

The general admonished the editors to look into the future logistics of the divided Kashmir, and the time frame he has set to iron out differences between the two parts which should not exceed more than ten years.

The opinion maker also cautioned the deadline of ten years and the anticipated outcome of the political space that can be created with the free movement of goods, services and people.

General Musharaff coming to India has changed the political matrix in India with the following details in the joint statement that proved more unique, as it interpreted the opening of trade across the Line of Control. The nine word sentence that made every South Asian analyst sit up "in the para 5 of the joint statement was" they determined that the peace process was not irreversible (The Hindu, April 26, 2006). The Jakarta summit on April 23, wherein both Presidents of Pakistan and India could be jointly proud of showing sincerity, the flexibility and courage, that could lead to bilateral achievement of peace and harmony.

The Jihadis have taken up the charge of targeting President Musharaff and the Karachi camps commander goes to prove that today Pakistan's own enemy is only the Jihadis and Jihadis cannot be used to achieve national goals.

The successful entourage of Pakistan's President to India vis-a-vis the visit of the one time city-banker and current Prime Minister Shaut Aziz speaks volumes of the related development of the former could bring in during his trip. The construction of the gas pipeline has become the hall mark of both

Indians and Pakistanis and as a stand will tell the entire world that they pursue projects in national interest and no power can veto as enhanced project to promote economic co-operation among nations. The Hindu also instigated the Petroleum Minister to show its spine to move ahead with the project.

The New Indian Express highlighted that two sides had difficulties drafting a joint statement at the end of the Manmohan - Musharaff talk reminds as once again about the depth of these differences and fragility of the peace process. The ceasefire along the segments of the dividing line in Jammu & Kashmir - the international border, the Line of Control and Actual Ground Position Line in Siachen had been one of the most important confidence building measures between India and Pakistan in recent years.

The Indian security forces are doing well against the militant and the other is that a ceasefire might allow the militants to re-group and fight another day. The New Indian Express insisted for a cease fire within J & K wherein he will be able to build on the current improvements in Indo-Pak relation and create the political space for engaging the various militant groups of Jammu & Kashmir.

In the Ramzan peace initiative at the end of 2000, Atal Bihari Vajpayee had decided that Indian forces would not launch military operations against militants except in self - defence.

The paper also cited instances wherein the Pakistan based commander of Hizbul Mujahideen, Syed Salahuddin, has told an Indian TV channel on the eve of Musharaffs visit that he will be prepared to put down 'if military operations are stopped, rebels released from jails and an atmospheres of good will generated.

The ceasefire along the dividing line another with militants - the political space will expand considerably and create stable conditions for peace in J & K. Reduction of Indian forces could be expected to feel positively into Indo-Pak peace process. The paper further eulogised political will among the Kashmiris and Manmohan Singh must boldly announce a ceasefire within the state of Jammu & Kashmir.

Pakistan Muslim League Chaudhary Hussain visit to India and the arrival of Musharafi' a day later has further driven all issues to parallel.

The regime hawks peace but only with Vajpayee Brajesh Mishra combine and Manmohan Singh Natwar Singh - Siphons off peace but with proper pat to women, the whole region awaits a smooth transition beckoning peace.

Jinnah the founder of Pakistan has been eulogised either as a icon or villain. But Jinnah never wanted hatred to be expressed by Pakistanis (The

New Indian Express, April 22, 2005). This enduring pride goes to Musharaff who has used the same tactics to elevate himself and his countrymen to such a stature. Musharaff on par with Ataturk hailing him a leader born out of a nation from the rump of a fallen empire as a nation stymied with moderate Islamic factors.

World over different seminars were being held to bring out a magic formulae for Kashmir. On any pretext it is a problem that pertained to India, Pak and Kashmir. The formula was suggested to manage the problem but not an end to the whole issue. Dublin has never turned its back on Republicans, nor the unionists are forsaken by the Irish. There is no travel document between Belfast and Dublin. Similarly the paras 6 to 12 in the joint declaration of Indo-Pak statement everything is facilitated except the resolution to Kashmir issue.

Media has amply portrayed the absurdity of the declarations with no concrete reminder to unresolved dispute.

The feature of the Hindu had predicted that the results of the encounter are inversely proportional that precede it. What transpired the 36 hours, the Pakistan president was in the capital was as momentious as anything the two countries have seen in recent years (The Hindu April 19, 2005).

The two governments stressed the irreversibility of the peace process and the self - imposed quartine India brought about by cutting all air, road, following the December 13, 2001 terrorist attack on parliament, will be hopefully not repeated.

Secondly, they committed themselves that India and Pakistan have jointly resolved not to give terrorists the right to veto the peace process through dramatic acts of violence.

The third stress during the encounter was the purpose of having discussions on the issue of Jammu and Kashmir is to reach a final settlement.

"The final Settlement" was taken directly from the Simla agreement of July 2, 1926 clause 6 of which both the governments to discuss further the modalities and arrangements for the establishment of durable peace and normalization of relations, including the questions of Prisoners of War and civilian internees. A final settlement of Jammu and Kashmir and the resumption of diplomatic relations".

India and Pakistan will eventually allow the economic geography of the region to revert to pre-partition days.

Fifthly, the joint statement undertook to speed up deliverables, such as an agreement on Siachen and Sir Creek and strive for greater business interactions.

Sixthy, Dr. Singh and General Musharaff have not only endorsed the proposed Iran- Pakistan - India pipeline in the face of U.S. criticism of the project but also expanded the scope for energy co-operations between their two countries.

During his stay in India, he drove home the point to India and bulk of media that "the (LoC) Line of Control cannot be permanent, border must be made irrelevant, and boundaries cannot be altered". Take the three together and now discuss the solutions, he said A soft border is the only administration arrangement that allows India and Pakistan to maintain their respective dejure or defacto. Sovereignities in Kashmir while not coming in the way of the people of the divided state enjoying the fruits of a unified territory.

The Pakistan President Pervez Musharaff for the first time after his visit to India was termed the borders soft and failed to accept the Line of Control as a permanent border. India considered soft borders a sop for maintenance of a political status quo, what General Musharaff probably means is that soft border is only a temporary solutions.

By constantly coming up with formulae and suggestions, in his iftaar dinner proposals he spoke of the divided state as consisting of seven distinct regions whose fate could be settled individually and now there is the endorsement of the soft border - General Musharaff aim is to focus India's approach in confidence building measure might end up in creating a new ground for that would weaken the demand for self - determination in valley.

Pakistan is also suspicious of the U-turn taken by the Indian government in settling issues by a meaningful and peaceful manner by invoking confidence building measures, which is seen as initiative to deflect the nation from other issues.

Three and half years after the Agra Summit, numerous proposals have come forward, this time around the president televised, conferences of "Kashmir freedom fighter" which sent the Vajpayee government to abort mode has changed considerably.

The change in the attitude of the general was explicit, and the maneouver he had used a mature politician after his first visit in 2001. He more of an astute politicians, comfortable with power of gun but this time around, he is neither peacenik. He proved himself to be a consummate politician by greeting the BJP President, Atal Bihari Vajpayee and elegantly side stepped the old trap, shifting the focus from the blood of martyrs in Kashmir to popular aspirations, such features were absent in the The New Indian Express.

Kashmir cannot be resolved on religious lines and that the borders have to be made irrelvant for the ultimate solution. Musharaff statements in

New Delhi about "Soft borders" and how Kashmir issue could be resolved only at the level of himself and Manmohan Singh did not go well back home (The Hindu, May 23, 2006). Implied in it was unambiguous statement that All Party Hurriyat Conference is welcome to give inputs but has no place in the dialogue table. There were comments on the free movement of journalists in Pakistan, but till date there has no been no such reciprocal measures.

Musharaff found the present junction is a fleeting moment in history largely leaves room for thought of moving closer and this moment has to be seized for establishing permanent peace at the earliest.

Pakistan renege its stand on terrorist on its soil as Sunday experienced a showdown from the different groups of separatists addressing a seminar on "Kashmir freedom movement" (The Hindu, August 11, 2005). Prospects of success, concerns and threats organized by Tehreek-e-Hurriyat Jammu & Kashmir. The Hizbul Mujahideen and Chairman of the Muttahida Jihadi council, Syed Salahuddin ruled any cease fire with Kashmir unless the Indian government treated it as a disputed territory and released all prisoners of war as a prelude to a dialogue with Kashmiris. Hizbul Mujahideen will not abide by cease fire unless these conditions are met either by President Musharaff or by any other world power.

The dais was also shared by Sheikh Rasheed Information Minister Pakistan, MMA Chief Aazi Hussain Ahmed.

The tenet of Jihad was announced in the meet and anyone, relinquishing the jihad came out of the ambit of the religion. The MMA chief accused the Pakistani government and its generals of confusing the Kashmir policy. And add on to the compounding allegations, Maulana Fazlur Rahman, Chief of his own faction Jamiat Ulema-e-Islam and leader of opposition in the national assembly alleged that Pakistan government was deceiving the west by helping militants enter Afghanistan through Waziristan. He is also prepared to open the pandora's box if pressured convinced the public at large the feckless attitude of the government which gives sweeping statements of effacing terror from its soil. This set back in dealing with terror indicated the murky state of affairs in the Pakistani establishment to bestow lethal blow to terrorists.

After an year and a half of bold experimentation in foreign policy Prime Minister Manmohan Singh emphasised the importance of implementation of the nuclear pact with the United State, making choice in Vienna on Iran's nuclear proliferation of taking risks in foreign policy. The lack of taking risks would amount to act of lethargy.

During Dr. Manmohan Singh's first trip to United Nations as Prime Minister in Sep. 2004, Manmohan Singh won the confidence of Pakistan

President Pervez Musharaff and initiated him to visit India in April 2005. This led to an unprecedented changes in Kashmir, including the launch of the bus service between Srinagar and Muzaffarabad, Singh's call for "thinking out of the box" on Kashmir (The New Indian Express, November 15, 2005).

Meeting Pervez Musharaff on New York in Sep 2005, caution came in the way of experimenting with Pakistan policy. The Delhi blasts that followed in the aftermath of earthquake India held its peace and did not blame Pakistan for the bombings and went ahead with talks to open up the five points on the Line of Control the terrorists have clearly succeeded in preventing India from doing has is its own best interests.

Mr. Singh declared that India would consider demilitarization or any re-deployment of troops in Kashmir only after the cross border terrorism comes to a complete halt. The feature also stated that Pakistan should not be allowed the luxury of negotiating with India with the gun on the table.

The clues to stop cross border terrorism are (a) a sophisticated policy response (b) recasting of the doctrine (c) organization (d) command and control of India's counter terror operations. The feature also added that the ultimate resolution cannot be easily obtained if wrapping intellutual lethargy in hard line rhetoric against Pakistan is followed in strait jacket manner.

(m) Newspapers Attitude on Conflict Resolution

There were three features in The Hindu and two features in The New Indian Express which dealt more on conflict resolution.

The Hindu has demonstrated that building a consensus against violence is the real challenge that confronts the dialogue process. Unless politicians are able to deliver an end to gunfire and bombings, the dialogue process will have little meaning to Jammu & Kashmir people. Some major steps taken up to be the newspapers are speaking out for the right of J & K people to live - not another interminable discussion on the state constitutional status ought to be the core issue for those who claims to care for its people.

The round table conference held on the eve of Bush arrival to sub-continent and the conference is held by Pugwash in Islamabad turned to be counter productive (The New Indian Express). The former lacked agenda and the latter the crowd was unwieldy with no concrete copy of the divergent views emerged during the course of the talk.

The New Indian Express is more concerned about the Pugwash in Islamabad.

As usual autonomy, between independence and self rule, joint management still a gray area, were the several opinions that cropped up. The feature adds if the mainstream parties step down from the goal of independence, the way out for them has not triggered the imagination of the many. Musharaff Solution is found to be short of Azadi.

The polit.cal solution to Kashmir is still pitched fork battle, but the comfort level of the Kashmiris can be a keynote—like releasing prisoners from jails.

The feature also delaying the process can buy time will only help in the transfer of guns to the next generation of men. So hasty solution becomes the hall mark is the course of political development in Jammu & Kashmir.

But the feature in The Hindu added that the Prime Minister after flagging off the bus to Nanasahib in Pakistan outlined a road map to peace that would have four distinct components. Two of these would be internal to those' areas of Jammu & Kashmir that are in control of India and Pakistan and two would be bilateral (The Hindu, March 25, 2006).

The latter would enable to encourage "co-operation, consultative mechanism" to solve the economic problems.

The internal dialogue is carefully crafted in such a manner that the entire territory of the erstwhile princely state of Azad Kashmir (PoK) and not just those areas under Indian Control would be the part of the peace process.

Secondly the unwillingness to include people of Kashmir as 'representatives' of the people of the state in the formal India - Pakistan dialogue on Kashmir. The two sides should be encouraged for cross border institutional mechanisms. These mechanisms provide the only practical way of making border irrelevant while keeping intact the dejure soverenity of both India and Pakistan. This is similar to the Agra test where the president during his interaction with the Indian (ditors, argued out that the two governments need to 'negate' solutions to the Kashmir issue that were unacceptable to others and focus on what would remain on the table once maximalist positions were abandoned. President Musharaff during his visit to New Delhi in April 2005, the borders would not be redrawn and the Line of Control cannot be made into a juridical border either, the only solution was to make the borders irrelevant.

That India appeared reluctant to give a precise shape to the notion of making borders irrelevant but instead the Indian bureaucracy was distrustful of the idea for the lack of sufficient fund of trust. The Prime Minister Singh desire to break away from the conservatism of Indian security establishment sufficient space had evolved to break a new phase in the J & K peace process.

There is ambiguity in the notion of the peace process expressed in the feature and the editorial of The Hindu with flagging off the bus to Nanasahib in Pakistan. The editorial hinged on both sides should begin a dialogue "with their people in their areas of control" and to improve the quality of governance" where else thf feature makes a stark difference wherein the Prime Minister Dr. Singh insisted on opening a ground for talks the entire territory of the erstwhile province state of Jammu & Kashmir and not just those areas in India. Control or within either the boundaries of "Azad Jammu and Kashmir". The means the so-called northern areas in Pakistan administered Jammu and Kashmir would also be part of the peace process. The editorial also pointed out that this is the first time that Government of India has spoken officially of the need for cross-border institutional mechanism.

Prime Minister mentioned of the fiery note of better approach of the Kashmir tangle while inaugurating the launch of the Amritsar - Nanasahib bus service at Amritsar would have been to allay the fears of the post partition of 1947. The Hindu failed to make the place or venue as a source of major importance.

The New Indian Express enumerated only three package to the Kashmir issue which differed with The Hindu which cited "two bilateral two internal packages" , "open borders" in The New Indian Express to "Border becoming irrelevant in "The Hindu". The Indian Express provided for a realistic package for further talks between key players like New Delhi, Srinagar, Islamabad and Muzaffarabad into split halves whereelse the Hindu gave importance only to "Pak administered Kashmir" and "Indian controlled Kashmir". Such glaring differences surfaced out especially in the after math of the launch of the Amritsar - Lahore bus service (The Hindu, March 26, 2006).

(n) Newspapers Attitude Towards Bilateral Peace

There were four features towards Newspapers attitude toward bilateral peace compared to the Hindu which carried only one.

The United States has now established itself defacto third party in India -Pakistan relations stated The Hindu. On the same day, the meeting of President Bush, Dr. Singh had asked for the ending of cross border terrorism. While General Musharaff harped on the reduction of troops in northern areas of Jammu & Kashmir. The reduction of troops in any area is the ultimatum of the government of that country. Similarly they may discuss the matter bilaterally, not involve a third party mediation which will be end up in chao (The Hindu, September 24, 2005).

Prime Minister Dr. Singh would be in Pakistan when the two countries are finally to deal with Siachen. Another proposal is issuing joint statement in third countries may not bring bigger outcomes.

Whereelse The New Indian Express emphasized the fact through a document in French archives which revealed that the Kashmir dispute is an unending saga. On September 22, 1965, Lal Bahadur Shastri the Indian Prime Minister ordered a ceasefire to the Indian army advancing on Lahore. In a letter sent by the French Ambassador to Pakistan to his Foreign Minister on Paris, the envoy reported a meeting held in July 1953 in Karachi between Nehru and Mohammed Ali, the Prime Minister of Pakistan. It had been announced before hand that Nehru had a compromise solution. In the afternoon of July 27, Mr. Nehru pointed out the final solution that he had chosen, the Kashmir territory would be divided between the two countries according to line of cease fire Line of Control laid down by United Nations authorities. It would mean that India would keep all territories with the exception of the Part known as "Azad Kashmir". Mr. Mohammed Ali spoke with shattered face and rejected the proposal of Mr. Nehru. One by one, Sir, Zafarullah (Foreign Minister), Mr. Malik, PWD Minister, Strove to bring back Mr. Nehru to a more sensible plan. It is in this atmosphere of helplessness and suppressed anger the meeting ended.

Even during civilian rule Pakistan had never been ready to accept the transformation of the Line of Control into an international border (IB). In 1972, a similar proposal was made in Simla and though Bhutto accepted it in principle, he made sure that it did not materialize during the following years.

The background of the 1965 conflict knowing that Delhi was not going to compromise further and that the US attitude was quickly changing after the 1962 war with China. The US administrations believed it was necessary to support Delhi to check communist China's advance on the subcontinent Ayub Khan sensed that the Pakistani dream to rule the valley was fading away. There was only one solution: to organize infiltrators of troops in Mufti (as in September 1947) and create popular insurrection. The people of the valley would then ask for their reattachment to Pakistan. It was to be on 'Algerian type' people's struggle for self - determination.

Pakistan Air force chief, Air Marshall Asghan Khan, wrote that operation Gibraltar was based on three assumptions. The raiders would receive the support of the local population, India would limit its retaliation to "Azad Kashmir" and finally most importantly the Indian troops would in no circumstances cross the (IB) International Border. The three assumptions were wrong.

The first assumption was wrong, the force did not know the language of the valley and were not aware of the metric system was not in use in the valley. The population of the valley did still remember the atrocities of the tribal raids of 1947, were not ready to accept foreigners as new masters. The Pakistan military rulers realised the failure of OP Gibraltar, as the strategic pass of Haji Pir opening the gate to "Azad Kashmir" fell into Indian hands. They had to implement OP Grandslam. The intention was to capture Aknoor bridge which was the umbilical cord between the valley and Jammu. Jammu could even be captured and become a bargaining chip to exchange against the valley.

Shastri took the boldest decision that nobody expected, India would cross the international border and advance towards Sialkot. On September 5, at 5 a.m. the corps XI moved into Pakistan.

Shastri agreed to a ceasefire under pressure from the United Nations Security Council and on September 22, India had occupied 1, 920 sq. km of Pakistan Territory and lost 540 sq. km.

Bhutto arrived in security council very late as the New York air port was closed by Snow storm. The dramatic council began very late in the night where Bhutto apprised all world leaders and their ideologies and in a voice breaking with emotion, asked. "Are the people of Kashmir some kind of pariahs to be denied the right of self - determination?" During the course of the talk Bhutto attended a phone call stating that it is from the President Ayub Khan. He took the seat with crest fallen face that I spoke of thousand years war, but my president over ruled me, but my people will garland me (The New Indian Express, September 25, 2005).

Prime Minister Manmohan Singh offered all possible assistance to the quake victims. But the foreign office headed by Natwar Singh had no clue as to how it could work to make the Prime Minister gesture an effective one.

The Indian army had placed a commendable role in doing the job by helping the counterparts in Pakistan during relief operation. The News and voluntary organizations are tepid.

Sources of NGO's with relief material loaded in trucks lining up at the Wagh a border and wanting to enter Pakistan for providing success would have had an impact on Pakistan is beyond words (The New Indian Express, October 14, 2005).

The relief work publicized by the UK press had the conspicuous absence of even a passing reference of Indian involvement, but the French and British aid had voluminous reports. The coming together may increase people - to people contact and obliterate the damage perpentrated by partition.

Indian government was ready to give assistance to Pakistan relief operations with helicopters but President Musharaff has refused it on grounds of sensitivities.

The feature quick enough to add that satellites have cornered the nook and corner and what compels them to talk about sensitivities.

The feature is also contradicting even if the NGO's arrived to safe the quake victims, they would be debarred from carrying on their activity by enunciatirg "sensitivity" as the core hindrance. Beheading the Hindu population amidst this catastrophe is sign of Xenophobic nature of the militants. Pakistanis never condemned this dastardly act speaks volumes of the disingenuous game perpetrated to protect their cause.

There was not sufficient organization on ground in Srinagar or in Muzaffarabad to process all help corning. An IC - 76 loaded with 20 tonnes of material could not take off from Palam Air Port because the air port at Islamabad was choked. When Turkey, Britain and China and host of other countries are already on the spot with post earthquake management teams. Prakash Karat, Sitaram Yechurry, Yasin Malik left for Muzaffarabad to help relief and rescue operations.

When Tsunami broke out December 26, 2004, it was on Boxing day. It was a holiday for naval officers. But within hours registering the naval headquarters, 37 Indian naval ships were diverted to Sri Lanka, Maldives and Ache in Indonesia.

The Ministry of External Affairs (MEA) had announced Tsunami as a model of co-operation in regional situation between India, United states and European Union. But Tsunami models are unheard of in the days of earthquake (The New Indian Express, October 14, 2005).

The impending announcement of the sale of F - 165 to Pakistan by the United States and big failure for India diplomacy and signal for American belt towards Pakistan. In the pre-nuclear age, India had every reason to oppose advanced arms sales to Pakistan from the United States, Europe and China since 1950s.

With the existential nuclear deterrence in place, bean counting of military air craft on either side makes little sense (The New Indian Express, October 15, 2005). While India has acquired Sukhors from Russia and Mirages from France, and Falcon air defence rader from Israelis, Pakistan has not purchased any new fighter air craft over the last decade.

Atal Bihari Vajpayee navigated the complex water India - Pak - United States relationship through 1998 - 2004. He had virtually used the American, pressure on Pakistan to vacate unconditionally the Kargil aggression of 1999. And give credible assurance of ending terrorism on the military stand off 2001 - 02.

There has been tacit military operations between the two countries in many ways.

Despite the sensitivities involved the two sides came closer, as Pakistan received all the assistance that India had given and thereby this coming together has to be steadily built upon.

Empathy and wisdom should guide India at this moment even as it makes a hard - headed assessment of the quake impact on the terrorist infrastructure in (PoK) Pakistan occupied Kashmir.

Growing American influence in Pakistan could be an advantage for India, provided New Delhi and Washington agree on next steps in changing the political dynamism in Jammu & Kashmir.

India must overlook the sale of F - 16 if Washington can come up with credible assurances from Pakistan the terrorist infrastructure destroyed Pakistan occupied Kashmir and if there is sustained evidence of change on Pakistan's approach to cross border terrorism.

(o) Features on Recent Past

During the period of study there were seven features in the New Indian Express kindling and justifying the past to bring about detente where else The Hindu carried only three features.

The movement of the bus service across the border and the influence of PoK to reclaims the properties has become a logical road to opened by the Indian government. (The New Indian Express, April 28, 2005) The resettlement Act of 1982 has stirred up the hornet nest with complaints once the rush of passengers picked up with the bus service. The Congress then in opposition severely opposed the bill and launched a rigorous attack winning the Hindu majority vote in 1983, but National Conference supported the Muslim voters in its favour. The bill was referred to the Supreme Court by B.K. Nehru but it was sent back without any advice on it in 2001.

The delay of 19 years is a sore in the throat for the reunion of people across the LoC is bound to create many more problems. The for and against the bill suffered from ignorance. It sets to resettle persons who were state subjects before May 5, 1954 who had migrated before March 1, 1947 to the territory now included in Pakistan. Even a cursory reading of the Act makes it clear that it applied to Pakistan and alloyed Pok administered Kashmir. The anxities of the refugees would be alloyed, if the evacuees property belonged to those who migrated to Pakistan and not Pakistan administrated Kashmir.

The intelligence agencies or the High Commissioner needs to disprove the citizenship if by now the migrant is a part of Pakistani nationality.

The entry 17 in 7th schedule of the Indian constitution that citizenship is a union subject and the state government has no power to restore citizenship to migrants to Pakistan.

That so called bill is outdated or no more in vogue. The Supreme Court directed the state government not to entertain any more claim for properties left behind by those who migrated to Pakistan as the 12 year limitation period prescribed in the evacuee 1949 was long over.

The features in The New Indian Express as well as many editorials. The features in the New Indian Express after the visit of Mr. Advani to Pakistan threw open the Pandora's box about the more its senior leaders affair unwavering allegiance to the fundamental tenets of the party only accentuated the appearance of being in denial over choices that have to be made. The feature also insinuated that few individuals in history have applied themselves with such single mindedness purpose as Jinnah did to accomplish a goal so unnatural within so brief span of time. Even Gandhi's rise to ascendancy in the Congress (pre - 1937) was more or less coincident with Jinnah's estragement from it (divide and quit 1961). The post 1937, Jinnah, virulent, passionate and unbending espousal of the two nation theory became a dramatic counter - point to the Mahatma's life long pursuit of Hindu-Muslim unity as the essential basics of Indian independence. The editorial also delineated on his personal behaviour and his uncompromising stand was the single most important factor contributing to the transformation of Pakistan from an undergraduate squib into a sovereign state. (The New Indian Express, August 12, 2005)

True Jinnah stand up, The Jinnah of 1916 Lucknow pact dubbed by Sarojini Naidu as the ambassador of Hindu - Muslim unity, Jinnah of the 1940 Lahore resolution and the two nation theory, Jinnah speaks of Pakistan a laboratory of Islam, Jinnah arguing for Pakistan as a bargaining counter in the constitutional round with Congress and the British; Jinnah was forced to accept the moth eaten Pakistan of the 3 June plan as the only realistic option.

Jinnah is thus the maligned other of Indian nationalism, the communal counterpart to Nehru secular vision of United India. Personal circumstances, the desire for power and the divide and rule policies of Raj have all been used to explain his 20 years transformation from Muslim nationalist to communalist.

For Jinnah, the secularist resplendent in the clarion call, Hindu will cease to be Hindus and Muslim will cease to be Muslims, not in the religious sense, because that is personal faith of each individual but in the political sense as citizens of the state.

It was during the period 1977-88 that a number of unconvincing attempts were made to depict Jinnah as wanting to establish Islamic state. Saeed R.

Khairi contrasted the Pragmatic and reasonable Jinnah with the utopian and irrational Gandhi who introduced religion into politics and insensitive Nehru who dealt a blow to Indian unity with the rewriting of the 1946 cabinet mission plan. In other words, Jinnah's secular vision had an Islamic rather western basics. This squaring of the circle enabled Ahmed to claim that Jinnah provided a paradigm for Muslim identity and leadership in a modern world obessed with western media images of Islamic fanaticism and terrorism.

Jinnah had entered the Indian National Congress even before Mahatma Gandhi entered the freedom struggle after his return from South Africa. An interesting assessment of Jinnah is given by none other than the doyen of the RSS H.V. Shedhari, "The tragic story of Partition" (Pages 106 & 107). Jinnah had no fascination for religion and he belonged to a sect in Islam which believed in ten incarnations of the Hindus. Gokhale had once expressed very high hopes in him". He (Jinnah) has true stuff in him". Sarojini Naidu complemented him liberally.

The Congress tried to chase away other Muslim League after the elections (United Provinces) episode in 1937, where the Congress went back on its word after winning clean majority the league felt cheated and its suspicious about the Congress bonafides. The very same view of H.V. Shedhri is reflected by Maulana Abul Kalam Azad in his book "India wins freedom".

Even as late as 1946, when Jinnah had agreed to the cabinet missions proposals for united India, Nehru convened a press conference on 10.7.1946 at Bombay the "the Congress world enter the constituent assembly completely unfettered by agreements and was free to meet all situations". The Maulana recounted in his book of Nehru going back on what was agreed upon between the Congress and the league on the cabinet mission proposals, made Jinnah retract from his earlier stand. The feature enlightened, on L.K. Advani courage, the leader envisioned on August 11, 1947 and the subsequent ruler and dictators ignoring the sound advice given.

Ever since Advani speeches hit the headlines, political analysts, journalists and those concerned about history have been interpreting them in different colours. How can Jinnah, the founder of Pakistan seen responsible for the partition of the country crowned with secular halo? Partition of the Indian sub-continent is a fact? But who is responsible for partitions is a matter of interpretation (The New Indian Express, August 28, 2005). One finger may point to Jinnah and the Muslim league, another to the British and third to the congress. It all depends of whose writing history.

This is what happened to Advani. He is looking afresh at the British rule and partition, free from nationalistic feelings and from broader perspective of history. Actually Advani was telling the Pakistanis to look at the other side of Jinnah, his secular face, which he had hidden from his people in order to find and head theocratic state. Having achieved the goal of new state for Muslims, Jinnah wanted his nation to be secular and that is what he articulated in his address to the constituent assembly of Pakistan on August 11, 1947.

Unfortunately his successor who came to rule Pakistan did not either believe in the vision of their leader or chose not to heed his advice. Equally unfortunate is the fact that most of Advani's own collegues in the party and the sangh parivar could not appreciate the purpose of his exposition of the secular doctrine in Pakistan by deriving support from utterances of its founder. Their reaction has done harm to India than to Pakistan.

Some blame Jinnah, others accuse the British for its divide and rule, the leftists ensure Savarkar and Hindu Mahasabha for provoking Muslim separatism through Hindu consolidation (The New Indian Express).

Jinnah secular and communal credentials has come under the ambience for much debate. Even in the 1937 provincial elections his party fared miserably in the Muslim majority provinces of Punjab, Sindh and Bengal that interestingly entered into Pakistan ten years later. In 1937, the Muslim League did not demand for Pakistan. But the fortunes of Jinnah and Muslim League changed in 1940 once the Pakistan resolution was adopted. Jinnah became the uncrowned king of Indian Muslims and the Muslim League swept reserved constituencies in the 1946 elections.

What was the pragmatism that led 90% of Indian Muslims to pitch for Pakistan in the last days of British raj? After the death of Aurangzeb in 1707, the Marathas, Rajputs, Jats and Sikhs were on the rise at the cost of Mughals or the Afghans, the British began to extend their power across India.

The Muslim League conducted propaganda that Muslims could not expect to love as equals in India.

Actually, Muslims were not looking for equality with Hindus that they had during the British rule. Muslims were aware of the atrocities they committed on Hindus and Sikhs during Muslim rule. Both these factors prompted them to demand for Pakistan strongly.

The most tantalising question of modern Indian history undoubtedly is "could the partition of India have been avoided" (The Hindu, August 28, 2005). Even feature in The Hindu, since August 15, 1947, the question has been asked by all kinds of Indians, who, naturally have given all kinds of answers. Even if the partition took place by 1946, could it come about with loss of lives. The Labour government in London announced that British would quit India by June 1948. It was Lord Mountbatten who foreshortened the date of departure to August 1947. His official biographer justified his decision thus". Once the principle of partition has been accepted, it was inevitable that communalism would rage freely. The longer the period the worse the tension would" prevail.

The tale of partition is estimated to be one million, some scholars have stated it to be 2 million. The understaffing, the Punjab boundary force and not supplying with aircover has been the major source of such mishap.

The British were paranoid as they hesitated to act as soon as they had orders to leave the country. The policy of the raj in the last days was to protect the British lives.

The Punjab boundary award was announced later by the Punjab governor, so that the district officers could be placed in their respective dominions, Indians in India, and Pakistanis in Pakistan. The earlier it was published, the more the British would have to bear responsibility for the disturbances which would undoubtedly result.

As the epitaph on the last days of the Raj was provided by the Punjab official who told a young social worker from Oxford "you British believed in fair play. You have left in the same condition of chaos those as you have found it."

The instrument of accessions signed by Maharaja Hari Singh of Jammu & Kashmir on October 26, 1947 long thought to be lost has generated considerable controversy among historians and others alike (The Hindu). The instrument of accession now available on the website is the original document as it was signed by the other 500 princely states of British India. Since 1947, it was with the government and later transferred to the national archives.

Scholars like Alster Lamb had already done damage by claiming that the document did not exist and even if it did not exist, Hari Singh claimed, may have never signed on it. More damaging for India, Lamb claimed that even if Hari Singh did sign any such document it was done after the first landing of Indian troops at Srinagar on October 27, 1947.

The document that Hari signed made it clear that he offered accession of October 20, 1947 and then it was accepted by the then governor - general of India, Mountbatten the next day.

As press Shankar Jha stages in his book, Hari Singh was persuaded by V.P. Menon to sign the instrument accession of the night of October 25 early morning of October 26, 1947. Menon also persuaded Hari Singh to leave Srinagar for Jammu, given the threat from the tribal raiders from Pakistan, which he did at around 2 a.m. After deriving almost non-stop the Maharaja entourage reached Jammu, palace around lunch time on October 26. There they waited for news from Delhi about the request for assistance. V.P. Menon did not come as his flight to Jammu was put off due to bad weather. But he had already handed over the instrument of accession to Lord Mountbatten on October 26 at the meeting of the defence committee of the cabinet.

The other document that is available at many sources is a letter written by Hari Singh to Mountbatten, also dated October 26, 1947. Actually, while Maharaja had signed the instrument of Accession, he had not agreed to bring in Shiekh Abdullah to head the emergency administration. To persuade Hari Singh to get Sheikh Abdullah in, Menon went to Jammu on October 27, soon after the first Indian troops were in, and got the Maharaj append his signature to letter dated October 26 and datelined "the palace, Jammu". This letter probably written originally on October 24 - 25 had to be redrafted to include at the end the paragraph about Sheikh Abdullah inclusion in government. This Menon took back to Dehli on the October 27 and then in the evening handed both both the Instrument and the letter offering accession to Mountbatten Jawaharlal Nehru. Thus the princely state of Jammu and Kashmir acceded to India.

The Atlantic charter carried a unsigned report, which stated that Ayub Khan had assumed power via military coup. Politicians were banned from the state and their very name is anathema". Many of the newly independent countries in Asia and Africa have tried to copy the British parliamentary system. The experiment has failed in Sudan, Pakistan and Burma and is under great stress in India and Ceylon.

Pakistan and poor, ex-colonial countries in general, were better served by unelected officers in uniforms than by elected politicians in Mufti. Democracy was the western import unsuited to the genius and culture of lands outside the west. Field Marshal Ayub Khan in 1965 brought them into war. In 1971, combined military defeat with break-up of the country there was restoration of democracy. ZA. Bhutto who came as the people's mandate was deposed by Zia-Ul-Haq and promised fresh elections. He remained in power and then passed away in an air crash.

If its issue of September 1999, the Atlantic monthly carried a report on Pakistan entitled "the lawless frontier". This report was signed by Robert D. Kaplan. Kaplan quoted a Pakistan intellectual "We have never defined ourselves in our right, only in relation to India. That is our tragedy" (The Hindu, September 11, 2005). In 1959, the Atlantic pitied India for not having a military dictatorship and in the same time in 1999 they praised India for democracy as it is a saving grace.

(p) Feature Coverage of Siachen Issue

During the period of study there 3 features in The Hindu and two such features in the New Indian Express.

The Hindu feature has emphasized Dr. Manmohan singh has sent a clear signal. In declaring that the mountain of war becomes the mountain of peace, the military establishment and the civilian administration to plan creatively to explore to settle two decade problems. The Defence Secretary level talks will not suffice the on going talks. The feature of the Hindu has during the course of discussions has suggested that this can be directly held between the Prime Minister and Musharaff (The Hindu, June 20, 2005). The soldiers may feel that the army at the top of the glacier may feel that there is no pressing need to disengage from the glacier. More than 700 soldiers have passed away. Today the ceasefire is in place along the actual ground position line (AGPL). It cost the exchequers more than 3 crores to 5 crores of money.

(q) Army Objections

The arguments put forward were there was no strategies value attached to Siachen. It is all invented. The army feared that the pull out from the glacier even if a bilateral agreement to redeploy forces would mean victory to Pakistan that they were not able to stand out. There is always the problem of distrust. Historians believed that the line of agreement along the ceasefire cannot be declared as there is no movement of troops across the border and the line drawn both north easternly direction they fear once the Indian army vacated the Saltro ridge the Pakistani forces will occupy the land.

Manmohan Singh has come a long way in solving the problem. Short of redrawing those borders partitioning any part of the territory on religious bias sky is the limit. Compromising on Siachen can help the peace process move forward. The purpose of authentication, the Prime Minister needs to stress that there is one way of securing cartographics commitment from Pakistan. Pakistan will not back its old position or re-occupy passes such Gyong la, Bil fond, Sia la to three passes currently held by Indian forces. The call for zone of disengagement along the border can be made so that after a pre-determined date that the presence of military on either side would be considered illegitimate. This could be jointly patrolled by the helicopter. The purpose of authentication is to ensure that after withdrawal has been effected Pakistan will not move back.

In 1992, India and Pakistan negotiators drew up such a zone a misshaped rectangle of saltoro range on the middle wherein Pakistan occupied the west and India in the east, such formula would produce a grid referenced map (that would be effective as a map authenticating the (AGPL) Actual Ground Position Line in the cartographic reference). The third issue is the question of thrust between two countries India and Pakistan that the peace process carried forward. If Pakistan cannot be trusted to keep an agreement on demilitarizing the Siachen glacier then authenticating Actual Ground Position Line will have no purpose other than taking the Indian army into false sense of security. Trust is not the soft corner from Musharaff but the rationality of Pakistan decision makers.

They have deliberate attempts to insure that military civilian establishment rapport to settle two decade long issue is defunct and the onus lies with the political establishment. This can be achieved by Dr. Manmohan Singh with Pakistani counterpart, president Musharaff.

The ceasefire agreement spoke of the ceasefire line going "North" to the glaciers from N 9842, Pakistan maps draw a straight line in a north easterly direction upto Karakoram pass. The features insisted that through the senior army officers that Pakistani forces night eventually occupy the saltora range to posts vacated by India. The authentication will help India merit an international attention if ever Pakistan reneges on the terms of withdrawal agreement.

Purport of media of Siachen issue. Given the regional and international realities of our time, Pakistan is unlikely to believe its core interests will be served by such an outcome. In diplomacy as well as in war countries must choose their battles wisely. Siachen is not a winnable proposition for either side but withdrawal will provide benefits to both.

After the meet between Musharaff and Dr. Singh the institutional mechanism should meet to find expeditions solution to Sir Creek Mission and the Siachen glacier, there has been no forward movement in the peace process (The Hindu, September 14, 2005).

The Indian government wanted assurances from the Pakistani establishment that the passes vacated by the army must not be occupied by Pakistan. Gyong la, Bilafond la, Sia la the three key passes along the Saltoro range.

The defence and the army institutions anxiously wait for the assurances to rely on Pakistan moves.

The newspaper quoted that the verification of any Siachen withdrawal is better accompanied not by democrating the triangular region bounded by NJ 9842 in the south (where the Line of Control ends), Indira Col. in the north, and the Karakoram pass in the east as demilitarized zone that neither Indian and Pakistani armed forces will enter except jointly or purpose of regular inspection.

Such an agreement with a signed map of zone appended would provide at least as much protection in international law as a signed map of the Actual ground position line, which Pakistan refused to agree to because it might prejudice the entire claim to the entire glacier.

The newspapers offered a number of solutions thereby easing the tension on both sides and the re-deployment of the troops, figured during the course of the talks leaving the much awaited controversy with receipt of solutions.

The feature also cited that the old reagan's phrase 'trust, but verify' in the context of Pakistani assurances on ending cross - border terrorisms.

The New Indian Express asserted that the record of negotiations there is a settlement at the earliest. There were earlier solutions of on May 1989 and 1992. But Islamabad and India never came close to defusing the conflict. Immediately after independence it was very difficult for them to extend beyond the Saltoro ranges where Siachen glacier is a part of it.

The Simla agreement of 1972 failed to draw the boundaries in the northern areas where it is inaccessible for either armies to travel across.

The joint statement issued by the Rajiv Gandhi and Benazir Bhutto in 1989, to defuse the conflict had the following statement, redeployment of the forces, avoidance of the chances of the conflict, determination of future positions on ground (The New Indian Express, May 17, 2005).

There were political reasons as well as technical issues - where the army had to be pulled upto, on how to acknowledge the current positions on ground and how to prevent either side form renewed occupation of the Saltoro range.

The domestic political compulsion in both nations did sap the morale of the statement reached by Benazir had to confront with army and Rajiv Gandhi with the ensuing elections.

The non-paper on Siachen that was presented to Islamabad in 2004 would take up the extension of the LoC without prejudice to the position held by either side. The two sides shall disengage from the authenticated position, they are presently occupying and the areas vacated will constitute a zone of complete disengagement.

The two sides also agreed that, they shall not seek to reoccupy the position vacated by either side and that in case of violation by one, the other side will be free to respond. The two sides also agreed to evolve a monitoring mechanisms and work out mutually satisfactory time schedules for military disengagements.

The feature quoted the dilemma of the Indian army and the guarantee they require to vacate the positions held at Saltro range by shedding money and the risk of losing superior position. The army needs trust worthy assurances after the Kargil invasion in 1999 when Islamabad tried to change the status quo on ground.

Disengagement along the LoC as well as ceasefire along the Saltoro ridge are the expected outcome but should be carefully weighed by prudence for successful agreement lies in credible verification mechanism. The feature also delivered another question to be sorted out in the next round of talks - the gulf between Indian insistence on authentication and Pakistan's reluctance to legitimize the Indian presence on Saltoro.

Pakistan refusal to sign maps has led to the breakdown of all previous talks (The New Indian Express, May 23, 2005). India tends to undervalue its Siachen advantage this must be evaluated through Pakistani eyes. An Indian pullback from Siachen will allow President Musharaff to present his people with what will be played as a triumph. The enormous cost paid by India to gain the advantage in Siachen must translate into benefits elsewhere on the LoC or against militant groups based in Pakistan.

The opinion columnist gives a quickie and a reminder to the conflict regarding the authentication their ground positions in Siachen. In 1992, Pakistan had suggested recording the position on an annexure that would be attached with the agreement, this proposal is expected to provide guarantees that there will be no re-occupation of Saltoro once demilitarization is completed. The authentication should not be by passed, no matter how it is inconvenient to Pakistan. In Kargil, Indian lives were battered to win back Indian territory. In Siachen the climate, the logistical difficulties mean that the territory is lost forever.

Human and emotions capital and authentication were the two main ingredients discussed during the course of Siachen issue.

But the feature in The Hindu is full of approbation for the coming of Manmohan Singh to the Siachen glacier for the first time by an Indian Prime Minister and the disengagement of troops and the either side of the border is to avoid future conflicts in the regime. The disengagement factor is widely discussed but that cannot find succor to the whole problem. Mr. George Fernandes as the Defense Secretary did not want disengagement on the borders as the perceived attacks any on the border. The army which has spent human and economical capital on the borders feels that at certain stage they can not fritter away money. As cited by Senior officials that safeguards to be placed on all points cannot be treated lightly for fear of incursion on the very same day. The whole discussion between Pakistan and Indian officials was going on the army men wanted it to make public whether withdrawal will be of help without authentication of the Actual ground line position N 9842 on LoC. Though the arrival of Manmohan Singh on the glacier is symbolic it has it must open up new vistas by convincing the institutional mechanism of conducting talks to settle issues like the Sir Creek mission and the Siachen glacier expeditiously. But the talks evolved so far are not conciliatory in nature here there is palpable solution. The authentication is necessary on two fronts one for the bigger reason of political and other military concern. It may be recalled that on the Kargil front international support was sought for as there was clear violation of LoC and the military generals would show the grids on the maps duly signed by the military general on both sides. Similar such steps evolved at this juncture may help to avert serious dangers in future. Pakistan has duly acknowledged in 1992 that it was prepared to include the authentication of the N 9842 in the main agreement but it was not receptive. Before any agreement an both sides is reached the disengagement on the both sides of the map of clearly indicated might help ease tensions. If on the contrary the present position is accepted India still fears reoccupying the territory.

(r) Features Covering Ending of Violence and Promotion of Peace

There were seven features in The New Indian Express where else The Hindu carried only two features.

The feature page The Hindu wherein feels at loss over the much perplexed remarks made Dr. Singh during the course of the interview with Washington Post. This sudden reversion to an evocation of stereotype to Pakistan loomed large in Prime Minister speech. The United Progressive Government failure to stick on the Promise of relationship with Pakistan and the confidence building measure took a great U-turn. And it will be a great set back to the much awaited peace process and the slackening of the pace of peace process.

However the trenchant remarks of adopting the guarded approach to Pakistan shows complacent nature in the developing context of confidence building measure.

The print media quoted that India is besieged democracy requiring Americas empathy in good measure (The Hindu, July 25, 2005).

In Singh remark during the meeting with editors of Washington Post regarding nuclear proliferation in the neighbourhood and painting India as marching ahead in nuclear disarmament posed a challenge and the condition of being inert in missile production. The nuclear control in our country is basically governed by civilian forces and their constant checks and balances.

Pakistani nature of strong nuclear assets does worry us with the proliferation of nuclear weapons and growth of extremists in Pakistan.

The fear of weapons transferred to the hands of Al-Qaeda and the massive destruction thereafter is predicted.

The picture of Pakistan as terror ensared cannot embolden the stand of India as the just remarks were later sidelined by the United States and they eulogized Pakistan being an ally of them in the fight against terrorism.

In the context of print media has stressed the need for emphasizing the Pakistan is using religious war as an instrument of state policy was widely quoted by P.M. Vajpayee, during his visit to United States. He also assured the US in having strong relationship and abiding trust in one another.

The peace process cannot be moved further if terrorism is not controlled and Pakistan reserve of terrorist should be highlighted for it defeats the purpose of peace process.

The media provided the edifice for patching up of relationship, did not mince words, constant effort to iron out difference and they don't elope away with the purport of the scheme leaving many in more consternation and formidable challenges ahead.

The special squads have been arresting Al-Qaeda which included Al-Qaeda third in command, Yassen Jazeeri, Abu Zubeia, but during a big United States. Congressional debate on the question of foreign aid to Pakistan as well as on delivering the F-16 fighter jets that had been held back by the Pentagon because of Pakistan's nuclear ambition. The Americans with the sale of F-16 to India, getting the right to interrogate Abdul Quadeer Khan is denied by Musharaff. The feature also commented on the nature of Pakistan's drawing from their reserves of terrorists, giving asylums to Taliban, the Pakistanis invented them.

The sincerity of Islamabad leader is being thoroughly questioned, when they present themselves as the best students of anti-terrorist class. (The New Indian Express, May 22, 2005)

Tle proclaimed change of heart of the general is discussed at length by many newspapers, rather they believe that it is ploy to buy time, or change the mood of the already disturbed to procure more strength, the nuclear arsenal and evolve long term plans to win laurels at home and international arena. The general can but with anybody with his kind of conciliatory remarks.

The hue and cry over Advani statement of Jinnah in the Pakistani soil and the letter to PM Dr. Singh by Mr. Vajpayee and the regret expressed by the National Democratic Alliance government the United Progressive Alliance govemment has given more concessions to Pakistani government has provoked the party henchmen as well as think - tanks to speculate on the wishful thinking of the BJP.

Sangh Parivar uses this ploy as an anti-Muslim consolidation to have an absolute hold on Hindutva stronghold and suppress the minorities on the other.

The RSS-VHP combine made a note to the Israelis that they join hands together by alienating the Muslims, would receive the patronage of the United States in their fight against terror.

But, Israeli government promptly replied back that for co-existence the Muslim nation cannot be loved but due course a spontaneous love may sprout. (The New Indian Express, June 24, 2005).

The post 9/11 world cannot be cast aside lightly for the embers are still more erractic. The world witnessed the pulling down of Saddam Hussain stature, which prompted Vajpayee to extend a hand of friendship fifteen days later. The equation received a new fillip without hampering the ordeal of friendship.

The policy of the bipartisan approach of the UPA government is circumspect for the way it is being handled but not the dialogue process.

The rumpus over Kashmir militant turned Pakistan Yasin Malik visit to Pakistan that once the Information Minister ran camps for the militants but with strong resentment from Indian government he clarified that these camps ran once shelter to refugees that arrived during Jammu & Kashmir violence. Ahmed was refused travel permit from Muzaffarabad to Srinagar he was constantly noted for anti-India rhetoric.

The Hindu determined the arrival of various other leaders who supported separatist violence for discussion.

Many might not come around with expressing regret over the past. Broad consensus need to be framed to treat such persons was the cautious note of print media. The Hindu, June 28, 2005).

We should never associate Islam with terrorism and terrorists have no religion, terrorism and terrorist element are supported from the Pakistani soil (The New Indian Express, July 8, 2005). Frequent terrorist strikes killings inside Mosques and secretarian conflicts including the encouragement to religious extremists and terrorism either as a component of Pakistani soil anti-India strategy or for Islamisations of Pakistan. It is for this reason that Pakistan had condemned the terrorist attack and the Hurriyat too has condemned the attack. The BJP President refused to blame the Pakistan government after the Ayodhya attack and the bold invitation from L.K. Advani to inaugurate the temple at Pakistan gives the spirit of reconciliation and mutual acceptance in a state of theocracy.

Richard Nixon became the president in 1967, largely on strength of bashing the communist regime and advocacy of containment of Soviet Union and ostracizing the people, Republic of China.

He was the first to visit China and Moscow immediately after the first world war. The USA is todays Vietnam trading partner, China - America, two way trade accounts for almost 30% of world trade. Former foes becoming friends and allies. India was kept off the security council by Russia and China vetoed of several times by both the countries inspite of having so many million pleas numbers. Both India needed Morarji Desai and Vajpayee to mend the broken relationship with Bangladesh and China. It was Vajpayee as the Prime Minister and the secular credentials that won him victory and who took the bus journey to Lahore summit 2004 and Simla agreement by Mrs. Indira Gandhi lead in settling the Simla accord. Pakistan had always been the breeding ground for sectarian violence as the country has been divided among themselves. The Pakistani sheltering of Taliban gives more credence to terrorism and the root cause of fanatics and the constant effort to shelter the secular fabric of India. Mao came to power with Sheer outcry of Anti-Americanism but after that he welcomed President Nixon after the Watergate scandal (The New Indian Express, July 17,

The discussion on nuclear explosion that was being carried out by both the countries evoked many ludicrous statements and illiterate jingoism.

BJP junior cadres have planned to take ash from the Pokhron site and carried across the country to mark the beginning of the text.

The media has opened up the diabolical game plan of inducing the government to think over the foreign policy and security of the country. As per the media portrayal of the issue, foreign policy has to be treated similar to the economic issue and considered for national debate. The different Prime Minster to like the issue of nuclear energy for its continuity and sustenance made it mandatory that the legacy is transferred to the successors.

With Pokharan Vajpayee had taken hold initiative of leaving apart from the old consensus of developing nuclear weapons. Especially after the anti - proliferation attitude of Clinton and the pressure exerted thereof on the NPT,

FMCT, CTBT, there is ambiguity on nuclear issue when it comes to public posture.

The idea of ending nuclear ambiguity and forcing Pakistan to come out in the open was an audicious one. The media emphasized the joint statement of the Talbott from wherein it is crystal clear after having engaged with Jaswant Singh and the diplomacy bomb that democracy has to be dealt. The purport of the report stated the Vajpayee government attitude to chip away from the sanction mind set and better acceptance by P5 countries. (tnie, July 23, 2005)

The parliamentarians say the nukes lie and the secrecy is not divulged. The fact that the unbecoming of the comment was what was military and what was civil was not clear to them. An anecdote to substantiate the statement wherein an IAS officer was appointed in the department of Atomic energy. The director insisted that he draft letters to parliament wherein he had to write or draft matters to parliament and tell no lie. If asked for your name, tell them first of your date of birth.

The separation of military facilities from installations and China being a permanent ally the nuclear preparations it is quite to think of nuclear defiance as warped sovereignty that the country is made to anoint with.

The United States has now established defacto third party in India-Pakistan relations. On the same day, the meeting of President Bush, Dr. Singh was assured for effacing of cross border terrorism. While General Musharaff harped on the reduction of troops in northern areas of Jammu & Kashmir. The reduction of troops in any area is the ultimatum of the government of that country. Similarly they may discuss the 'matter bilaterally, not involve a third party mediation which will end up in chaos.

The Prime Minster Dr. Singh would be in Pakistan when the two countries are finally to deal with Siachen. Another proposed is issuing joint statement in third countries may not bring bigger outcomes.

(s) Features on Third - Party Mediation

There were two features related to third party mediation in The Hindu wherelse four features in The New Indian Express during the period of study.

The visit of President Bush to Pakistan was not efficacious for though Pakistan was one the front line ally and elevated to the status of a major non-NATO Ally for its role in the "war against terror" the visit only helped an expression of gratitude by the sole super power.

The Anti-American, anti-west sentiments plagued the Pakistani establishment. The religious parties and the opposition party were peeved by the kind gestures, extended by Bush for patronizing military ruler at the cost of democracy. The feature (March 4, 2006, The Hindu) reflected that America continued to harbour suspicion in Pakistan's role in combating terrorism and the seriousness with which Islamabad has approached the fundamentalists.

The feature demarcated the word "Push" used by Bush to close all terrorist camps in Pakistan. In diplomatic parlance, "Push" would mean "encourage" only when you cannot "push" has been derided by the media.

President Musharaff feels the necessity to pull Pakistan from the edifice of India centric ideas. (March 9, 2006, The Hindu) He has also unravelled the enigma of India centric ideas that hailed from the foreign office, the Pakistani army. The onus of removing the India fixation from the minds of the Pakistani public lies with the government, the media, the foreign office.

The feature dwelled on impractical factor of other institutions in the country to get rid of their India - fixation either the feature also enunciated on the pre-eminence of the military which shapes the government policy where the government nor the foreign office may be on the fringe to decide on policy matters.

The New Indian Express features also began with the lead wherein how newspapers like the New York Times has summed up the visit of the President Bush to the subcontinent.

The New York Times summed by saying that he gave a hug to India and a pat to Pakistan similarly the German MPS Del'.spirigel daily quoted that he bought roses to India and thorns to Pakistan. Bush arrival was venture to determine the trails of path towards war on terror. In the meantime to make realistic, according to reports in the operation that started the day before the arrival of Bush a hundreds have been worked in Himanshah in Washington by Pakistani troops. When interviewed by the BBC, a young man reported that the most of killed included civilians too. Democracy, pipeline, can nuclear deal Bush clarified the American Stand.

On issue of Kashmir, a strange U-Turn has taken place where the American craved to internationalise the issue at various forums a notable tacit approach has emerged on the Pakistan soil by Bush (March 19, 2006, The New Indian Express) This time he heralded only to "encourage" as distinct from "facilitate" talks between the two countries.

The Bush administration ought to be extra - careful that when it does with Pakistan does not harm either Indo-US relations or the Indo-Pak process. Avoiding a little towards either on Indo - Pak issues, de-hyphenating relations with India and Pakistan, maintaining pressure on Islamabad to end cross - border terrorism, the Bush administration created a sound basis for expanding ties with both, as well as creating a conducive environment for the Indo-Pak process. In New York, both Singh and Musharaff had conveyed their respective concerns about the peace process to president George W. Bush. Singh's emphasis was on Pakistan taking additional steps to curb cross - border terrorism and Musharaff in term focused on India moving forward.

Musharaff decision to raise the issue in the United Nations and Pakistan side's unfortunate attempt at specifying the reduction of troops in Kupwara and Baramulla prevented India from moving down a path. Natwar Singh discussion with top US officials on Pakistani question, Pakistan national security adviser Faroq Aziz in Washington, US National Security advisor Stere Harley in Pakistan and Afghanistan revisiting the multi-dimensional US - Pakistan relations wherein each adopts a strategy to smoothen the relations further. A wide variety of different national concerns has to be calibrated to keep the equation with in full momentum.

The attributes are the American interest in Musharaff's political future, Indian apprehensions about the credibility of Musharaff steps against terrorism, Musharaff fear that India will string out Pakistan on Kashmir, the continuing instability in Afghanistan and the links between interests in the sub-continent and global terrorism.

Islamabad's pressure on Washington to extend nuclear energy co-operation to if on terms similar to those being offered to India, add dynamism in the triangular ties 2001, Musharaff is found to be serious as the forces responsible for terrorism in Kashmir is also responsible the ones trying to get Musharaff himself. The United States is also concerned that many involved in Kashmir terrorism also have links with larger networks of terrorism operating in the western world.

The spurt of militancy across the border the extended engagement in the Gurez sector one of the largest infiltrations across the Line of Control did room for thought for questioning on the legitimacy and patronage that terrorists received for carrying out their nefarious activities. (August 5, 2005, The New Indian Express) As a consequence two schools of thought emerged, one the militants were freelance in nature two there were residual terrorists. The pragmatic leaders believed in the residual and this is controlled by Islamabad. The Afghanistan could be stabilised, causing the Americans to depart, there would be an option to resume compact with Islamists. But this is not happening. The New Delhi - US relationship has conclusively de-hyphenated the US - Pakistan from the US framework. The only option for Musharaff is to increase peace momentum. Such features demonstrate the strength of peace in agonizing global terrorism and Musharaff's ultimatum relinquishing ribaldry to peace.

General Musharaff's visit to India was the occasion when Manmohan Singh could have used all strategies to bring about a amicable solution to bring the never ending dispute. (April 19, 2005, The New Indian Express) The United States has recognized India as knowledge power for the 20th century and China too has shown its willingness for improving speedy economic relations.

Pakistan has so far depending on United States & China to use the retrieved energy to be hardliner on Kashmir.

The sale of F -16 by United States to Pakistan need not be taken as a cause for worry as United States may take them as hostage until delivery. There is another grand design of the United States wherein 126 advanced figher bombs will be transferred to India with co-productions in India.

The Kurdish demand for a separate state but today, Dr. Jabel Talabari has been installed in multilingual, multicultural, multi ethnic Kurdish majority. Autonomy and demilitarization are the catchwards the United States uses as its ploy to democratise the fractured Islamic status.

The general himself faced threat from terrorists and the surveillance along the Line of Control has been strengthened to avoid the infiltration of terrorists across, the border.

The United States government expected Musharaff to give a clean chit of A.Q. Khan nuclear black market and the Pakistan govt. involvement in it. Pakistan can improve its working climate by opening joint trades, economic co-operation across the Line of Control.

The general who had received ultimatum from the United States would use the pro-Taliban support to one of lukewarm support to the United States.

The editorial cited that Dr. Manmohan Singh is clean to come up with talks to continue the composite dialogue.

(t) Features of PoK

During the period of study there was one feature in The Hindu and one feature in the New Indian Express.

The feature in The Hindu concentrated on the men living across the Line of Control in Pakistan occupied Kashmir (PoK) who opted for militancy but later abandoned it after getting disillusioned with the gun. The feature on (March 5, 2006, The Hindu) had identified many more men left in the quandary and wishfulness to return to their native land.

The feature abhorred the return of men who pioneered the gun culture in Jammu & Kashmir would never be easy due to the baggage of the past. In the complex Kashmir tangle, the problem of ex-militants and their urge to return home would require a combined humanitarian approach from both India and Pakistan.

The feature in The New Indian Express (July 11, 2006) explored the conduct of polls within Pakistan occupied Kashmir will be it free and fair and the contradiction within the PoK politics has been examined further. The feature reinforced that 'democracy should however be judged by certain standards, rather than by whether polls were held at regular intervals, that is where the 'Azad' Kashmir becomes an occupied one, given the limited powers of the assembly and the pre and post poll political manipulations to which it is subjected.

The composition of the elected assembly for Azad Kashmir consists of (48 seats -now 49) - 28 to be elected from the districts of Azad Kashmir, 12 from refugees - 8 reserved seats - 8 seats out of this five for women, one each for technocrats, ulema / mushaikh and overseas Kashmiris. The election process could be seen in three categories. Numbers directly elected within PoK those elected by Kashmiri refugees elected by electoral college. Northern areas are exempted from this list. The contest is between NC, PDP- AJK, JK-PML, MMA & MQM. Intelligence agencies with the support from Islamabad also manipulatd the post - election political scenario in Pakistan occupied Kashmir.

The feature lamented on the obstacles, with militants raising the level of violence and terrorizing the local people against participation during the 2002 J & K election, where else elections in PoK carried out without a whimper. The northern areas is exempted from elections, and the reticence of the international community on the Azad J & K is understandable.

(u) Features Related to Human Rights Violation

During the period of study there was one feature. The feature in The Hindu on March 4, 2006 narrated how Tasleen been paid price and her finance was beheaded when she refused to marry a local Hizbul Mujdlideen commander. In war fatigued Jammu & Kashmir, it figured only in the footnotes of public discourse and later ignored. On the other hand the four boys who were killed in the Handwara shoot out by Rashtria Rifle received compensation as well as jobs - in stark contrast with more typical fate of Tasleema family which did even a word of commiseration. The feature highlighted, the Hondwara incident received wielded such importance.

On the morning of February, Rashtria Rifle received a telephone cell about (LeT) Laskar-e- Toiba group the village of Doodipora and the security forces apprehended Abdul Samad Mir, a covert Lashkar operative.

The feature investigated the nature of the shoot out when Doodipora villagers have told police investigators a single shot rang out. It is still unclear if it was fired by one of the terrorists as a signal to warn the rest of the group of the presence of the troops or if a soldier fired his weapon by accident.

Whatever the truth, the troops opened fire in response, Mir and other local residents nor and four others aged between 8 and 18 were shot dead.

The feature also re-examined the available date and ensured on the improbability of captain Datta shoot Mir in the presence of large number of eye witnesses.

The All Party Hurriyat Conference had taken up addressed the United Nations that was "catch and kill" policy and the Indian forces have been given full authority by the government of India to act with impunity, unleashing a reign of terror and oppression on the innocent people of Jammu & Kashmir.

The legitimacy of the Delhi Conference was stripped off when Mirwaiz demonstrated the conference was vain activity and the Islamist leader went on a step further it was a part of "genocide conspiracy". The feature evaluated the conspiracy of genocide as claimed by the hardline faction of the Hurriyat with available data.

From 1988 to 2005, period composite dialogue, between 12 to 15 years of 15, 101 civilians died were the genuine exchanges of fire between security force personnel and terrorists. The human right violations have been in steady decline:

1. From 142 in 2001
2. 74 in 2004
3. 25 in 2003
4. 16 in 2004
5. 7 in 2005

The security forces also received life sentences for Human Rights violations between 1990 - 2004.

Eg. The court held Major Rehman Hussain for criminal use of force during search operations raping the mother and her daughter. Though the ambiguous DNA test led to his acquittal of charges, the military court expelled him. The All Party Hurriyat Conference has maintained with stoic silence on the murders on Tasleem, state education minister G.N.L. one, MJ. Tarogami, Nephew of assassinated by the (LeT) Laskar-e-Toiba.

Using the tragedies that took place in Handwara to attack the dialogue process is as best disingenuous - and at worst plain dishonest.

(v) Features related to Baglihar

The Baglihar project, across the Chenab, about 120 km. from border, is located upstream of the existing sable project and is one such project being executed by India conforming to these provisions. However, in spite of furnishing all data about the project features and discussing in several meetings of the Permanent Indus Commission (PIC) and secretary level meetings, Pakistan said the design of the plant did not conform to the criteria laid down in (IWT) Indus Water Treaty (The New Indian Express, June 8, 2006).

India for its part has been clarifying the treaty has not imposed any ban on the height of the dam it provided for pondage adequate to meet the power load variations and to take due account of the requirement of secondary power than firm power. There is no restriction on the free board though there is limit to the storage to be retained; any flooding action would first affect Indian areas and also the India's sake project before affecting Pakistan. Provision of sluice spill ways is a technology driven need for any dam and the heavy silt flows in the river reaching Pakistan would be reduced with a dam.

Conditions rather than without ignoring the clarifications, Pakistan took up the matter with the World Bank, charging India with the flouting of Indus Water Treaty and seeking the appointment of neutral expert to examine the issues. It never tried to substantiate its objections before approaching the bank. However, its real intentions got exposed when during the meeting between the two countries it stated its willingness to resolve the differences bilaterally, provided India stopped all construction activities at the site.

Eighteen years and numerous meetings later, Pakistan is still to agree to the project proposals, thereby stalling the benefits to the people of Jammu & Kashmir. Hence India informed the World Bank that Pakistan's recourse was premature and the Bank should not appoint the *Ne* at this state. However, ignoring India contentions, the expert (NE) Neutral Expert was appointed by the Bank. Both countries have submitted their views in writing to the (NE) Neutral Expert and have made oral presentations at the hearings in London in May. One more chance to present the case will be given in the meeting scheduled in Paris in October and the verdict is expected in November this year.

Raising the bogey of (IWT) Indus Water Treaty violations, Pakistan has succeeded in stalling or delaying the Indian projects, about 30 in all, with the result that out of 8169 MW of estimated hydro-potential from that part of the basin flows which India could utilize, only about 1500 (MW) Mega Watt could be tapped by India so far.

The Hindu extensively covered on two features even the technical details wherelse the New Indian express had only one feature.

The neutral expert Raymond Lufotte, appointed examined the differences over the construction of the Baglihar dam issue.

Baglihar is no more a water sharing dispute. (June 9, 2005, The Hindu) The water sharing proposal was settled down in 1960 (in the Indus water treaty) the Baglihar issue is on technical disagreements between the two countries over certain features.

The treaty divided the Indus systems into two segments, the eastern rivers (Ravi, Beas, Sutlej) and the western rivers (Indus, Jhelum, Chenab) and allocated the former to India and latter to Pakistan. Whether allocating the westerns rivers to Pakistan, it did allow India some limited use of them, including run of the river, hydro electric schemes, subject to western conditions and parameters. The term run of the river means the Project does not involve any shortage. India is not allowed to build storage on the western rivers except to a very limited extent.

A project of the western rivers by the Indian side will have to submit their projects before the construction and the question of differences does really arise. The hydro electric project was settled at the inter governmental level. If it is not settled their, the issue is referred to the neutral expert. The neutral expert fails and the dispute is referred to the international court of arbitration.

The third point is the nature of the difference, the question is not about the need for the project, its precise location, the height of the dams, the planned capacity of the project (50 MW). The treaty has nothing to say about such things. Pakistan may have reservations about some of these matters, but the question it can raise is only about comformity to the treaty provisions. The main treaty and several annexures and appendices lay down the conditions and parameters to which the Indian projects on the western rivers must confirm.

These include matters such as the calculation of firm power, the extent of pondage, prohibition of raising artificially. The water level in the operating pool, permitted range for daily variation in water flows below the structure (within the weekly flow), placement of the crest of the spill way gates (if a gated spill way is considered necessary).

Role of neutral expert as challenging and need to be carefully worded. If it does not conform to the conditions laid down in a particular clause of the treaty or one of its annexures or appendices. The Neutral Expert has to answer these questions 'yes' and 'no' in terms of the provision of the treaty. Equal hearing to both sides and make sweeping judgements. But at the request of the parties, he can suggest measures to compose a difference or to implement his decision. The Neutral Expert can also take the view that the matters referred to him are not within his purview or that the recourse to a court of arbitration will follow.

Leaving aside the various points that come up during the discussion at the meeting of Indus commission the specific points of difference over Baglihar relate to :

(a) the design of the project

(b) the extent of pondage

(c) the placement of the spill way gates and the water intake

(d) Pakistan feels that the free board that is the space between the maximum water level and top of the dam is excessive and will enable India to store more water level than the full pondage level.

India says that the free board is a standard safety feature, and that using it to store more water would compromise the safety, the structure and cannot be done.

Pakistan argued that the planned pondage of 37.7 is more than what the treaty permits.

India says of its calculation of the pondage required is correct.

Pakistan says the placement of the spill way gates and of the water intake do not confirm to the treaty provisions.

Indian justified the placements on certain technical ground that need not gone, into here.

The answer will be given by Prof. Laffitte on the findings in the discourse.

India may offer great attention in spirit of than letter. India attached greatest importance to technical soundness, common viability and satisfactory operation.

Pakistan, on the other hand, is primarily concerned with safeguarding its own interests and tends to insist on stringent and literal interpretation of the treaty. Was India wrong in stating construction in this case without waiting for Pakistan's agreement? That is the Pakistan's view the Indian reply is that the treaty does not specifically say that construction 'should not start without Pakistan's clearance. That if Pakistani's concurrence is held to be necessary for the start of the work, it can use the power of raising objections and rejecting the answers given to stall a project indefinitely.

Some commentator say that given the history of bad relations between two countries Pakistan, distrusts India on deep security concerns, others agree that any lower riparian is bound to have visceral activities vis-a-vis the upper riparian. The answer to the concern and anxieties cannot be found in the treaty.

(w) Newspapers Attitude Towards Conflict Management and Peace

Conflict management in the backdrop of the disaster had five features in the New Indian Express and two features in The Hindu.

The New Indian Express, October 15, 2005 appraisal of the situation calling forth this much loved intellectual an American ancestry chairman, crescent investment management, New York, fiercely loyal and Patriotic American of the Islamic faith feels that the President should come out and stay in one of the make shift arrangements set up during the ravage time to feel the plight of those living under harsh conditions.

At the regional level, the President Musharaff had accepted India's help. But at the same time he must invite the Prime Minister of India to visit Pakistan occupied Kashmir when the ground is more stable, so the Indian leader can console Muzaffarabad in person. The finance wizard of Prime Minister, Shaukat Aziz must be sent to every Arab country and those who enjoy Paskistan's countryside for hunting and falconry to cough up the cash needed for the reconstruction plan.

Japan and China can provide the heavy machinery and skilled forces to complete the task of reconstruction.

One being that let us marshall our resources to help Pakistan rebuild the lives of its Kashmiri citizens - as one people of a civilization to another with respect and dignity that honoured their sacrifices.

President Bush should call on the mayors of a representative list of major cities across the US to each adopt one small village or town in Pakistan occupied Kashmir for reconstruction.

It is time the world ventured to set up a multinational natural disaster management organization to save from eventualities. Accessories need to be kept on demand at strategically located points around the world, and the arrests could be paid for on a GDP ratio basis that puts the burden on rich countries. Overtime to insure there is a ready pool of assets for on demand situations like earthquakes and tsunamis. Multinational companies like caterpillar, John Peer, or Mitsubishi and Daewoo for contributing assets to these global pools.

Indian helicopters were a welcome step whereas the Indian pilots were not welcome rhetoric over F-165, A, (Khan, Gulgat) lace the air degenerate confrontanist positions.

Shruti Patnark has highlighted in her study of international relations that policy arises out of elitist discourse: (October 29, 2005, The New Indian Express)

Perceptional biases have created a stereotype image of each other within which the expectation of each other are formulated. In relationship characterized by emotionalism gains tend to get interpreted as strength and compromise and equated with weakness. The slackening of mutual response is during the relief operation is due to the sterility of the on-going process.

International codes of conduct are to be served while giving relief operations and offer assistance to the people on either side of LoC. It should be based on race, religion, class, struggle for the humanitarian assistance for the people. It is time that the Pakistan and India do not have much time to think that they want to be recorded in history as matters that they rise above parochial ends and effectively carry out relief operations.

The October 8 earthquake that arose from Afghanistan to India marked one of the worst sites on the face of earth as it manifests itself. The human dimension of such colossal tragedy cannot be minimized unlike the December 26 Tsunami, which hits tourist friendly regions and therefore rang alarm bells in every capital of the world, there are inhospitable regions to all but the most intrepid journalist and relief organizations. Pakistan, construct of Azad Kashmir is today in shambles. Pakistan's proxy regime in PoK has been reduced to cipher. But state stood as solid as rock between people on both sides.

Foreign journalists and brave tourists had their way to Srinagar, but not to Muzaffarabad. (October 31 ,2005, The New Indian Express) But today the whole landscape is dotted with Americans doubling troop deployment in PoK British troops, foreign and workers, United Nation as officials, global contractors, western media crew were permanent feature of the soil. Their presence can curtail Jihadis an (ISI) Inter Service Intelligence elements also. The opening of Line of Control at major three locations, - five if India accepts Pakistan's proposal - is a nuanced, creeping movement towards the idea that dare not speak its name border. The acceptance of Line of Control as an international border

The collateral gains from earth quake have culminated a year of three diplomatic landmarks for India. One of them is well known of course, the July 18, nuclear agreement and the mutual courtship of New Delhi - Washington axis.

Tsunami had brought about many changes like they were able to recover faster than other nations as conceded by the United States and the Human rights watch group.

They send ships to Sri Lanka, even before the US navy could reach the spot. By the afternoon of the Tsunami an Indian air force pilot had made a heroic landing on Andaman and Nicobar Islands.

Before the (UN) United Nations took over the four democracies, the Japan, Australia and the United States which formed the Asia Pacific concert of democracies, a sub group in the proliferation of the security initiative against Weapon of Mass Destruction traffiking took change. Thus the mantle of leadership change hands.

The landmark pact between India and Pakistan on the opening up the LoC to enable people to take part in relief and rehabilitation took nearly 23 days to materialize. (October 31, 2005, The Hindu) The key elements of the pact were at after nearly 15 hours of talks. It envisaged two way involvement of people across LoC for relief and reconstruction and the ambiguity on this score is further removed on the assertion that the parameters and procedures already agreed upon for the Srinagar - Muzaffarabad bus service would be used for additional crossings identified in the agreement. The accord is envisaged as a long term agreement. The next day Gen. Musharaff had qualified his proposal saying that facility would be open only to Kashmiris. The joint statement makes no such reference.

The foreign office in Pakistan had conveyed to India that it was ready to provide any assistance to the quake affected on the other side of the LoC. Three days before the LoC pact was signed.

Pakistan Prime Minister Shaukat Aziz told journalists on the sidelines of (SCO) conference. "We have as of last night opened relief centre on various proposed points of movements across (LoC) Line of Control. Thus aid will be going in both directions, not one way traffic". Mindsets cannot be changed overnight.

The army had played an enduring role to restore normalcy in the far flung areas. (November 4, 2005, The New Indian Express) The army role in helping out the victims of the October 8 earthquake has been thanks giving. Many people especially the Defense Minister and the well meaning Americans have warned against being 'romantic' for Pakistan would raise objections. The feature quoted that there were objections when they started building three relief centres on this side of LoC.

The Indo-Pak script has always been placed by the New Delhi - Srinagar script.

The factors in the Hindu referred the calamity on Kashmir to be "Wound on a wounded body".

The decision of the Indian and Pakistan government to open the points along the LoC is belated, but welcome. (November 15, 2005, The Hindu).

The people in "United States and Britain have started asking whether the disaster will help? The help here indicated sink their differences to make an end to the Kashmiri question.

India offered Pakistan helicopters, but Pakistan refused it to be flown along the LoC with Indian pilots. This tested for quite some time and the quake victims went right dying.

The recent murder of moderate politician and Delhi blasts goes to prove that India - Pakistan peace will come to stand still, unless they are given sanctuaries in the neighbourhood nation. Though many anticipated - world over, a change after quake diplomacy there is hardly any change except the exchanges on the different points.

The arrangement were made by the Pakistan's foreign office to send people shattered by the earthquake in PoK to meet relatives in India, it had taken 16 days to finalize the first list after the agreement was reached in India. This laid back approach typics the state government and the military to the aftermath of the quake.

The Pakistani establishment and the military had not taken many forays in rehabilitating the quake hit victims. Instead embarked on other developments take the acquiring of F-105 from United States, an early warning system moving six SAAB at the cost of billion dollars from Sweden particularly at a juncture when Pakistan is urging the international community to chip in more funds for the massive construction work.

There was no consensus over holding customary all party meeting to take stock of the impact of the earthquake. (November 16, 2005, The Hindu) Musharaff instead of calling the opposition has given the taste of relief and reconstruction to the army and has been criticized.

The civilians have lost trust in the army as the army entered into different spheres of life leaving the barrack. The resurgence of militant outfits in the earthquake zone, has also alarmed the international community.

President Bush's Assistant Secretary of State Christina Rocca is leaving a business delegation to the earthquake hit areas for an assessment. Jamaat-Ul-Dawa, an affiliate of Lashar-e-Toiba opened a major field hospital weeks before an American wash Unit was up and running.

Pakistan president has been talking to the world leaders that the money was not enough and Pakistan needed more funds for relief and rehabilitation.

(November 23, 2005, TNIE) But the Indian leaders remained mum. Both Mrs. Sonia Gandhi and Mr. Singh who were careful not to step into others shoes, thus delaying actions in sensitive areas depriving speedy development works. The delay in announcing the change of guard in Jammu & Kashmir had further made the process dilatory.

It is at this moment that the leaders express their ingenuity to save the state from further deluge. The Prime Minister is shy of speaking beyond the brief and so does the Congress president who doesn't step into the domain of the Prime Minister.

Due to the dual power at the centre we see the spectacle of one waiting for another, be it an relief operations or the change of guard in Jammu & Kashmir. The administration is quiet on the change of winter capital from Srinagar to Jammu on Oct. 26, the arrangements for which commences on October 22. Uncertainty in the air in the change of guard had delayed the process further.

(x) Features Abhorring (UN) Resolutions and other Proposals Mooted

Dvring the period of study there two features in the Hindu abhorring the resolutions and other proposals mooted but the New Indian Express had no such features.

Prime Minister Manmohan Singh, according to an official spokesman asserted that Jammu and Kashmir already enjoyed autonomy under the Indian constitution and has an elected Government. There was clearly a lack of autonomy in the Pakistan occupied Kashmir and there has been no popular elections at all in Gilgit and Baltistan. Pakistan's latest claims are a reflection of President Pervez Musharaff's proactive approach to improve ties with India. This has been the case ever since of peace process gained momentum in January 2004 after the parleys between him and the Prime Minister Atal Bihari Vajpayee. On the sidelines of South Asian Association for Regional Co-operation summit in Islamabad. Days before the 2004 summit General Musharaf indicated that his country was ready to set aside the United Nations resolution. (December 9, 2005, The Hindu) It was no ordinary offer considering the whole edifice of Pakistan's case on Kashmir rested on the United Nations resolution. His concept of division Jammu and Kashmir during the 2004 Ramzan did not win the approval of the Kashmiris. There is an absence of clear direction from Pakistan. Pakistani establishment does not appear to have done sufficient homework on the proposals. All the proposals emanate from one individual. The result is the top and other layers of the establishment do not concur.

Take for example the proposal on self-governance where the Pakistan foreign office spokesperson had a tough time fielding questions from the media whether it meant Pakistan occupied Kashmir is being governed from Islamabad.

The Pakistani establishment and large sections of the media have highlighted demilitarization and self-governance towards resolving the disputes with India over Jammu and Kashmir. Prime Minister Shaukat Aziz spoke on November 20th about the proposals to Minister of State for External Affairs Ahmed. The next day it was the main story in most of the Pakistani press. The categorical assertions by the external affairs ministry spokesperson in New Delhi, the following day that no such proposals were made has done little to dampen the enthusiasm of Pakistan's foreign office or media in debating their merits.

The demilitarization proposal also suffered a setback owing to the heightened Indian concerns after the serial Delhi blasts. He has been fighting shy of addressing or appealing to the militant outfits. To the (SAFMA) parliamentarians conference General Musharaf himself acknowledged the linkage between demilitarization and militancy and the need to tackle both issues together. Pakistan has gone public with new proposals for the resolution of the dispute over Kashmir even as negotiations were going on with India.

Mehbooba (PDP) People Democratic Party at the November 16 meeting in New Delhi threw her support behind the pre - restoration of the 1953 states in Jammu & Kashmir, which would give the state near complete auntonomy other than in matters concerning, defence, communications and external affairs. (December 15, 2005, The Hindu) The restoration of the pre-1953 status would render inapplicable the section of the constitution of India on fundamental rights and remove the supervisory authority of the Election Commission of India.

Ms. Mehbooba support for autonomy constituted a stunning ideological volte-face. The National Conference during its term in office from 1997 to 2002 had set up an official committee that made detailed proposals for autonomy legislation. But the successive central governments have rejected North East demands for dialogue on these proposals. The sharp departure from the traditional People Democratic Party position - a rejection of the autonomy idea and support instead, for three way dialogue among India, Pakistan and representative of Jammu & Kashmir came in the course of a conference addressed by Mehbooba, organized by a newspaper group and the common platform shared by Omar Abdullah, Mirwaiz. Such initiatives were taken to establish to position People Democratic Party as ethnic Kashmiri entity to defend the dominance of regional elites.

(y) Features on Political Development

During the period of study there are six features in the New Indian Express and two in The Hindu.

The meet of Prime Minister Dr. Manmohan Singh and President Musharaff in New York would hasten the process of reworking the core strategies on Kashmir. The representation of Hurriyat leaders to Islamabad was part of well though out design or one of the many thought through moves that did not work. The decision to discuss matters on Kashmir policy lies with the (PM) Prime Minister and (PMOS) Prime Minister Office, but if authority and clout lies with the members of Home Ministry one can expect coherence and imagination in handling situation but ideal conditions do not prevail. The result is that Kashmir has fallen between two stools. (August 3, 2005, The Hindu) There is no gainsaying the fact that the National Democratic Alliance government was in power, the All India Congress Committee had constituted the Jammu and Kashmir committee.

Besides Dr. Singh, there were other senior Congress Committee members and the office fell into complete disuse once the United Progressive alliance assumed office. In October 2002, understanding between the People Democratic Party and the Congress, the Mufti to be (CM) Chief Minister for the first three years and thereafter a congress nominee would head the coalition government.

Mr. Azad does have the stature who can take over the reins in Sri Nagar. Though Mr. Azad hailed from Jammu & Kashmir has no base in Jammu.

The features in The Hindu have on to say that Mufti's continuation in the office as Chief Minister and the non-replacement Gen. Sinha did complicate matters for the elected government. The question of accommodating Kashmiri sub-nationalism within the constitutional and philosophical framework of the larger Indian nation state can be alarming. The Mufti once the Home Minister of India has long standing as the voice of Kashmiri sub nationalism need not replaced but a hand picked Chief Minister will not the refrain from media.

But the feature in The New Indian Express discussed how Kashmiri sub-nationalism can be materialized to keep the fulcrum of polity at work.

They must use their faculties to persuade the pandits to return home, snub Pakistani intervention in the affairs of the state, distinguish the Kashmiri struggle for identity and autonomy from suicidal jihad, language of growth and reform in the economic sector, reparations, and justice in the political arena, and with intelligence and decisiveness without dithering in a fog of outdated slogans and entranced positions. (August 4, 2005, The New Indian Express).

The New Indian Express feature also argued for a Naya Kashmir with young generation of leaders who is of in the age of 20-40 in the driver's seat inheriting much of the legacies from their forefathers. The roles they have to play in a dilapidated economy, publicly fractured, strife torn state to one of prosperity and peace lies in the hands of these young politicians who wield power.

The Srinagar - Muzaffarabad, bus service and the outlay from the government in swinging a hefty Rs. 24,000 crore package and the pro-active role played by Mehbooba, whenever crisis broke out helped him.

There were other perceived incongruities in the change of leadership and places of their origin. (September 27, 2005, The New Indian Express) Azad hails from Jammu but the candidate for Chief Minister post has always been in the valley.

The Congress may act as proxy by New Delhi and this may upset the delicate balance of power in New Delhi. The people in the valley no more believe that it is an extension of the central rule.

As the opinion that governs Kashmir is greater normalcy, fewer incidents of violence, one million tourists and the youth are looking beyond orchards, to fields like (IT) Information Technology the Hurriyat is talking of dialogue, not about referendums and United Nations resolution. Sonia Gandhi's decisions entails not just choosing between two leaders but may well influence the future trajectory of the state and the peace process currently underway.

The features in The New Indian Express discussed elaborately on the pros and cons of change of guard in Srinagar. Anti incumbency factor had not set in and Mufti was preferred to be the tall leader in the crowd. A Congress Chief Minister would be synonymous with the centre. Mufti played a pivotal role in bringing about normalcy in the state by preparing ground for talks with the Hurriyat, even when Congress was wary of the protest that may result with the opening of the Srinagar - Muzaffarabad bus service, one million tourists visited the country, the situation in Jammu & Kashmir started to deteriorate in the situation when the Congress imposed its own men in Srinagar, which converted an anti-centre sentiment into anti-India movement for succession. Mufti at the head of the regional party, is not seen as a Chief Minister planted by Delhi. The congress has constraints being a national party and cannot do or say things that the state outfit can do, catering to regional aspirations.

The New Indian Express feature stressed that the talks in the valley are in favour of Mufti government though after three years tenure the onus is on the Congress nominee. Azad as per the decision taken by the coalitional government after assuming office. But the present scenario called for a wider debate on this issue as the most in the valley has undergone a change in 2002 after the elections. Earlier the situation started to deteriorate in the mid eighties when the Congress imposed its own rule.

The people have begun to feel that they are of more an extension of the Delhi rule. (October 3, 2005, The New Indian Express) A leader from Jammu to head the state will create the problem as it will divide the state on religious state. Mufti has emerged as the tallest leader among the mass but the change of guard should being about a larger peace processes with Hurriyat and Pakistan.

Manmohan Singh attitude that Pakistan take additional steps to curb cross border terrorism but instead Musharaff focussed as India moving forward on Kashmir. (October 4, 2005, The New Indian Express) Since then all sides have had the opportunity to review the state of the triangular relationship.

Musharaff who had raised the Kashmir issue at the United Nations hours before the meet with Manmohan Singh has made the Indians counter part more irate and specifying the reduction of troop maintainence at Kupwara and Baramulla has added more feed to fire, thereby the New York Man Mohan Singh talks unproductive. Besides cracking down on terrorists Musharaff has made very serious inroad in tackling terrorism as they are getting at Musharaff himself.

The United States feels that it must crackdown on Kashmir terrorist as they have global links. Unlike in 2001, when Musharaff did take some cosmetic steps against the sources of terrorism in Pakistan, Washington believed that he is more reasons this time.

The Congress party's coalitional arrangement are under strain in most of the states. (October 24, 2005, The New Indian Express) The only state where the Congress has preferred well and enhanced the credibility of the party is Jammu & Kashmir. All Jammu & Kashmir Chief Minister used to be derided by the Delhi's as puppets and stooges of the government. The coming together of the Congress PDP for the first time in the state the Pakistan establishment had to acknowledge the legitimacy of the elected government Mufti's government was not only offered a healing touch to winning estranged Kashmiri Muslims but this included reducing corruption, prevailing a responsive government fostering a process of dialogue across political divides, revitalizing the economy of the valley, 50,000 jobs through merit, recruitment in the police, school teachers and engineer, ten lakh tourists mostly Hindus from various parts of Jammu & Kashmir and many more developments.

The hartals have come down drastically where people no more agitate against human rights abuses by security forces, and the callous attitude of the government against people's grievances.

The voters participation in various election has gone up steadily. Mufti acts as a credible champion of Kashmiri rights without being anti India, and a non confrontational approach towards the centre. This is a winning combination for India.

A section of the Congress feels deeply perturbed and unhappy at PDP's growing creditability. The Congress believed that they would playing second fiddle to PDP, as they are forced to do in Bihar vis-a-vis the RJD. Although state Congress men use every opportunity to humiliate him, Mufti dextrously deflects attention by emphasizing in all his public meetings the valuable support he has received from Prime Minister and the United Progressive Alliance chairperson, as well as Atal Bihari Vajpayee and L.K. Advani when they headed National Democratic Alliance government. Mufti acts as a credible champion of Kashmiri rights without being anti-India and a non-confrontational approach towards the centre. This is a winning combination for India.

Congress should remember that Kashmiris turned against India because they were denied the opportunities of self-governance by puppet chief ministers appointed by the centre. Without the assent from the party supreme, the Congress leaders believe that their position is not safe and the decision are taken by Sonia Gandhi.

The former research and analysis wing (RAW) chief, A.S. Dulat, for example, argued that the national interest demanded the Mr. Sayeed be giver another three years in office - or for national conference leader Omar Abdullah to be installed in his steed.

The Hindu on (October 31, 2005) has argued out how credible is this position? A close study of the results of the 2002 elections in the province of Kashmir offers semi interesting insights. Although the People Democratic Party won 16 seats in the valley, and the National Conference won just two more seats than the People Democratic Party, making it the largest singular political party in the state. The Congress for its part only 15% of the seats.

As important, the election results showed strong region fractures within the Kashmir province. Much of the People Democratic Party support came from the central Kashmir district of Badgam and southern district of Palwama and Anantanag. The National Conference demonstrated the highest levels of support in the northern district of Kupwara and Baramulla. Congress politicians did well in areas with the presence of ethnic minorities the 2002 elections demonstrated that not a single voice represented the region.

Jammu and Kashmiris accession to India union skewed democratic practices in the state. Leaders from Sheikh Mohammed Abdullah to Bakshi Ghulam Mohammed and Syed Mir Quasim were brought to power or removed from power not-because of democratic legitimacy but in other words they were seen as instruments to contain secession. It was kind of sub-contractor J & K to rule the state from Delhi. This policy was adopted by Nehru after 1947-48 war. Pakistan backed sub-conventional warfare skewed the political discourse on the state. For Mr. Dulat to argue for a CM to be installed by New Delhi rather than elected representatives, illustrated profound contempt for democracy in Jammu & Kashmir. The smooth transition of Chief Minister designate Azad has to meet this challenges. The core areas identified where he has tough decision to make the choice between being tough (Hurriyat) and soft line (BJP).

Out of 250 Newspapers:
The percentage of 0 features in The Hindu = 49.28%
The percentage of 0 features in The New Indian Express = 50.72%
The percentage of 1 features in The Hindu =83.33 %
The percentage of 1 features in The New Indian Express = 16.67%
The percentage of 2 features in The Hindu = 0%
The percentage of 2 features in The New Indian Express = 100%

Table 7.1 : Frequency Distribution of Features

Features	*The Hindu*			*The New Indian Express*		
	Count	*Col%*	*Row%*	*Count*	*Col %*	*Row %*
0	240	96.00	49.28	247	98.80	50.72
1	10	4.00	83.33	2	0.80	16.67
2				1	0.40	100.0
Total	250	100.0	50.00	250	100.0	50.00

N.H: There is no association between features and types of newspapers
R.H: Theff; is association between features and types of newspapers
P value is =.04008.

P value is less than = .05

Null hypothesis is rejected at 5% level of significant

Hence there is association between features and types of newspapers

Table 7.2 : Features by Paper Type of Newspaper

Features	*The Hindu*	*TNIE*	*Chisquare*	*P Value*
0	240	247		
	49.3	50.7		
1	10	2		
	83.3	16.7	6.43395	0.04008
2		1		
		100.0		
	250	250		

T value = 1 .52

P value = 0.129

The p value 0.129 is less than 0.05%. Hence the null hypothesis is rejected at 5% level. There is significant difference between the features in The New Indian Express and The Hindu.

Table 7.3 : T-Test for equality of Means

Variable	*Number of cases*	*Mean*	*SD*	*SE of Mean*	*T Value*	*P Value*
Feature						
The Hindu	250	0.460	0.196	0.012	1.52	1.29
The New Indian Express	250	0.0160	0.154	0.010		

8

Letters to The Editor

Coverage of Letter to The Editor

During the period of study there were mainly five stories in The Hindu and twenty four stories in The New Indian Express.

The readers Hindu appraisal of the situation after the militants attacked the tourist reception centre in Srinagar on April 6:

1. The India - Pakistan peace process has isolated the militants
2. The bus journey provided oxygen to the dying patient.
3. PoK PM sardar sikander Hayat Khan remark that the gun has failed in a unction organized to honour the first batch of passengers.

Though the readers appreciated the good expressed by both the countries, there were apprehensive of the final result of the resolution they also expressed the desire not to abndon caution inspite all the positive moves. (April 7, 2005,The New Indian Express)

Letter in The New Indian Express, The Jihadi mindset of Jinnah is with instances wherein Jinnah's direct action day pogroms against Hindus in Calcutta, Naokali, Sikh, Hindus reveal that sJinnah was demagogue. (June 25, 2005,The New Indian Express)

The reader remained that Ambekahar evaluation of Jinnah's politics, thoughts on Pakistan, Ambedkhar called Jinnah's type of politics and politics of goodaism.

The letters in The New Indian Express are grateful advani's for resurecting Jinnah recalled the historical blunders of Nehru, the two nation theory etc.

The letters in The New Indian Express have applauded the electronic media showcase the face value scenario the prime media take stock of the situation especially The Hindu for the respect of facts on the ground. (April 15,2005)

The letters in The New Indian Express appreciate the India - Pakistan cricket services two countries in the south Asian region, converting LoC into soft border avoid training of militants on the pakistan's soil, etc. The letters in the Hindu were apprehsive of the several tunnels and bridges enroute the proposed Jammu - Udampur rail line, but The New Indian Express has praised the interest taken by the central government for free toward and national integration.

There were plenty of letters in the Hindu praising the service rendered by the both the governments and also condemned the acts of terrorist. The bus service was a fervour on the PoK but no attempts were made by the militants to sabtoge the process speaks of the insidious game of the militants.

The letter of The Hindu has cited an instance wherein the spokesperson of for the Al-Mansoor outfit that the purpose behind the attacks was to expose the security lapse in the valley that the terrorists too give too many cues before they resort for any attack.

The letter emphaised the invite given to HC leaders to tranvel beyond pok, indicated that such moves may usher more strength and disavowed the government's call of backtracking from the issue. During the visit of president Musharaff to India, the readers of the Hindu compared the coming together of both nations like the pot boilers of the Hollywood in which bitter enemies become friends at the end and the rest love happily after. India and Pakistan are conjoined twins and they can never be separated. The letter also opined that crores of rupees remain dead locked in security matters foreign policy needs mature thinking.

The letters of The New Indian Express have give a few suggestions during the visit of President Musharaff to India,

1. The focus to introduce peace studies in the school curriculum.
2. Exchange programmes among the student community.
3. E-pals in schools to share their country's social, cultural, religion, political issues.

4. Leading newspapers in India and Pakistan can play a great role in furthering friendship between India and Pakistan.

The letter very much applauded the move taken Dr. Singh in demilitarizing part of Kashmir. But his cautious note is also appended of such promising step is not a stragegic compromise and does not give any undue advantage to the militant outfits. Dr. Singh is extolled as leader par excellence, for he has shunned the jingoism and rhectoric that characterized India - Pakistan in the past. There was satirical comment from one of the readers regarding the much debated autonomy which the reader feels can be extended to this vast sub - continent which can have autonomous state with strong binding of common history and heritage.

The Hindu coverage of the Hurriyat claim has not won the approval of the mass for they fear and suspect the demand of the Hurriyat for Kashmir being integral part of India and Kashmiris need not be included in the dialogue process. The welcome givens to Hurriyat leaders is also seen with much suspect for the reader claims that after terrorisms, thesenon-elected representatives are the next foe that Pakistan may use as trumph card to smite the Indian establishment, (June 4, 2005,The Hindu) The letter circumspect the Hurriyat's claim and the welcome extended to the Hurriyat. The readers don't deny calling the utterances of Advanji and the demotion of the Babri Masjid a blatant lie as soon as he expressed that the saddest day in his life.

Advani's visit, the steady increasing people-to-people contact, softening of the Kashmir problem, reduction of armed forces across along the border, and the willingness of those across the border to adopt fresh moves towards peace and reconciliation. The letter vehemently seek for the acceptance of LoC as IB. for practical reasons. They are also hopeful that people on both sides have become increasingly loyal to their countries. The readers were very much apprehensive of Mr. Advani's respectful homage to Jinnah for he was instrumental in partitioning the country. How could Mr. Advani, himself a refugee from Pakistan, forget the Mayhem of those days.

Jinnah was essentially an irreligious individual with a penchant for western life style, and it was his thirst for power more than his championship of the muslim cause that made him speak in favour of partition. (June 7, 2005,The Hindu)

Mr. Advani's recognition of Jinnah as a secularists portends a positive sign for bilateral relations. Jinnah's utterances between 1945 and 1947 hardly betrayed his faith in secularism. (June 7, 2005, The Hindu) He branded Nehru a peter pan and an arrogant Brahmin, and he called Gandhi a 'cunning Hindu fox' the rate at which Mr. Advani is changing his stand, it will not surprise if he unveils a statue of Jinnah in Admedabad. History is testimony to the fact that the muslim league fought tooth and nails to frustrate congress efforts for united India and freedom. As the chief architect of the two nation theory Jinnah was responsible for the loss of millions of lives of both Hindus and Muslims living on either side of the border.

There were rave reviews from the readers regarding to the visit of Mr. Advani to Pakistan.

Mr. Advani's decription of Mohammed Ali Jinnah as a secular leader and his regret over the Babri Masjid demolition should not be misunderstood as political camonflage or stunt. Jinnah alone was not instrumental in partioning the country. The congress and the right wing are to blame. (June 9, 2005, The Hindu)

How can lasting peace be achieved if Indians do not tolerate one of the political leaders saying something good about Jinnah to his hosts. Jinnah could well be held responsible for his premature and catastrophric call for Direct Action which resulted in a colossal human tragedy but the fact remains that even if the league had softened its stand on partition, the congress would not have been very comfortable in an undivided India with a national assembly consisting of a substantially huge segment of Muslim legislators from the cast and west. (June 9, 2005, The Hindu)

Advani resignation drama in the wake of his visit to Pakistan and utterances on Jinnah has catepulated him but as an hardliner or hawk but instead hailed as a wiseman from the readers.

The letters blamed the Indian government of driving Jinnah to the wall Mahatma suggestion of making Jinnah the PM of India fell on deaf ears. None can deny that the Jinnah represented hard core muslims. (June 10, 2005, The Hindu)

Jinnah refused to join the Mislim league in 1905 when it was founded. He was strongly against Khilfat movement, If Indians want Gandhi to be respected by others, they should treat leaders of other countries with respect. Let Advani's praise for Jinnah signal a new chapter in India - Pakistan relations. (June 10, 2005, The Hindu)

Both India and Pakistan must strive to make Siachen a symbol of peace. Demilitarising the Siachen glacier will put an end to problems our jawans face manning The post under in hospitable conditions.

So many decades have passed since partition was effected and it is time people of the two countries forget the past and got adjusted to realtity.

The letter leaves a pragnent note that though the army has claimed that it has identified the Hizb-ul-Mijahideen as responsible for the blast by intercepting the outfit communations, the army should have committed before it was too late.

The letter abhors the people whose secular credentials are doubtful have put themselves in the position to certify the secular character of others. The New Indian Express as people know very little about Jinnah, he needs a through assessment. During one of the congress session, probably at Nagpur, it sums that due to some differences of opinion, Jinnah walled out of the meeting. Those was considered to be the turning point of souring relationships. The letter showers praise on Jinnah as India still holds people like Modi, and orgnisations like RSS, VHP and Bajnang Dal in India. (June 16, 2005, The New Indian Express)

Mr. Advani utterances on Jinnah and his expression of regret over the Babri Masjid demolition are well though out plan to give a new avatar to his Hindusvata image.

Even smallanecdote were elaborated in different columns like a spoonful of honey smeared by the satan brought two countries into war made interesting reading of how leaders behaved immaturely to project themselves to be above blunders. (June 17, 2005, The Hindu)

The culture of Hindusim and Indians was indicated using a brief note on how Ram himself offered to perform the last rites of ravana when his brother Urbeeshna hesitated. Cultural ethos was speculated to keep the unrest at bay. (June 17, 2005, The Hindu)

The letter Dr. Manmohan Singh by Mr. Vajpayee has created a lot of flutter among sangh parivar and even the public who feed cynical of the activities carried out by Mr. Vajpayee. The whole nuclers has been carried out to pacify the sangh parivar and they denigrate the attitude of the Vajpayee as he seems to condemn the good will gesture by its own president vouched on the Pakistani soil. (June 18, 2005, The Hindu)

The letter condemn the double speak of attitude of the BJP leaders for the issue though leaves a striking note as a discardant note as 'Kashmir centric' it is because the kashmiris are getting frustrated at being side lined. The demand for trilateral talks those who do not have faith in Indian constitution should have no say in the discussions leading to a settlement of the Kashmir dispute. (June 18, 2005, The Hindu)

By inviting the Hurriyat to travelto any part of Pakistan and allowing them to travel beyond Musaffarabad, both Islamabad and New Delhi have compromised the understanding reached while opening the srinagar - musaffarabad bus service. The elected representatives should be called for any discussion and not the Hurriyat. (June 18, 2005, The Hindu)

The New Indian Express (June 18, 2005) Pakistani's information minister Rasheed who gave shelter to Jehadis and "India poses a potent threat" are indicators of how Pakistan still perceives India in the midst of CBMS. Malik's relevation is an eye opener to Indian establishment that Pakistan president who swears by the peace process, has no qualns in having Rasheed occupy a coretons post and a grim reminder to his faltering commitment.

The letter bemoaned that instead of harping on the past, we should learn a lesson or two from Israel that does not mind dealing with Germany and Japan that enjoys good ties with the US even after the Hiroshima, Nagasaki bombings. (June 22, 2005, The Hindu) Jinnah is condemned to be a irreligious person and died with the idea of Pakistan extract maximum concessions for Muslims from the congress. The New Indian Express, (June 22, 2005) one of its letter has unfailingly adores Jinnah and bestows three cheers to Advani. The readers that the UPA government has not registered a formal protest over the breach. Only when Mr. Vajpayee wrote it to Mr. Singh, he made his stand very clear. (June 24, 2005, The Hindu) The third party in the bilateral talks being ignored can take a new U turn stating the people who have taken interest in the people cannot be completely ignored and BJP is making tall claims in opposition.

The Hindu (June 27, 2005) The letter comply with the decision of the Indian government in denying a visa to the Pakistan. Information minister Rasheed after the relevation of Yasin Malik goes to tell the world that if Narndra Modi is denied Visa by the US government in the walk of Gurajrat carnage, India at this juncture has shown enough prudence and rejection of Rasheed's application as a relief there were others who termed Rashed's speech as 'Rhectoric' and wish that he be permitted to travel legally and morally. The New Indian Express (June 27, 2005) gives a better reply to the skewed problem of Hurriyat recent visit to Pakistan.

The Hurriyat visit to Pakistan with or without passport is insiginificant because they used to meet Pakistan dignitaries. The reader is forced to comment that lettering Pakistan renege on its commitment lacks.credence. (June 27, 2005, The New Indian Express).

The Hindu. Therewere extremely differing views regarding the rejection of the application field by the Pakistan information minister Rasheed. The claims of Malik unfounded as he confessed that the media has distorted his own view. The reader bemoans such calms rejection may destroy the camenadric established among nation. (June 27, 2005, The Hindu) Such rejections are admissible to some, but to others feel it is knave to take a decision with specious statements dished out by media.

The Hurriyat leaders travel to PoK and Pakistan is seen with much disdain by readers for they may takes sides at opportune mement and can be misleading . (The New Indian Express, June 25, 2005).

The letter of the Hindu coverage (July 7, 2005) have given a good account of the security forces who saved themselves during the encounter and the innocent pilgrims unhurt. The misadventure was obviously to destroy peace in the sub-continent. The grand design was threatened by the apt hadling of the situation. The letters of The New Indian Express of the heinous crime perpenetrated at the Ayodya complex reveals how terrorists become a stumbling block in the on going crises and peace process. (July7, 2005)

The alarming increase in the dangerous trend to establish state sponsored terrorism beyond J & K will cast a dark shadow on India - Pakistan détente. The fears instilled proves beyond doubt the high handness of the terrorists to target any area in the Sub-continent must be abhorred at all levels. (July 8, 2005, The Hindu).

The moderate faction of the Hurriyat conference in Kashmir condemned the attack is a welcome sign of Muslims in general by one by the The New Indian Express (July 8,2005)that public is not asleep over the good will gestures extended by various leaders is commendable. The new Indian Express, the letter admonitions Indian government to take merciless action to stop terrorism as it is not correct to say that terrorism has come down.

The letter fear that the existence of terrorist camps in Pakistan and the reports are true, won't the terrorists disguised as genuine travelers enter into India. Will they fan out to different parts of the country, are the concerns of the common men. "Ties with US" When Pakistan decision to step up its joint ventures on defence production with China, Ukraine and Turkey. (July 14, 2005, The New Indian Express) Non alignment of 1950 has to be set aside and not so - friendly neighbours around us, a defence understanding with a power ful country is must. There are other inquisite questions from the readers like "where we could not wrest PoK in spite of three wars, how can we form "Akand Bharat"? suspend all peace talks is the vehement stance taken by the reader with relevation of terrorist camps on Pakistan soil. (July 14, 2005, The New Indian Express) Pakistan is bestowing financial and moral succour to militant outfits to retaliate against India for the Kargil fiasco and there other wars. (July 19, 2005, The New Indian Express) In the appreciate reality coverage in life Hindu makes a sensible reading. The shooting down of Jan charles de memezes by London metro politan police and the three children in a Kashmir village on par. "The men in olive green are also human beings and they canerr is justified through the letter. (July 27, 2005, The New Indian Express) There are other letters which counter balances the above by stating that memezes cannot be compared with what happened in Kashmir. Unless a person has lived in high attitude, it difficult to understand the harsh climatic conditions where it becomes ultimately difficult to distinguish between even men and women. The readers still extend their sympathy through the incidents cannot be justified.

The privileges endowed to the J & K state by the government with central assistance is much more when compared to other states. While all other states get central assistance in the ratio of 70% loan and 30% grant, J & K gets 90% grant and 10% has been waived. Greater autonomy for Kashmir which is stated to be present in article 370 of the Indian constitution.

The Hindu coverage of geelani acquittal makes many readers to oppose the move of the court . For not having provided a clean chit to S.A.R. Geelani and warrants capital punishment it is not utopian. (Aug 6, 2005, The Hindu)

The high body says Mr. Geelani role is not above suspicious, remember he has only been given the benefit of doubt. The verdict was not an obiter Dicta as it referred to his untruthful pleas about his contacts with the guilty. The editorial welcomed the Supreme court modifying the High court, emphasis on the letter vis - a - vis Mr. Geelani seemed misplaced.

The courts promulgation is observed with suspicious for it more or less vindintive and not vendicative wide publicity is given to Sarajit case, the reader feels why they have not taken up the cases of Indian convicted in Pakistani jails? (Aug 29, 2005 The Hindu) Or it ia matter dictated by the media or decided by the political climate. Indians are jailed in Pakistani jails for year. Whether any help was rendered to him and his family members since the beginning of the case is not clear.

Sarabjit case was highlighted by the media and people showered encomiums that the media are responsible for walking up the establishment.

54 armymen who were missing after the 1971 war, many more Sarabjit's languishing in Pakistani jails, the fate of these defence personnel should be ascertained. (Aug. 31, 2005, The Hindu)

There were laments on the number of ISI agents killed - without even establishing their identity through legal process, let alone granting consular access. The number of alleged ISI agents llanguishing in Indian jails is anybody's guess. The release of prisioners languishing in the jails of the two countries is the most humane of all CBMs. The two countries can show greater anxiety by re-defining the modalities. And release prisoners charged with trivial offences such as crossing the territorial frontiers and overstaying on visa. In the Sarabjit Singh issue the government would be cautious. It should not do anything that may amount to interfeference or Pakistani judicial system. (Sep 1, 2005, The Hindu)

Mehbooba's plea that mohammed Afsal a Kashmiri sentenced to death for his involvement in the parliament attack should be pardoned if Pakistan grants sarabjit singh clemency. (Sep 1, 2005, The Hindu) The enormity of the crime committed by Afzal is inexcusable and his sentence cannot be equated with that of Sarabjit Arundati roys candid remarks on the withdrawal of army from Kashmir and her observation that Indian media are suffering from schizophrenia is uncharitable. The readers claim that outspoken journalists and photographers have died reporting news from the valley. They have advised her to stay in Kashmir to see the challenges faced by common - men and the army. Ms. Roy can no more admonition the army - but continue to do her interesting job of writing fiction is the mainstay of many readers, and day to day confrontation with the mayhem in J & K. (Sep 2, 2005, The Hindu) India occupation of Kashmir is unacceptable, India is defender and not an aggressor. She should stop making irresponsible statemention on real life issues.

Making idealistic statements on what ought to be is not the same as having Ak - 47s and grenade explode on our faces.

What is worse is her comparision of the 'Indian Occupation' atrocities with Pinochet regime in Chile. Our soldiers certainly deserve better. Ms. Roy seems to revel in playing to her gallery of fellow activists. (Sep 2, 2005, The Hindu) The controversial statement made by Arundoth distortion on real life issues received much flak from the common men.

Her statements paints an ugly picture of India and its army abroad particularly in the west, which has been keen on faulting our human rights record in Kashmir Ms. Roy has stated Indians have no right to talk about Iraq and Palestine unless they highlight the atrocities in valley. (Sep 5, 2005, The Hindu) It is amusing to hear intellectuals telling us what are the conditions under which we should take, what we should critise and what should be the order criticism. Roy trivializing the issue covered by media on the issue of army. The oft repeated exercise for the PM to invite the APHC leaders for talks has become ritual. This is because many leaders of the hardline factions in the Hurriyat do Pakistan's bidding. (Sep 7, 2005, The Hindu)

The letter plea of asking PM Manmohan Singh to prevail upon Pakistan president Pervez Musharaff to Sarabjeet Singh's life when they meet. A witness has said on television that the prosecution forced him to identity Sarabjit. His family has also said his is a case of mistaken identity.

There were more or less similar claims from other readers who plead his case in several other ways. Had Sarabjit been ISI agent lodged in the Indian prisons and indicted for so many bombardments in the city; would citizens and the media accept the plea by some sections of Pakistanis (after 15 years) that he is a victim of mistaken identity? The only thing that can save him is a elemency appeal on the ground that he had spent 15 years in jail, equivalent to life imprisonment. (Sep 15, 2005, The Hindu) The reader becomes the death of political parties after losing power especially after RSS persuaded to step down as the party chief for his reference on Jinnah being secular on the Pakistani soil. There were other claims condemning such act as battle of waterloo, especially Jinnah's speech shrugged off his hardcore RSS ideologic image. The US reduction of troops in Baramula and Kupwara areas is drewed with suspension even by the hreadrs as these are the polical are insiders strategy to identity terror activities. More over, America is viewed as an interloper. (Sep 17, 2005, The Hindu)

Even Indira Gandhi's stress on peace was quoted to the letter to the editor of (The New Indian Express Sep 20, 2005) We need movements and arrangements which will mobilise a collective will for peace of the entire people of the world and to consolidate, harness and put it to purpose. India believes in tolerance, not bigotry, in acceptance, not rejection, in affirmation, participation and involvement, not negation, withdrawal and self - imposed isolation. It should must be difficult, therefore, for us to work logically in worthy cause.

In the LNG gas deal, there were very letters in The Hindu which abhorred inletter and spirit the voting against Iran which may thwart the fate of the ambitious India - Pakistan - Iran gas pipeline project and the consternation in carrying out an independent foreign policy.

The letters of The Hindu appraisal of the LNG deal and Tehran and Tehran wriggling out of all compulsions not to rescind the LNG deal despite voting against it at the IAEA meeting is the sine non quo of its success in the world fora. The cartoon depicting the success, also won aplandit from the government. (Sep 29, 2005, The Hindu) Iran prevailing on Pakistan before the UN over the resolution in Kashmir and wreak the bullying by U.S. have been identified by the reactor. (Sep 30, 2005, The Hindu) India's voting in favour of

IAEA resolution on Iran's controversial nuclear programme has also been criticized by them. The leftists do not take a view on the basis of merits of the issue on hand, but on the basis of the person involved. India cannot afford to have a nuclear power in the near vicinity. Iran is known to be champion of Islamic extremism and so there is real chance that Iran's nuclear arsenal may fall in the hands of Islamic terrorists. So, India has finally done the correct thing by voting in favour of the resolution. The remedies under the gamut of nature's fury found several opinions.

1. The united nations can ensure an effective mechanism to warn on the impending disaster.
2. Government plans to join the global seismic network. (Oct 11, 2005, The Hindu)
3. Developed nations should help countries such as India set-up quake prediction mechanisms.
4. Indian government as well as common people to contribute liberally.
5. India should rush earth - moving equipment to its neighbour.
6. The relief package of Rs.100 crore should reach the real victims.
7. Indian government a generous package for Pakistan.

Letter in The Hindu have expressed concern over the relief material that did not reach PoK, Pakistan, Kashmir in time anywhere else in the world the supply is faster. India and Pakistan should forget LoC for the year, the time had come for mankind to realize the fatility of spending huge amounts of money on preparing for war, the noor effect saw Indians contributing generously for treatment of Pakistani children, it should help the military establishments to realize in Pakistan realize the fulility of running terrorist camps and waging proxy wars, (Oct 15, 2005, The Hindu) Indian troops responded to a plea far assistance by Pakistani soldiers by lending them implements, armed forces rose to the occasion and did an excellent job despite the inclement weather and death of their colleagues makes a suggestive, well keaded arguments to cope up with unprecendented natural calamity.

In the case of replacing Mufti, nothing should not alienate the people of the valley which is bound to happen if Mufti stepped down came the verdict from the reader. (Oct 15, 2005,The Hindu)

The loss of life can be considerably reduced if seismological and meterological equipment are modernized to ensure advance warning.

Ashoka realized the facility of war only after the Kelanga war. The quake should act as an eye-opener for both nations. (Oct 17, 2005, The Hindu) The money that can be saved from hosting or attending iftaar parties can be donated to the PM's relief fund. The money that is spent for of activities during diwali can be send for relief and rehabilitation.

The continued killing even during the post quake entails, terrorism reared across the border for over two decades, cannot melt away in the sentiments , military with an iron hand 3. militancy rears its ugly head when there is forced lowering of guard by the security forces.

4. Promises of suspending operations of terrorists outfits such as LTTE and united Jihad council are more often than a mere eye wash, meant to lull authorities into letting down the guard. (Oct 20, 2005, The Hindu)
5. Such acts show how desperate the terrorists are to break the momentum of the good work being done by the army and elected government in the state.
6. The killing of innocent people and monsters is not the solution to the Kashmir issues.

Musharaff throws opens the different points on the LoC for relief and rehabilitations shows that Musharaff proposal is aimed at undoing the damage done by Pakistan's earlier refusal to accept joint relief operation. Assassination of lone demonstrates, Islamabad has not dismantled the terror infrastructure on its soil. India should concentrate on rehabilitating the earthquake victims than fritter away appeasing the unwilling Pakistan what are the sensitivities Gen. Musharaff keeps referring to the fear of exposing terrorists training camps. When several countries are jointly pooling and operating helicopters for rescue and relief operations. Why should India alone dealt with differently.

This will mark a view high in India - Pakistan relations. It is worth recalling the words of Donald Williams. "The thing that we share in our world are far more valuable than those which divide us. (Oct 11, 2006,The Hindu)

4. Pervez Musharaff offer to throw open the line of control to allow Kashmiris on both sides to take part in the reconstruction work of quake ravaged PoK, the mounting pressure both inside and outside Pakistan to accept the Indian offer help, president Musharaff's proposal and New Delhi response have kinled hope among the people. (Oct 21, 2005, The Hindu)

The question soft borders and the hiccup to make the borders irrelevant have been traced by many following the post - quake relief across the border. The general has already put impossible riders to accepting Indian help - helicopters but not pilots for instance.

General rejected New Delhi offer of joint relief operations. Had he agreed to the proposal, it would have made substantial difference.

The proposal implies safeting the fight against terrorism.

No major private corporation operated in the state and the few brave souls who invested there have been chased away by insurgents.

The dastardly killing of Ghulam Nabi work, at a time when thousands of Kashmiris are desperately coping up with the after math of the killer quake, is highly reprehensible.

The heinous act was perpentrated during Ramzan - shows the terrorist are not true believers of Islam. It is time the majority of Muslims unanimously rejected the so - called Jihadis as un-Islamic. (Oct 21, 2005,The Hindu)

Pakistan Presidents Pervez Musharaff appeal to make borders irrelevant will be a pipe dream without Pakistan working out modalities without wasting time and work towards breaking the man-made barrier the Pakistani establishment should set aside its prejudices and welcome Indian relief teams. Gen. Musharaff declaration that he would accept helicopters from the Indian side is amusing. The letters boldly state there is lot to conceal on the other side of the border, beyond the flimsy facade of sensitivities. India's offer of help to a nation that keeps discrediting is insulting to its people. Constant rejections and borders only be little the given and leave him unacknowledged. The people of PoK have been devastated by earthquake. And when help is only a few minutes away, their rulers turn it down, the united nations has called relief in PoK, the biggest logistical challenge. (Oct 22, 2005, The Hindu).

Jihadi terrorism is just another aspect of human behaviour that is driven by revenge, retaliation and violence. Peace and prosperity cannot prevail unless human nature and consciousness evolve to transcend barriers of religion, race, languages and territory.

The gruesome terrorist attack that killed minister Kashmir Ghulam Nabi lone is tantamount to attacking the people of the state who have reposed their faith in democracy.

Firstly militancy, for whatever cause has no human face and secondly it exposes the hollowness of the militants claim that they are fighting for people's cause. The killing of lone send the clear message that so called Jihadis are mercenries incited by hate and money. By gaining entry into high security area and achieving the mission of killing a minister, the terrorists have sent a clear message that earthquakes can shake only buildings and not their resolve.

The letter of 'The Hindu' on the opening the LoC may help people to come in contact with one another but at the same time India should ensure that it does not lower its guard because terrorist have proved post quake.

India should undertake relief operations for the PoK victims only if it is accepted unconditionally and gracefully.

In the change of guard in J & K, the readers had then own apprehension in installing a congress nominee. The stuation on the valley has improved when Mufti Mohammed Sayeed was the CM. Theloss may be greater if the states quo is changed. (Oct 26, 2005,The Hindu).

There was also hesitation founds in the congress leadership to assume leadership and a rebuitance to risk challenges in the state.

There were two diametrically divergent views on the change of guard in J & K. One to wanted to remove the impasse over the suspense and the delay in naming a Ghulam Nabi Azad as the next new CM and other view pertained to maintaining the status quo in J & K, keeping in mind the fragile peace process and the clout of PDP as a regional party.

Mr. Sayeed has earned the goodwill of the people in the three years he has been the CM, but for this credit should go to the congress too, This belongs to the first category of which congress has been under dispensation. (Oct 29, 2005,The Hindu) Now that congress is in the driver's seat it is the PDP turn to extend co-operation to ensure smooth functioning of the party.

Arm twisting by the congress MLAs who threatened to resign if the party did not stake claim to power seems to have desired result. It is the most inopportune time to demand the reins of power.

The right choice for the post of CM is often debatable, the congress had taken the right decisionin appointing Gulam Nabi Azad as the CM of J & K. But his leadership is fraught with risks for Mr. Azad govern the decade old insurgency, the additional responsibility of strengthening the peace process.

There were other leaders who implored on the change of CM midstream is neither orthodox coalitism politics nor does it make administrative sense. It is a concept the congress borrowed from the BJP at a time when its prospects at the national level were uncertain and it could not afford to lose an opportunity without a caveat. (Oct 31, 2005, The Hindu)

There has been over drive in the Indo- Pakistan peace process. The pre-notification of the missile test and the demilitarising of the siachen glacier have taken a new course. The retirement on India - Pakistan - Iran gas pipeline is effective CBM and will open up new vistas for regional co-operation. The Pakistan - Israel ties has come under flak by readers. For the anti-Israeli sentiment within Pakistan has been nurtured not only by mullabs but also by the state.

The current thaw in the relationship which Pakistan has initiated and hopes to sustain, is facade to thwart the growing Indo - Israeli ties - a relationship even the UPA government whole heartfully supports. (Oct 6, 2005, The Hindu)

The perpentrators of the heinous crime struck in Delhi turning the festive bazaars into morgues of innocent shoppers.

The PM Says he is shocked by the blasts. I do not understand why he is shocked. Does he not know that he is living in a country that is a source of world wide terrorism. General Musharaff wants to have demilitarised zone for looking after the quake victims and on the other hand, he has no hesitation in saying 'he is not in for reduced military spending. Is it not an open secret that Pakistanis defence spending is India centric. (Nov 3, 2005, The Hindu)

If adopting a soft policy is going to result in innocent civilians becoming soft targets, should we not start talking tough.

Reinforce the need for strong anti-terror laws.

The death penalty awarded to mohammed asif, the LeT terrorist in the Red Fort attack caseis laudable the thought of going to the gallows will at least send a chill down the spine of others.

When cold blooded murders are committed against humanity, there can be no alternative to captain punishment.

Given the healted debate surrounding death penalty, the opinion of the families of about 1000 victims of cold - blooded murder. (Nov 3, 2005, The Hindu)

If a majority of them is for capital punishment, its abolition will amount to rubbing salt on their wounds. All the talk today ismade of valley and Jammu and no talk on Ladakh. But Ladakh is totally cut off from the rest of the state as there is no communication between different quarters. The CM Is made to pay special attention to Ladakhis.

The death penalty given to Mohammed Asif is welcome, though the verdict comes after 5 years. But the accomplies who knew the crime are given rigourous imprisonment for seven years and life long imprisonment. The readers feel that those who have killed innocent people must be given equal verdict. The sympathsiers have to be weaned away and bring them back to mainstream. With plenty of hate philosophy, based on blatent lies and twisted history directed against the Hindus and India being target in Pakistan madrassas brain washing generations of Pakistanis to grow up India haters who are we dealing with in the so-called peace talks. (Nov 4, 2005, The Hindu)

Despite the enormity of the suffering of people of India and Pakistan, the two countries have not come close as expected. The future will bind bond us together to face not only terrorism but also natural calamities. (Nov 16, 2005, The Hindu)

The requisition to have five points on the LoC to remain opened for their will be continuous exchange of people across the borders. (Nov 16, 2005, The Hindu)

The readers of The Hindu, realities positively towards the Tsunami - affected people, we have been comperatively less concerned for the kashmiris. Kalpana Sharma's writing about children who survived the killer quake of October 8, 2005 is a window to the world of sufferings our children in modern times. The reader implores to extend a helping hand to the suffering million of children in this country.

The victims of the quake on both sides of the LoC just half a century ago belonged to the same country. The reader exhausts and that this is a golden opportunity for India to provide relief and won their hearts so that permanent peace can prevail in the whole of Kashmir.

The letter consider the liberalized visa regime as detrop as the denouncements of trial chief nawab akbar of the role of ISI in distributing weapons to Afhanistan, Iran and J & K goes to prove that Pakistan is the abetter of violence. The abolition of TADA and POTA, undue importance to Hurriyat, maintaining porus border with Bangladesh has helped the growth rate of terrorism. (Jan 13, 2005, The Hindu)

The letter felt that they were deprived of the cricket match between India and Pakistan and the miserable state of doordarshan which could barely telecast for 90 minutes where Chennai city is forced to have conditional access system instead set topper boxes. (Jan 13, 2005, The Hindu)

For peace with Pakistan the article, 'who is afraid of peace with Pakistan?" is enlogised by the reader that India's ability to defeat any kind of militaristic or jihadi take over of Kashmir and the obligation to ensure that the people do not lose faith in democracy.

They were letter acknowledging self - governance that apart from the subjects acceded in 1947, defense, foreign affairs, communication currency - to the central government, the rest of the subject will rest in the J & K government. They also condemned the Indian agencies and the army of having a 'strong institutional stake in continuation of a conflict with Pakistan is highly irresponsible. The Indian army stays in the barracks and is totally under the control of civilian leadership. This has been further justified that the ingrained hostility in Pakistan towards India is well documented and not perceived.

The other letters have argued out that it is the Pakistani army that has strong institutional stake in the continuation of conflict with India.

The New Indian Express, The terror blasts in India may be to test - obeck India for its preparedness and the way in which India reacts. The readers also state that terrorists attacks in srinagar or else where in India, the government of India finds itself voiceless.

Haven't the citizens of this country heard all this before with nothing being done to combat Islamic terrorism the reasons cited by the readers were,

1. The loosening authority of the PM
2. In past blasts.
3. Appeasing minorities.
4. Finding fault of Hindus always.
5. Tolerating attitude as way tosolution.
6. Poor screening at entry points and opening up of more of them in the name of normalization of relationship with neighbours.
7. Ignorance of grand design of neighbours until they come out in the media.

The letters have paid much attention to tackling of terror. Some of have raised have and cry over the 'Z' category security cover to politicians, tall proclamations of the government, the government a mute spectator, policies like repeal of POTA, class for lifting the ban on organisation like SIMI, leaving the innocents billions to the lunch of the terrorists. (July 13,2005,The Hindu)

The letter feels that though the preliminary investigations have revealed the terrorist orgnisations such LeT, Tabliq, Alic - , SIMI, the main perpentatives J. Ansari, Mohammed Fazal, Imtax Bafkal, and Riza, it seems too of two of this men have been trained on the Bangladesh soil, nothing has been done to curtail the activities of this organization.

The NDA government banned it in the year 2001 and the SIMI involvement is confirmed in the Mubai blasts, Varanasi blasts. The U.P. CM Maulana Mulayam has given a clean chit to the outfit that they had no direct role in Ayodiya or Varanasi attacks and the height of appeasement has to be condemned by one and all. (July 13, 2005, The New Indian Express)

The letters on the response to terror in the Hindu has suggested various alternatives and cautioned Indians from further kneeling down to Pakistan stop appealing to Pakistan, emulate Israel model, widen the intelligence network, monitor the activities of the various madarassa are the suggestions that hail from the country men in the wake of blasts in Mumbai and response to terror.

There were other steps like cultivate a security culture similar to what exists in Israel, Strengthen security infrastructures, complacency, and the histrionic behind the schedule like the people blame the police, the police balme intelligence agencies, intelligence source blank politicians, and politicians blame Pakistan were the comments from the citizens.

The fight against terror has evoked many a formulas from the public to tackle the menance of terrorist in sabotaging the normal life as well as peace process.

Firece Bheetoric during the G-8 summit by PM Manmohan Singh to win international support against terrorism has shibboleth and the onus lies in the hands of the Indian establishment to takle terror.

Avoidance of riding two horses, sponsoring terror and continuing peace process. Organise a separate terrorist cell; public short memory, expected scientific investigation, enhanced intelligence apparatus, and justification drawn from MISA, TADA, POTA which are draconian in nature but insists that "Preventive detention has been given constitutional status in India. (July 18, 2006, The Hindu) The sinister looking feature is incompatible with the promise of the preamble. But it has doubtedly been designed to prevent an abuse of freedom by anti-social and subversive elements which might endanger the national welfare of the infant republic.

9

Interviews

During the period of study there four interviews in The Hindu and four in The New Indian Express.

There were only very few coverage of interview with the leaders in both the news papers. But the Hindu had an exclusive coverage of an interview with Yasin malik JKLF Chairman. It was an op-Ed of the Hindu giving remarkable space for the ensuing dialogue and the on-going composite dialogue. He reiterated the Need to involve the Kashmiris in the dialogue (The Hindu, June 20, 2005). His recent vist to Pakistan did find a differential treatment than his earlier visit to Pakistan as militant in 1989. The pro-Pakistan line then adopted has given way for pro-Kashmiri stance. He also cited that belonging to the separatists pursuing the same goal took an entirely different line but moved in for a consultative process to admit that a transparent agenda has evolved. A complete independence is the desired goal which the Pakistanis are also happy about of. The representation at the peace table can be done only by the leader who is talking on their behalf of or no extension of the card of favoritism.

Though there were reports which stated that Kashmiris have been accepted as a party to dispute by Mirwaiz. It will be modus operandi when Tariq Aziz (Pakistani national security adviser) and Narayan (India's National security adviser) talk and an Kashmiri representation is there then this shall stand finalized.

The appraisal of PoK leaders figured during the course of the talk wherein the set back in their relationships were delineated for their distance on Pro _ Kashmiri stand. As the question of representing Kashmiris was bestowed to the clected representatives by the Indian government where else

Pakistan never had a say on this. Assembly elections and parliament elections are not the mainstay but a leader elected from district or another can be provide effective and efficient administrative set-up.

The Hindu coverage of the interview with Najan Sethi, Editor - in - Chief of the Friday times and Daily Times and his wife Jugna musha publisher and Managing Editor of the Weekly Newspaper represent the independent and courageous face of Pakistani journalism. (The Hindu, May 6, 2005)

The peace process is irreversible especially when it comes a more wanted hawk in the Pakistani military establishment. Musaharaff has given two reasons after the September 9/11 attacks and India and Pakistan joint stake holders in peace. The interview also stated that Musharaff could not carry on Jihad in Kashmir because he was hitting at one element of the recruitment base, which was linked to Afganisthan, Al - Quida and Jihad began to see Musharaff as an obstacle to their development.

The interview also stated that Pakistan Jihad activites in India failed to achieve its objective and also Indian army did not brow beat the Kashmiris because of the changed context of the World.

Tackling terrorism is alone not a pro-active issue but also a proposal that with soft borders theHurriyat and its role re-defined today in the changing socio-economic matrix had to be taken into account wherein not only Hurriyat represent the mass, but also omar Abdullah, Mehbooba and Former CM Mufti where the tie needs to constructed between the government and the centre, the centre and the Hurriyat.

The interview stressed on water issues and misunderstanding over Baglihar issue hogged the lime light.

The second area which found prominent stress where that India can demilitarize Kashmir demilitarization of Siachen is called for which reduce the strain of the conflict.

The political side, India needs to talk to Hurriyat and facilitate their trip to Pakistan, Hurriyat can act together and then talk to other groups in Kashmir.

The New Indian Express with the editor in chief Shekar Gupta seeks an with the RSS Chief Kuppp halli Sitaramyya Sundarshan who persided over the organization at the time of RSS-BSP relationship and he made vicdictive remarks on peace talks with Pakistan. If Pakistan keep promoting terrorism we will not support the peace talks. The final solution for India and Pakistan, Pak should leave PoK. It is the one and only solution. (The New Indian Express, April 17, 2005)

The Hindu coverage of the dialogue, between a senator and minister in three federal cabinets in Pakistan. He has been a part of Trace II process between India and Pakistan, known as the Neerana Dialgue, since 1992.

The two countries seem to look at each other and has been successful expecially after 16 months. The subterranean context is that India has the great advantage of being an older historial entity with a pre 1947 identity, even though it may not have existed as a singular nation states. The subterranean context therefore, is that we are working out the capacity to recongise our respective identities and hopefully through a period of time and through a period of listening to them.

The way forward for Kashmir question is the two sides engage in a closed - door processes, Track II and the Track III is media and people - to people contest) processes need to start looking at actual options and start preparing people in both countries for what could be the various solutions that the governments eventually can accept or present to people as possible alternatives.

The likely solutions were spelt out there is a talk of regionalisation of the devolution process, looking at Kashmiri's identity in terms of ethenicity, in terms of religion and in terms of territory. There is the semultancity processes on both sides of the line of control and creating mechanisms for interaction between thems whether through bus service, whether through the respective ligislator, whether through joint enonomic initiatives.

The third is to look at not similar but equally problematic places like Agdorra, Spain, and France and also the way in which Itally and Austria worked out issues of territory.

The extent of instant terrorism goes beyond conventional definition of terrorism and both countries are pursuing growth, both as an objective and as a mirage. The relationship between growth and creation of jobs is not a fully tested and will refuse to accept disparity of any kind. These disparities create distortion.

In an interview with Javed Jabbar to the Hindu (June 1, 2005), during his recent visit to Hyderabad recently, to attend the south Asia Editors forum about the India - Pakistan peace process and its future. The right ambience can be created to instill there is thaw in relationships between the two nations. The Kashmir question will have to be recognized at two levels. Ther is therefore closed level meetings within doors, the Track II between the non - official members and Track III media and people to people context processes need to start looking at actual option and start preparing people in both countries for what could be the various solutions that the governments eventually can accept or present to people as possible alternatives.

Union defence minister and leader of the house in LoK sabha Pranab Mukerjee is virtually the No. 2 in the union cabinet an is acting PM whenever Manmohan singh is abroad. During the course of the interview, the position of infiltration from Pakistan side, he remarked that the infiltration has come down dramatically. It has come down by 61%. From 2003, the situation started improving and from 2004, there has been further improvement. In May this gear there has been slight increase in infiltration but our jawans had either liquidate or frustrated the infiltration bids from across the borders. In june and July it has further increased. It came down in September but we have to wait till October 15, when the snow started forming making it difficult for them to infiltrate. Only then we will assess the situation in its entirely.

On the move as unilateral ceasefire during the month of Ramzan in Kashmir, the PM has already stated that we will consider if the situation improves on the border and if violence stopped completely.

With regard to demand of the Hurriyat to withdraw the army from Kashmir and let the police force handle the law and order situation in the valley. So long as terrorists and violent activities are these in the valley, we will continue to have the army. (The New Indian Express, September 18, 2005).

Swapping of prisoners from both countries figured during the course of the interview and the exchange of powers. Releasing of prisoners by both the countries is carried out in phased manner, but no agreement has been reached between the two countries on the exchange of pows yet. The Hindu coverage of an interview with Gulam Nabi Azad, the CM of J & K of the measures that will be taken to strengthen bilateral ties and the challenges ahead of the government gives an in-depth study into the major changes that would implemented shortly was the focus of the interview. (November 10, 2005).

For reseolving Kashmir issue a broad based dialogue which every region and community of J & K should contribute to make it more meaningful and effective. In situation have to be strengthened at every tier so that a feeling of neglect whether at regional level or sub-regional does not exist. A process of decentralisation is important towards empowering the people right at the panchayat level.

Opening up of five posts along the LoC is to help the earthquake affected people on both sides which may prove to be big CBM. On Kashmir, Pahari speaking families living along our side LoC and on PoK were the bulk of victims of the earth quake.

Regarding militancy, he promised that we would form in dealing with them, security forces have being directed to be extra cautious in avoiding collateral damage to any civilian.

The interview with Azad promoted development and infrastructure, custodial death being taken into account. Azad unveiled plans for transforming Kashmir. The deployment of the army, ensuring the corrupt ministries don't go scot free and form the framework of the interview. The Hindu coverage of the interview with Kasuri, Pakistani's foreign minister, immediately after the blasts endorsed the view that foreign securities talks will strengthen those who do not want the peace process to succeed and asserted that Pakistan could help at all countries in south Asia have gone through similar trauma of nation building (The Hindu, July 19, 2005). The reassurance can be derived from the compliments united States and France has paved on the war against terrorism.

The US is so extra- sensitive that they make their own assessment and they have designated JOD as a specially designated global terrorist.

The post ponement of the foreign secretary - level talks in inimical to the interests of Pakistan and an insinuation on SAARC which remained a hostage to Pakistan - India tensions. Mr. Kauri during the course of the interview with the paper that the more state holders in the peace process and the preemptory role of media at the forefront breaking the strong mindsets that exist.

Coverage of Cartoons in NPS

During the period of study there are eleven cartoons in The New Indian Express and five cartoons in The Hindu.

The Hindu had a cartoon with Pakistan president Pervez Musharaff Dr. Singh at the opinion makers column. Both stand to greet the peace process with sign board indicator and proclaim that peace process is irreversible. "Trust me, Mr. President, I have knack for making things irreversible".

The Hindu clearly analyzed the growth rate with the Foreign Minister from China representing the economy growth rate which received a fillip after the solidarity of friendship between the two countries whereas the caricature representing Musharaff made a reference to Kashmir which indicated that "our aim is K%" (April 14, 2005). More than trade the conditionality was expressed of the irreversible peace process which formed the main stipulation of the cartoonists. But such targets were not found in The New Indian Express.

The cartoon in the Hindu represented the peace bus with two buses with R.S.S. Head quarters to BJP headquarters where the bus service between musaffarbad and Srinagar. (The Hindu, April 23, 2005)

The cartoon that appeared in The Hindu which indicates General Musharaff extending a warm welcome to Mr. Advani and smugness expressed through the caricature speaks volumes of the warmth expressed by the General during the reception. (June 1, 2005).

The New Indian Express, had a cartoon representing the Indo-Pak peace process, where a Snail's pace is shown by representing the caricature of snail where its back is burdened with the peace process and a new leaf is carried by the snail on its lips. The peace process is utterly slow with hullbo around peace making. (June 2, 2005).

The New Indian Express, depicting the Rath Yatra wherein Advani pulling the Rath Yatra and openly acknowledging and that it was a brazen act of his and the worst incident I saw in my life. (June 5, 2005).

The Hindu coverage of Advaniji and the sangh parivar with exchange of marks shows how they fail unravel truth under compulsions, but conveniently avoiding harsh reality.

The The New Indian Express (June 18, 2005), the Bush intervention in the Iran - Pak - India gas pipeline is shown with an elephant with its trunk meandering through the relationship that exists between Indian and Pakistan. Both the leaders perpeturbed by the pace with which it reaches the landscape with trunk etched with US opposition to Iran - Pak - India gas pipeline project goes to tell the public at large the unhindered interference of the super power.

The cartoon depicting "Peace process" was split into "piece process" gives the ambit of the on-going dialogue process. A placard held by Mushraff Dr. Singh and the Hurriyat with Ka-Sh-Nir in their respective hands goes to indicate the irony peace process and its fate (The New Indian Express, June 24, 2005).

The cartoon in The New Indian Express reflect how would leaders stand in unison especially with telescope for the extradition of much wanted criminals and the onus of the government to identity these criminals is seen. (August 31, 2005).

The coverage of the Indo - Pak talks ina cartoon reveals how imploring and distancing from the main area. The two men astride helping one another and trying to reach one another by means of a ladder indicates the lackadaisical attitude of the government or its is a dilatory process. (The Hindu, September 1, 2005).

The Hindu coverage of PM Manmohan Singh steering the wheels in the direction of light at the end of the tunnel shows the remarkable, painstaking efforts to find a resolution in the available realm, especially after math holding parleys with the Hurriyat conference the Hindu coverage of post - quake relief measures extended to quake hit families from India and the warring issued thereof that the Indian soldiers not to cross the LoC indicates the ridiculous fashion with which the rehabilitation activities were carried out.

The under coverage of the change of guard in J & K after November with part stuck between the PDP and the congress. J & K cm Mohammed Sayeed sitting posture on sun dial glass structure Azad standing near the seated Sonia Gandhi todecide on the future CM of the state indicate dilemma faced by the leaders with the coalition government. The word 'toss' and 'we well abide by your decision" shows to a remarkable extent the hierarchy in leadership and the musical chairs after every election. (The Hindu, October 26, 2005).

The Hindu coverage of the on going change of guard in J & K with the carrcature of mufti behind Azad who is on his heels bearing a torch to light the flames indicated how course of history changes with every new leader in the scene. (October 20, 2005).

The Hindu coverage of the peace process in J & K which is respresented with by revolver with a pigeon on the trigger indicates the kind of peace process that has gained momentum all these year. The pigeon on the trigger shows the noterity of peace among the 'peace brokers' on 'mongers' who do not believe in peace without gun. It is a symbol of gesture to the gun wielders in the game. (November 4, 2005).

The cartoon In the Hindu just below the feature who is afraid of peace with Pakistan? May help sincere readers of issues to identify what holds store in the cartoon. Otherwise it may not be very obvious to the lay readers. The theme of the cartoonist deserves praise for he has enclosed some leader of J & K in bottle with cork which indicates nothing but 'self governance' under the frame work of the Indian constitution as the strategy for meeting the aspiration of J & K. (August 28, 2006).

The Hindu coverage of the war on terror and the difference sign boards with war on terror especially on the LoC indicates more than the bilateral disputes, enough spade work has to be carried by all nations to eradicate war on terror. (July 13, 2006).

Photos in The Newspapers Identifying Militancy in The State During The Period of Study there were 19 Photos in The New Indian Express and 33 Photographs in The Hindu.

THE HINDU

Daughter of Aliquallah Shah, Slain nephew of Jammu and Kashmir CM Mufti Mohammed sayeed, being consoled in Bijbehiara. But in TNIE as photos were largely absent. The trauma of the victims got highlighted in the Hindu. (May 3, 2005).

School girl injured in a grenade explosion in the heart of srinagar being rushed to hospital. It is pathetic to see the girl carried by her own relatives and writhing in bloody pain. (May 13, 2005)

A broad spectrum of people streaming and filling the air with their outcries on the death of the suspected militant commander Mohammed Yousuf, in Burwah. (May 28, 2005).

Relatives of those seriously injured in the Dulwama Car Bomb blast outside the Srinagar hospital where they shifted for treatment. (June 14, 2005)

Policeman take position when militants opened fire on Minister of State for Irrigation Syed Bashir Ahmed at Lal Chowk in Srinagar. One policeman and four civilians were injured in the attack. (July 7, 2005).

A Border security force personnel guards a section of the Jammu - Srinagar National Highway near nandani, as vehicles carrying Amarnath pilgrims (July 10, 2005).

Relatives mourning a civilian killed in a shooting accident involving a policeman in Srinagar (July 22, 2005).

An Indian Border security soldier standing guard during a cordon and search operation where common men squat on the floor indicates the security scenarios ahead of the idependence day celebrations. (August 14, 2005).

Children awaiting on of LoC attending regular classes in the Battok sector, LoC proves beyond doubt that Kashmirs are yearning for peace to lead a normal life in the state. (August 14, 2005).

The new Indian express coverage, a screaming with mouth wide open when the militants opened fire on a family in sajroo village, of Jammu suggested the alarming situation in the state where heinons crimes are committed irrespective of people. (July 7, 2005).

Terrified school children after an (IED) improvised explosive device outside Bakshi stadium in Srinagar burst causing panic among school children gives the deliberate singular act of the militants ignore human capital. (August 16, 2005).

The army officials present surrendered Harket - Ul - Jihad - e- Islami militant Mohd. Amin alias Wasim before the media relates to the presence of training camps in PoK to forment Jihad on this side of the LoC. (September 2, 2005).

The paramilitary jawans in action during a gunfight between militant and security forces at Shatrashahee in Sri Nagar indicated how militants seep into blow up the establishments. (September 9, 2005) And damage public property. The suicide squads are in full swing at unguarded moments.

An injured SPO along with son in a hospital. The SPO battled terrorists for more than one hour at Dharmari area of Udhampur district. The fate of Barkat's family gives a glimpse of the difficulties endured by villagers who refuse to support Jihadis. (September 11, 2005).

The Hindu coverage of the ponies being usedby locals how explicit and obvious the transport of ammunition are being carried out inspite of the joint statement of January 2004 commitment to wipe out terrorism from Pakistanti soil. (September 25, 2005).

The women learning self defence in telikata near surankote to join the battle againt militancy shows how aggressive the populace has turned to be in Kashmir to keep the militants at bay. Women too risk in horrendous games of retailating the onslaught of militants by training themselves. (September 27, 2005).

Police canecharging processionists, whowere protecting against the killing of Ibrahim dar indicates that the state machinery did not support terrorism or terrorist high handness. (September 2, 2005).

Counterng militancy where the lay press photographer could identify a live grenade where the armymen go about their task during an encounter with militants in Kathna 83 kg from Jammu narrated how army men either neglect the on the spot inspection of further explosives or they meekly accept such challenges. (October 16, 2005).

Indian soldiers at the last post along the LoC in manjakote ara of Rajuveri district in J & K indicate the army his constant vigil across the border thereby trying to register the infiltration of militants in the valley. (October 23, 2005)

Troops on vigil on the LoC in Bimber beach. Sector of J & K indicated how the army patrolling across the border can help to control the militant activity in the state. (October 6, 2005).

The police examining the wreckage of a car used by militants for a bomb explosion at Nowgam on the outskirts of Srinagar. (November 3, 2005)

Six persons were killed and 20 injured in the blast which came hours before new CM was to be sworn in indicates that they beleaguer every opportunity to express their clout and perpenetrate any act to disturb the normal course of life.

The relatives mourn the death of Shabir Ahmed in the cross fire as the army engaged militants in a gun battle. (November 14, 2005).

The Hindu coverage of the CRPF Jawan taken by his colegue during a shoot out at Lal Chowk in Srinagar indicated the callousness and the deliberate act of the militants to achieve their ends and moreover reflects the brutality and beastity of the militants. (November 15, 2005).

The Hindu coverage of one of the victims of the grenade attack at Tangmarg in J & K taken to hospital when he sustained injuries when the militants targeted the former tourism minister Ghulam Hussain Mir, who was addressing a rally. (November 16, 2005).

Child warriors where in a child shows what he learnt in handing gun indicates various terrorist groups in J & K are using an alarming number of children as "terror tools". (November 20, 2007).

A man injured in the car - bomb attack in Srinagar being removed from site There is no end to tenure inspite of all joint statement arrived at by Vajpayee and Musharaff. (November 17, 2005).

The army men round the body of the suspected militants after gun battle in Khur, The militant is suspected to be member of a Pakistan based guerilla group in Kashmir who the police said a man conspirator in the serial blasts in New Delhi indicates the horrendous activity of the militant. (June 17, 2006).

Work in progress near Kulagam on the New Delhi - Kashmir railway line. Contractors on this and other infrastructure projects in south Kashmir have been targets of extortion by terrorists. (June 24, 2006).

Police and villagers clearing the bodies at an army camp at chokbal. Eight molilants were killed when they tried to infiltrate. (November 14, 2005)

Students of Tynadle school Biscoc school offering prayers paying homage to the victims of the grenade attack outside the school was portrayed in depth of field size of the photo wherelse the Indian express had a very small size photo of the school children. (May 17, 2005) Violence in the valley where the reader expouses the statement of spokesman for Al-Mansoor outfit that the purpose of the attack is to expose the security lapse in the valley. (November 15, 2005)

The New Indian Express

Jawan carring the coffin of major salman Ahmad Khan of 6. Rastriya Rifle, who lost his life after killing two militants in a gun battle in North Kashmir. (May 9, 2005).

A school girl injured in the grenade explosion being taken to a hospital. The glory picture in colour portrays amplified militant attacks in the recent months. (May 13, 2005).

A man who was critically injured in a grenade blast being dragged along the road depicts the kind of violence unleashed by the militancy in the state. (May 29, 2005).

Jawans carrying the coffin of major Salman Ahmed Khan of 6 Rastriya rifles, who lost his life after killing two militants, in a gun battle. (May 9, 2005)

An exclusive photograph of the BSF personnel dowsing the fire on police jeep, enumerates the atrocities committed by the militants on public prosperity. Leave alone human lives. The new Indian expres coverage of the sentinel guarding a local police station after the militants devasted the area determines the concern shown by the state admini stration in maintaining law and order. (August 6, 2005).

An eight old boy undergoing treatment. For bullet injuries in a hospital in srinagar pronounced. The dastardly act of the militants and cold heartedly wreak vangenance of anyone, including children. (August 9, 2005).

Soldier keeps vigil near the barbed wire fencing along the LoC in Baraf post, 165 km north of Srinagar has made them to protect the sovereignty and integrity of the state. (August 9, 2005).

The same incident more on the car of th state former minister as man Majeed in Srinagar than on human beings. This shows express attitude in protecting the state property more than innocent civilians in the state. (August 15, 2005).

Soldiers stand near the wreakage of vehicle where blast occurred near srinagar Airport indicated that militants have used every juncture to raise hue and cry against every opportunity available to wreak havoc and mayhem among the public.

The paramilitary personnel checking the identity lands of people at Lal Chock in Srinagar indicates the role of state security in protecting the lives of the innocent people even after the third round of composite dialogue indicates that the governmental parleys cannot hold back the act of militancy. (November 3, 2005).

Security jawans keeping vigil at High court Bar association called for complete strike reveals how the security is beefed up to avoid tensions during the escalation of conflict. (February 7, 2006).

The Police personnel inspecting the wrekage of the car that was blown up by militants in Srinagar. That the state police took every possible initation to monitor the havoc perpetuated by the terrorists. (January 25, 2006).

A paramilitary soldier tries to retrieve luggage from a burning vehicle as a body of a tourist lies on the ground following a general explosion in central srinagar, talks the whole community they target innocent civilians without any qualms. (July 12, 2006).

An injured goal being helped after agreenade attack at Lal Chowk in Sri Nagar terrorists every day target at least a civilian a day. (July 12, 2006).

Paramilitary personnel checking the identity cards of people at Lal Chowk in Srinagar. Security has been beefed up in the valley in view of the Republic day celebrations. (January 25, 2006).

A woman consoling the grand daughter of Atequ-al-Allb Shah, nephew of J & K CM Mufti Mohammed Sayeed (May 3, 2005).

Photos in Both the Newspapers Identifying The Spirit of Militancy in The State

The Hindu and The New Indian Express

TNIE portrayed only battalion of police officials dispersed by tear gas shells, but Hindu depicted the woman brcast beating which makes it more sensational to the readers. The Hindu coverage of a woman wailing consoled by her relatives. Tells the grisly act of the terrorists.

The Hindu and TNIE coverage of the bus that was damaged in an explosion in srinagar where none soldiers of an army convoy were cited 24 injured in the blast killed in an explosion. (June 25, 2005).

The heavily guarded terrorist reception centre set ablaze by militants, and the skies filled with crimson red flames reveals the plight. Of the tourist who are trapped inside, wher...... TNIE indicated that the building in srinagar where passengers of the historic bus to PoK goes up in flames. Civilian and security personnel take cover during the militant attack. (April 7, 2005).

The Other Photos That Covered During The Period of Study.

There Were Sixteen Photos In the New Indian Express and Thirty Five Photos in The Hindu.

The Hindu

Surya Kiran team performing at Rangreth on the outskirts of Srinagar, with its act of devil delivery ranging from inverted runs to the 'heart loop' and wings over by Indian Air force to motivate Kashmiri youth to join the force, shows the kind of attempt to bring the youth to the mainstream of life. (September 22, 2005).

School boys participate in an AIDS awareness campaign in Jammu. India had 5.13 million infected with the HIV virus in 2004. Inspite of the militant artivity and irreparable damage on public property and human life, the state has lost no time to propogate measures that can safeguard the interest of the people of the state.

Jammu and Kashmir CM Mufti Mohammed Sayeed during the 9th All Inda Public golf tournament at the Royal Spring Golf Course in Srinagar, the photo journalists have not failed to pin even a small happening in the state. (September 28, 2005).

Former J & K CM, farooq Abdullah with CM Mufti, Hurriyat leader Bhat Share the same dais during the centenary celebrations of their Alma mater indicate a strange emui and longing for a peace. (October 4, 2005).

The earthquake and its after math when it was black Saturday in J & K when a powerful earthquake rocked the state flattening houses and shattering lives. A man ruminates over collapsed house in srinagar even as policeman surveys the damage to a police station in Uri town, which bore the brunt. Supore town, near srinagar, presented a pricture of suffering - an anguished women crying her heart wounded being taken to hospital and children are inconsolable. (October 9, 2005).

Family surveys its destroyed home in the hamletof Kurkhot, near Tanghdhar town.

Hamida Begaum awamid the debris of her home in Gundishot, where five of her seven children were buried alive. (October 17, 2005).

The children who survived the October 8 earthquake in a makeshift classroom at a camp in Musaffarabad the capital of PoK indicates a new beginning. (December 14, 2005)

The New Indian Express

Jammu and Kashmir and Mufti Mohammed Sayeed teering off broadway golf tournament at Royal spring Gol course along the banks of the Dal lake in Srinagar, the CM taking detour from his official duties for disport. (September 28, 2005).

MP Naveen Jindal flags off a two wheelers expedition to Ladakh The expedition attempts to set a world record of crossing the world's highest motorable passes.

Two Braeli chat by the window of the house boat in Nigeen lake in Srinagar There has been an influx of foreign tourists following the return of peace to the valley. Tourists still abound Sringar inspite of constant threats.

Faiza babi, a kashmiri girl, talks to the media after coming back to her native place in Aknoor where she had spent 27 years in PoK. That media men are keen to garner the state reality to smoothen the life of common man and the life that abounds them in a divided country. (September 29, 2005).

A group of Senior citizens from Kargil, Dras and batalik comes out after darshen at the golden temple in Amritsar shows even slightest developments go reported in the media. (September 27, 2005).

An emotional upsurge when Jameet Singh (L) who survived killer quake in Musaffarabad greeted by his grand daughter on his return to Jammu indicates that the TIE did not bother about the victims of the tragedy but more with survivors, when media fails to expose the succour for the victims realing under the unprecendented calamity . (October 15, 2005).

Earthquake affected villages at Salemabad, 104 kms next of Sringar, sift through clothes donated by relief agencies. The wait for relief material at kamal kur village near the border. Soldiers using batons to make victims queup for supplies in Jabori, Pakistan, Hands are extended for aid in Muzaffarbad, capital of PoK, worker removing boulders off what used to be a road at Teetwal 200 km from north of Srinagar. (October 16, 2005).

Coverage of a distribution point near Uri, 100 km. north of sringar, an earth quake victim carries relief material under a plastic sheet the death toll in J & K is reclaimed to be 1199. (October 17, 2005).

A Kashmiri girl carries food supplies in Neelam valley north of Musaffarabad more than one million quake survivors spent the night exposed to the elements. (October 17, 2005).

A boy in front of his sheltered house in Kamalkote in Uri, 100 km north of Srinagar, two weeks after the October 8 earthquake. About 150,000 people in J & K are to reported to be homeless. (October 24, 2005).

Both The Newspapers

The woman taking a salute at the flag gives the impression of normaly in the state, expecially after the Azad's government. The New India Expressalso covered the same feature. The New Indian Express coverage of Pakistani children in traditional dress holding national flags during a ceremony to celebrate the Nations independence day celebration at the Jinnah convention centre. A new headline hoping for a new begining beyond Kashmir draws insight into a better plan to pull Pakistan from retrogressive step of pursuing relentless Proxy war to one of development and progress.

Very less number of photographs compared to the Hindu which was with a surplus number of photos. The condition of patients in local hospital remained outdoors after tremors was given a significance. Wherelse the Hindu had mothers and relatives wailing and beating the chest. The wall of the historial mubark mandi complex in J & K collapsed during the earthquake that shook several parts of north India and Pakistan, and a kashmiri woman cries with folded hands in Baramullah, 60 km north of srinagar were other reliable photographs.

Three days after a powerful quake hit the sub-continent ripping apart the land and lives, the focus was on rescue and relief. The death graph continued to shoot up but hope for the injured rose too. The armed forces were on their foes reaching succour to the wounded and helpless, even as heroic talks of people, themselves affected, rushing to others and were not rare A Kashmiri stands mute witness to the destruction of his house at Uri, 110 kg from srinagar. A girl is being rushed to hospital at Tatwal while a baby finds comfort in the hands of a rescue team. There was also the sad spectacle of the body of a boy being dug out of a house at Udoosa village near the LoC. The plight of quake victims and the myriad forms of devastation nearly filled more than half of the page of the Hindu the school children mourning for the earthquake victims in Amirtstar was the only photograph in the Coverage of TNIE.

The Hindu and the TNIE hae covered the rubble of a land slip the Uri - Musaffarabad road, under the caption endurance test, survivors of the earthquake tread on the Srinagar - Musafarabad roadlittered with rocks following landslip near the Kemanpost Uri, With a caption where will I go'. A survivor of the family in the earth quake - hit Ibkaot village in Kashmir with her belongings. (October 11, 2005)

The vehement coverage of the stark reality of the quake victims made a striking contrast to the onces covered in TNIE. TNIE of a girl smiles holding her doll in a shelter camp in Rawalpindi . (October 16, 2005)

During The Period of Study there were Seventeen Stories Human Rights The Photographs Indian Express and Fourteen Stories in The Hindu.

The Hindu

Human rights violation included even the graves were target of a qubod bhat co-founder of the JKLF being desecrated. (July 22, 2005).

Sapandeep Kaur and Poonam, daughters of Sarabjit Singh, performing 'hawn' with students of Gurikal college at Philkhiwant, near Amirtsar, praying for the over turning of the death sentence given by the paskitan court to their father shows the empathy for the closs of innocent men. (August 26, 2005).

The members of All India Muslim Council raise slogans during a demonstration in New Delhi. Hundreds of Muslim participate in the demonstration demanding memory from Pakistan President Pervez Musharaff showed how vigoursly the common public react when innocents are being prosecuted. (August 25, 2005).

The compatriots signing on a 75 m long canvas in Bhopal to appeal to Pakistan president Pervez Musharaff to release Sarabjit from jail. There were constant pleas from various sources to release Sarabjit Singh. (September 2, 2005).

Sarabjit Singh's sister Dalbar Kaur reads out a letter written by him as his wife Sukhpreet Kaur holds his latest photograph at Bhikiwaond village near Amritsar The letter and photographs were given to the Indian High Commission officials. The letter and photo graph to the Indian High Commission officials when they met Sarabjit in Lahore jail indicates the sincere and magnamous role played by the Hindu transport the anxiety expressed by the family members to welcome the man lodged in Pakistani jail and inadvertently crossed the LoC.

J & K CM Sayeed with he south Assam foundation founder and UNESCO goodwill ambassador madanjeet singh will provide long-term care to orphans, most of whom are victims of violence in Kashmir. (September 30, 2005).

The migrants from Talwara camp stage a mock sale of their children in Jammu to highlight their plight. Forced to abandon their homes due to poverty and conflicts in the region, the migrants said they had received little help from the government there are reports that some of them were forced to sell their children. (May 30, 2005).

General J.J. Singh of the army staff, declared open a model village at Teethwal for the earthquake affected people indicate the army playing a significant and contributory role in saving the lives of the people. (June 23, 2005).

The group agonises over the destruction of their homes in an exchange of fire between security forces and militants in Pulwara indicates how innocents are being targeted and rendered homeless in the ensuring battle. (June 25, 2005).

People run for cover as the body of the youth killed lives on the road during his funeral procession in Srinagar.

The New Indian Express

TNIE where the traders protested VAT implementation being lathi charged in Srinagar.

A child smiles during a cultural programmee presented by Muslim, and orphanage for the militancy affected children. (June 6, 2005).

JKLF leader Javed Mir and his supporters to a protect rally against terrorist attacks stand to tell the grim reminder to Indian government the public has been patient enough to contain the onslaught of terrorism and wants immediate reprieve from such atrocities. (July 18, 2005).

School girls on a rally orgnaised by all India Rajiv Gandhi Brigade near Dal Lake, reminds us of the courage, grit expressed by women folk against terrorism. (June 22, 2005).

Relatives mourning the death of teenager shot dead by the army who mistook him for a militants shows the callousness or caveliar attitude of the army while handling encounters in the strife torn area. (July 23, 2005).

Shkhpret Kaur, wife of Sarabjit Singh with her daughters Sepandeep Kaur and Poonam at march in death how innocents caught receive much wide public support for human rights violations. (August 24, 2005).

Pakistan's interior secretary syed Kamal Shah being received by the High Commissioner of Pakistan to India, Aziz Ahmed Khan on arrival in New Delhi, established the official contacts during the meetings. (August 28, 2005).

The union home secretary V.K. Duggal speakes hands with Pakistan's interior secretary syed kamal shah, brings rapprochement among the conflicting nations. (August 30, 2005).

The Hizbul Commander identified as Mohammed Rafiq has been active for the last eight years was killed in an encounter with security forces during search operation sat Dugga - Bhaderwash area of doda district. Acting on the tip off, security forces cordoned off the Patrhi Behak area of bandi pura in Baramulla distict, leading to a gunfight with hiding extremists.

Deepak Kaur seen outside of Lakhpat jail in Lahore. The Indian government the High commission officials trugged ahead to save Sarabjit from death sentence after reclaiming his identity. (August 31, 2005).

Separatist leader Yaseen Malik and Shabir Shah leading a demonstration at Lal Chowk to protest against the Supreme court order confirming death sentence to Mohammed Afzal impleies the kind of solidarity and alacrity expressed when there has been serious violations against human rights in the state. (September 25, 2005).

Actor Smirti Irani, social worker Nafisa ali and MCA Navyot singh Sidhu to a protest demonstration by releatives of POW in New Delhi, that the active co-operation of people belonging to different strata of life demonstrate their capacity to protect human life. (October 3, 2005).

The police blocking a Muharram procession by Shia muslims in Srinagar. Several of the protestors were arrested for violating a ban on procession in the heart of the city.

The Indian prisoners released from Pakistani jail crosses the Wagh border, A Pakistani prisoners released from the Indian jail waves to Indian officials before crossing over to Pakistan. The vice-versa exchange of prisoners were the most prominent feature coverage of CBM.

Both The Newspapers

BSF soldier standing guard on a deserted street in Srinagar as shops and government offices were closed on the day, against the killing of three boys by the army that the pubic near feared to attack anything that will against the will of the people. Wherelse a photograph on the same day TNIE depicted vacant streets with only one man walking at the end of the street is clear sign of lapse of security in the area. (July 28, 2005).

Actress Nandita das and Pakistan human right activitist Asma Jehangir along with peace activist of India and Pakistan during a candle light vigil at the Wagh border emboldens both the governments to curb terrorism and allay the fears of people living in these areas. (August 16, 2005).

The family members of Sarabjit Singh, facing death by hangings in Pakistan on spying charges, threatened to hang themselves if sarabjit was not saved, shows the orgy of human feelings and desperate bid to die provided justice is not noted out to them. Wherelse the new Indian Express only highlighted the sister of Sarabjit Singh talling to media persons. (August 23, 2005).

The Indian prisoners and Pakistani prisoners cross the Wagh border check post as the two countries began exchanging over 500 prisoners highlights the concern over how governments make the move easier to hand over the country-men to their respective countries. But in the TNIE the photo coverage was millimeters in width and length and not very suggestive of the on going transaction between two countries and render may ignore see the small file photo. (September 13, 2005).

Photo Coverage of Baglhar A Issue

During The Period of Study There Were Four Photographs in The Hindu and only and Photograph In The New Indian Express.

The Hindu

The water inundating the banks of the Tawi river in Jammu indicates the magnitude with which over flooding can cause severe damage to the area. (July 8, 2005).

The army jawans keep a watch on the rising water levels of the chenab in Akhnoor indicates the kind of vigilance taken by the security forces to keep the area well protected. (July 9, 2005).

The Baglihar hydel power project site with chenab in full flow indicates that water is on rise in the dam; which can be used for power generation. (October 3, 2005).

The New Indian Express

The houses in Gujar nagar,Jammu, were nearly sub-merged by the over flowing of Tawi. This brings to the fore front, the objections expressed by the Pakistani government, on the nature of dam and fears of over flooding. (July 8, 2005).

The army jawans keep a watch on the rising water levels of the chenab in Akhnoor indicates the kind of vigilance taken by the security forces to keep the area well protected.

The Baglihar hydel power project site with chenab in full flow indicates that water is on rise in the dam; which can be used for power generation.

Photo Coverage of The Separatist Talk

During The Period of Study There Were Eleven Photographs in The Hindu and Five Photographs in The New Indian Express.

The Hindu

The Hurriyat conference chairman Mirwaiz Umar Faroq addressing a news conference with senior Hurriyat leaders Abdul Ghani Bhat and Maulana Mohammed Ansari. (May 11, 2005).

Hurriyat supporters participating in a procession to observe the death anniversary of Monlvi Mohammed Farooq and Abdul Ghani Lone is Srinagar. Supporters greeting PC leader Sajjad lone as he arrives to commemorate the death anniversary of his father Abdul Ghani lone the people involved in greeting the leaders, with people in a more jubilant mood. (May 23, 2005).

The Chairman Mohammed Yasin Malik talking to press persons in Srinagar regarding their travel to Pakistan after meeting the people of erstwhile princely state of J & K (PK). (May 22, 2005).

The HC leaders according a warm welcome to Kashmir pandits after 16 long years is another milestrone achieved in the on-going composite dialogue. JKLF leader Yasin Malik and NC leader Omar Abduallh undermined the dogged determination of both the leaders in the demand for autonomy. (August 1, 2005).

Hurriyat conference chairman Murqaiz Omar Farooq flanked by Abdul Gheeni Bhat and Fazal Hq Quarshi address the media in New Delhi shows the unanimous resolution adopted by the conference on the eve of the talks with Home Minister Shivaraj Patil. (September 5, 2005).

The PM Manmohan Singh and the separatists like Moulur Abbas Ansari, Abdul Ghani Bhat, Mirwaiz Umar Farooq Prior to the talks he had with them at his residence in New Delhi indicates the steps taken by the UPA government to resolved the tangle. (sep 6, 2005).

The Chairman of the Hurriyat conference mirwaiz Umar Farooq addressing a congregation at Jammu Masjid in Srinagar, very vehemently and convincing the populace on the positive signals and assurance from the heads of governments indicates how he tires to forge a better relationship bring closer home the message of new emerging trends in the peace process. On the airport with luggaged Hurriyat leader Abdul Ghani Bhatt shows a commendable role in being a part of the amalgam of leaders to meet all other members during the parleys with the PM. (September 10, 2005).

The New Indian Express

Maulana Mohammed Abbas Ansari, for mer chairman APHC, with Umar Farooq APHC chairman during the course of talks with the centre. (May 26, 2005).

Hurriyat leaders Mirwaiz and Yasin Malik offering prayers at the mausoleum of Mohammed Ali Jinnah. (June 10, 2005).

The Delhi Jama Mazid Oam Syed Ahmed Bukari welcoming the Hurriyat leader at the AIRC on the promises of the Ul-century Jama Masjid, the moderate wing of the separatist grouping in J & K indicates the rapport with Muslim clerics.

Syed Geelani, the hard line faction of the HC slowly refusing to board the bus to Musaffarabad as well the invitation of Pak government to visit PoK reacting the need to implement self determination at a pres conference eludes the interest of the on-going composite dialogue.

The kashmiri pandits performing as Bhajan on the occasion of "Ram Navami" in Sringar that the Pandit community which fled from the state during insurgency made every attempt to celebrate every hour in their home land. (April 19, 2005).

Photo Coverage of Siachen Issue

During The Period of Study There Five Photos in The Hindu and one Photograph in The New Indian Express.

The Hindu

An Indian army soldier at Siachen monitoring the Siachen glacier indicates the security cover offered to protect those anmmanned spaces. (June 9, 2005).

The chief of northern command Lt. General Hari prased and other senior officers pay homage to Kargil heroes at drass. 160 km from Srinagar shows the relentless effort taken by the Indian government to defend the sovereignty of the Nation at hour of need and a day too observed to honour them is exemplary. (July 25, 2005).

Soldier crossing a crevasse at the Siachen glacier at the height of 20,000 feet the fait accomplish of the soldiers who traverse such paths to protect the territorial integrity of the nation daring such high posts. (July 29, 2005)

The soldiers of the 8 J AK LI (Siachen) battloon at a farewell function in New Delhi before their departure on a UN peace keeping mission to suntan that the government is taking serious effort to guard the frontiers. (August 26, 2005)

The biodigester installed at a post on the Siachen glacier enumerates the kind of effort to protect the environment. (August 26, 2005)

The New Indian Express

Hindustan aeronautics limited re-engined and upgraded Chetek helicopter chetan, lands on the siachen glacier during an attitude test. (September 5, 2005).

Photo Coverage of Leaders

During The Period of Study There Were 36 Photographs in The Hindu and Twenty one in The New Indian Express.

The Hindu

Former PM Benazir Bhutto offering "chadder" in Dargah brings round the message that the countries former Pakistan PM's pard a visit to India during the composite dialogue reinforcing that only elected governments can sustain peace process. (April 2, 2005)

Gen. Musharaff meeting the leaders of opposition Ms. Sonia Gandhi, L.K. Advani and Dr. Abdul Kalam at New Delhi indicates a new momentum has taken after a lull of 2002.

The BJP president L.K. Advani, accesompnied by his family members and Pakistani officials walks out of the Allama Iqbal International Airport on his arrival in Lahore.

The BJP president and opposition leader L.K. Advani with Pakistani President Gen. Musharaff in Rawalpindi.

Javed Jabbar commited to peace while attending the south Asia editor's forum in Hyderabd. (June 1, 2005).

PoK Prime minister Sardar Sikander Hayat Khan greets leaders of the all parties Hurriyat conference delegation Mirwaiz Umar Farooq during a meeting the team had with the legislative assembly members. The former president of PoK, Sardar Abdul Ayyam this shows both sides have expressed solidarity oin the on-going peace momentum.

A Sikh devotee presenting a shawl to BJP Leader L.K. Advani at a gurdwara in Lahore.

The BJP present and leader of the opposition L.K. Advani paying floral tributes at the mausoleum of Pakistani founding father Mohammed Ali Jinnah. (June 5, 2005).

The former J & K CM Farooq Abdullah during international gold tournament says that the leaders adjust to the changing atmospheres in Sringar and pave the way for attracting the tourist potential. (June 5, 2005).

The BJP president and leader of the opposition L.K. Advani and his familyu embers at his ancestral house at Parsi colony. PM Manmohan Singh with army and Air Force personnel in Leh. (June 6, 2005).

JKLF leader Mohammed Yasin malik who runs a rough shod not to show favoritism on the leaders of Kashmir and rigorous on 'independence"

Home Minister Shivraj patil one day's visit to Jammu and Kashmir to discuss the peace process with the state government officials. Shows the eagerness with which the centre is often sending different ministers to improve the situation. (July 11, 2005).

Union minister of state for Home Sri Prakash Jaswal at the BSF head quarters in Srinagar reveals that the centre has taken imminent measures to protect the life and property in the state in spurt of infiltration across the border. (July 24, 2005).

PDP chief Mufti Mohammed Sayeed and his daughter illustrate the kind of initiative they would willingly take to retrieve peace in Kashmir. Or (peace brokers). (August 12, 2005).

PM Manmohan Singh and Pakistan President Pervez Musharaff at the joint press conference in New York reveals that the heads of government have used every forum to arrive at consensus, though every meetings were retrogressive. And failed to be efficacious. External affairs minister Natwar Singh and his Pakistani counter part Khershed Mohmed Kasuri were part of the delegation that arrived in New York. (September 16, 2005).

National conference leader Farooq Abudllah with the supreme head of All J & K Muslim conference Sardar Mohammed Abdul Quayyam Khan internal the good rapport that emerges as result of the Kashmiris coming together. (September 21, 2005).

The former PM of PoK, Sardar Abdul Aayaaum Khan with the former PM A.B. Vajpayee re-opens the history of Struggles and the curiosity to raise hope. With large bold caption over the photograph peace process must go on. (September 23, 2005).

The J & K CM Mufti Mohammed Sayeed after submitting his resignation to the governor, Lt. Gen. (retd) S.K. Sinha, at the Raj Bhavan in Srinagar. Eschews leadership and good governance and the spirit of the pact inked after the 2002 bye elections. (October 30, 2005).

The leaders when Azad was sworn in as minister where they greeted each other after a massive victory for the congress - led PDP coalition that every event in J & K is carefully tapped to sent right signals to all states of India regarding the smooth transition of power, and how leaders bind themselves to the pact in letter and spirit.

The New CM of J & K, Ghulam Nabi Azad with his predecessor Mufti Mohammed Sayeed and Farooq Abdullah at the swearing in ceremony. (November 3, 2005).

PM Manmohan Singh with his Pakistani counter part Shakat Aziz during a bilateral meeting on the side lines of the 13th SAARC summit in Dhaka how leaders exchanged pleasantries during international summit to resolve the issue. (November 13, 2005).

U.N. Secretary General Kofi Annan and Pakistan PM Shankat Azaiz greet each other as President General Musharaff looks on during the world conference of donors in Islambad, talks on the international community imminent to the region devastated by quake. (November 20, 2005).

The CM of Gujarat and J & K Narendra Modi and Ghuylam Nabi greet each other at an interactive session among states at the Porvasi Bharatiya Dwan 2006 in Hyderabad reveals that the J & K is more a part parcel of India or bringing closer home J & K to other states. (June 9 2006).

J & K governor S.K. Sinha, CM Azad, Dy. CM Baig welcomed president A.P.S. Abdul Kalam Azad at the Rinagar airport and later addressed a joint session of legislature. The leaders have taken from the centre to improve the conditions in J & K becomes more emphatic. (July 29, 2006).

The leader of Pakistan Pervez Musharaff bidding a farewell after his visit to India is portrayed as in the Hindu as if a new messiah of peace had arrived to give people more peace and rest.

The Pakistan president Gen. Musharaff during an interview in Rawalpindi quoting that peace process is fairly irreversible at interview with Reuters since the summit in Agra in July 2001.

The New Indian Express

Railway minister Lalu Prasad hugging former PM Shujaat Husain

The Railway minister hugging former PM Shyaat Hussain before the launch indicates that democratic leaders made way to India wherelse the Hindu had given prominence to the arrival of Benazir Bhutto and the restoration democracy as the Hall mark for sustaining the on going peace process. (April 2, 2005)

Dr. Singh presenting a momento to Gen. Musharaff, and meeting between the foreign Minster Dr. Natwar Singh and Mr. Kasuri expressed more quest for peace in the sub-continent.

Former PM I.K. Gujral with people's Democratic party president Mehbooba Mufti during a workshop on "Jammu and Kashmir women in Governance : Changing power equations organized by women's political watch group. (May 11, 2005).

Leader of the opposition in the Lok Sabha L.K. Advani posing for photographs at the Lahore Fort Museum in Lahore.

BJP president L.K. Advani laying a wreath at the mausoleum of Mohammed Ali Jinnah in Karachi. The good will gesture L.K. Advani expressed at Pakistan. (July 5, 2005).

The soldier watch former Miss. Universe Sen as she arrives to participate in the opening of golf tournament. (June 5, 2005).

Advani outside what used to be his pre-partition residence. (June 6, 2005).

The leader of opposition and BJP President L.K. Advani on his arrival from Pakistan at the Delhi Airport.

Azad as addressing an audience of the membes of CCP meeting of the J & K assembly elections.

The external affairs minister K. Natwar Singh at a hotel with the dignitaries from Karachi indicates in spite of the imbroligo, there were constant meetings between the leaders. (October 6, 2005).

The Indian council for cultural relations chairman Karan Singh with J & K former CM Farooq Abdullah at a gawali evening in New Delhi states they are not only storages of the Delhi government but also they share the views among themselves at nevertheless of the constant reentrance of puppet of regime in J & K. (December 24, 2005).

APHC chief Umar Farooq injter acting with the boy who survived the October 8 quake in PoK indicates that though restriction were placed across governments, there is a change of mood in the air (January 5, 2006).

Pakistan president Gen. Musharaff meetings all the leader APHC from J & K Mirwaiz, Bhat, Lone indicates that there exists a good rapport among the separatist and Pak government though the Indian government Identifies hiatus in the relationship.

The foreign secretary shyam saran with his Pakistan counter part Riaz mohammed khan before their talks indicates the alacrity expressed in building new infrastructure along the Loc. (January 18, 2006).

The former CM Kasuri Mufti Mohammed Sayeed, PDP Mehbooba Mufti Dy. CM MusaffairHussain Beigh at the PDP executive meeting in Jammu indicates the conglomerate is still lacking consensus as each political proceeding unfolds.

There were special photograph with cricketer turned politicians BSP MP Navjot Singh Sidhu listening to the problems of porters of wagh border, considered to be a life line of cross - border trade with Pakistan at Wagh. (July 22, 2006).

Pakistan President Pervez Musharaff, the then external affairs minister Jaswant Singh and PM Vajpayee in Agra on July 15, 2001 indicates that the stress of the former government policies (NDA) was heightened to disparage the UPA and manifestations of terror looming large and inchoate ideas of the present government.

Both The News Papers

The ICCR President dances with the folk artist suggested that even the visits were not spared by the government and hospitality accorded with state honours in spite on the prevailing hostilities. The Hindu has mocked at the presence of Dr. R. Singh and President Musharaff at the ODI where the beauty and nuances of cricket are being taught by one another on the stadium. TNIE indicated as livekt spectators from Bullet proof box.

The signing of (Mov) on the establishment of communication look in Islamabad by the Indian coast guard general vice - Admiral Arun Kuma Singh and his Pakistani counterpart Admiral Baktral Mohasin that heated has come down with agreements on either side where else TNIE had the two ministers sitting closely on chair. (October 4, 2005).

Gen. Musharaff and PM Dr. Singh after making the joint statement at Hyderabad house reveals the bonhomic expressed by both leaders indicate a high level encounter is inversely proportional to the expectation that precede it.

Wherelse TNIE the president looks on the joint statement read at the Hyderabad house shows the crux of the situation.

Coverage of CBM Related Photographs.

During The Period of Study there were 28 Photographs in TNIE Wherelse The Hindu Had Forty Nine Photographs.

The Hindu

The photos do commit a lot of peaceful atmosphere that prevails even after the terror unleashed every now and then which instigates the governments in power to find a amicable solutions.

Bollywood actress interacting with the inmates of the shelter for orphans and widows organized by the CRPF in Sringar shows the interest shown by the film dom which buries the horrendous pact by setting new trend in reinforcing on going peace momentum. (June 19, 2005).

Pakistan girl Karan bari with her family after a successful surgery for a complex cardiac disorder at frontier life line hospital shows the hospitality and generality expressed by the Pakistani government in perpetuating violence across the border. (June 19, 2005).

The Hindu coverage of the Khari Rawalkut road which will become motoable till the last point on the Indian side, will become a transline of control connecting a number of divided families. (June 26, 2005).

Deheraj Gurunath in Srinagar especially a boy on his bicycle shows the horrific past and realm of harmony that prevails in the state after heinous crimes. (June 29, 2005).

Even the visit of vice - chief of army Lt. Gen. B.S. Thakur interacted with students from the border region of Akhoor (J & K) as a part of operation sadbhawar, tells the efforts extended by the army. (July 19, 2005).

Pakistani porters collection garlic fallen on the ground as Indian porters line up to hand over sacks containing the spice to thing Pakistani counter parts at wagah. Gives an improved relation in trade. (July 27, 2005).

Ladakhi children standing along the LoC, gives a deserted look of the place should draw considerable amount of attention from the state government.

The devotees on their way to the cave shrive of Amarnath crossing a glacier on horse back indicates the throes of the pilgrims in the post modernism Era. (August 3, 2005).

Children on the barren land portrays the indifference and isolating, people living in these areas face.

The Lama standing near the sign post reveals that the Buddhist too has surfaced for political empowerment or expressing solidarity over who should govern their ethnic majority. (August 6, 2005).

The Batti - speaking families in Kargil waiting to get recruited with their relatives shows the lack of in these development areas to be tardy. (August 7, 2005).

The deputy director general of Pakistan rangers bird Sakhi Margazan (left) presenting flowers to command out of 12 battalion of BSF Pradeep Kalyat on occasion of Pakistani's independence day celebration at the zero line on the joint check post at wagh demonstrate their no reversal to the policy towards India and the capacity of the army is n less to their neighbour. Vain glorious assortment nevertheless they assent their might. (August 15, 2005).

The Shanti Stupa constructed by the Japanese is a tourist attraction in Ladakh, tells how places of attraction has been neglected for long which can bring bigger turn over of income for the governments. (August 21, 2005).

The Lok Saba speaker Somnath Chaterjee welcoming a delegation of Pakistani parliamentarian at Parliament house brings to the fore the camaraderie across the border. (August 25, 2005).

The Union Commerce Minster, Kamal nath with the Pakistani counter part, Humayun Akhtar Khan, at an interactive in New Delhi denote show trade sanctions are being carried out successfully. (September 20, 2005).

Mukhtar Ahmed talks on the phone from the telecommunication exchange in Jammu to a relative in Musaffarabad which will enable the people of J & K to contact the relatives across LoC free of charge for the next fortnight tells us of the bringing together people who have boldly affected by the quake and the post - quake reconstruction work. (October 20, 2005).

Porters from the other side of LoC carry relief material from the Indian side for the earthquake victims indicates how relief material is carried out among the victims. (November 10, 2005).

Pakistani army officer Shehar and Indian army officer J. Nair meet on a foot bridge connecting J & K and PoK during a relief exchange at Teetwel. But they were seen approaching face - to - face but express expressed the bonhomie with the hug.

Women on the Indian side Loc as they watch relatives on the other side during the opening of the fifth crossing point for aids brings to the force the suppressed emotions of divided families and thin longingness to meet the near and dear ones across the border. (November 17, 2005).

Pakistani driver Mohammed greets a BSF officer at Wagh. The bus was on travel run to Amritsar. (December 14, 2005).

Pakistani dancers perform on the front of the bus as it crossed Wagh border post. (January 26, 2006).

The bus passengers who boarded the Srinagar Musaffarabad bus being escorted by police to a high security area in Srinagar. (April 5, 2005).

Kashmiris use the foot bridge to enter the PoK. For the first time in several decades, 24 people from J & K were allowed to meet their relatives. The historic opening of LoC though has facilitated a section has not made way for the free flow of people across the LoC. (November 20, 2005).

The Pakistani official Tariq Usman harder receives Dilip Sinha chief of the Indian delegation at the foreign ministry to agree on the finalization of 'Border ground rules' for implementation along the international border as part of the conventional (CBMS) between the two countries. (April 28, 2006).

Ladakhis making mud bricks near the famous change la pass near the LoC Locals are pinning there hopes on the re-opening of the road conles with china , as Ladakh is cut off from the rest of the country for the next six months. (July 31, 2006).

The Srinagar - Musffarabad busses to set to roll on April 7 passes its way to Srinagar from Jammu and the Bus route highly guarded reveals the state of security deployed by the state administration. Wherelse TNIE had covered security guarding the inaugural area of the flagging of the bus sher-e-kashmir cricket stadium. (April 3, 2005).

ICCR President, Najma Heptullah dancing with a folk artist during a reception hosted by her for Pakistani girl students who are on a goodwill and friendship visit to India indicates an all occasions the Indian government have expressed their concern for their neighbour. (April 3, 2005).

College girls looking at the hoarding displaying the pictures of the Pakistan president Musharaff PM in Srinagar reveals the goodwill gesture of the Indian government. (April 3, 2005).

Enough initiative to portray the tunnel too, indicates the painstaking effort of the print media to avert all risks and give comfort to people on both sides.

THE NEW INDIAN EXPRESS

The girl getting married off to Ajmel Haswant which shows how relationship between theYouth have culminatied after the opening of the routes, (May 2, 2005).

Bonhomie expressed during the hour of the visit of former cricket captains wasim Akram during his visit to his ancestral village at Chavenda dew, 25 km from Amritsar. (May 4, 2005).

An army jawan stands guard at the 20jila pass, after the srinagar - keh road was opened to traffic after six months. This shows the promptness and the security arrangement made at LoC to protect the integrity sovereignty of the nation. (May 21, 2005).

Residents of PoK accorded a warms welcome to leaders of Hurriyat conference 20 km beyond LoC, south of Musaffarabad, was recognized a full fledged message of peace moving along with convoy of vehicles with men sprinkling flowers over him be denied with much favour and the spectacular event reminicils all leaders were beheld during the postpartition days.

A man removing weeds from Dal lake in Sringar acts as a harbinger of hope in troubled times. (June 7, 2005).

A Ladakh artiste in a traditional attire at the Sindhu festival in Leh. (June 12, 2005).

A Buddhist monk narrating the history of thi ksy monastry. (June 12, 2005).

Sadhu protesting the J & K governments decision to not open the regular pilgrims route through pahlagam to Amarnath. (July 22, 2005).

The Hurriyat leaders welcoming the pandit leader prior to the commencement of first - ever - meeting reveals cameradarie expressed among the separatists to evolve a draft plan to restore peace and confidence in the minds of the people. (July 20, 2005).

Suresh babu released from Pakistani jail embracing his father at the wagh border shows the necessity of reunion of family members for no fault of theirs, the harm unleashed by partition. (July 24, 2005).

BSF Jawans distributing sweets to civilians on the occasion of independence day celebrations at the joint Indo - Pak border post at Wagah gives credence to the spirit of camaraderie expressed from the other side. (August 16, 2005).

The road path was not clear and there was upheaval of sands dones An Indian police officer and his Pakistani counterpart hug each other at a bridge connecting Kashmir and PoK at Ketwal, 195 Km west of Srinagar. A

Pakistani porter brings relief material to Teetwal in Kashmir. (November 13, 2005).

The BSF official greeting their counter part on border problems, shows there is flexibility on either side to take decisions.

Pakistani Army Brigadier Lahir Raza Nagur shakes hand with his Indian counter part A.K. Bakeshi during the opening of one of the points on LoC in Pole, about 180 km east of Islamabad portends the coming together of army generals especially after many decades.

The former Indian cricket player and BJP MP Navjot Singh Sidhu addressing Amritsar international bus terminal to inspect the facility for passengers and to hi surprise he did not find a single passenger on Amritsar Sahib bus which indicates that though much evoked fanfire among the public at large did not promote the real cause.

Concerns to dispel of fear from the minds of the public by depicting photographs wherein the cops made a though search before the passenger boarded the bus. (July 22, 2006).

Both The Newspapers

The entourage of the Najam Aziz sethi Editor, the Friday times and the daily times, Pakistan along wife Janu sethi at the convecation ceremony of the Asian College of Journalistm gave a fillip to the already perceived peace process. Both the newspapers acknowledged the goodwill gesture extended by the Editor in chief, the Friday times an Daily times of Pakistan. (May 4, 2005).

Amidst the hoop-hopla created by both the governments with the travel of Hurriyat leaders to PoK, tourist enjoyed surfing in the Dal lake in Srinagar. (May 24, 2005).

Pakistani's first cruise missile test fired was full blowncompered to TNIE. (August 12, 2005).

The external affairs Minster K. Natwar Singh and his Iranian counter part Manocharr mottaki during their meeting in Tehran ignoring pressure from US, India and Iran decided to go ahead with the proposed gas pipeline project to supply the much needed natural gas through Pakistan and sign a frame work agreement December indicated the momentum gained even during an atmosphere of opposing forces. (September 4, 20005).

Pakistani policemen fire teargas shells and chase away attempting to cross LoC at trinote. A policemen intercepts a man and his child as they try to cross the LoC. The opening of the LoC points made great significance when people felt free to meet one another after gap of 6 decades. The entire shown by the divided families is well portrayed by both the New Indian Express as well as the Hindu.

PM Manmohan Singh flagging off the bus to Wanasbib in Amritsar that the CBMS had a smooth sail inspite of the tensions between nations. The New Indian Express of highlight passengers of the inaugural Amritsar - Wankana sahib bus being welcomed upon their arrival in Nankaa Sahib in Pakistan but the statues of the Indian PM and officials flagging off did not find prominence. (March 25, 2006).

The hoardings of displaying the pictures of Musharaff and PM Singh in Srinagar which indiecate the the coming together of both the government after a long period of strife and distrust.

Dr. Singh greets the passenger before flagging off the bus to Musaffarabd wherelse the TNIE portrayed instead of Pak general Musharaff greeting the passenger PoK PM Sardar Sikander Khan greeting passenger who arrived. In India the PM of the country unfailingly addressed the move wherelse such mutual response was not reciprocated shows the awardness of belitering the whole venture behind such move. (April 18, 2005).

The Hindu had given importance to passengers on the bridge but TNIE portrayed PM Dr. Singh flagging of the bus with the Ms. Sonia Gandhi flanked to his side. TNIE expressed through the photos the strong protest expressed by women members of against the Srinagar - Musaffarabad bus service during a rally in Jammu; the antagonism of the party members (opposition). (April 8, 2005).

10

Conclusions and Suggestions

Soft borders don't simply increase people-to-people contact. They normalize the rules of engagement between two neighbours. The way this process has played of this far, new routes have given the peace process an increase...... character.

On terrorism, the Prime .... did not accuse the attack on April 6, as the accusation would undermine a process of reconsilation progressively .... by New Delhi and Islamabad. The .... Appear to discept the service because they believe that the people-to-people contact will defect the movement for self-determination.

The ad.............. Srinagar - Musaffarabad bus service journey confidence of the travellar would mean managing the fear factor and managing the fear factor would require substantive engagement between India and Pakistan on Kashmir and concealed attempt on the part of both the countries to defeat the terrorist agenda.

.... the bus service is the key to re-ignoting the kind of alienation that gives them and their cause oxygen. Alienation between people and the government and alienation between the two governments.

There is nothing that the Manmohan Singh government has done which amounts to a serious deviation from the line laid downin the Indo-Pak joint statement of January 6, 2004, and the Prime Minister did well to clarify this in his response to Vajpayee letter.

Stand on Pipeline :

The Prime Minister must immediately clarify that his government has every intention of persuing the Iranian pipeline because it is an excellent project and because India makes its own sovereign decisions.

Pakistan to open road line between Kargil and Skarich (Northern areas occupied by Pakistan)

Bus service - It is Pakistan, in any case, that had the problem with Passengers of the srinagar - Musaffarabad bus service entering it s territory without adequate travel documentation and India should not raise unnecessary objections to their traveling wherever they wish. This should simplify not just national self - confidence but an internal in furthering the peace project in the region.

Buses can ferry people across the border, it follows that lorries can transfer goods. And an increased movement of goods across borders is a good mar.......... of the state Indo - Pak ties, just as unleashing of .... energy is an affection way to help wind down hos............

For détente to maintain its momentum, India and Pakistan need to generate concrete outcomes in areas that can meake a material difference to people's loved, particularly in J & K.

General's visit to India in 2001, and the visit and also well - merited reversal of .... Fortunes since the Indian team made a .... visit to Pakistan in March - Aril 2004. It is only in the fitness of things that Islamabad which in the past has seen .... As a temp that might compromise its basic position on the cure 'issues' which would come around in appreciating the big difference in economic, cultural and potential interactions.

Terrorism - the government of India's refusal to deny Pakistan's information minister a visa to travel to India can be restricted if only he demonstrated convincingly that he had contributed in dismantling the terrorist machinery, there would be compromise.

Avoiding gloating over the pressure created by the world community on Musharaff, India should not like a laser beam to bring about structural changes in Indo - Pak relations. The inner contradiction, like re-grouping of Taliban in Afghanistan and its favourite Kashmiri militant shut shop are routed in Pakistani's ambiguities on terrorism adopted after Sep. 11, 2001.

Trade - India must be prepared to go an extra more in boosting the level of bilateral trade, if it means granting unilateral concessions for certain products Pakistan is keen to export. The Indian establishment is has tended to see border as sites of tension and danger rather than as windows of opportunities and promise.

Curb Terrorism - This is the time to close ranks against the terrorist design to store up diversine forces and not the moment to howl fur resignations which may be similar to VHP's .... which lamps Pakistan, Jebadi terrorism, votobank politics, reservation far muslims into a seamless spectre.

The process of reconciliation - The process of reconciliation should not always be mediated through the state. Instead of should be based on irect contacts and .... between different groups. If reconciliation with the pandits and a comm............ to help them get back to Kashmir is now part of Hurriyat's strategy, this will for the good.

LoC - Bush was ready to say publicly what the Indians wanted to hear- that the US has no desire to see a territorial distribution of India.

Terrorism - Singh and Bush identify the importance of promoting values of plarilism and tolerance which they identify as the key to winning war on terrorism.

Curbs on terrorism - In time of spreading insecurity, it must assure the people of its unrelenting vigil an of its capacities to mount a co-orientated response. There must be a systematic follow-up through evidence and an unfussy pursuit of culprits.

Pipeline - The project that promises to transform the geo olitics of south Asia and person galf by country them firmly in arrangements for an ergy an economic independence. This agreement between India and Pakistan would also be a model for similar arrangements for the transport of gas from central Asia.

Defense for Security forces -

Terrorism

But the inflow of terrorists into India is more robust evidence of the first that Americans pressure. An Pakistan to curb terrorism is not yielding the desired result. Pakistan should recognize in................ needless suffering on the Kashmiri people cannot help their cause.

A handful of Pakistan seminaries are certainly associate with militant Islam - these app............ More in need of a firm an then refers.

The sub-continent's enduring insecurity is rooted in the nature of Indo-Pak politics and with the character of weapon systems the two nations acquire- Security, Kashmir, Peace.

Ceasefire option - Singh should offer a simple deal to Musharaff and the Hurriyat - Delhi were cease fire within Jammu and Kashmir, If Islamabad and its insurgent friends in the state agree to end violence on their part. (Repeated).

Terrorism - Indian military official note that the limited pull back of troops in 2004 did not yield on reciprocal decline in .... violence, there is relatance to repeat the exercise.

Dialogue process - Notwithstanding the decline of violence, at least five people die everyday in terrorism, related evidents - the real test for the dialogue process will be its ability to more beyond being an idea, and start dec............ peace on the ground.

HC - the moderate wing of the Hurriyat has come to presence the role of the hawdlonus as obstruction counter .... and dangerous in so far as they appear compulsively opposed to any initiative.

While none of the major issues in contention is settle after two rounds of composite dialogue - what is uncalled for at this stage is hyped - up frustration over the absence of a break through.

The central makes people ponder on - To those .... without compromising its core interests. On Paskistani side, Musharaff will have to prepare the Pakisthani establishment to accept the significant alteration in tits traditions position is not loss but a gain for Pakistan.

Natwar Singh - Kasuri joint statement does not offer new insights - the .... to address mutual concerns on Kashmir (for Pakistan) and LBT (for India) might have begun to slow the pace of the peace process.

The earthquake the terrible tragedy has offered New Delhi and Islamabad a greater opportunity that of establishing an .... between the two countries The New Indian Express, ways can always be worked out to address Pakistan's sensitivities and protect its interest.

Tactical changes made recently by the security forces, especially the transfer of responsibility for urban counter terrorism operations from the BSF to central reserve police force, have provided some space to militants, The CRPF which does not passes the kind of arrangements or the intelligence resources the BSF does, will be at a disadvantage in the transtonal phase. This might cause a sparke in militant activity in the short term. The militants wanted to arrest the process

Reconciliation between people and security forces

The only thing that can be stated with absolute certainity is that there is no scope for complacency - even at an abnormal time ...... the present are, when an earthquake .... havoc. It now needs to be more pro-active in joining India in identifying and isolating these brutal agents of terrors.

LoC -Even if the interaction across the LoC will be only for the short term, it will represent significant movement towards the acceptance of the proposal of 'soft border' between India and Pakistan. This proposal is a compromise between Pakistan's refusal to make the LoC the permanent international boundary and India's rejection of any change in the territorial states quo.

Diplomacy - General Musharaff's announcement that Pakistanis willing to allow an open LoC to allow Kashmiris "to meet relatives and assist with the reconstruction effort" is just such as example of gimmple diplomacy.

An "open LoC" whole a .... Idea in thereby, can as easily be an open invitation to the Laskar version of the Trujan horse.

They need more than ever, in this hour of calamity are grief, to be given the opportunity to reconnect with each other and participate in the relief and reconstruction of a ravaged region.

Both the PDP and the Congress need to demonstrate to the people of the state and their future lies in co-operation, not .... rivalry. The challenges before the new regime are obvious - notably the need to strengthen the peace process by initiating a b.......... - base dialogue among representatives of the states highly regional and religious communities and to ensure a transparent, corruption free administration.

Siachen - In dividing to tackle the issue in an integrated fashion rather than sequentially,the two governments have given themselves an excellent chance of making progress. New Delhi want Islamabad to certify that the Indian army held the .... Before the pullback. Pakistan has refused to do on ground that if would be tantamount to certifying aggression.

Terrorism - Can the man who invaded Kargil please show courage to lead his troops into Miderika? If not, should the world do his job for him. General Musharaff has promised India all help in trenching down the culprits- a cyclostyled resolve that is reissued each time.

LoC - A sort of compulsion from the The New Indian Express - The concern that terrorist right misuse it had a lot to do with Indian relactance to allow free movement across the LoC. Yet, given to scale of the tragedy and the scope of new opportunities in .... diplomacy, India must find ways to make of easier for ordinary people to go back and forth the dividing line.

Terrorism - Indian policy - workers have hoped that confidence building measures would persuade Pakistan to come to the table without a green tacked under its combat fatigues.

CBM - Given the potential the new bus service has for enhancing people - to - people exchanges, the two governments need to think seriously about making arrangements for issuing Visas in Lahore and Amritsar.

Terrorism - Laskar Commanders are increasingly using secure satellite phone based communication technologies that Indian intelligence organizations do not have the resources to decrypt.

CBMS - Islamabad concern remains that New Delhi is using (CBMS) to sidestep consideration of Kashmir the core issue.

Dialogue - Dialogue, after all, is a process - not a tool to deliver a pre - concerned end.

For the full potential to be realized however, India and Pakistan must begin practicing a rational Visa policy that aims to encourage rather than restract the flow of people between the two countries.

Hurriyat - The solution would be to stay the course, and so strengthen dialogue with follow-up on the ground that boycott would be statement only about the absentees ....

US - Pakistan - India relations - Bush underlines the growing, economic, political, strengthen and nuclear differentiation between India and Pakistan, it is now up to New Delhi to demonstrate leadership on regimal peak and reconciliation.

LoC - A fact of life in one disputed regions such as south ...., cross - LoC arrangements would allow borders - which everyone agrees cannot redrawn - gradually to become irrelevant. Territoral, ... Sover............. would remain intact, of course, but these would not be allowed to come in the way of people in the region moving and trading freely.

The PM's emphasis on good government open borders and consultation mechanisms between the two Kashmirs provides a realostrobases for further talks between all the key players. New Delhi, Srinagar, Islamabadand Musaffarabad.

Kashmir - In rightly painting out to the many ..... of Pakistan's rule in PoK, India should not, however become complacent about its own constitutional and political obligations to the people of Kashmir and a commitment to find an early resolution to the dispute with Pakistan conflict resolution.

Terrorism - Terrorism has specific local dimensions, define by both local policies and socieity. India now needs to compile a dossier that would argue its case before the world. If terror was communalized by onc by .... in power, the current fashion is communicating anti - terror policy.

Terrorism groups threatening India's security now can easily murph into outfits that undermine Pakistan.

Army - But it is a good context in which to remember now without sectarianism infecting its professionalism.

Diplomacy - The longer the PM, who is increasingly burdened with the complex management of domestic policies avoids opportunity full time monster the greater wall be the damage to India's long term interests.

The process is made all the mere difficult by a complicate set of political factors that has made the UPA government seem hard of should be on terror.

Index

O

P

Y

Z